D1397096

LAURA LEMAY'S
WEB WORKSHOP

DESIGNING WITH STYLE SHEETS, TABLES, AND FRAMES

LAURA LEMAY'S
WEB WORKSHOP

DESIGNING WITH STYLE SHEETS, TABLES, AND FRAMES

Laura Lemay
Series Editor

Molly E. Holzschlag

201 West 103rd Street
Indianapolis, Indiana 46290

Copyright © 1997 by Sams.net Publishing

FIRST EDITION

All rights reserved. No part of this book shall be reproduced, stored in a retrieval system, or transmitted by any means, electronic, mechanical, photocopying, recording, or otherwise, without written permission from the publisher. No patent liability is assumed with respect to the use of the information contained herein. Although every precaution has been taken in the preparation of this book, the publisher and author assume no responsibility for errors or omissions. Neither is any liability assumed for damages resulting from the use of the information contained herein. For information, address Sams.net Publishing, 201 W. 103rd St., Indianapolis, IN 46290.

International Standard Book Number: 1-57521-249-8

Library of Congress Catalog Card Number: 96-71502

2000   99   98   4   3   2

Interpretation of the printing code: The rightmost double-digit number is the year of the book's printing; the rightmost single digit, the number of the book's printing. For example, a printing code of 97-1 shows that the first printing of the book occurred in 1997.

Composed in Frutiger and MCPdigital by Macmillan Computer Publishing

Printed in the United States of America

All terms mentioned in this book that are known to be trademarks or service marks have been appropriately capitalized. Sams.net Publishing cannot attest to the accuracy of this information. Use of a term in this book should not be regarded as affecting the validity of any trademark or service mark.

Publisher and President:	Richard K. Swadley
Publishing Manager:	Mark Taber
Acquisitions Manager:	Beverly M. Eppink
Director of Editorial Services:	Cindy Morrow
Managing Editor:	Mary Inderstrodt
Director of Marketing:	Kelli S. Spencer
Assistant Marketing Managers:	Kristina Perry
	Rachel Wolfe

Acquisitions Editor
Beverly M. Eppink

Development Editor
Kelly Murdock

Software Development Specialist
Bob Correll

Production Editor
Brice P. Gosnell

Indexer
Johnna L. VanHoose

Technical Reviewer
Brad Seifert

Editorial Coordinator
Katie Wise

Technical Edit Coordinator
Lorraine Schaffer

Editorial Assistants
Carol Ackerman
Andi Richter
Rhonda Tinch-Mize

Cover Designer
Alyssa Yesh

Cover Illustration
Eric Lindley/
Partners Photography

Cover Production
Aren Howell

Book Designer
Sandra Schroeder

Copy Writer
David Reichwein

Production Team Supervisors
Brad Chinn
Charlotte Clapp

Production
Lana Dominguez
Ayanna Lacey
Chris Livengood
Tim Osborn

Dedication

For Wil Gerken, who taught me to know the code.

—*Molly E. Holzschlag*

Overview

Contents

Acknowledgments

From Molly E. Holzschlag

The following people have been fundamental to this book's process as well as my own:

Lee Anne Phillips, who always provides a steady and supportive hand as my research assistant; Matt Straznitskas, for continuing professional support and personal friendship; Tim Huddleston, for teaching me how to write books.

From Sams.net: Beverly Eppink, whose warmth, vision, and intelligence make my job a joy; Kelly Murdock, who provides the voice of reason; Brice P. Gosnell, who is a rare talent that makes me laugh and guides my words to be the best they possibly can be; Rachel Wolfe, for her assistance and whose wisdom belies her years; Sandra Schroeder, for the book's design; Macmillan Computer Publishing staff and reps, who have an unflagging amount of energy and are dedicated to producing only the highest quality product. Thank you all for your efforts on behalf of my endeavors.

My family, Dr. Phillipa Kafka, Ollie Kenen, Linus Holzschlag-Kafka, and Morris Holzschlag-Kafka; fellow management, staff, and members of the Microsoft Network; *Web Publisher* editor Jerry Coffey for offering me a home in a great new magazine, *Web Publisher;* and *Goldmine Magazine* editor Michael Metzger, for allowing my music-on-the-Net column, "Line Noise," to not only survive, but thrive. You're tops in my book, Michael, and you know I love you dearly. For keeping me in mind, body, and spirit, a very sincere thanks goes to Andrea Morken, Jeff Rogers, and Patricia Hursh, Ph.D. To my partner in music, Patty Sundberg, who helps me reach heaven every time we're together. To C. Scott Convery for his contributions to this book and my life. To all of my personal friends and family: Your daily lives demonstrate the true meaning of love.

Credits

Chapter 9: Matthew Bardram and Atomic Media for permission to use and alter code and employ graphic elements from the Atomic Media Web site for the limited purposes of this book and accompanying CD-ROM.

Chapters 12 and 16: Wil Gerken, Doug Floyd, Amy Burnham, Nathan Hendler, DesertNet, The Film Vault, Paperboy, and *The Tucson Weekly* for permission to use and alter code and employ graphic elements from The Tucson Weekly Online, the Film Vault, and Paperboy for the limited purposes of this book and accompanying CD-ROM.

Chapter 13: Ed Roemke for permission to use code and graphics from the Sedgwick China Web site; Frank Huffman, Director of Communications, Sedgwick, Incorporated, for express permission to reproduce the trade-marked name and logo of Sedgwick, Inc.; C.Scott Convery for detailed explanation of the non-static frame code he wrote; Matt Straznitskas for graphic design of the Web site.

Chapter 15: Robert Cohen and Evan Goldberg of Core Wave for permission to use the code and design created by me for the Glass Bead Game Web site. Tom Bates for the final design and colorization of "The Symbol." Erik J. Lundquist for iconographic reproductions.

Chapter 16: Fine artist and cartoonist Joseph Forkan for the "Paperboy" logo design.

About the Author

Molly E. Holzschlag is an author, columnist, and new media designer. The common themes throughout her work are holism and humanism—offering a balanced view of the Web medium as being one of both science and art, technology and humanity, and function and form.

These ideas reach a broad audience through her vibrant, colorful, and popular design book, *Laura Lemay's Guide to Sizzling Web Site Design*, also by Sams.net Publishing. Monthly offerings include two columns: "The Web Designer," in *Web Publisher Magazine* (www.informant.com) and "Line Noise," in *Goldmine Magazine* (www.krause.com/goldmine/). Molly acts as a design consultant for a number of high-end media firms, as well as continuing to help build and design community on the Microsoft Network. She enjoys teaching seminars, workshops, and classes on Web design and is currently developing an online masters-level course in Web design at the progressive New School for Social Research in New York.

Molly holds a B.A. in writing from Prescott College and an M.A. in Media Studies from the New School for Social Research. She plans on pursuing a Ph.D. program—when she can find one—that will support her studies on the consciousness of cyberspace and the use of non-linear environments as tools for human evolution.

Visit Molly's Web site at http://www.molly.com/.

Tell Us What You Think!

As a reader, you are the most important critic and commentator of our books. We value your opinion and want to know what we're doing right, what we could do better, what areas you'd like to see us publish in, and any other words of wisdom you're willing to pass our way. You can help us make strong books that meet your needs and give you the computer guidance you require.

Do you have access to CompuServe or the World Wide Web? Then check out our CompuServe forum by typing GO SAMS at any prompt. If you prefer the World Wide Web, check out our site at http://www.mcp.com.

NOTE: If you have a technical question about this book, call the technical support line at 317-581-3833.

As the publishing manager of the group that created this book, I welcome your comments. You can fax, e-mail, or write me directly to let me know what you did or didn't like about this book—as well as what we can do to make our books stronger. Here's the information:

Fax: 317-581-4669

E-mail: newtech_mgr@sams.samspublishing.com

Mail: Mark Taber
             Sams.net Publishing
             201 W. 103rd Street
             Indianapolis, IN 46290

Introduction

When Days Are Months and Years Are Decades

If time flies when you're having fun, the world must be having a blast on the Web! One week can offer up enough news and industry revisions to dizzy even the most calm of Web designers. A shift in policy by Microsoft or Netscape can turn an entire site development plan on its ear; a policy change in the ever-evolving standards can upset the virtual apple cart. The profession of Web design requires an almost manic ability to keep up with trends, much less lead the pack.

How do you keep up in such a fast-paced industry? It's a tough question, but the answer lies in the ability to understand as much about the design process as possible. That means keeping aware of trends, surfing the Web daily to see what your competitors are up to, and spending time mastering the many techniques involved in the creation of Web pages.

When Web design first began to emerge as a profession only a handful of years ago, HTML, browsers, and the delivery of media over the various available pipes were all quite limited. We've been witnesses to an enormous explosion in this industry; the years literally do seem like decades in terms of the fast-paced growth of the possibilities now available to designers of the Web medium.

This book takes a look at a critical and evolving area for designers—control of Web page layout and style. The objective is to familiarize designers with current trends, but also provide a task-oriented workshop that will teach both the basic and more complicated elements of controls. These controls will invariably become more sophisticated as time goes on, but the value in learning them well is that you will have a strong foundation upon which to build for future, new media design applications.

Book shelves will quickly fill up with books on how to create and employ tables, when to use—and not to use—frames, and what cascading style sheets are and why you should be studying them closely. The point of this book is to take these elements and combine them with savvy design tips. The reason is simple: The Web is not only about technology, it is also about art. The blending of the two enables designers to capture the true crux of any medium, which is to communicate your given point with lasting impact.

A Web designer will only enhance the opportunities offered by this new and powerful medium by combining his or her skills in both the technological requirements and design-oriented concepts presented here. Furthermore, as you work through the process of learning how to best achieve this meeting of art and technology, you will be exposed to ideas that will serve to empower how you use the medium to reach your audiences. You will learn time-honored media formulas to convince Web site visitors that the ideas being expressed therein are in fact worthy of using, remembering, and returning to time and again.

Why can this book provide you with such a well-rounded educational experience? The answer is simple—the clear, concise, and friendly style of Laura Lemay Web Workshop books makes the process of learning even advanced applications simple. Moreover, the workshop environment allows you to learn hands-on. You'll step through tasks that immediately put you in direct contact with skills, rather than merely *telling* you how to do the job. My writing teachers always told me, "Show, don't say." That's the most impor-tant underlying theme of this book—to show you how to get the most out of the *design* experience.

What This Book Will Teach You

Ideally, you will learn many aspects of Web design through the experience this book provides. The most significant lessons include

- ❏ The HTML tags and attributes necessary to achieve high-style design with tables, frames, and cascading style sheets

- ❏ How to create specific individual page layout using a variety of techniques in an easy-to-follow fashion

- ❏ To functionally employ these techniques as part of entire, real-world examples of Web sites

❏ Elements of Web design

❏ Adding interactive content to Web sites

❏ Shortcuts to enable you, as a designer, to perform high-level work in a time-productive, cost-effective fashion

How to Read This Book

This book uses the familiar series of Tasks, Margin Notes, Tips, and Cautions to give you quick-and-easy reference points to highlighted issues. I've also added a Design Note option, which will pull your eye to a concept or technique related specifically to Web design. Design Notes serve to enhance all tasks and activities by providing esthetic as well as logical design tricks to strengthen the task at hand—as well as future projects.

Please note that a variety of tools, as well as graphics and code, have been placed on the CD-ROM. As you work through tasks in this book, you'll need to copy the files onto your own computer. The files are arranged by chapter; this will make the tasks easy to accomplish.

For each task-oriented chapter, you'll want to create a folder with that chapter's name and a sub-folder called `images` on your hard drive. For more information on how to do this, please see Appendix D, "What's on the CD-ROM."

You'll also see several terms that I use throughout when referring to tasks. These are

❏ Code refers to HTML as well as programming selections.

❏ Container, Container Method: This refers to the placement of HTML tags, creating a "container," followed by the introduction of the graphics, text, and other elements between those tags.

❏ Shell refers to the HTML basics that are specifically related to a given task. This is typically made up of beginning and ending `HTML`, `HEAD`, `TITLE`, and `BODY` tags and attributes.

❏ A "string" describes a series of attributes within a tag.

❏ Syntax is interchangable with "code" in the context of this book.

The First Rule of Web Design

Well, it's my first rule, anyway, and it comes out of the experience of seeing design as an expression of ideas. Web design is, as I've suggested before, as much a creative process as it is one of technology. I encourage Web designers to consider my first rule as an important part of that process, and that is to **have fun**. In the end, your enjoyment of the time and effort put into the job will shine through, and visitors to your Web site will invariably notice the difference!

-Molly E. Holzschlag

PART

I

Quick Start: Elements of Tables, Frames, and Style Sheets

one

Good Manners: Basic Table Elements

No one planned for the Internet to become a significant means of communication for people outside of military and educational institutions. Similarly, HTML table tags were not introduced as a means of controlling the entire layout of pages, nor were they to go on and become a primary structure upon which complete page design—including graphic placement, color arrangement, and text control—would rest. In fact, until very recently, HTML was still thought of as a means of defining overall page structure and, specifically, *not* elements of visual style. However, the remarkable evolution of HTML is showing that it has, in fact, become increasingly involved with page style and design.

New ideas will force change to what is the standard, and often narrowly defined, way of doing things in both the real and virtual worlds. Savvy but disrespectful designers caught on to clever ways to employ table tags to create progressive design. Then, renegade browsers pushed ahead of standards, and instability reigned on the Web until HTML 3.0 specs were allowed into standards and common browsers caught up.

This is not to say that the process is over; it has only just begun. However, in terms of tables becoming a major aspect of page layout design, well, the process has been quite a rocky highway. It is easy to see, at least in retrospect, how disrespect of manners in Web design has changed the literal face of HTML and broadened the design options available to Web authors.

Evolution and Revolution: Tables as Technological Advancements

The study of biological evolution provides an excellent metaphor for the natural process that is occurring with Internet technology. In nature, new characteristics are introduced by random mutation. Often, the results do not endure, but natural selection will usually allow the mutated plant or animal to survive when its adaptive qualities are strong. This process typically takes years, or even a millennium, but it can occur quickly when conditions are unstable. If natural selection allows the new trait to survive, that attribute can rapidly become commonplace.

Sound familiar? It should! HTML tables are an excellent example of a mutation that survived natural selection in the technological mien and went on to become a fundamental aspect of the technology. Consider the environment of the Internet in 1993. Academic papers were being published with increasing regularity on the Net, and commercial access to the Internet was growing in leaps and bounds. Mosaic, the first graphical Web browser, arrived the same year.

Many individuals were frustrated because there was no definable means of placing data into visually well-organized rows and columns. The only available way of doing this was to use preformatted text, defined with the <pre> tag, and results were less than attractive—defaulting to a monospaced font and often forcing horizontal scrollbars, as Figure 1.1 demonstrates.

Figure 1.1.

The only way to table data before the introduction of HTML table tags was with the limited <pre> *tag.*

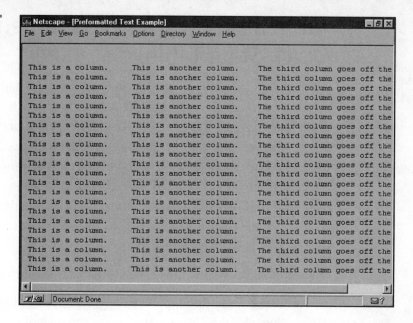

In November of 1993, discussions regarding HTML began to reflect the frustration people were experiencing in regard to HTML limitations. Included in such discussions was how to handle visual data without having to use graphic file formats. Dave Ragget, a Hewlett Packard engineer in Bristol, England, proposed the logical concept of tables. Soon thereafter, Netscape released a browser in which tables were supported. Although a controversial move, considering the unstable progress of standards, Netscape made some significant and revolutionary advances in terms of how to meet the public's increasing demands for HTML flexibility.

Although some of the aspects that Netscape originally introduced, such as the <caption> tag, are rarely used in Web design, the fundamental elements of specs are not only a standard employed to create actual tables, but are, in fact, a standard that has become a conventional means of designing entire Web pages. To follow the biological metaphor, natural selection has allowed new characteristics to not only survive, but become commonplace and, in the case of tables, dominant. Realistically, change continues to occur, but a certain stability has been reached, allowing Web designers a new level of confidence and exciting, variable layout options as a result.

Table Basics: Three Tag Elements for Quick-Start Tables

The first step in learning how to use tables as a fundamental tool in Web design is to understand the basic tags used to create them. Note that tags often have a variety of arguments that call advanced controls. *Only the most immediate and common* to Web design will be introduced in this chapter. As you proceed through this book, different and more advanced applications will be offered. For your convenience, Appendix C, "Current HTML Standards," provides a comprehensive guide to current table standards. I recommend that you refer to it regularly as you work, as the related information will cater to your individual skill level and learning pace.

There are really only three critical tags required to create a table. These include

A helpful companion guide to use with this book is Laura Lemay's *Teach Yourself Web Publishing with HTML 3.2 in a Week*, also published by Sams.net. Tables are described from a technical standpoint as opposed to the more design-centric applications provided here.

❑ **`<table>`** This is the tag that determines the beginning of a table within an HTML document. As with the majority of HTML tags, after all of the elements are placed within a table, the process is concluded with the companion tag `</table>`.

❑ **`<tr>`** Table rows are identified with this tag, which literally determines a row—the left-to-right, horizontal space within a table. As with the `<table>` tag, table rows are closed with the `</tr>` tag.

❑ **`<td>`** Individual table cells are defined by this tag, also referred to as the "table data" tag. As I demonstrate various applications of the table cell tag, you'll see that it is particularly critical—for a number of reasons. For this elementary introduction, remember that the `<td>` tag and the information contained therein *determines the columnar structure* of a table. The `<td>` tag closes with the logical `</td>` tag.

You've just learned the most important HTML requirements to create tables. It really is that simple! What becomes challenging is adding attributes, using tables to design in unusual and attractive ways, and adding interactive multimedia to the mix. As with all HTML, the basics are easy. Using it *well* is where the challenge lies.

Making a Simple Table

The first task, then, is to take these simple table elements and make a table. Before you begin, set up a workshop folder on your computer; you will use this to save files you make for future use. Also, have the companion CD-ROM available. There are files on it you'll need to access during various tasks within this chapter.

1. In your favorite HTML editor, set up a basic Web page, with `<html>`, `<title>`, and `<body>` tags in place. In between the `<title>` tags, type the table's title, "A Basic Table." Most HTML editors will offer a basic template page with these tags provided for your convenience. The results should look like this:

```
<html>
<title>A Basic Table</title>
<body>
</body>
</html>
```

TIP: It's a good idea to work with HTML within what I call the "container" method. To do this, you always create the starting and ending tags necessary for the job you're doing, and then you work *within* the tags as you proceed. The container method helps you avoid missing critical tags and gets you into the habit of micro-managing individual areas within an HTML document. This becomes more and more necessary as HTML documents become equally more complex.

Still looking for a good HTML editor? A witty and resourceful place to look is the Internet Bag Lady's site at `http://www.dumpsterdive.com/`. Not only are there excellent links to current versions of freeware and shareware HTML editors, but this humorous site also offers up a variety of Web design tools, tips, and tricks.

2. Now, add the `<table>` tag below the `<body>` tag. This alerts the HTML browser interpreting your code that a table is beginning. Above the `</body>` tag, place the closing `</table>` tag. You'll notice that I've included an attribute, `border=1`. This will enable you to see the final product clearly. Do keep your eyes open for the border tip just ahead, which helps to explain how you can best use this attribute.

```
<html>
<title>A Basic Table</title>
<body>
<table border=1>
```

```
</table>
</body>
</html>
```

TIP: Table borders control the number of visual pixels surrounding the table. Many designers, myself included, prefer to turn borders off (`border=0`), allowing the table to quietly control placement of text, graphic, and multimedia elements without "boxing" those elements into the space. In fact, turning table borders off is *precisely* the moment when a table ceases to be a table in the standard sense, and takes on the job of controlling a Web page's format. However, there are occasions where you might decide to use borders as part of your design. I'll look at this issue in detail in Chapter 4, "Table Controls and Site Interface." While working with tables for page layout, you'll find it extremely helpful to turn on borders by adding a value of 1 in order to see the fields you are creating. Then, turn them off to see the results!

3. Directly underneath the `<table>` tag, place the `<tr>` tag. This defines the beginning of your first table row. Directly above the `</body>` tag, place the closing `</tr>` tag.

```
<html>
<title>A Basic Table</title>
<body>
<table border=1>
<tr>
</tr>
</table>
</body>
</html>
```

4. Drop down to the next line and type in the tag to determine the starting point of your first table cell, `<td>`. Below this, add a line of text as I have, and then close the cell with the `</td>` closing tag.

```
<html>
<title>A Basic Table</title>
<body>
<table border=1>
<tr>
<td>
This is my first table cell, located in the first row of the
➡table.
</td>
</tr>
```

```
</table>
</body>
</html>
```

5. Repeat step four, adding a second table cell. (Remember, cells determine columns!)

```
<html>
<title>A Basic Table</title>
<body>
<table border=1>
<tr>
<td>
This is my first table cell, located in the first row of the
table.
</td>
<td>
This is my second table cell, which also creates the second
column of the table.
</td>
</tr>
</table>
</body>
</html>
```

6. Save this HTML file in your workshop directory as ex-01.htm, and then open it and view with your Web browser, as I have done in Figure 1.2. Voila! You now have a basic table.

Figure 1.2.
You've just created a basic table.

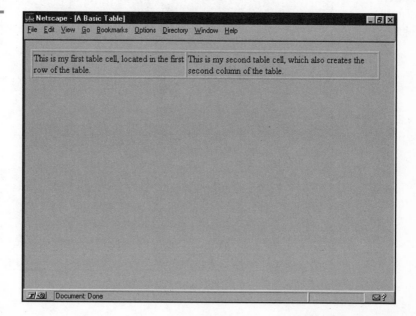

CAUTION: Remember that Web browsers are essential to the way HTML is interpreted. Out-of-date browsers will cause confusion. To further complicate the issue, computer platform, monitor size and type, and screen resolution all influence the way an HTML page ultimately appears. Be sure to keep up with the latest browser, and where possible, try and view your work on a variety of platforms.

Using Common Table Tag Attributes

The table you've just created isn't just a bare-bones starting point; it is ready to be immediately employed. You can add a graphic to one of the table cells in place of text (see Figure 1.3), add another row of table cells, or add another table cell to each row, as I went on to do in Figure 1.4, making the table more complex. I've placed a simple photo into one of the cells of the table. You can begin to see what early Web designers first saw—that a new method of controlling the placement of visual elements was at hand.

Figure 1.3.
*Adding an image
enhances the look.*

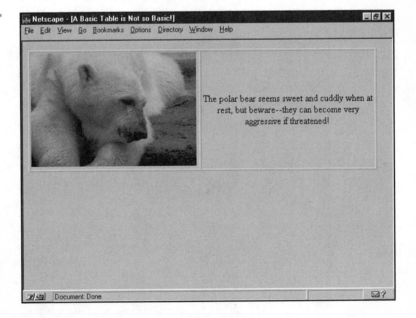

Figure 1.4.
A simple table becomes more complex.

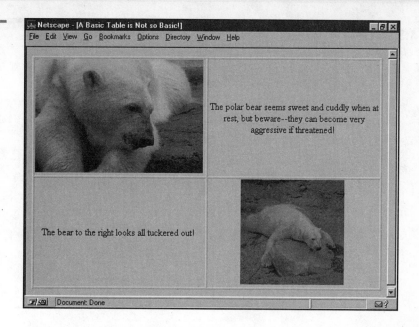

I'll now shift the focus a bit to look at the various common attributes you might wish to use in regard to these core tags. There are many, and their use begins the departure away from straightforward coding to the complicated job of using HTML as an advanced design tool.

NOTE: In the following example, you find a table with a border value of 2, a cellspacing value of 10, a cellpadding value of 10, and a width of 75%. I've used the `align=right` attribute to force placement to the right of the browser's visual field.

The `<table>` tag has a variety of related attributes that turn it from a simple tag into a series of powerful attributes that will alter the look of a table considerably. The ones most commonly used by Web designers include

❏ `align=x` Align tables on a page with this attribute. Options allow "x" to equal `left`, or `right`. Because the latest browsers default alignment to the left, and it's commonplace to center tables using other tags, the only effective use of this attribute is when you specifically want an entire table placed to the far right of the browser field (see Figure 1.5).

Figure 1.5.
This table aligns to the right.

❏ **border=x** The x is replaced with a value from 0 on up. This value defines the width of the visual border around the table.

❏ **cellspacing=x** Cellspacing defines the amount of space between each individual table cell (in other words, between visual columns). The x requires a value from 0 on up.

❏ **cellpadding=x** This attribute calls for the space around the edges of each cell within the table—its literal "padding."

❏ **width=x%** or **width=x** To define the width of a table, you can choose to use a number that relates to the percentage of browser space you wish to span, or a specific numeral that will be translated into pixel widths.

NOTE: There are several legal ways to center entire tables. The two most simple ways include placing the table between the <center> tag and its closing tag, </center>, or using the <div> tag. This elegant way of handling divisions of data within an HTML page will allow a variety of alignment attributes. In this case, place the <div align=center> tag and attribute before your table, and after you've closed the table, close the division with </div>.

NOTE: You might be thinking: "I've seen these attributes before, but the values always have a quotation around them, such as `width="100"`. Why haven't you done that?" The answer is simple: Style. Each individual designer develops his or her own coding style. An excellent resource is the Yale C/AIM Web Style Guide available at `http://info.med.yale.edu/caim/manual/index.html`. A guide is sometimes just a guide, however, and as your Web design and HTML skills expand, you'll notice your own style emerging. As long as your style doesn't interfere with legal HTML coding—go with it!

TASK

Using `<table>` Tag Attributes

The following task will show you how to use `<table>` tag attributes.

1. Begin by opening the `ex-01.htm` file in your HTML editor. Change the title to `Task: Table II`. You should see the following:

```
<html>
<title>Task: Table II</title>
<body>
<table border=1>
<tr>
<td>
This is my first table cell, located in the first row of the
table.
</td>
<td>
This is my second table cell, which also creates the second
column of the table.
</td>
</tr>
</table>
</body>
</html>
```

2. Because you're going to focus on the `<table>` tag, I'm going to isolate that here:

```
<table border=1>
```

3. Just for fun, change the border value to a higher number. I'm going to select 2.

```
<table border=2>
```

4. I want the table to have spacing and padding, so I'm going to add a value of `10` for each:

```
<table border=2 cellspacing=10 cellpadding=10>
```

5. You'll want to try out the width value. I encourage you to experiment with both pixels and percentages. For this example, I've chosen a percentage:

```
<table border=2 cellspacing=10 cellpadding=10 width=75%>
```

6. Save your file as `ex-02.htm` and view it using your browser.

NOTE: When given the option of defining a table by percentage or pixel width, I prefer to use pixels. The reason is I can then count each used pixel in a space. For example, if I have a table that is 600 pixels wide, I must be sure that all of the elements within that table *do not exceed* 600 pixels. Percentages are less accurate, yet they can be handy when you want to use a visual portion of a space that is not dependent on literal pixel count. An example of this would be to create a table, as I did in Figure 1.5, that is 75% of the browser area; this table will remain proportionately the same no matter what screen resolution at which I'm viewing the page.

Now that I've described some of the specific table attributes, let's move on to the table row. The only two attributes I've ever seen used within rows include `align`, which controls the row's spatial alignment, and `valign`, which determines the vertical placement of all the data within a row. However, I rarely use table row attributes, preferring the surrounding HTML, `<table>` attributes, and `<td>` table cell data attributes to control my table layouts. The following illustrates attributes available to the table row:

❏ `align=x` Here, the values for "x" are not numeric; rather, they are literal and include `left`, `right`, and `center`.

❏ `valign=x` Again, the values for vertical alignment are not numeric. Vertical alignment can be `top`, `middle`, `bottom`, or `baseline`.

NOTE: Not every browser supports or handles attributes, pixels, or percentages in the same fashion. For browser-specific descriptions, visit the browser company's home page. The two most important browsers for Web designers are Internet Explorer, which provides information at its home on Microsoft at `http://www.microsoft.com/ie/`, and Netscape Navigator, which can be reached by pointing your browser to `http://home.netscape.com/`. Be sure to read the latest release notes applicable to your browser version for specific and timely information regarding that browser's technology. Ultimately, you must test your work in different browsers to see the results first-hand.

You'll find some of the greatest flexibility in terms of layout control and style within the attributes allowed in the `<td>`, or table cell string. Table cells attributes are as follows:

❏ **`align=x`** When you use this attribute within a table cell, the data inside the cell will align with the literal value you assign to the attribute. In other words, a `<left>` value will left-justify the text or graphic you place within the cell, the `<middle>` value will center the information, and a value of `<right>` will justify the information to the right of the cell.

❏ **`colspan=x`** Colspan refers to the number of columns the cell you are working with will span.

❏ **`rowspan=x`** As with colspan, rowspan refers to the span of the cell, in this case, how many rows the cell will stretch.

❏ **`valign=x`** The vertical alignment of a table cell will place the information therein to the `top`, `middle`, or `bottom` of the cell.

Designers will need to think very carefully about `rowspan` and `colspan`. The introduction of these attributes critically changes the way tables can be used. I now can have one cell spanning multiple columns or rows, or many cells, using a variety of span attributes to create all kinds of visual field options.

I encourage you to play with these and all table attributes on your own, as well as following the tasks set out within this chapter and the book. You'll discover all kinds of exciting ways to use these simple attributes to powerfully enhance your control over page layout.

TASK Adding Width and Alignment to Table Cells

Now you're ready to build a table using a number of the described attributes.

1. Begin by opening up the first basic table file you created in your HTML editor (ex-01.htm). Change the title to Task: Table III. You should see the following:

```
<html>
<title>Task: Table III</title>
<body>
<table border=1>
<tr>
<td>
This is my first table cell, located in the first row of the
table.
</td>
<td>
This is my second table cell, which also creates the second
column of the table.
</td>
</tr>
</table>
</body>
</html>
```

2. In the <table> tag field, add a value for the border, cellpadding, cellspacing, and width attributes. I've chosen to leave out alignment values here; you can experiment with centering or justifying the table according to the note comments provided earlier. Also note that in this example I've chosen to use pixels for my width rather than percentages. I encourage you to play with individual attribute values and try different pixels and percentages to see the types of variations that will result. A final string will look like this:

```
<table border=1 cellpadding=10 cellspacing=10 width=400>
```

3. As I mentioned, I don't feel that aligning table rows is particularly useful in the common application of tables for Web design, so I'll add the tag, but without any attributes.

```
<html>
<title>Task: Table III</title>
<body>
<table border=1 cellpadding=10 cellspacing=10 width=400>
<tr>
</tr>
</table>
</body>
</html>
```

4. The next step is to add the first table cell, <td>, and a string of attributes. Here, I've chosen to align the text within to the left and the vertical alignment of the cell to the top of the table. I'm going to add a width, this time in percentage value, that covers 40% of the table space.

```
<html>
<title>Task: Table III</title>
<body>
<table border=1 cellpadding=10 cellspacing=10 width=400>
<tr>
<td align=left valign=top width=40%>
This is my first table cell, located in the first row of the
table.
</td>
</tr>
</table>
</body>
</html>
```

5. Add the final <td> table data cell, this time changing the attributes somewhat:

```
<html>
<title>Task: Table III</title>
<body>
<table border=1 cellpadding=10 cellspacing=10 width=400>
<tr>
<td align=left valign=top width=40%>
This is my first table cell, located in the first row of the
table.
</td>
<td align=middle valign=top width=50%>
This is my second table cell, which also creates the second
column of the table.
</td>
</tr>
```

```
</table>
</body>
</html>
```

6. Save the table as `ex-03.htm` in your workshop folder.

The final results of this table can be seen in Figure 1.6.

Figure 1.6.

The table you have just created includes a variety of tag attributes, including alignment, cell padding and spacing, and control of table width.

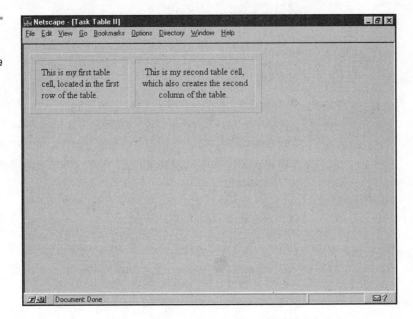

Look closely at this table and try to imagine the simple cells you've just created becoming splashes of borderless color, or areas in which you can place graphics, common gateway interface (CGI) scripts, ActiveX controls, and other plug-in, multimedia technologies. Suddenly it becomes clear just *why* tables are so useful to control placement of visual elements!

 Adding Rows and Columns

Now you can expand on the basic techniques you've just learned by adding rows and columns. Each row and column added to a table will increase its potential to be used as a page layout system.

1. Open your HTML editor and begin the table. You'll note I selected a background color with the Hexadecimal value of FFFFFF, which is white. I've also planned and implemented a table scheme that

includes a border of 1, cellpadding and cellspacing of a value of 10 individually, and a width, in pixels, of 600.

```
<html>
<title> Task: Table IV </title>
<body bgcolor="#FFFFFF">
<table border=1 cellpadding=10 cellspacing=10 width=600>
</table>
</body>
</html>
```

2. I'll begin by adding rows. I want two, so I'll place the following tags inside the table I just set up:

```
<html>
<title> Task: Table IV </title>
<body bgcolor="#FFFFFF">
<table border=1 cellpadding=10 cellspacing=10 width=600>
<tr>
</tr>
<tr>
</tr>
</table>
</body>
</html>
```

3. Now, add two table cells, <td>, inside *each* row, with some text to fill the cells.

```
<html>
<title> Task: Table IV </title>
<body bgcolor="#FFFFFF">
<table border=1 cellpadding=10 cellspacing=10 width=600>
<tr>
<td>
This is my first table cell, located in the first row of the
table
</td>
<td>
This is my second table cell, which also creates the second
column of the table.
</td>
</tr>
<tr>
<td>
This is my third table cell, which is in the first column of the
second row.
</td>
<td>
This is my fourth table cell, located in the second column of
the second row.
</td>
</tr>
</table>
</body>
</html>
```

4. Save the file as ex-04.htm. Now view the table in your browser and see if it resembles the table in Figure 1.7. If so, good job! If not, go back and carefully review your syntax to see if you've left a tag out.

Figure 1.7.
This table has two rows and two columns, with table cells that are padded and spaced.

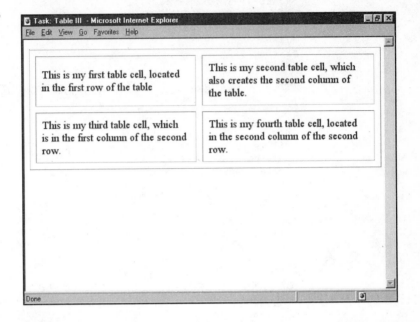

It's important to remember that while logic would suggest a row's span would be determined by an attribute within the <tr> (table row) tag, the fact is that all spanning is controlled within the table data cell tag, <td>.

NOTE: When you don't add attributes to a tag, browsers will seek the default. Table borders default to 0 cell padding, and cells pacing default to 1. Alignment defaults to the left and width becomes *dynamic*, meaning that the width of a table and the cells within adapt to the combination of browser space and the data you've placed within the cells. You can see in Figure 1.7 that I haven't yet defined attributes for <td> table cells, and the browser has adapted accordingly.

Working with Column and Row Span

Column and row span can be tricky but very powerful design attributes. I'll begin by introducing a simple span for a table.

1. Add a row span (`rowspan`) to the first cell. Because I have only two rows possible and I want to span both rows, I'll use a value of 2.

```
<td align=right rowspan=2>
This is my first table cell, located in the first row of the
table.
</td>
```

2. Now I'm going to take the second table cell and span it across columns:

```
<td align=right colspan=3>
This is my first table cell, located in the first row of the
table.
</td>
```

CAUTION: Remember that a table data cell creates a column. Because I have *four* table data cells in this table, I have to account for *four* individual cells. I'm going to span the second cell, and I want it to stretch from the cell's beginning along the full horizon of the table. Therefore, I will use a value of 3 to create the span. This can be very confusing, because it really appears that there are now only three *total* columns and the logical span for this cell would be 2. The trick is to always count the cell you are working from as being the first part of a span. Then you simply add to that number in order to reach the total number of cells, without getting confused by the visual results.

If you work using the "container" method I described earlier, you'll find you make fewer errors while coding. However, a good syntax checker can help. Many HTML editors have these built right into the software. HotDog Pro has a good one; you can find a shareware version on the CD-ROM accompanying this book.

3. Save the file as `ex-05.htm`.

Figure 1.8 demonstrates the results. If your results don't match, go back and look carefully at your code. Are you missing any of the tags or attributes?

Figure 1.8

With the addition of alignment and span, you've completely changed the look of your table.

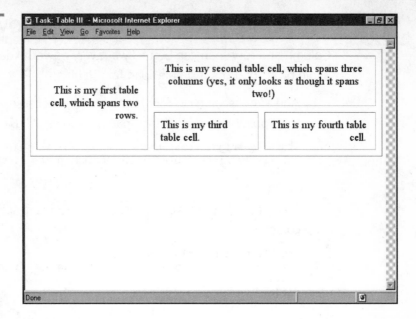

TASK Adding Background Color to Table Cells

To add color to cells, you'll use the `bgcolor` attribute and a hexadecimal value to the string within the `<td>` table cell string. Follow my lead in adding a different color to each table cell.

TIP: Graphic designers will often already have an idea of the RGB (red-green-blue) values of color palettes for a given project. RGB values can easily be converted to hexadecimal using a scientific calculator—the Windows OS has one built right in. Simply enter each individual color and then select hex. Combine the three values to get the six, alphanumeric, hexadecimal color values. Web designers will be familiar with the "safe" palette; you can use the safe palette provided on the CD-ROM. This palette helps ensure that your color selections will be stable across different browsers and platforms. I've included the complete palette with the hexadecimal values written right in for easy selection.

1. Replace the table data information in the first row of the table with the following code:

```
<td align=right rowspan=2 bgcolor="#CC9999">
This is my first table cell, located in the first row of the
table.
</td>
<td align=middle colspan=3 bgcolor="#FFCC99">
This is my second table cell, which also creates the second
column of the table.
</td>
```

2. Now replace the table data information in the second row of the table with the following code:

```
<td align=left bgcolor="#CCCCCC">
This is my third table cell, which is in the first column of the
second row.
</td>
<td align=right bgcolor="#FF9966">
This is my fourth table cell, located in the second column of
the second row.
</td>
```

3. Save the file as ex-06.htm, and then view it in your browser. Figure 1.9 shows the results.

Figure 1.9.
Background color can add a range of visual texture to tables.

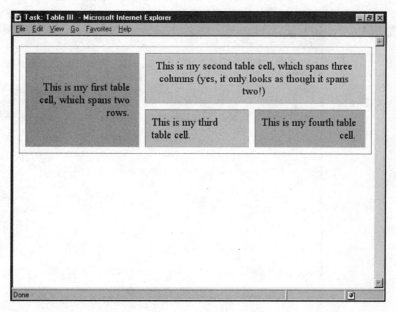

DESIGN NOTE: Color is an essential part of design, and Web designers should study color combinations carefully. Graphic designers will come to the field of Web design with a good deal of information on how to work with color, but for those designers without a great of experience, I recommend looking for books on color use for graphic designers. One such book is *The Color Source Book for Graphic Designers* by Sadao Nakamura, published by Mitsumura Suiko Shoin Publishing, Co., Ltd. Although the book is published in Japan, you should be able to order it from your local bookseller. Its ISBN is 4-8381-0110-4.

A basic color resource for HTML authors can be found at `http://colors.infi.net/colorindex.html`.

Now, if I drop the table's border, cellpadding, and cellspacing values to 0, I'll end up with each field snug against the next (see Figure 1.10). Furthermore, depending on what background color I use, I can literally create a mosaic of colors on which to place my images, text, and multimedia options.

Figure 1.10.
Drop the border, cellpadding, and cellspacing values to create borderless color fields.

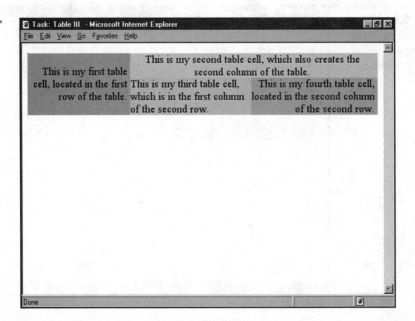

As you move through the workshop tasks in this book, you will learn different ways of using these techniques as the basis for almost all your Web design.

There are currently very few, if any, advanced page designers not using tables to control page layout. Obviously, some layouts are more advanced than others, but they all begin with the fundamentals that you have just now mastered.

To prove this point, all you need to do is simply add rows and cells, play with spans and colors, and alter alignments to the basic tables in this chapter to see how rapidly you can achieve a wide range of powerful options.

NOTE: Using background colors in body and table cell tags not only makes attractive and interesting design possible, but answers a fundamental problem in Web technology: Speed. Browser-based color loads much faster than colors based on graphic files (background graphic tiles, graphic headers, and so on.). Exploiting browser colors as a significant part of your design will place you far ahead of competitors by enabling interesting design *without relying* on time-consuming extras. The kilobytes (and, therefore, download time) you save by using browser-dependent color can better be put to use with graphic, programming, and multimedia features to make your pages the most exciting they can be.

I'd like to leave you with one more task that will excite your imagination in terms of how to begin applying table techniques in design immediately. The following exercise will focus on adding media to the basic table you've just created, giving it a different look and hinting at some of the exciting details that will be covered later in this book.

 ## Adding Media to Tables

Multiple media is what makes the Web interesting for Web site visitors and challenging for its designers. Individual books are dedicated to the range of applications available in current Web design, including animation, database applications, CGI scripts, ActiveX, and Java applications. For the following exercise, I'm going to add three pieces: an animated GIF, a graphical header, and a JPEG photo. Each of these can be found on the CD-ROM, so you can simply drop the graphic or code into the correct spot of your HTML page and see how exciting the possibilities of table-based layout are.

1. Begin, as usual, by opening the last table that you just created in your favorite HTML editor.

2. From the CD-ROM, copy the `01ani.gif` graphic from the Chapter 1 `images` directory into your current working folder and add the command into the first cell of your table:

```
<table border=0 cellspacing=10 cellpadding=10 width=600>
<tr>
<td align=right rowspan=2 bgcolor="#CC9999">
<img src="images/01ani.gif" width=150 height=100>
</td>
</tr>
</table>
```

3. Also from the CD-ROM, find the `01-hed.gif` graphic in the `images` directory, and copy it into your current working folder. Replace the earlier text with the following command in the second cell of the table:

```
<td align=middle colspan=3 bgcolor="#FFCC99">
<img src="images/01h-ed.gif" width=300 height=50>
</td>
```

4. Now change the text in the third table cell to match the field in the following code:

```
<td align=left bgcolor="#CCCCCC">
I had a lot of fun putting this table together! I hope you did
too.
</td>
```

5. Copy the `pic.jpg` file into your working directory and add the following syntax between the `<td>` and `</td>` tags of your final, fourth cell:

```
<td align=middle bgcolor="#FF9966">
<img src=images/surf.jpg>
</td>
```

6. Save the file and view it in your browser. It should match Figure 1.11.

I encourage you to take some time and really play with the various tags and attributes explained within this chapter. Although I can teach you how to do things in a progressive and logical fashion, only you can bring your own sense of style and imagination to your work!

Figure 1.11.

Are you having fun yet? The simple table becomes a lively page with the addition of various media.

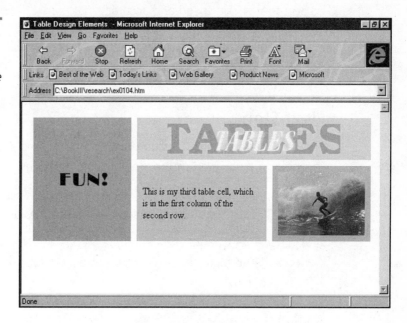

Workshop Wrap-Up

Although my most sincere hope is that you found the tasks in this chapter easy to do, and that they inspired you to spend time experimenting on your own, do remember that everyone learns at his or her own pace. Therefore, if you found yourself hung up on a task, go back and study the task closely. Redo your work, if necessary, to find out where you might have missed an important concept.

If it does seem a bit overwhelming, remind yourself that it starts very simply, with three absolute fundamentals, as mentioned early in the chapter. All complex table layouts begin with these fundamentals, and you, too, will find yourself doing complicated tables if you put in the time and practice.

For those of you who are a bit more comfortable with tables, or already have a working knowledge of how they are used, rest assured that as you practice both the basic and more advanced applications of table layout for design, you will not only strengthen your general understanding of the practice, but also be able to work on speed and accuracy.

Also, be sure to read the margin and design notes, tips, and cautions, and CD-ROM references in this and future chapters. They will greatly enhance your experience of the tasks and the process of Web design.

Next Steps

The next chapters in this section move to frame and cascading style sheet technology. If you want more time to work on tables, you can

❏ Jump ahead to Chapter 4, "Table Controls and Site Interface," where you'll learn about using tables for interface design.

❏ Check out Chapter 12, "Multiple Menus and Non-Linear Navigation." The focus there is how to work with table-based color for site navigation.

Q&A

Q: I've seen other tags for tables, such as `<th>` and `<caption>`. Why didn't you teach tags like that here?

A: The primary learning within this book concerns how to use HTML to create pages that are equivalent to or more advanced than current design trends. Although this book uses HTML to help teach the Web designer how to use HTML *for design*, it doesn't go into explicit detail about tags that are perfectly legal—and important to know— for the HTML coder. Please refer to the many HTML references available to enhance your own knowledge regarding such tags.

Q: I've noticed that some people actually put tables inside of tables. Is this legal, or should I be using only one table to achieve a page layout?

A: Actually, a table-within-a-table is a legal option. It's referred to as "nesting," and can be used to great success in more advanced table layout design. You'll see me using them later in the book, but for now, try playing with the tags you've learned in this chapter and seeing what types of results you can achieve. Just remember to work from the "container" method, check your syntax, and if you run into trouble, use a syntax checker.

Q: Sometimes I'm working with tables and when I go to view my work in a browser I see a blank page. What does this mean?

A: Most often this occurs when you've done the following:

❏ You've forgotten to close your table with the `</table>` tag.

❏ You have one or more table cells that have not been closed with the appropriate `</td>`. Check your work, and then recheck it!

Q: I'm trying to make a table, but suddenly, instead of running vertically, it is running left-to-right, creating a horizontal scrollbar. What happened?

A: This is the result of a missing `</tr>` table row-end tag. Check your syntax and try again. Another reason is that you may be trying to create a table that is simply too wide for your browser, and this is forcing a horizontal scrollbar. Make sure your ultimate length is no longer than 640 pixels wide. Even if your monitor supports higher resolution, many others do not, so designing to the 640 pixel width maximum keeps that ugly horizontal scrollbar from appearing.

two

Strong Foundations: The Basics of Frame Technology

Designers and Web visitors alike have both praised or criticized frames technology. Not only is there the literal and technical division of browser space that frames create, but a philosophical division as well. The rift, which has been argued on each extreme since Netscape released frames, is as logical as it is unnecessary. Fortunately, the churning surf has not stopped the progress and development of frame-based models. Most Web designers are beginning to agree that the survival of frames is a fortunate twist of fate, for frame technology now has moved to the forefront as a very powerful page formatting device.

But why so much disparity? The reason is primarily both the curse and the blessing of what frames do: the breaking up of space. Look at your computer monitor. It is highly likely that you fit into the common population of computer owners, and your screen will be an average of 15-17" diagonally, with an available resolution of either 640x480 pixels or 800x600 pixels.

Take this space and add to it the pixels that a Web browser's interface takes up, from about 5 to 15 on either vertical margin, anywhere from 25 to 150 on the top margin, and about 25 on the bottom margin. At best, on a 640x480 resolution screen, the number of used pixels reduces your viewing space to 630x430, at worst, 610x305 pixels or less, leaving you with a very small amount of viewing space.

Now add a bordered, frame-based design to the mix, as seen in Figure 2.1, and you can quickly see why some individuals have gotten upset. Frames literally take what is a small, contained space and break that space up into smaller, even more contained spaces. Until borderless frames became available, only the most technologically adept and design-savvy could use frames well, and even then at the risk of upsetting visitors who visit their pages. It is still good protocol to provide "no frame" options for Web browsers that do not support them and for Web visitors that maintain a passionate dislike for frames.

Figure 2.1.
Frames with borders take up a significant amount of viewing space.

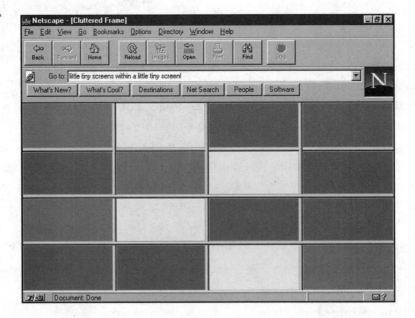

Web Without Borders

Borderless frames have bridged the churning waters, however. When Microsoft's Internet Explorer Web browser introduced the <frameborder=x> attribute, with Netscape Navigator 3.0 introducing a similar feature quickly thereafter, the face of frames changed. In fact, the face of frames can now disappear altogether, if a designer so desires. Setting the frame border to a value of 0 makes the three-dimensional frame borders go away, offering seamless integration between frame divisions (see Figure 2.2).

Figure 2.2.

The same frame-based page as Figure 2.1 but without borders.

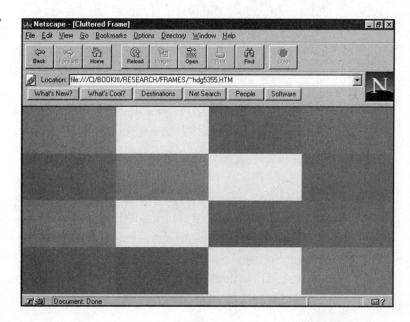

This seamless integration moved frames from their position as an organizational tool to one of page format control. With borderless frames, as with borderless tables, individual sections of a page can be defined and controlled. But where tables can only be used on a page-by-page basis, frame technology introduces *static* and *targeted* aspects, allowing portions of the visible screen to remain static while others can be targeted, or changed, with the simple click of a link.

With the control that borders allow, a designer can now make better choices about how to employ frames. Whether he or she uses dimensional borders for an attractive interface, or to create pages with frames as the silent and strong foundation beneath a complex and multifaceted design, the Web designer is ultimately empowered by the new and ongoing additions to frame technology.

Frame Structure: Columns and Rows

Before I introduce the practical aspects of how to design a framed page, I'd like to demonstrate a fundamental aspect of frame design. Much like tables, frames are built by thinking in columns and rows. Tables, as you've seen in Chapter 1, "Good Manners: Basic Table Elements," get a bit complex in the ways columns and rows are spanned, creating some confusion between horizontal and vertical reference points. Frames approach the issue in a much more straightforward fashion—a column is an overtly vertical control, a row is a horizontal one.

Moreover, the syntax is very clear. Rows are *rows*, columns are *cols*. Both columns and rows can be defined in terms of pixels or percentages. For example, `cols=240, *` calls for a left column with a width of 240 pixels; the right column, called by the asterisk, will be the remainder of the available viewing space. To add more columns, simply define each one in turn. For example, if I wanted to create four columns of equal percent, the syntax would read `cols=25%,25%,25%,25%`. The results are shown in Figure 2.3.

Similarly, if I wanted to create rows rather than columns, I would simply change the syntax to `rows=240, *`, and the results would be a top row with a height of 240 pixels. To create four individual rows of equal percent, I would call for `rows=25%,25%,25%,25%`, as shown in Figure 2.4.

To create combinations of columns and rows, the values are simply stacked into the appropriate tags and pages of the framed site.

Figure 2.3.
A four-column frame.

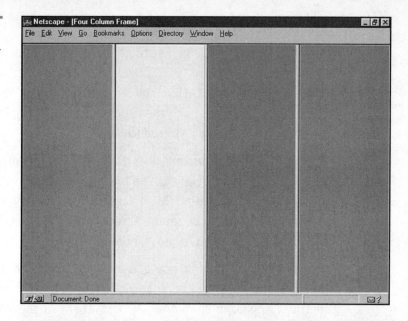

Figure 2.4.
A frame with four rows.

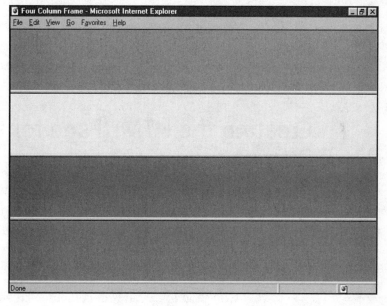

Elements of Framed Pages

A well laid-out, frame-based site offering up-to-date HTML information, including beginning to advanced level frames data, is Sizzling HTML Jalfrezi. Point your browser to `http://www.woodhill.co.uk/html/html.htm` for all the HTML tags fit to print!

There are only three elements absolutely necessary to build a framed page. It sounds too easy, I know! And, as I advance through various aspects of working with frames, you will see that they can get a bit complicated, depending upon the ways you wish to employ them. But, at the most basic level, all framed sites begin with the factors I'll introduce here.

So, how many basic elements does it take to make a framed page? The answer is simple: one HTML page *plus* the total number of frames. Any framed page will require a controlling HTML document that gives the instructions on how the framed page is to be set up. This control is called the *frameset*. Then, an HTML page is required for each individual frame.

Remember your sums! A framed page requires one HTML page per each individually defined area, *plus* one HTML page for the control, or frameset, page.

In the following tasks, I'm going to show you how to create a simple, framed page. For logic's sake, I'll begin by working with you to create the actual pages that will appear in each given frames. Then, I'll show you how to pull it together using the frameset control page. This basic framed page breaks up the viewing space into two sections. What, then, is the total number of elements necessary to create this page? If you said "three," you're right: two HTML pages for the viewable sections and another HTML page, the frameset page.

Creating the HTML Page for the Left Frame

Each section of a frame requires a standard HTML page containing the data you wish to provide in that section. My aim is to design a two-column page, with the left column serving as a simple menu that could eventually be used to guide a visitor through the site. In this exercise, you'll create the HTML page for the left column.

The choices listed within this menu are currently inactive, but you'll be changing them as you progress through frame-based tasks within the chapter.

1. In your workshop folder on your computer, create a subfolder named `frames02` from the CD-ROM. Copy all files from the directory `frames02` into that folder.

2. In your HTML editor, type the following:

```
<html>
<head>
<title> Menu for Frameset I</title>
```

```
</head>
<body bgcolor="#000000" text="#CCCCFF">

<img src="02-hed.jpg" width=200 height=100 align=left>
<br clear="all">
<pre>

</pre>
<div align=right>
Choice I
<p>

Choice II
<p>

Choice III
<p>

</div>
</body>
</html>
```

NOTE: You'll notice the use of the `<pre>` (preformatted text) tag within these documents. In Chapter 1, I briefly described how this tag was the only original way to create columnar data. It is used now by designers to create white space when working along the vertical axis. To get a better idea as to how it controls space, remove the tags, or change the amount of carriage returns between them and then view them within the browser.

3. Save the file as `menu.htm`.

4. View the file in your browser to see how it looks before you apply the frameset to it.

DESIGN NOTE: Note that the attractive header I've created for this page was made quickly and easily in Photoshop. Although there are many Web graphic design tools available, and you will be using a variety to perform different jobs as a Web designer, no single tool will be put more to use than Photoshop. Make this program first on your list of required graphics programs, regardless of what platform you work on.

Creating the HTML Page for the Right-Column Frame

Now you'll create a right-column frame.

1. In your HTML editor, type the following:

```
<html>
<head>
<title>Main Section Frame I</title>
</head>
<body bgcolor="#000000" text="#CCCCFF">

<pre>


</pre>
<img src="frame.gif" width=150 height=220 align=right hspace=20
vspace=10>
<br clear="left">
<pre>

</pre>
<p align=right>

In this, the "main" section of the frame, you can put a variety
of media,links, or text—whateverickles your fancy. Here I've
added a JPG graphic of a log cabin's window, which is itself a
frame!
</p>

</body>
</html>
```

2. Save the file as main.htm.

3. View the file in your Web browser to see what it looks like before adding the frameset command file.

CAUTION: It's important to remember that, as you create HTML frames for individual pages, the width and height you choose for images or table fields are appropriate for the frame space you are designing. For example, if your image is 250 pixels wide, but the frame column in which it will appear is 25% of a page, a horizontal scrollbar will appear at common resolution or the image will be cut off, depending on what attributes you call for. Always be aware of space considerations; otherwise, you can fall into the problems that frames are notorious for rather than using them to enhance design.

The Frameset

The frameset is the control page of your framed site. In it, you'll argue primarily for the rows or columns you wish to create, and the HTML pages that will fill those rows or columns. This is done using two major tags:

- ❑ **`<frameset>`** This tag for the frame, and its basic arguments, define rows and columns. The frameset information is closed with a corresponding `</frameset>` tag.

- ❑ **`<frame>`** The frame tag argues individual frames within the frameset. This includes the location of the HTML document required to fill the frame, utilizing the `src=x` (where x equals the relative or absolute URL to the location of the HTML page). A variety of other `<frame>` attributes will be covered later in this chapter.

NOTE: There's an old saying, "What you open, close." This is an excellent guideline when coding HTML, but there are exceptions to that rule. One such exception is the `<frame>` tag; there is no real counterpart `</frame>` tag. All the information for individual frames is placed within the tag and it is considered closed when the right-angle bracket (>) is reached.

 ## Creating a Frameset Page

This task will help you create the foundation of all framed pages: the frameset.

1. Open your HTML editor and begin a new page. Type in the following, and remember that you are working with the "container" method described in Chapter 1:

```
<html>

<frameset>
```

```
</frameset>

</html>
```

2. Now you'll add the appropriate syntax to create the columns as mentioned earlier in the chapter. Add the following to your page:

```
<html>

<frameset cols="240, *">
</frameset>

</html>
```

NOTE: You'll notice that I chose to make the first column of this frame 240 pixels wide. I wanted to buffer my graphic with some white space (in this case, actually black). The 240 pixel width provides that space. Instead of coding the exact size of the remaining space, I've chosen to allow the browser to define that dynamically by using the * wildcard. The browser will now dedicate the remaining space to the second column.

3. Now you'll add the individual frames with their corresponding HTML pages:

```
<html>

<frameset cols="240, *">

<frame src="menu.htm">
<frame src="main.htm">

</frameset>
</html>
```

4. Save the document as `frame-01.htm`.

5. Load the frameset page (`frame-01.htm`) into your browser and view the results. Does it match Figure 2.5? If it does, congratulations!

DESIGN NOTE: It's important to remember that the `<frameset>` tag is a conceptual replacement for the `<body>` tag in the frameset HTML page. Therefore, be sure that any instance of `<body>` tags appearing before the `<frameset>` tags are removed.

Figure 2.5.
The results of your first frameset.

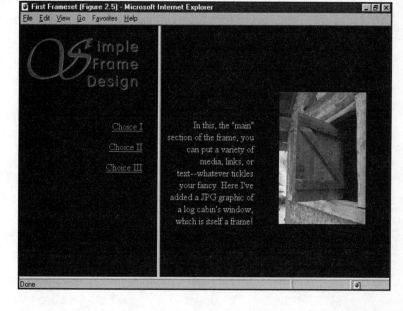

Pages not matching the examples? Look over your syntax very carefully first, and then refer to the glossary directory on the CD-ROM for syntax clarification.

Frameset and Frame Tag Attributes

There are several powerful attributes available for the `<frameset>` and `<frame>` tags. Not only do these attributes control the way a framed page is laid out, but offer some interesting design options that you'll see unfolding as the book progresses. I'll introduce attributes here that are either common to both the Netscape Navigator 3.0+ and Internet Explorer 3.0+ browsers, or that are required for designing in either browser. Then you'll have the opportunity to perform tasks in order to see them at work. Please refer to Appendix B, "HTML Quick Reference," for a complete reference of attributes.

Frameset Attributes

The following are commonly used attributes for the `<frameset>`:

- ❏ **cols=x** This attribute creates columns. An x value is given for each column in the framed page; it will be either a pixel value, a percentage value, or a combination of one of those plus the *. The star creates a *dynamic* or *relative* size frame. This is whatever the remainder of the framed space size turns out to be. That size will be different for different browsers and screen resolutions.

- ❏ **rows=x** This attribute is used to create rows in the same fashion that the column attribute is used.

- ❏ **border=x** The border attribute is used by Netscape Navigator 3.0 and above to control border width. Value is set in pixel width.

- ❏ **frameborder=x** Frameborder is used by the Internet Explorer browser to control border width in pixels. Netscape Navigator 3.0 and above uses the attribute with a yes or no value.

- ❏ **framespacing=x** Used by Internet Explorer, this attribute controls border width.

Entirely confused between border, frameborder, and framespacing attributes? The disparity is a result of rapid browser development and slower standards being passed. Designers trying to design across browser lines have long been frustrated by the instability in browser technology. The good news is that there are workarounds, and I'll cover frame border techniques in the final part of this chapter.

Frame Tag Attributes

Use these tag attributes for individual frame control:

- ❏ **frameborder=x** Use this attribute to control frameborders around individual frames. Netscape Navigator requires a yes or no value, whereas Internet Explorer will look for a numeric pixel width value.

- ❏ **marginheight=x** Argue a value in pixels to control the height of the frame's margin.

❏ `marginwidth=x` This attribute argues for a frame's margin width in pixels.

❏ `name=x` This critical attribute allows the designer to name an individual frame. Naming frames permits targeting, or the precise placement of an HTML page into a frame, by links within other HTML pages. Names must begin with a standard letter or numeral.

❏ `noresize` Simply place this handy tag in your string if you want to allow resizing of a frame. This fixes the frame into the position.

❏ `scrolling=x` By arguing `yes`, `no`, or `auto`, you can control the appearance of a scrollbar. A `yes` value automatically places a scrollbar in the frame, a `no` value ensures that no scrollbar ever appears. The `auto` argument turns the power over to the browser, which will automatically place a scrollbar in a frame if it is required.

❏ `src=x` The x value is replaced with the relative or absolute URL of the HTML page you wish to place within the frame.

At this point, it is easy to see how, between the various ways individual browsers work and the variety of attributes common to contemporary browsers, frames can easily confound the less adventurous of designers. The next task is designed to allow you to feel more comfortable with `<frame>` tag attributes.

TASK Creating a Frame with Margin, Resize, and Scroll Controls

In this task, you'll learn how to offer maximum flexibility for your site visitors with margins, resizing, and scroll attributes.

1. Open the frameset HTML document you created earlier (`frame-01.htm`).

2. In the first `<frame>` tag, add the following arguments:

```
<html>

<frameset cols="240, *">

<frame src="menu.htm" marginheight=5 marginwidth=5 noresize
scrolling=auto>
```

```
<frame src="main.htm">

</frameset>
</html>
```

3. View this page in the browser of your choice. Note that the appearance of your framed page hasn't changed, but the mechanics have. You cannot resize the frame!

4. Change the scrolling value to yes.

5. View the change in the browser. You'll see that the browser assumes that a scrollbar will be required. It, therefore, places one there, even if it isn't actually needed, as shown in Figure 2.6. Because this is unattractive from a design standpoint, change the value back to auto. See the following tip to clarify how scrolling is best used.

Figure 2.6.
A yes *value for scrolling creates a scrollbar, even if it isn't necessary.*

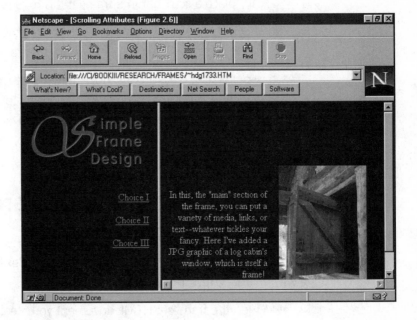

6. In the second `<frame>` tag, add the following:

```
<frame src="main.htm" marginheight=15 marginwidth=15 noresize
scrolling=yes>
```

7. View the results in your browser. Now the browser has put in scrolling for the right frame. Again, I find this unattractive, so I'll ask you to reset the scrolling value to auto.

8. Save the final page as `frame-02.htm`. Your code should match this:

```
<html>

<frameset cols="240, *">

<frame src="menu.htm" marginheight=5 marginwidth=5 noresize
scrolling=auto>
<frame src="main.htm" marginheight=15 marginwidth=15 noresize
scrolling=auto>

</frameset>
</html>
```

TIP: Make good decisions when choosing scrolling. A `yes` value for scrolling is rarely attractive, but is extremely useful when the frame in question contains a long document. My advice is to use it sparingly and only when necessary. A `no` value is most valuable for fixed-column frames used for menus. If you have done your math and are absolutely certain that you have allowed for enough viewing area to contain the HTML information, use the `no` value. Setting scrolling on `auto` is usually the favorable choice because it allows the browser to make the decision. An `auto` value is especially favorable wherever you've argued for dynamic or relative size (a `*` value) rows and columns.

For a good example of scrolling and resizing frame attributes at work, visit Buffalo Exchange at `http://www.desert.net/buffalo/`. Enter the frame version of the site and view the frameset source for any of the individual pages. Look for the `<frame>` tags. Notice how the designers of this site employed various attributes to achieve a sophisticated, attractive frame-based design.

Interested in how to accomplish a variety of frame interfaces? Visit Chapter 5, "Frame-Based Interface Design."

Now I'll move into a more detailed frame technique critical to frame-based design. Linking, or targeting individual pages to load in specified windows, is perhaps one of the more confusing aspects of designing with frames. The following information and tasks will demonstrate the basics of how to accomplish targeting.

DESIGN NOTE: To resize or not to resize? From a design standpoint, resizing can foul up your attractive, well thought-out framed page. As a designer, I truly dislike resizing and almost always prefer to use the `noresize` attribute. However, as a visitor to Web sites, I've noticed that resizing can be very valuable, especially if I want to see a particular frame's data in its entirety. Usually this occurs when a certain frame contains a lot of data. It's a tough call, but my recommendation is to think about a page from both the design and practical use standpoint before making resize decisions.

Targeting Windows

In order to effectively use frames, a designer must decide where link options will load. For example, in the frame page you've developed in this chapter, I've guided you in creating a menu on the left and a larger frame field on the right. This is a natural start for effective design using frames.

There are two basic ways to link, or target, HTML pages to specific windows:

❏ Combine target and name attributes to work in harmony with the frame interface.

❏ Use what is commonly known as magic target names. Magic target names are a series of preset names that you can implement to do specific functions.

To see the first method in action, you'll need to have the following elements:

❏ A frameset page with the `name` attribute argued in the appropriate `<frame>` tag.

❏ One HTML page per frame window.

❏ One or more HTML pages to link, or target.

Creating a Frame Using Target and Name Attributes

Before employing the `name` and `<frame>` tag attributes, you'll need to have an extra HTML page to target. This first part of the process is especially easy! The HTML page in question requires no special tags. You simply need to do the following:

1. Start with a blank page in your HTML editor.

2. Type the following basic HTML:

```
<html>
<head>
```

```
<title> Choice I</title>
</head>
<body bgcolor="#000000" text="#CCCCFF"
link="#CC99CC"vlink="#999900">

<h2>Choice I</h2>
```

This page is loaded into the right frame. I used the `name=col2` attribute in the frameset page to achieve this result.

```
</body>
</html>
```

3. Save the file as `choice1.htm` in your frames folder and set it aside.

4. Now open the frameset (`frame-02.htm`) code in your HTML editor.

5. Add the following syntax to name the right frame:

```
<html>

<frameset cols="240, *">

<frame src="menu.htm" marginheight=5 marginwidth=5 noresize
scrolling=auto>
<frame src="main.htm" name=col2 marginheight=15 marginwidth=15
noresize scrolling=auto>

</frameset>
</html>
```

6. Save the file.

Now you'll need to add the corresponding target syntax to the `menu.htm` file. To do so:

7. Open the `menu.htm` file and add the target syntax:

```
<html>
<head>
<title> Menu for Frameset I</title>
</head>
<body bgcolor="#000000" text="#CCCCFF">

<img src="02-hed.jpg" width=200 height=100 align=left>
<br clear="all">
<pre>

</pre>
<div align=right>
<a href="choice1.htm" target=col2>Choice I</a>
```

```
<p>

Choice II
<p>

Choice III
<p>

</div>
</body>
</html>
```

8. Save the changes and open the frameset in your browser. You should see the original frame page created earlier, but the first link, Choice I, is now hot and ready to be clicked.

9. Click the link and watch what happens. If `choice1.htm` loaded smoothly into the right frame, you've successfully completed the process. The results should match Figure 2.7.

Figure 2.7.
The target for Choice I has loaded smoothly into the right frame.

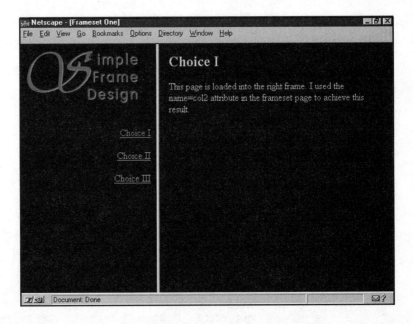

To nullify a target window created with a `<base target=x>` value for a specific link, simply target that link using any target convention. The `<base>` creates a default, so it is the final argument that a browser will look for. Anything else you argue for will be interpreted first.

TIP: Want all of a site's pages to load into the same window? Follow the `name` and `target` convention. Within each document you want to load into that window, use the `<base>` tag. Place the following syntax within the `<head>` of every page to be loaded in that window: `<base target=col2>`.

Magic Target Names

There are several predefined target names that will cause certain actions to occur when a target link is created.

Because magic target names always begin with an underscore (_blank, for example), you must avoid naming targets with anything other than an accepted alphanumeric character. An underscore, or any other symbol, will be ignored.

- ❏ **target=_blank** The _blank argument causes the targeted document to open in a new browser window.

CAUTION: The magic target name _blank always forces a new browser window to open. Be careful to use this only when a new window is absolutely necessary; otherwise, you run the risk of angering Web site visitors who will end up with numerous, resource-draining browser windows on the desktop.

- ❏ **target=_self** The targeted document will load in the same window where the originating link exists.

- ❏ **target=_parent** This will load the targeted document into the link's parent frameset.

- ❏ **target=_top** Use this attribute to load the link into the full window, overriding any existing frames.

DESIGN NOTE: The target=_top argument is a wise design choice when a link takes the visitor out of your framed site into a new site, which may or may not use frames. Some designers like the idea of keeping external sites inside a targeted frame, allowing the native site's menu or advertisement to remain live while surfing elsewhere. Although this can be an effective option, use it sparingly to avoid upsetting visitors, who may not appreciate your site following them wherever they go!

 ## Using Magic Target Names

This task will show you how to add two types of magic target names to your existing framed page.

1. Begin by opening your HTML editor. You'll need to create two more pages to target. Copy the following into one instance of a blank editing page:

```
<html>
<head>
<title> Choice II</title>
</head>
<body bgcolor="#000000" text="#CCCCFF" link="#CC99CC"
vlink="#999900">

<h2>Choice II</h2>

This page is loaded into the left frame, using the <i>magic
target name</i> "_self"


</body>
</html>
```

2. Save the file as choice2.htm.

3. Open another blank editing page and enter the following:

```
<html>
<head>
<title> Choice III</title>
</head>
<body bgcolor="#000000"text="#CCCCFF"link="#CC99CC"
vlink="#999900">

<h2>Choice III</h2>

This page loads into a new window using the <i>magic target
name</i> "blank"in the referring syntax.


</body>
</html>
```

4. Save this page as choice3.htm. You'll notice that both pages are plain HTML pages, without any target or name attributes.

5. Open the `menu.htm` file you made earlier. This is the file where the links to the pages that will be targeted appear. You should see the following:

```
<html>
<head>
<title> Menu for Frameset I</title>
</head>
<body bgcolor="#000000"text="#CCCCFF"link="#CC99CC"
vlink="#999900">

<img src="02-hed.jpg" width=200 height=100 align=left>
<br clear="all">
<pre>

</pre>
<div align=right>

<a href="choice1.htm" target=col2>Choice I</a>
<p>

Choice II
<p>

Choice III
<p>

</div>
</body>
</html>
```

6. You're going to add the syntax for Choice II, which will target into the menu frame. The syntax is as follows:

```
<a href="choice2.htm" target=_self>Choice II</a>
```

7. Save the file and open the frameset page. In the menu frame, you will notice that Choice II is now hot. Click that link and watch how `choice2.htm` loads into the menu frame.

8. Return to your HTML editor and add the following syntax:

```
<a href="choice3.htm" target=_blank>Choice III</a>
```

9. Save the file, and open the frameset page in your browser. Choice III is now hot. When you click this choice, you'll notice how `choice3.htm` is loaded into an entirely *new* browser window (see Figure 2.8).

Figure 2.8.
Clicking the Choice III link loads the corresponding HTML page into a new browser window.

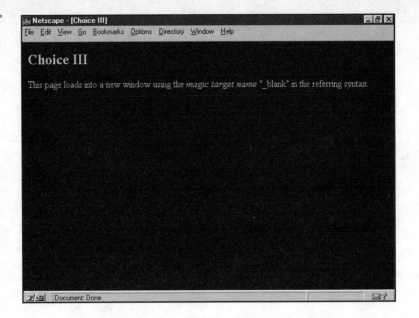

Sensitive, sensitive! Be sure when you are naming your own targets to keep your case consistent. It's always wise to figure out a style that appeals to you and *stick to it!* This will aid you from running into problems because of frame and target case sensitivity.

Need the latest browser? Visit `http:// www.microsoft.com/ ie/` for Internet Explorer releases, and `http:// home.netscape.com/` for the most recent release of Netscape.

You've now tackled some of the most difficult aspects of coding for frames. I encourage you to try a few designs using various targets and attributes of your own selection. You'll learn a lot from experimentation, as well as have fun in the process!

I mentioned earlier in the chapter the confusion surrounding borderless frames. It's a critical issue because using, or not using, borders is the point where the designer makes decisions about how to use frame technology as a format tool. Removing borders makes formatting a page seamless, and this is a powerful as well as popular method of designing pages.

Creating Cross-Browser Borderless Frames

The first rule in cross-browser design is to know which browsers you are attempting to reach. With frames, that rule is clarified by the fact that only certain browsers interpret frames, and some do so with very limited capabilities. At this point in browser history, it's safe to say that if you're developing framed sites, only two browsers are going to interpret the advanced visual results you are after: Netscape Navigator (3.0+) and Internet Explorer (3.0+).

The challenge of borderless frames doesn't necessarily lie in the coding, but in the differences the way popular browsers *interpret* the code, or require the code to read. Fortunately, you can stack attributes within tags; if a browser doesn't support that attribute or its value, it will ignore it and move on to the attribute and related value that it does interpret.

The difference, which I touched upon earlier when discussing `<frameset>` tag attributes, appears in the way browsers control borders and spacing between frames. Here are the individual browser requirements:

❏ **Netscape Navigator** The Netscape browser (3.0+) will allow for borderless frames when it does the following:

The `border` attribute is set, in pixels, to a numeric value of `0`.

The `framespacing` attribute is assigned a `no` value.

❏ **Internet Explorer** Microsoft's browser, referred to as "IE" for short, will produce borderless frames if it does the following:

The `frameborder` attribute is set, in pixels, to a numeric value of `0`.

The `framespacing` attribute is assigned a width, in pixels, to a numeric value of `0`.

If it seems like there's a conflict, there isn't, because each browser requires either a different attribute to control width or a different value to control spacing. It looks confusing, but if you stack attributes, you can easily create borderless frames that will be read by both browsers without difficulty. This technique results in two legal syntax options:

```
<frameset frameborder=0 framespacing=0 border=0>
```

or

```
<frameset frameborder=no framespacing=0 border=0>
```

Either one is correct, and it's just a matter of personal preference as to which you'll use. Remember to add your columns and rows to the string in order to create a full range of frameset arguments.

Making a Borderless Frame

Because you already have a fully operational framed page, you can simply add the appropriate syntax to the frameset string in order to achieve a borderless effect:

1. Open the `frame01.htm` file in your HTML editor.

2. Add the following to the `<frameset>` string:

```
<html>

<frameset frameborder=0 framespacing=0 border=0 cols="240, *">

<frame src="menu.htm" marginheight=5 marginwidth=5 noresize
scrolling=auto>
<frame src="main.htm" name=col2 marginheight=15 marginwidth=15
noresize scrolling=auto>

</frameset>
</html>
```

3. View the results in both Netscape Navigator 3.0 or above or IE 3.0 or above. Your results should match Figure 2.9.

Figure 2.9.
A frame without borders!

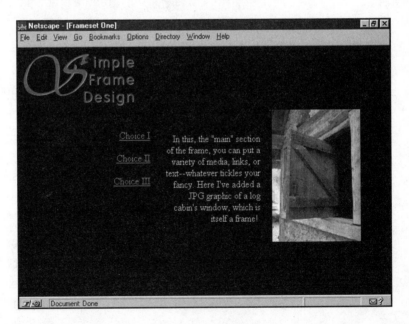

Ensuring Support for Non-Frames Browsers

Most Web aficionados keep up with current browser trends. However, there is a large population of people who either don't use the Web enough to worry about the latest versions, are new to the Web and aren't yet aware of the need to keep in step with the rapidly changing trends, or are simply disinterested in the design of a page. From a design standpoint, I've always encouraged using advanced browser-based techniques, because I think Web designers help push technological development. This rapidly offers new options for Web designers, even if it disregards people not in step with the latest and greatest available tools.

DESIGN NOTE: Designing across browsers can be challenging, and many people like to place links on pages so that the latest browsers can be accessed. The wise designer will either design so efficiently as to reach every browser that comes past his or her virtual doorstep or will concede to offer links to current browsers. The very first page is not a good choice for browser links. What if your visitor surfs off to get the latest and greatest in browsers and forgets you ever existed? If you do choose to place links to browsers, do so as sensibly as you can.

However, there is a smaller population that is of extreme concern to me, and that is the blind and certain disabled who require text-only access. The Internet, with its vast wealth of information and communications opportunities, has been very empowering for such individuals. However, the graphically rich environment of the Web is at best cumbersome and at worst inaccessible to people who use screen readers and similar access tools. Those technologies, while certainly advancing, are still expensive and unsophisticated in terms of Graphic User Interfaces (GUIs).

Netscape and Internet Explorer are GUIs. There are browsers, such as Lynx, which are text-only, and deliver Web pages as text without a graphic interface environment. Designers can usually incorporate text access with great ease in general Web design. Frames introduce additional Graphic User Interface information, but, fortunately, there is a powerful option to allow for non-frame and text-only browsers to access information within a frame-based site. Keeping to the current trends and incorporating no-frame and text access addresses cross-browser issues by enabling not only those who require text access, but those who prefer it as well.

The way to achieve this in a framed site is by employing the logical <noframes> tag. This is placed in the frameset page. Critical information can then be provided at the same URL as the frameset page, and an entirely accessible site can be formed using the same pages as the framed site.

Employing the <noframes> Tag

When you must be sure your framed site is accessible for people who may not have frame-viewing capabilities, you can use the technique in this task.

1. Open the frameset (frame01.htm) in your HTML editor.

2. Add the <noframes> tag and its companion </noframes> in the following fashion:

```
<html>

<frameset frameborder=0 framespacing=0 border=0 cols="240, *">

<frame src="menu.htm" marginheight=5 marginwidth=5 noresize
scrolling=auto>
<frame src="main.htm" name=col2 marginheight=15 marginwidth=15
noresize scrolling=auto>

</frameset>

<noframes>

</noframes>

</html>
```

3. Now you'll add all of the HTML syntax necessary to create a fully functional page within the <noframes> tag:

```
<html>

<frameset frameborder=0 framespacing=0 border=0 cols="240, *">

<frame src="menu.htm" marginheight=5 marginwidth=5 noresize
scrolling=auto>
<frame src="main.htm" name=col2 marginheight=15 marginwidth=15
noresize scrolling=auto>
```

```
</frameset>

<noframes>

<body bgcolor="#000000" text="#CCCCFF"link="#CC99CC"
vlink="#999900">

<img src="02-hed.jpg" width=200 height=100>
<p>

<blockquote>

Welcome. We're happy to provide this non-frames access to our
Web site. If you prefer to view our site using frames, please
upgrade your browser to a recent one that fully supports frames.
Otherwise, please select from the following options:
<p>

<a href="choice1.htm">Choice I</a>
<p>

<a href="choice2.htm">Choice II</a>
<p>

<a href="choice3.htm">Choice III</a>
<p>

</blockquote>
</body>

</noframes>

</html>
```

4. Save the page. You've now made the page completely accessible to non-frame browsers. Notice how the syntax within the `<noframes>` tags has been properly adjusted for a standard, non-framed style page. For example, I've removed targets within links, added block quotes to create margins, placed the image appropriately, and included all of the body information for background and link colors.

> **TIP:** To see how a browser without frames will interpret the code, simply copy all of the syntax within the `<noframes>` tags into a clean HTML editing environment. Add the appropriate beginning and closing `<html>` tags and view the page (see Figure 2.10).

Figure 2.10.
This is how your page will appear in a browser that doesn't support frames.

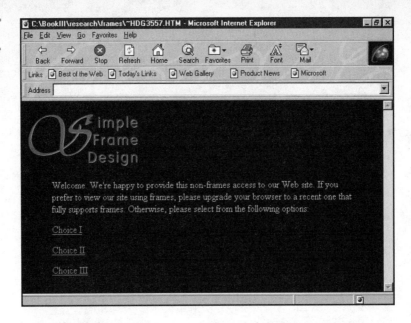

The framed page you've designed here is already an employable, effective interface. Additional frame-based interfaces using multiple rows and columns, a variety of complex frames, and how to use floating or independent frames will all be introduced throughout this book.

Workshop Wrap-Up

The tasks in this chapter have been designed to walk you through building a frame step-by-step. It may occasionally appear as if I've stepped backwards, or asked you to wait before approaching a given issue that would seem immediate, such as the discussion of borderless frames. By giving you information incrementally, I have done this in order to clarify a seemingly complicated technology.

If at any time the process has become confusing, go back to the beginning and remember how frames are built. Simply stated, frames involve a relationship between standard HTML pages and the frameset page, with attributes that allow for more complicated aspects such as targeting or offering borderless options.

As you work through the various chapters in this book, you will find the tasks, while sometimes resulting in more complex frames, are actually more logical because of the strong foundations laid in this chapter. Your ability to build framed sites will not only become stronger as a result, but you will also become wiser as you come to understand the historic and technological difficulties involved.

Next Steps

The next chapter moves on to examine the basics of another design and format tool: cascading style sheets. Should you wish to move on and try your hand at more advanced frame exercises, you can

❑ Practice tasks in Chapter 5, "Frame-Based Interface Design."

❑ Move to Chapter 7, "Designing Interfaces Combining Tables and Frames," to read about borderless frames for high-style interfaces.

❑ Discover a powerful frame technique in Chapter 8, "Progressive Interfaces with Floating Frames."

❑ Continue on a chapter-by-chapter basis through the book, which offers expanding opportunities to learn about format options for Web designers, including advanced frame techniques and combination techniques using tables, frames, and style sheets.

Q&A

Q: I've tried to print the information in the right frame, but the left frame is printing. What's going on?

A: Click on a dead space within the frame you wish to print. The browser will then send the correct frame to the printer. If you have detailed information in a frame window, thorough designers and good browser developers recommend offering downloadable options so the visitor may quickly retrieve the data available on the site.

Q: How come my frame pages look different in Netscape and in IE? I'm following your cross-browser advice and using the latest version of each. What am I doing wrong?

A: If your syntax is correct, you aren't doing anything wrong. The two browsers have notorious differences in the way HTML pages are displayed, in general. These disparities will appear within framed pages also. One specific difference is that Netscape Navigator handles the bottom and right side of frames differently, cutting off visual data. This makes the pages appear larger in IE. The trick is to learn as much about cross-browser techniques as possible, and be sure that your designs look attractive within each. At that point, vive la difference!

Q: The more I work with designing framed pages, the more pages I generate. How can I control the amount of HTML pages I create?

A: Aside from being careful with syntax and designing frames from a logical as well as design standpoint, the answer is a sad, but true, *not much.* The amount of data necessary to create multiple frames on a page is reliant on individual HTML pages. So, think about how many windows you really need. Don't fall into the trap that because something looks cool that it *is* cool. Balancing appearance and functionality is one of the hallmarks of a truly good Web designer.

three

In Vogue: Cascading Style Sheets

Style is the name of the game now! For the first time in Web design history, designers have one of the components long denied: the ability to control how both text and design elements are laid out on pages through HTML, with a good amount of sophistication.

Style sheets are basically a means of controlling the way HTML tags are formatted. Because many Web designers have come from a graphic design or desktop publishing background, style control is part of the natural approach to design. But a common tool to do style control has been missing from HTML. Historically, the scripting process of HTML specifically avoided advanced style options, offering instead only very standard or rudimentary means of creating style elements such as color, headers, and margins. Special effects, such as text shadowing, have required the use of graphics, slowing down pages as the data is shuttled between server and browser.

Although this book looks at design aspects of HTML and browser-based technology, there is no other current trend in Web design that will overtly separate the technologists from the artists than style sheets.

This means that, now more than ever, Web designers must seek out a balance in skills in order to compete within the New Media industry.

The word "cascading" refers to the fact that not only can multiple styles be used in an individual HTML page, but the browser will follow an order—a cascade—to interpret the information. Out of the three types of currently available style sheets, a designer can choose to use all three simultaneously. The browser will then look for information in an orderly fashion in delivering the pervading style sheet.

Full Control? Not Entirely, Not Yet...

Style control with HTML has been clumsy at best, and non-existent at worst. Cascading style sheets change that. Not only does a Web designer have better ways of working with such style-critical issues as fonts, he or she has the means by which to control such text-related style issues as font face, size in several measurement types, font weight, font style, and leading (pronounced "led-ing").

Needless to say, the enthusiasm surrounding style sheets is so strong that the World Wide Web Consortium—the organization responsible for introducing new technologies into the HTML standard—has responded with great enthusiasm and unprecedented support. At the time of this writing, Netscape is incorporating style sheets into its 4.0 release. Internet Explorer set the pace by introducing them in the 3.0 release. This browser disparity is the only reason designers have been somewhat hesitant in going hog-wild with the technology.

NOTE: Ironically, when a page using style sheets and no other HTML style controls is viewed by Netscape 3.0 or below, the page appears as a visual throw-back, reverting to that horrible gray background and demoting fonts and other styles to their bare-bones defaults (see Figures 3.1 and 3.2). It is the Web designer's good fortune that the time gap between compatibility from both major browser developers has been relatively short! However, the pre-release version of Netscape Navigator 4.0 shows some very inconsistent problems with CSS implementation. Because of this, the information in this chapter is geared primarily to the Internet Explorer 3.0+ browser, whose support of CSS (cascading style sheets) is fairly stable.

Figure 3.1.

A page using cascading style sheets as it appears in Internet Explorer 3.0.

Figure 3.2.

The same page will revert to bare-bones defaults in any Netscape browser below a 4.0 level release.

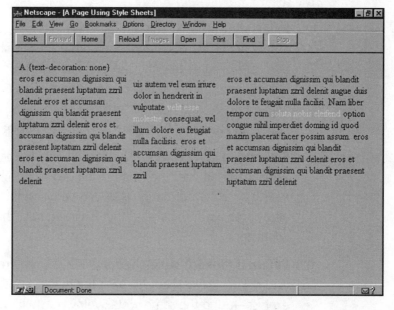

Be sure to take a preliminary look at Part IV of this book, "Sophisticated Pages Using Format Control," which focuses heavily on sophisticated layout using style sheets.

This is not to say that there aren't challenges inherent in cascading style sheets. Of course there are, and they include issues such as the fact that my machine invariably has different fonts loaded on it than yours does, and your selection of fonts is somewhat different than your coworker's, and hers is different from her neighbor's. Font style, including face and weight, can be called by a style sheet, but if the font and font weight aren't on the visitor's machine, the browser cannot interpret the style you've set up.

A variety of techniques, books, and online resources are mentioned throughout the margin and design notes in this book. Appendix A, "Directory of Resources," provides a thorough listing of such resources. Make note of these resources!

Conveniently, there are workarounds for this type of problem. Wise designers will stack information into the style argument strings, and the browser will seek out the information it can interpret. This is good, but the designer still loses some control as a result, because he or she cannot ever be absolutely certain that a page is going to remain consistent no matter where it's viewed. As ever, a designer should be careful, and, wherever possible, test the results of his or her work by viewing it in a variety of browsers and on different platforms.

Style Sheet Essentials

There are three primary ways to use style sheets: the inline method, the individual page or embedded method, and linking to a master, or external style sheet.

❑ **Inline style sheets.** This approach exploits existing HTML tags within a standard HTML document and adds a specific style to the information controlled by that tag. An example would be controlling the indentation of a single paragraph using the `style="x"` attribute within the `<p>` tag. Another method of achieving this is with the `<span>` tag and the `style="x"` attribute combined.

❑ **Embedded style sheets.** This method allows for control of individual pages. It uses the `<style>` tag, along with its companion tag, `</style>`. This information is placed between the `<html>` tag and the `<body>` tag, with the style attributes inserted within the full `<style>` container.

❑ **External (linked) style sheets.** All that is required with this method is to create a style sheet file with the master styles you would like to express—using the same syntax you would with embedded style. This file uses the `.css` extension. Then, simply be sure that all of the HTML documents that will require those controls are linked to that document.

NOTE: With embedded and linked style sheets, the attribute syntax is somewhat different than standard HTML syntax. Attributes are placed within curly brackets, where HTML would place an = sign, a colon (:) is used instead, and individual, stacked arguments are separated by a semicolon rather than a comma. Also, several attributes are hyphenated, such as `font-style`, or `margin-left`. A style sheet string would then look like this: `{font-style: arial, helvetica; margin-left}`. Still, as with HTML, style sheet syntax is very logical. As you practice the tasks in this chapter, you should become quite comfortable with the way style sheets work.

The following tasks will introduce you to the basics of each one. Although you'll be using some style sheet syntax to create the examples, detailed syntax will be covered later in the chapter.

TASK Using Inline Style

To begin using style sheets inline, follow these steps.

1. To begin, open up your HTML editor to a clean page.

2. Type the following, paying attention to the `style` attribute and the `<span>` tags used.

```
<html>
<head>
<title>Style and Span</title>
</head>
<body bgcolor="#FFFFFF">


<p style="font: 14pt garamond">
This paragraph was created using inline cascading style sheets
with the style attribute used within the paragraph tag
</p>


<span style="font: 32pt arial">
This section's style was created with the span tag and the style
attribute combined.
</span>


</body>
</html>
```

3. Save the file as span.htm.

4. Review your work in a browser that supports cascading style sheets. Figure 3.3 shows the results.

Figure 3.3.
The results of inline style sheet commands.

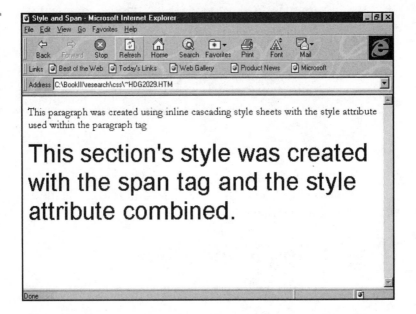

TIP: The <div> (division) tag can be used like the <span> tag for inline control. The <div> tag is especially helpful for longer blocks of text, whereas <span> is most effective for adding style to smaller stretches of information, such as sentences, several words, or even individual letters within a word.

NOTE: In a sense, the inline method of style sheet control defeats the ultimate purpose of cascading style sheets. The main point of the technology is to seek style control of entire pages or even entire sets of pages. The inline method should only be used where touches of style are required.

Using the Individual Page Style

This task focuses on what is known as "embedding" a style sheet. Embedding enables control for an entire page.

1. Open a fresh page in your HTML editor.

2. Enter the following, paying close attention to where the `<style>` tags are placed. You should begin taking note of style syntax, which will be covered in depth as this chapter progresses.

```
<html>
<head>
<title>Embedded Style Sheet Example I </title>
</head>

<style>

BODY {background: #FFFFFF; color: #000000; margin-top:.25in;
➥margin-left:.75in; margin-right:.75in}
H3 {font: 14pt verdana; color: #0000FF}
P {font: 12pt times; text-indent: 0.5in}
A {color: #FF0000}

</style>

<body>

<h3>Embedded Style Sheet Example I</h3>

<p>
In this example, the body background color has been set to
white,the text color to black.The entire page's margins are
controlled with the embedded style sheet to 3/4 of an inch on
either side of the page.
</p>

<p>
All third-level headers (H3) will appear in 14 point Verdana, in
the color blue.
</p>

<p>
You'll note that individual paragraphs will each be indented 1/2
of an inch, and will appear in 12 point Times.
<ahref="other.htm">A link</a> will appear in red.
Also note that the top margin has been set to 1/4 of an inch.
</p>

</body>
</html>
```

3. Save the file as `embed.htm`.

4. Open the file in your browser. Your work should match Figure 3.4.

Figure 3.4.
The results of individual, or embedded, style sheet commands.

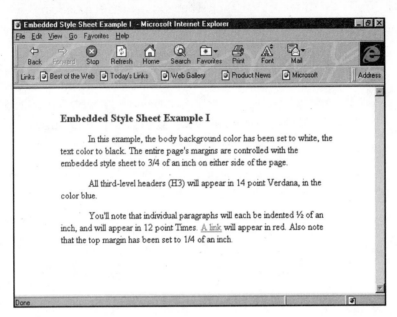

Embedded style sheets will likely be the ones you find yourself using most often. Because of their page-by-page control, they enable a designer to modify the look and feel of pages within a site. However, if strong uniformity is required, linking to a master style sheet is in order.

DESIGN NOTE:

What's this? Paragraph tags being used as containers, with beginning `<p>` and ending `</p>` tags? Yes, it's true. If you've avoided using paragraph container coding in the past and you intend to use cascading style sheets, it's time to change your style! Style sheets won't recognize a paragraph until they see an indication that one has begun. Moreover, if you choose to use inline style, you'll need to use the container code for paragraphs, as well.

Creating the Cascading Style Sheet Master File

Linked style sheets are the focus of this task. This type of style sheet is a master document, controlling all documents that link to it.

1. Open a plain file in your HTML editor.

2. Type in the `<style>` and its corresponding `</style>` tag in the "container" fashion:

   ```
   <style>

   </style>
   ```

3. Place your style requirements between the tags. I'll use the style attributes from earlier:

   ```
   <style>

   BODY {background: #FFFFFF; color: #000000; margin-top:.25in;
   ➥margin-left:.75in; margin-right:.75in}
   H3 {font: 14pt verdana; color: #0000FF}
   P {font: 12pt times; text-indent: 0.5in}
   A {color: #FF0000}

   </style>
   ```

4. Save the file as `style.css`.

This file can now be used to control the values it is arguing, for as many individual HTML pages as you'd like to link to it.

Linking an HTML File to a Master .css File

After you've created the master file, you'll need to use the following steps in order to ensure that it will interpret the commands within that file:

1. Select any existing HTML file that you'd like to have styles applied to using the linked style sheet you've created.

2. Open the file in your HTML editor.

3. Place the following syntax within the `<head>` tag, below the `<title>`:

```
<head>

<title>Linking to Master File</title>

<link rel=stylesheet href="style.css" type="text/css">

</head>
```

4. All the data within the actual HTML file will now interpret the styles you've set forth in the `.css` file. An example of an HTML page using externally linked style sheet controls is shown in Figure 3.5.

Figure 3.5.
This page calls on an externally linked style sheet for style control.

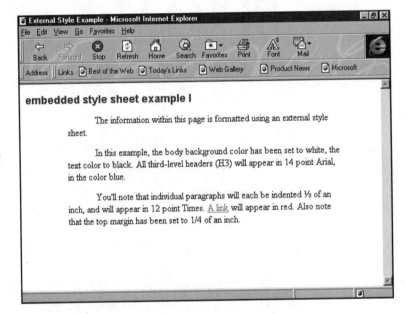

If your server requires you to register the MIME (Internet Media) type for style sheets, note that the suffix is `.css`, the MIME type is `text/css`, and it is considered an 8-bit (ASCII) file type.

Combining Style Sheet Techniques

Designers who have complex requirements are going to benefit from mixing style sheet techniques. Mixing takes full advantage of the cascade element of style sheets. When multiple techniques are combined, the browser will look for the information in the following cascading order:

❑ Linked style sheets will be employed globally.

❑ If an embedded style sheet exists on a page with a linked style sheet, the embedded style sheet will override a linked style sheet.

❑ Inline styles will override the preceding two points.

This way, you can set a single style sheet for an entire site, change a few pages here and there for individual style with embedded style, and use inline style to override both.

DESIGN NOTE: With so many sites, it's difficult to keep up with which style overrides which, and it can become confusing! Designers and developers using style sheets do recommend that you select a favorite technique and stick with it; apply other style sheet techniques only if they are required for distinct assignments.

Text-Specific Style Attributes

Some graphic designers spend entire careers dedicated to the study of typography. It is undeniably an art, comprised of not only being familiar with countless font faces but, also, related attributes such as weight, size variations, styles, families, and how to artistically use all these aspects in attractive combinations.

Beg, buy, or borrow the appropriate version, for either Mac or PC, of Robin Williams' fantastic introductions to typography: *The Mac is Not a Typewriter*, or *The PC is Not a Typewriter*. Published by Peachpit Press, and no Web designer should be without a copy.

The face of the Web cannot change for the better if designers don't understand some text-based fundamentals before putting style sheets to use. I'll offer a number of tips and notes as I progress through this chapter, but be sure to refer to Part IV, "Sophisticated Pages Using Format Control," where I discuss style as it relates to text styles in greater detail.

The following text and text-related attributes are available for use in all methods of style sheets:

❑ `font-family` This attribute controls the face of the font by arguing for either

the name of the typeface you wish to use. Here is a sample-style specification for Times:

`{font-family: Times}`

the addition of a series of alternative fonts in those cases mentioned early in the chapter. Because an individual computer might not have the installed font of your preference, you may want to add a similar alternative:

```
{font-family: times, garamond}
```

the name of a typeface family name:

```
{font-family: serif}
```

The following typefaces, or type *families,* can be called for with style sheets:

Serif Serif fonts are a good choice for long sections of text. Popular Serifs include Times New Roman and Garamond.

Sanserif This font family includes popular choices such as Arial, Helvetica, and Avante Garde.

Cursive These are script fonts—fonts that appear as though they have been hand-written.

Fantasy Fantasy fonts are decorative in nature and very useful for stylish headings and titles. They are typically not practical for body text.

Monospace You're most likely to be familiar with monospace fonts from the days of the typewriter—assuming you've ever used one of those dinosaurs! Monospace refers to the fact that every letter takes an equal amount of space. An `a` takes as much space as an `m`. Most fonts are proportional; each letter takes up a space that is proportional to the individual letter's size and style, rather than forcing it to fit in an exact amount of space.

DESIGN NOTE: The standard design guideline for selecting Serifs versus Sanserif fonts is to use Serifs for body text, Sanserifs for headers or small blocks of text. However, although studies suggest that Serif fonts are easier to read—probably due to the way the strokes guide the eye along—Sanserif fonts are becoming increasingly popular as common text fonts within Web browsers. It's an interesting phenomenon, but no one quite understands why it's occurring! Designers have to use good judgment, basing the use of Serif or Sanserif fonts on whether the pages are easy to read as well as attractive.

TIP: Using a typeface family as a default is an excellent idea, because it covers the designer's font choices as completely as possible. Even if a specific font face is unavailable on a given computer, it's likely that a similar one in that font's family is available. A savvy designer will place his or her first choice first, second choice second, and so forth, with the family name at the end. If I'm arguing for two Serif fonts, my final string would be: `{font-family: times, garamond, serif}`.

❑ `font size` Sizing in style sheets offers the designer to size his or her fonts using five size options:

Points To set a font in point size, use the abbreviation `pt` immediately next to the numeric size: `{font-size: 12pt}`.

Inches If you'd rather set your fonts in inches, simply place `in` and the numeral size, in inches, of the font size you require: `{font-size: 1in}`.

Centimeters Some designers might prefer centimeters, represented by `cm` and used in the same fashion as points and inches: `{font-size: 5cm}`.

Pixels Pixels are argued with the `px` abbreviation: `{font-size: 24px}`.

Percentage You may wish to choose to set a percentage of the default point size: `{font-size: 50%}`

DESIGN NOTE: Designers will most likely find themselves more comfortable with the point and pixel values for setting font sizes. However, if you prefer another method and find yourself at ease with it, that's fine. The only concern I would have is to be certain that if you choose a method, you stick to it. Consistency is a smart approach to the creation of your own individual design and coding style.

❑ `font-style` This attribute typically dictates the style of text, such as placing it in italics. The appropriate syntax to do this would be the following:

`{font-style: italic}`

DESIGN NOTE: Another font style would be `bold`, but interestingly, there is no current style sheet attribute to achieve this. The only other legal attribute for style is `normal`, which simply places the typeface in normal, default status. When support for more font styles will become available is questionable, although it only seems natural that they will at some point be added to the specs.

❑ **font-weight** The thickness of a typeface is referred to as its *weight*. As with font faces, font weights rely on the existence of the corresponding font and weight on an individual's machine. A range of attributes are available in style sheets, including the following:

```
extra-light
demi-light
light
medium
extra-bold
demi-bold
bold
```

TIP: Before assigning font weights, be certain that the font face you are applying the weight to has that weight available. Always check your work on a variety of platforms and machines, where possible, to see whether you have been able to achieve strong design despite the fact that some machines might not support the font or the font weight in question.

❑ **text-decoration** This attribute decorates text, including such options as the following:

```
none
underline
italic
line-through
```

DESIGN NOTE: Do you dislike underlined links? With cascading style sheets, designers can now use the `{text-decoration: none}` attribute and argument to globally shut off underlined links. In embedded and linked style sheet formats, the syntax would follow the A value: `A {text-decoration: none}`. For inline style, simply place the value within the link you wish to control:

`<a style="textdecoration: none" href="my.html">; this link has no underline!</a>`. There is one caution: Using the Netscape Navigator Professional Preview 4.0, this trick didn't work.

Another important text-related aspect is leading. This refers to the amount of line spacing between lines of text. This space should be consistent, or the result is uneven, unattractive spacing. The line-height attribute allows designers to set the distance between the baseline, or bottom, of a line of text.

❏ **line-height** To set the leading of a paragraph, use the line-height attribute in points, inches, centimeters, pixels, or percentages in the same fashion you would when describing `font-size` attributes:

```
P {line-height: 14pt}
```

Now I'll give you the chance to take a break from text details and put the learning to use!

Using Text Attributes in Embedded Style Sheets

Now you'll get to employ these attributes in an embedded style sheet.

1. Begin by opening a fresh page in your HTML editor.

2. Type in the following shell syntax (note container method):

```
<html>
<head>
<title>Text Style Example: Embedded Style Sheets</title>
</head>

<style>


</style>
<body bgcolor="#ff9933">

</body>
</html>
```

3. Add the following style syntax between the `<style>` tags. You'll see that I've argued for font family, size, weight, and style in headers, family, size, and style in paragraphs, and I've removed underlining from links with the text-decoration attribute. Also, note the stacking of font faces and families for broad coverage:

```
H1 {font-family: lucida handwriting, arial, helvetica, cursive,
➥san-serif ;font-size: 16pt; font-style: normal}
H2 {font-family: lucida handwriting, arial, helvetica, cursive,
➥san-serif; font-size: 14pt; font-style: normal}
P {font-family: garamond; font-size: 12pt; font-style: normal;
➥line-height: 11pt}
A {text-decoration: none; font-weight: bold}
```

4. Add the following text and HTML to the body:

```
<h1>Duis Autem Vel</h1>

<p>
Duis autem vel eum iriure dolor in hendrerit in vulputate velit
esse molestie consequat, vel illum dolore eu feugiat nulla
facilisis at vero eros et accumsan et iusto odio dignissim qui
blandit praesent luptatum zzril delenit augue duis dolore te
feugait nulla facilisi.
<a href="other.htm"> Nam liber </a> tempor cum soluta nobis
eleifend option congue nihil imperdiet doming id quod mazim
placerat facer possim assum.
Accumsan et iusto odio dignissim qui blandit praesent luptatum
zzril delenit augue duis dolore te feugait nulla facilisi.
</p>

<h2>Vendrerit In Vulputate</h2>

<p>
Eros Et Accumsan dignissim qui blandit praesent luptatum zzril
delenit augue duis dolore te feugait nulla facilisi.
Nam liber tempor cum soluta nobis eleifend option congue nihil
imperdiet doming id quod mazim placerat <a href="other1.htm">
facer possim assum. </a>  Iusto odio dignissim qui blandit
praesent luptatum zzril delenit augue duis dolore te feugait
nulla facilisi.
Nam liber tempor cum soluta nobis eleifend option congue nihil
imperdiet doming id quod mazim placerat facer possim assum.
Accumsan et iusto odio dignissim qui blandit
</p>
```

5. Save the file as `text-st.htm` and view it in your browser. Note how the headers, paragraphs, and links have obeyed the style sheet's commands, as demonstrated in Figure 3.6.

Figure 3.6.

Using an embedded style sheet; the text on this page has a variety of text controls applied to it.

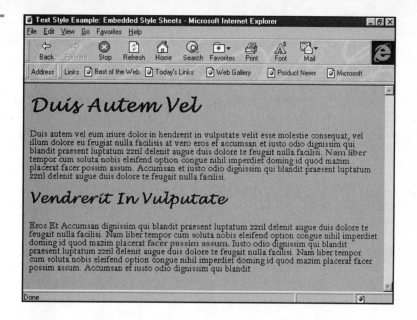

What's that gibberish she's using in place of text? It sure looks like Greek to me! If this is what you're thinking, you're not far off. Although referred to as greeking, it's not really Greek, but a latinesque style of word placement designers use when creating mock-ups and dummy text.

NOTE: Remember, a linked style sheet is simply the information in an embedded style sheet placed in its own file and given the extension `.css`. Then, all pages you wish to have draw from the information in that file are simply linked to that file.

Now you have a page that has successfully employed embedded style sheets. But the page is boring! So, in the next lesson, I'm going to cover margin, indent, and text alignment attributes. These will help add texture and white space to the page.

Margins, Indents, and Text Alignment Attributes

All critical elements of controlling page layout, margins, indents, and text alignment can help bring a sophisticated look to your pages.

❏ `margin-left` To set a left margin, use a distance in points, inches, centimeters, or pixels. The following sets a left margin to ³/₄ of an inch:

```
{margin-left: .75in}
```

❏ **margin-right** For a right margin, select from the same measurement options as provided for the `margin-left` attribute:

`{margin-right: 50px}`

News flash! Internet Explorer allows for negative margin and text indent values. This exciting feature enables the designer to create interesting and unusual effects, including overlapping text for contemporary, stylish design.

❏ **margin-top** Top margins can be set using the same measurement values as for other margin attributes:

`{margin-top: 20pt)`

❏ **text-indent** Again, points, inches, centimeters, or pixel values can be assigned to this attribute, which serves to indent any type of text:

`{text-indent: 0.5in)`

❏ **text-align** This long-awaited feature allows for justification of text. Values include left, center, and right:

`{text-align: right}`

DESIGN NOTE: Text alignment is a powerful layout tool, and designers will enjoy being able to place text in a variety of alignments without having to rely on tables, divisions, or other less graceful HTML workarounds that existed in the past. Designers should remember that justification of text requires a fine eye. Left justification is the only reasonable choice for long selections of text, as its readability is much more accessible to the eye. Right justification comes in handy for short bursts of text, such as pull-quotes. Centered text should be used sparingly. Even though it seems natural to want to center text, it is actually more difficult to read, and it looks cliché and ungainly.

The following tasks will assist you in using margins and text alignments with style.

Margin Control with Embedded Style Sheets

This task shows how to control margins within a style sheet.

1. Open `text-st.htm` in your HTML editor.

2. Add the following margin syntax alongside the BODY attribute within the `<style>` tag section:

```
BODY {margin-left: 0.75in; margin-right: 0.75in; margin-top:
0.10in}
```

3. Save the file and view. The results should match Figure 3.7.

4. For a different view, attempt changing the margin values.

NOTE: Although I've added the margin values to the entire page with the BODY attribute, you can add margins to any HTML tag you'd like. For example, if you want to control the headers with different margins, place the margin values in the string next to the header of your choice. Similarly, you can adjust margins on individual paragraphs by adding the margin values you seek to the paragraph string.

Figure 3.7.
Margins create attractive white space.

Now you'll add justification in order to create more visual texture on the page.

 # Adding Justification

Alignment, or *justification*, plays an important part in design. This task will show you how to get the visual texture you desire.

1. Using the same file, add the following justification syntax to the headers:

```
BODY {margin-left: 0.75in; margin-right: 0.75in; margin-top: 0.10in}
H1 {font-family: lucida handwriting, arial, helvetica ;
➡font-size: 16pt; font-style: normal; text-align: left}
H2 {font-family: lucida handwriting, arial, helvetica; font-
➡size: 14pt; font-style: normal; text-align: right}
P {font-family: garamond; font-size: 12pt; font-style: normal;
➡line-height: 11pt}
A {text-decoration: none; font-weight: bold}
```

2. Because I want to justify actual paragraphs, I can go ahead and place that information inline, and the browser will know to justify those individual paragraphs. The full HTML code will look like this:

```
<html>
<head>
<title>Text Style Example: Embedded Style Sheets</title>
</head>

<style>

BODY {margin-left: 0.75in; margin-right: 0.75in; margin-top:
➡0.10in}
H1 {font-family: lucida handwriting, arial, helvetica ; font-
➡size: 16pt; font-style: normal; text-align: left}
H2 {font-family: lucida handwriting, arial, helvetica; font-
➡size: 14pt; font-style: normal; text-align: right}
P {font-family: garamond; font-size: 12pt; font-style: normal;
➡line-height: 11pt}
A {text-decoration: none; font-weight: bold}


</style>
<body bgcolor="#ff9933" link="FF0033">

<h1>Duis Autem Vel</h1>

<p style="text-align: right">
Duis autem vel eum iriure dolor in hendrerit in vulputate <a
href="other.htm"> velit esse molestie </a>consequat, vel illum
dolore eu feugiat nulla facilisis at vero eros et accumsan et
iusto odio dignissim qui blandit praesent luptatum zzril delenit
augue duis dolore te feugait nulla facilisi.
</p>

<h2>Vendrerit In Vulputate</h2>

<p style="text-align: left">
Eros Et Accumsan dignissim qui blandit praesent luptatum zzril
delenit augue duis dolore te feugait nulla facilisi.
Nam liber tempor cum <a href="other1.htm">soluta nobis
eleifend </a> option congue nihil imperdiet doming id quod mazim
placerat  facer possim assum.
</p>
```

```
</body>
</html>
```

3. Save this page and view it in your browser. The look and feel is becoming much more interesting, as shown in Figure 3.8.

Figure 3.8.

Visual texture makes a Web page more interesting, even without graphics.

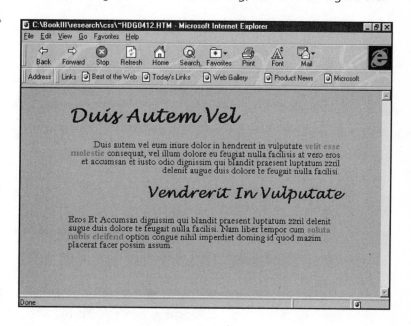

Another method to justify individual paragraphs is by defining classes. I'll introduce style sheet class variations toward the end of this chapter.

Color and Background

If you've checked these pages with the examples on the CD-ROM, or noticed the <body> tag syntax, you'll have noticed that I'm using a background color within the traditional HTML rather than in the BODY attribute available to style sheets. Internet Explorer 3.0+ has a bug in the software that results in the browser ignoring this basically legal attribute. Sadly, the bug appears to also exist in the Netscape 4.0 pre-release. As a workaround, I'm defining background color for the body in a traditional fashion.

All bugs and browser headaches aside, background color can be added to actual attributes including other HTML tags used in style sheet formats. For example, I can have a paragraph or a header splashed with color simply by placing the appropriate syntax in that area.

Furthermore, I can change the text color in any field I specify. This is particularly satisfying for Web designers who are constantly seeking to employ browser-based color to enliven pages rather than rely on graphics that are time-consuming.

The syntax required to create background color—again with the one exception that Internet Explorer versions below 4.0 will ignore the attribute if placed in the BODY string—is the style sheet background: convention and a hexadecimal color argument:

```
{background: #FFFFFF}
```

Similarly, background graphics can be called upon using this attribute. Merely replace the hex argument with a URL:

```
{background: http://myserver.com/cool.gif}
```

For text color, simply use the color attribute and a hex argument:

```
{color: #FF6633}
```

DESIGN NOTE: Internet Explorer allows for the use of color names in the case of color and background arguments. Such color names include black, silver, gray, white, maroon, red, purple, fuchsia, green, lime, olive, yellow, navy, blue, teal, and aqua. My advice is to stick to hexadecimal values. You not only have a better selection, but it helps keep your coding consistent and professional-looking.

TASK   Adding Background Color

Now you'll add splashes of background color to fields in the file you've created:

1. Open text-st.htm in your HTML editor.

2. Add the following syntax to the <style> variable:

```
BODY {margin-left: 0.75in; margin-right: 0.75in; margin-top:
➥0.10in}
H1 {font-family: lucida handwriting, arial, helvetica; font-size:
➥16pt;
font-style: normal; text-align: left}
H2 {font-family: lucida handwriting, arial, helvetica; font-size:
➥14pt;
font-style: normal; text-align: right; background: #99CCCC}
P {font-family: garamond; font-size: 12pt; font-style: normal;
➥line-height: 11pt}
A {text-decoration: none; font-weight: bold}
```

3. Save the file (`text-st.htm`) and view it in your browser (see Figure 3.9).

Figure 3.9.

Notice the splash behind the text. Is it distracting or enhancing? Designers must choose background splashes carefully.

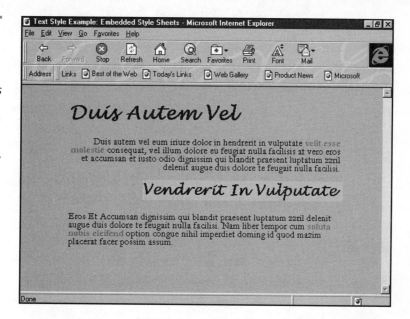

To see full-color versions of the files, please check on the CD-ROM for the corresponding chapter. In this case, all of the files you need to view these pages are in the Chapter 3 folder.

CAUTION: Contrast gained by using background splashes can be very effective, but designers can quickly get in trouble by overusing them. Be careful and consistent with your color palettes, and select splashes that provide visual accents rather than detracting the eye from what's important. You'll note that I selected the header to highlight; in another case, maybe only a line or phrase of text would be important.

TASK

Adding Text Color

To liven up sections of text, simply follow the same style guidelines to set for background color, but use the `color:` attribute:

1. Open `text-st.html` in your HTML editor.

2. Add the following syntax:

```
H2 {font-family: lucida handwriting, arial, helvetica;
➥font-size: 14pt;
font-style: normal; text-align: right; background: #99CCCC;
➥color: #FF0033}
```

3. Save the file and view it in your browser. You now have an interest-ing, textured page completely designed with style sheets!

Additional Functionality

There are two additional techniques that can assist you in making style sheets more functional. The first is *grouping*, which allows for the reduction of attributes and arguments by creating logical groups. Another way to expand function is through the use of *classes*. This technique allows you to assign variations to individual HTML tags, giving you tremendous flexibility in terms of creating variations within page attributes.

Grouping Style Sheets

To group style sheets, you can

❏ Group multiple tags together. If I want to assign the same attributes to all header styles, I can group them together. Here's an example without grouping:

```
H1 {font-family: arial; font-size 14pt; color: #000000}
      H2 {font-family: arial; font-size 14pt; color: #000000}
H3 {font-family: arial; font-size 14pt; color: #000000}
```

Here's the same example grouped:

```
H1, H2, H3 {font-family: arial; font-size 14pt; color: #000000}
```

❏ Group attributes by dropping them into specific families of informa-tion. Without grouping, an example of font attributes and arguments would be

```
BODY {font-family: arial, san-serif; font-size: 12pt; line-
➥height: 14pt; font-weight: bold; font- style: normal}
```

With grouping, I can simply name the attribute `font:` and then stack the arguments like this:

```
BODY {font: bold normal 12pt/14pt arial, san-serif}
```

NOTE: When grouping attributes, be sure to remember that attribute order is significant. Font weight and style must come before other font attributes; the size of the font will come before the leading, and then you can add additional information to the string. Note that there are no commas between the attributes, except in the case of font families.

Want to make sure that your embedded style sheets are hidden from non-CSS browsers? Simply use comment tagging around the <style> tags as shown in Figure 3.10.

Grouping attributes can be done with margins, using the `margin:` argument followed by the top, right, and left margin values in that order. Be sure to specify all three values, unless you want the same value applied to all three:

```
BODY {margin: .10in .75in .75in}
```

Note again that there are no commas between the attributes.

Figure 3.10.
Comment tagging around style tags.

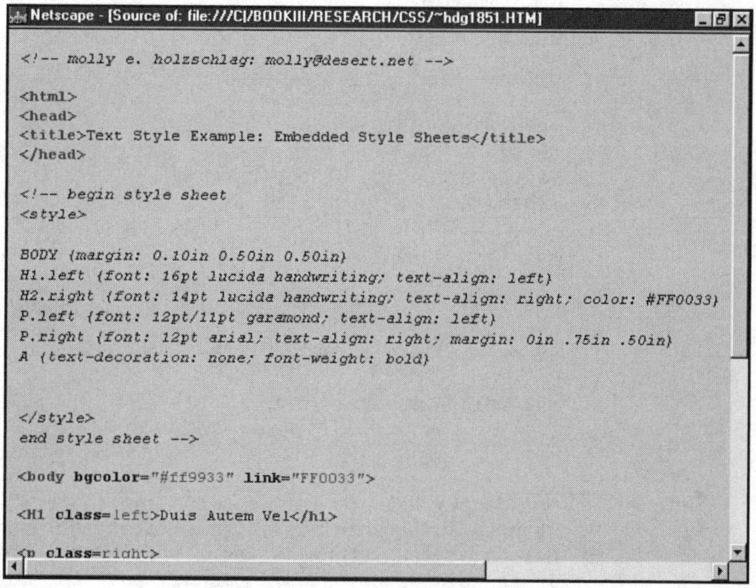

```
Netscape - [Source of: file:///C|/BOOKIII/RESEARCH/CSS/~hdg1851.HTM]

<!-- molly e. holzschlag: molly@desert.net -->

<html>
<head>
<title>Text Style Example: Embedded Style Sheets</title>
</head>

<!-- begin style sheet
<style>

BODY {margin: 0.10in 0.50in 0.50in}
H1.left {font: 16pt lucida handwriting; text-align: left}
H2.right {font: 14pt lucida handwriting; text-align: right; color: #FF0033}
P.left {font: 12pt/11pt garamond; text-align: left}
P.right {font: 12pt arial; text-align: right; margin: 0in .75in .50in}
A {text-decoration: none; font-weight: bold}


</style>
end style sheet -->

<body bgcolor="#ff9933" link="FF0033">

<H1 class=left>Duis Autem Vel</h1>

<p class=right>
```

Assigning Classes

To get the most variation, assign classes to individual HTML tags. This is done very simply by adding a named extension to any HTML tag. If I have two headers and two paragraph styles that I'd like to attribute, I can name each one and assign style to the individual paragraphs. I then call on the name within the specific HTML tag in the body of the document:

```
H1.left {font: arial 14pt; color: #FF0033; text-align: left}
H2.right {font: arial 12pt; color: #FF6633; text-align: right}
```

In the HTML, I would place the class name:

```
<h1 class=left>This is my Left Heading</h2>
```

All of the H1 headers I name class=left will have the H1.left class attributes. Similarly, the H2.right headers named class=right will have the attributes defined for that class.

TASK

Creating a Style Sheet Using Grouping and Class

Grouping and class allow for very flexible use of style sheets. This task gives you a first glance at how to use the techniques.

1. In a fresh HTML, copy the original information from text-st.htm without the style attributes:

```
<html>
<head>
<title>Group and Class</title>
</head>

<style>

</style>

<body bgcolor="#ff9933" link="FF0033">

<h1>Duis Autem Vel</h1>

<p>

Duis autem vel eum iriure dolor in hendrerit in vulputate
<a href="other.htm">velit esse molestie </a>consequat, vel illum
dolore eu feugiat nulla facilisis at vero eros et accumsan et
iusto odio dignissim qui blandit praesent luptatum
zzril delenit augue duis dolore te feugait nulla facilisi.
</p>

<h2>Vendrerit In Vulputate</h2>

Eros Et Accumsan dignissim qui blandit praesent luptatum zzril
delenit augue duis dolore te feugait nulla facilisi.
Nam liber tempor cum <a href="other1.htm">soluta nobis eleifend
</a> option congue nihil imperdiet doming id quod mazim
placerat  facer possim assum.
</p>
```

```
</body>
</html>
```

2. Within the `<style>` tags, create an embedded style sheet using class and grouping:

```
BODY {margin: 0.10in 0.50in 0.50in}
H1.left {font: 16pt lucida handwriting; text-align: left}
H2.right {font: 14pt lucida handwriting; text-align: right;
➥color: #FF0033}
P.left {font: 12pt/11pt garamond; text-align: left}
P.right {font: 12pt arial; text-align: right; margin: 0in .75in
➥.50in}
A {text-decoration: none; font-weight: bold}
```

3. Within the appropriate tags, place the class names:

```
<H1 class=left>Duis Autem Vel</h1>

<p class=right>
Duis autem vel eum iriure dolor in hendrerit in vulputate
<a href="other.htm">velit esse molestie </a>consequat, vel illum
dolore eu feugiat nulla facilisis at vero eros et  accumsan et
iusto odio dignissim qui blandit praesent luptatum
zzril delenit augue duis dolore te feugait nulla facilisi.
</p>

<h2 class=right>Vendrerit In Vulputate</h2>

<p class="left">
Eros Et Accumsan dignissim qui blandit praesent luptatum zzril
delenit augue duis dolore te feugait nulla facilisi.
Nam liber tempor cum <a href="other1.htm">soluta nobis eleifend
</a> option congue nihil imperdiet doming id quod mazim
placerat  facer possim assum.
</p>
```

4. Save the file and view it in your browser. Style, style, style—you're sure looking good (see Figure 3.11).

TIP: If you're placing margins in the BODY attribute as well as the P attribute, be sure that your paragraph margins are larger than those you've selected for the entire body of text; otherwise, the point is moot. The browser will ignore the lesser margins and use the greatest value that's available.

Figure 3.11.

The resulting page is stylish.

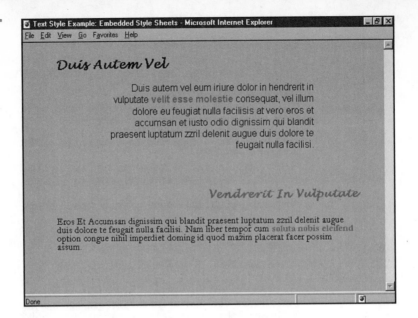

Workshop Wrap-Up

Style sheets are simultaneously sophisticated and infantile in their behavior. The concept is extremely advanced, allowing designers tools with which to do things never dreamed possible—at least in the young history of HTML. However, the actual application is in its infancy. This is, as with many layout options available to designers, more the fault of browser technology than the reality of the tool.

If you begin to use style sheets to work with your design, you are certain to be challenged by the limitations of browsers. That problem will last for some time; however, what is invariably in your corner is that you started learning and using the technology early. This gives you the competitive edge! I encourage you to think about the power of the system rather than the limitations, because those limitations will gradually subside. Your skills can only improve with time and practice.

Moreover, there's the thrill of being able to actually design without ever opening up a graphics program! Color, font, text control—they're all yours now, to use and enjoy.

Next Steps

The next section of the book moves into interface design, and how to employ tables and browsers to create effective interfaces. This is an excellent stepping stone for designers interested in ultimately applying style sheets to an already strong and appealing site foundation.

Those readers desiring to work more with style sheets immediately, please

- ❏ Read Chapter 17, "Creating Professional Presentations."

- ❏ Visit Chapter 18, "Combining Tables, Frames, and Style Sheets," to learn how to combine table and style sheets.

- ❏ Follow the tasks in Chapter 19, "Style Sheets at Work and Play," to master text-heavy documents with style sheet control.

- ❏ Enjoy Chapter 20, "Real-Time Example: MainStay Communications— Style Sheets in Action," which demonstrates a real-time corporate Web site that employs style sheets.

Q&A

Q: I've tried to use leading with the line-height control, but every time I do so my headers end up as far from the text as the text. I want my headers to be closer to my body text. How can I accomplish this?

A: Remember that leading works in style sheets by referring to the baseline of a piece of text. To avoid how this function places extra space between heading and body attributes, set the paragraph's top margins to 0. You'll still get some space, but it'll be a natural amount rather than the leading's equivalent. Another trick is to make sure that your leading is less than your body-text point size.

Q: Can I set defaults for an entire page?

A: Style sheets work on a concept known as inheritance. This means that if you set a BODY attribute first, every tag you place underneath it "inherits" from that attribute. Simply said, what you place in the BODY is essentially the default value. So, load up the BODY attribute with your global values, and set other specifications elsewhere in the style sheet.

Q: Is there a way to justify text without alignment, creating smooth edges rather than ragged ones?

A: Unfortunately, not yet. The only current workaround to achieve this is to place the text on a graphic image and load that image where you want the justified text. It's awkward and unfortunate, because smoothly justified text has been shown to be easier to read. Eventually, this will be an easy option, but for now, it's more important to make sure your Web pages have nicely defined margins and plenty of white space to gently lead the eye where you want it to go.

II
Designing a Welcoming Interface

four

Table Controls and Site Interface

Interface is the most critical visual and functional aspect of any multimedia design. With Web sites, this fact is intensified because if an individual isn't finding the information he or she requires, or isn't having an enjoyable time on your pages, he or she can simply choose to take a sharp turn off the road and visit another site—one, perhaps, that will be more interesting, informative, and profitable.

One step to avoid creating sites that act as pit stops or U-turns on the Web's highways and byways is to be sure that the sites you build welcome the visitor. This is done via a number of methods, including intelligent design as well as attractive and useful site interface.

As tables become one of the major components of layout tools available to the Web designer, the role they play in the creation of powerful interface is enormous. In this chapter, I'll look at how to use tables to create a site that is not only visually pleasing, but practical as well. The techniques in this chapter can be applied immediately to current projects of your own. In the following hands-on tasks, you'll learn step-by-step table codes to create everything from a splash page to a multiple-column page.

The Front Door

The first part of interface design is deciding what the virtual front door of your site is going to look like. Some designers prefer to have a page that is predominantly graphical in nature—much like a traditional magazine cover. Other designers like a functional greeting, or splash page, with graphics as well as navigational options available. Then, there are designers who take the stance that because people want to get to the information fast, a splash page is a waste of time.

I feel that each individual client and site is going to have unique needs. Therefore, it's advisable that designers research the client's preferences, the content type, and the audience demographic. What is going to work best in each scenario? The best designer will do his or her homework and have a strong idea of what is required before sitting down and doing the hard work.

TIP: A good splash page should hint at or convey the site's intent, as well as give an introduction to some of the site's design elements including color, shape, typography, and texture.

For the purposes of this chapter, I'm going to take the middle road with the splash page concept. I'll provide you with a means of creating a front door that is both visually attractive and functional. You can then subtract or add to the concepts shared here to achieve what your client and audience require.

TIP: Although download time and graphic size considerations are always foremost on a site designer's mind, these issues are especially important for splash pages. The front door is going to be a major player in keeping the visitor interested. Pages that load too slowly are going to offer a perfect excuse for people to leave your site—without ever seeing what might be behind door number one. Generally, pages should be no more than 60 kilobytes at the high end. Half that for a splash page, or better, and you're in good shape!

Creating a Splash Page Using Tables

As introduced in Chapter 1, "Good Manners: Basic Table Elements," tables are a strong tool for layout. This task is the perfect example of a simple table; although it is much like what you've already created, it has a specific goal in mind. An important concept being introduced with this task is how designers can exploit browser-dependent color and break up graphics into individual pieces, rather than using a full page of graphical information. This helps cut down on download time by reducing size. The following tasks will help you create a splash page using tables.

1. Begin by making sure the book's accompanying CD-ROM is available to you. Create a Chapter 4 folder on your computer, with a folder inside called `images`. This will get you used to calling images from their own directory rather than having everything jumbled up in the same folder.

2. After you have the folders made, copy all of the images from the CD-ROM Chapter 4 `images` directory into the `images` directory you just created.

3. Open a fresh page in your HTML editor.

You'll note that I've centered task one's table using the `<div align=center>` option mentioned in Chapter 1. You can also place the table between a `<center>` tag and its counterpart, if you prefer. Either is legal.

4. Working with the container method, first enter all of the necessary syntax, including the `<table>` tag and its associated `</table>` tag counterpart. I've also added attributes for the body and the table itself:

```
<html>
<head>
<title>Chapter Four: Splash Page</title>
</head>
<body bgcolor="#FFCC99" text="#000000" link="#FF9966"
vlink="#999999" alink="#FFFFFF">
<div align=center>
<table border=0 cellpadding=0 cellspacing=0 width=550>
</table>
</div>
</body>
</html>
```

5. Now add the table row and table cells. Note that I'm only going to require one row and two cells. You'll see that the cells have each been given a width of a value that anticipates the width of the graphics you'll be loading into those cells.

```
<tr>
<td width=274>
</td>
<td width=175>
</td>
</tr>
```

6. Add the syntax that references the first images. Notice the use of width, height, and alternative text attributes:

```
<td width=274>
<img src="images/sv-spl.jpg" alt="southwestern voices splash image"
width=274 height=256>
</td>
```

7. Now, you'll add the syntax that references the stack of linked images that create the menu. You'll see I've placed a `border=0` attribute in these strings because they are referenced hypermedia:

```
<td width=175>
<a href="fp.htm">
<img src="images/1.gif" alt="go to front page" width=175
height=25 border=0>
</a>
<a href="fe.htm">
<img src="images/2.gif" alt="go to features" width=175 height=25
border=0>
</a>
<a href="col.htm">
<img src="images/3.gif" alt="go to columns" width=175 height=25
border=0>
</a>
<a href="voice.htm">
<img src="images/4.gif" alt="go to your voice" width=175
height=25 border=0>
</a>
<a href="class.htm">
<img src="images/5.gif" alt="go to classifieds" width=175
height=25 border=0>
</a>
</td>
```

TIP: When is it best to use the `border` attribute around images? Regardless of the value, use border attributes whenever you are creating hypermedia. In other words, if the image is going to be linked, argue the border. If not, you can leave out the `border` attribute.

8. Save your file as `splash.htm` in the main Chapter 4 directory you've created on your computer. Open up the file in the browser of your choice; your results should match Figure 4.1.

Figure 4.1.

A splash page made with tables.

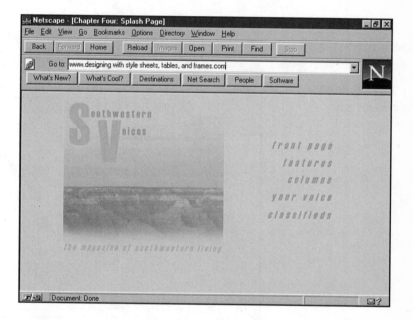

<TASK> The Border Trick

This task will show you exactly how the table you are creating controls graphic and text placement.

1. Open `splash.htm` in your HTML editor.

2. Change the `border=0` value to `1`.

3. View the file in your browser. You will see the table's cells, rows, and outline defined.

DESIGN NOTE: Some designers prefer borders around any hypermedia. I'm personally not a big fan of this technique, but if you turn the image borders to a value of 1 and view in both Netscape Navigator and Internet Explorer, you'll see the results, as shown in Figure 4.3. Decide which you prefer and then save the file—your first splash page with tables.

Figure 4.2.
Change the border attribute to a value of 1 or greater and you'll see the table behind the layout.

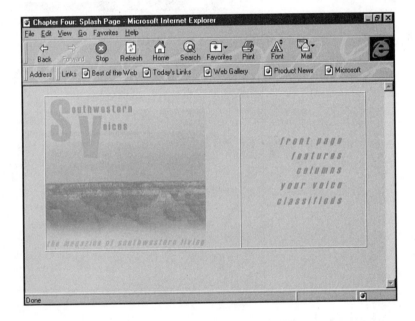

4. You can now change the border value back to 0.

NOTE: Notice how the images are stacked within a table cell, rather than a table being built to separate each one. A common mistake is to make a grid out of a table and then fill it in. Tables can be much more simple. Always build cells with the vertical axis in mind. You can stack images, text, and even multimedia objects, on top of each other. Rows and spanning only become necessary when you begin working on a combination of the horizontal axis and vertical axis.

Figure 4.3.
Borders around images can be attractive or distracting.

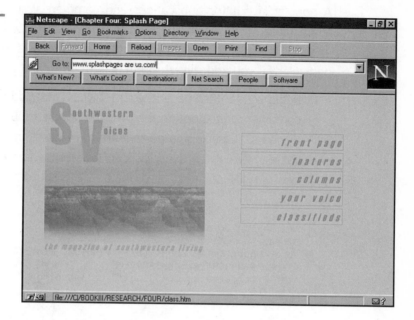

Internal Pages

As a person continues to move through a site, each page should offer a combination of consistent and new features. Consistency can be achieved with traits such as color palettes and fonts, which you'll learn more about in Chapters 17, 18, and 19. Fresh components can be added using a variety of layouts, graphics, and other multimedia options.

Visit Core Wave's A Glass Bead Game to see a variety of layouts, use of fonts and browser-dependent color, and interesting graphic treatments— `http://www.ybi.com/corewave/`.

The objective in terms of interface is to keep each page interesting so that visitors are compelled to see what's coming next—not just in terms of the information you have to impart, but in terms of the visual panorama that unfolds as they move throughout the site.

With the next tasks, I will begin to introduce a variety of layouts and some uses of graphic media, as well as offer ideas for design that are inherent in the HTML that helps create tables.

Creating a Two-Column Borderless Table

A popular layout for publications and commercial sites where there is a combination of text information and graphical data is a two-column borderless effect. This is easy to achieve with tables, and creates a sophisticated look—particularly if you add style through palette, font, and graphic choices.

1. Begin with a fresh page in your HTML editor. Add the following container syntax, noting the title, the body attributes, and the table attributes. Especially important are the cellpadding and cellspacing values. Here, I've argued for 10 pixels each. This creates the cushion between the columns. Also, the border is set to a value of 0:

```
<html>
<head>
<title>Two-Column Internal Page</title>
</head>
<body bgcolor="#FFCC99" text="#000000" link="#FF9966"
vlink="#999999" alink="#FFFFFF">
<table border=0 cellpadding=10 cellspacing=10 width=600>
</table>
</body>
</html>
```

2. Now add the table row and table cell values. Because the objective is to create two vertical columns, only one row is required. However, you will need two table cells. Here, I've attributed alignment values to the table cell arguments, <td>. This will bring the text within the cells flush with the topmost margin of the cell. The align=left attribute and value will align the text with the cell to the left margin:

```
<tr>
<td valign=top width=250 align=left>
</td>
<td valign=top width=250 align=left>
</td>
</tr>
```

3. Because I want to create a refined look, I'm going to add font attributes to each cell. Unlike style sheets, using font attributes is ungainly, as you must open and close the <font> tags around each instance of text you'd like to change. However, as with style sheets, you can stack font face values, which allows for some coverage of

cross-platform viewing consistency. You can use the following syntax for both table cells:

```
<td valign=top width=250 align=left>
<font face=arial, helvetica size=2>
</font>
</td>
```

4. Now add text to the cells:

```
<td valign=top width=250 align=left>
<font face=arial, helvetica size=2>
The news is in! It's spring, and the desert is in bloom. Cactus,
succulents, native as well as international plants are flowering
in all their glory.
</font>
</td>
<td valign=top width=250 align=left>
<font face=arial, helvetica size=2>

Be sure to visit the <a href="desert.htm">Desert Museum</a>,
the<a href="bg.htm">Botanical Gardens</a>, and the
<a href="zoo.htm">Desert Zoo</a>for an experience of the
southwestern desert's spring celebration.
</font>
</td>
```

5. Save the file as `fp.htm` and view. You'll see two short columns of text, as shown in Figure 4.4.

Figure 4.4.

Two text columns created using tables.

If your fonts look too large or too small in Internet Explorer, you can adjust them by simply selecting the font options from the View menu on the toolbar. Both Netscape Navigator and Internet Explorer allow for setting of font style and size within the prefer-ences and option sections; however, it's wise to leave these at default.

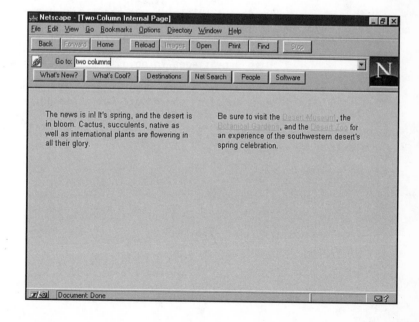

6. To add typographical, color, and visual interest, graphic headers and images are added to the individual cells, links are added within the text, and text is fleshed out using greeking:

```
<td valign=top width=250 align=left>
<font face=arial size=2>
<img src="images/fp-new.gif" alt="what's new?" width=88
height=75 align=left>
The news is in! It's spring, and the desert is in bloom. Cactus,
succulents, native as well as international plants are flowering
in all their glory
<img src="images/fp-flow.gif" alt="cactus flower" width=75
height=75 align=right>

Duis autem vel eum iriure dolor in hendrerit in vulputate velit
esse molestie consequat, vel illum dolore eu feugiat nulla
facilisis at vero eros et accumsan et iusto odio dignissim qui
blandit praesent luptatum zzril delenit augue duis dolore te
feugait nulla facilisi.
<p>
<a href="other.htm"> Nam liber </a> tempor cum soluta nobis
eleifend option congue nihil imperdiet doming id quod mazim
placerat facer possim assum. Accumsan et iusto odio dignissim
qui blandit praesent luptatum zzril delenit augue duis dolore te
feugait nulla facilisi.
<p>
</font>
</td>
<td valign=top width=250 align=left>
<font face=arial size=2>
Be sure to visit the <a href="desert.htm">Desert Museum</a>, the
<a href="bg.htm">Botanical Gardens</a>, and the <a
href="zoo.htm">Desert Zoo</a> for an experience of the
southwestern desert's spring celebration.
<img src="images/fp-go.gif" alt="goings on" width=88 height=75
align=left>
Duis autem vel eum iriure dolor in hendrerit in vulputate velit
esse molestie consequat, vel illum dolore eu feugiat nulla
facilisis at vero eros et accumsan et iusto odio dignissim qui
blandit praesent luptatum zzril delenit augue duis dolore te
feugait nulla facilisi.
<p>
</font>
<p>
</td>
```

There is never a valid excuse for not using height and width values in image strings. They are an essential aid to the browser's capability to logically deliver information. Don't be lazy; use them and get more professional results.

DESIGN NOTE:

I've found it very helpful to think of each table cell as its own HTML body field. This assists me in remembering that I can apply a wide range of design attributes, place graphics and multimedia, as well as insert programming options within that cell—just as I would within a full HTML body area. Obviously, the difference has to do with width and height; a table cell is a significantly more controlled area than a full body of text.

7. Save your file and view. You now have a visually attractive, two-column table, as shown in Figure 4.5.

Figure 4.5.

Graphics and text enliven the page.

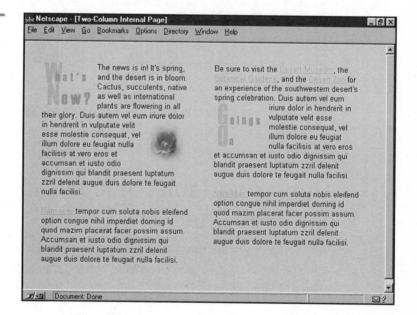

I'd like you to now experiment on your own with the table attributes. Change the border, the cellpadding, cellspacing, and width within the `<table>` tag to any numeric value you like, and see what happens. In Figure 4.6, I've dropped the cellpadding and cellspacing values to 0. Note the lack of white space. This causes a readability problem. Without enough space to ease and guide the eyes, it's difficult to discern columns or follow the text without being distracted.

Figure 4.6.
With no cellpadding or spacing, white space decreases significantly.

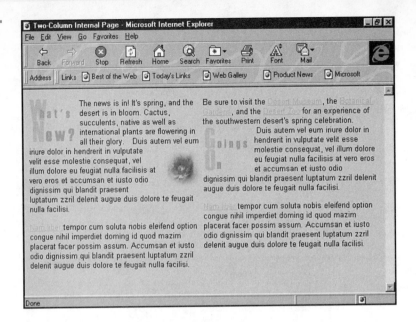

TIP: To avoid horizontal scroll bars, be sure that your total width, including cellpadding and spacing, does not exceed 640 pixels.

TASK

Using Two Tables Side-by-Side for a Textured Effect

Very often, there are times that a designer will want to try different effects using tables. In this task, you'll combine two separate tables in order to achieve a visually interesting look:

1. Open up a fresh editing page and place the following container syntax within it:

```
<html>
<head>
<title> Side by Side Table Example </title>
</head>
<body bgcolor="#FFCC99" text="#000000" link="#FF9966"
vlink="#999999" alink="#FFFFFF">
</body>
</html>
```

2. Add the following syntax and greeking for the first table, paying special attention to the width and alignment values in the `<table>` tag:

```
<table border=0 cellpadding=10 cellspacing=10 width=400
align=left>
<tr>
<td valign=top>
<font face=arial, helvetica size=2>
<img src="images/fe-hed.gif" alt="feature of the month"
width=150 height=50 align=left>
Duis autem vel eum iriure dolor in hendrerit in vulputate velit
esse molestie consequat, vel illum dolore eu feugiat nulla
facilisis at vero eros et accumsan et iusto odio dignissim qui
blandit praesent luptatum  zzril delenitaugue duis dolore te
feugait nulla facilisi.
<p>
<img src="images/canyon.jpg" alt="canyon vista" width=110
height=157 align=left>
Duis autem vel eum iriure dolor in hendrerit in vulputate velit
esse molestie consequat, vel illum dolore eu feugiat nulla
facilisis at vero eros et accumsan et iusto odio dignissim qui
blandit praesent luptatum zzril delenit augue duis dolore te
feugait nulla facilisi.
<p>
Duis autem vel eum iriure <a href="fp.htm">dolor in hendrerit</
a> in vulputate velit esse molestie consequat, vel illum dolore
eu feugiat nulla facilisis at vero eros et accumsan et iusto
odio dignissim qui blandit praesent luptatum zzril delenit augue
duis dolore te feugait nulla facilisi. Duis autem vel eum iriure
dolor in hendrerit in vulputate velit esse molestie consequat.
</font>
</td>
</tr>
</table>
```

3. Immediately below the previous table, add the following table. You'll notice I've set the border to a value of 1, and the width to 100. You will also see the use of italic and bold text attributes, which have added to the visual elegance of the page:

```
<table border=1 cellpadding=10 cellspacing=0 width=150
align=right>
<tr>
<td valign=middle>
<font face=times size=2>
<i>
Duis autem vel eum iriure dolor in hendrerit in vulputate velit
esse molestie consequat, vel illum dolore eu feugiat nulla
facilisis at vero
```

```
<p>
<b>eros et accumsan et iusto odio dignissim qui blandit praesent
luptatum!</b>
<p>
zzril delenit augue duis dolore te feugait nulla facilisi.
<p>
Duis autem vel eum iriure dolor in hendrerit in vulputate velit
esse molestie consequat, vel illum dolore eu feugiat nulla
facilisis at vero
</i>
</font>
</td>
</tr>
</table>
```

4. Save the file as `fe.htm` and view. You now have a side-by-side table layout that is visually interesting to the eye.

5. To add even more visual texture, you can use the `bgcolor` attribute in the second table's table cell. Place the following syntax in the `<td>` tag:

```
<td valign=middle bgcolor=#CCCCCC>
```

6. Save the file and view the results, as shown in Figure 4.7.

Figure 4.7.
Two tables side-by-side create an attractive, visually rich layout.

Typically, borders belie the quiet power of tables as a layout control. However, designers can choose to use them to achieve refined design if they do so very thoughtfully, and keep their use to a minimum.

Nested Tables

As mentioned earlier in this chapter, using tables inside tables can sometimes produce interesting results. This is called *nesting.* Nesting allows for any full-table attribute to be applied to the internal table, with different attributes applied to the external table.

Remember, anything you place within a table cell can be placed in the cell along with another table. For example, if you want a bit of text before the table, simply place the text within the standard HTML area, and then begin the table syntax. Just be sure to use standard formatting, once again treating the table cell as though it were its own body text environment.

The primary thing to remember about the technique is that a nested table must be placed within one of the containing table's cells. Here's an example of the basic syntax:

```
<table>
<tr>
<td>
    <table>
    <tr>
    <td>

    <td>
    </tr>
    </table>

<td>
</tr>
</table>
```

Tables can be nested fairly endlessly. Here's a stack of four, and as you can see, each is placed within the individual table's cell:

```
<table>
<tr>
<td>
    <table>
    <tr>
    <td>
        <table>
        <tr>
        <td>
            <table>
            <tr>
            <td>

            <td>
            </tr>
            </table>

        <td>
        </tr>
        </table>
```

```
<td>
</tr>
</table>

<td>
</tr>
</table>
```

NOTE: To add multiple rows and columns in any given nested table, simply place the required syntax within that individual table.

DESIGN NOTE: Getting confused about which nested table is doing what? Turn that border value into your best friend. A value of 1 gives you the outline of the individual table in question. You can turn them on and off during development, whenever you want.

TASK   Creating a Nested Table

The following nested table will allow you to separate information from the main body of text, and employ borders on the nested table to take advantage of the separation borders can create:

1. Open a clean editing environment in your HTML editor and add the following start-up container syntax:

```
<html>
<head>
<title>A Nested Table </title>
</head>
<body bgcolor="#FFCC99" text="#000000" link="#FF9966"
vlink="#999999" alink="#FFFFFF">
</body>
</html>
```

2. Place the basic syntax for a single table, being sure to follow the attributes and images I've included:

```
<table border=0 width=600 cellpadding=5 cellspacing=0>
<tr>
<td valign=top align=left>
<font face=arial, helvetica size=10>
climb it?
```

```
</font>
<p>
</td>
<td valign=top width=200>
<font face=arial, helvetica size=10 color="#999999">
yes!
</font>
<p>
<font face=arial, helvetica size=2>
<b>September 14:</b> in an unprecedented rock climb, world-class
mountaineer Lucy Jones made it to the top of one of the world's
most difficult peaks.Not only has Jones done the near-
impossible, but she's also helped make history by being the
first woman to scale the sheer rock face leading up to Donald
Duck Rock, pictured to the left.
<p>
For details of the climb, read on!
</font>
<p>
<a href="next.htm"><img src="images/arrow-r.gif" alt="right
arrow" width=150 height=25 border=0 align=right></a>
</td>
</tr>
</table>
</body>
</html>
```

3. Now you can add the following under the `climb it?` text within the
   first table cell:

```
<td valign=top align=left>
<font face=arial, helvetica size=10>
climb it?
</font>
<p>
    <table border=0 cellpadding=10 cellspacing=10>
    <tr>
    <td valign=top bgcolor="#FF9966" align=right>
    <font face=arial, helvetica size=5 color="#999999">
    extreme fun:
    </font>
    <p>
    <font face=arial, helvetica>
    world class rock climber <b>lucy jones</b> rocks on
    </font>
    </td>
    <td valign=top bgcolor="#FFCC99">
    <img src="images/n-roc.jpg" alt="rock" width=200 height=132>
    <p>
    <font face=arial, helvetica>
    this interesting and seemingly random jumble of rocks sits
    atop a 9,600 foot climb.
```

```
      <p>
      lucy knew no fear…
      </font>
      </td>
      </tr>
      </table>
</td>
```

4. Set the main and nested table border values to 1 to see the underlying layout structure shown in Figure 4.8.

Figure 4.8.
The underlying structure of a table within a table (nested tables).

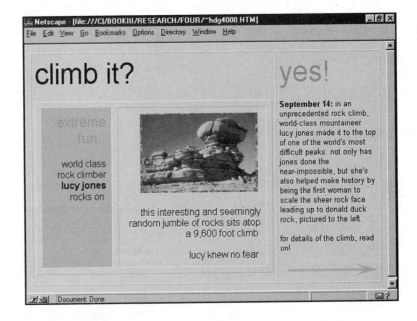

5. Reset the borders to 0, save the file as column.htm, and view the end result, as shown in Figure 4.9.

The final outcome is a functional table layout that offers an HTML page with a variety of design options such as white space, font control, graphic imagery, links, and—last but not least—information!

Figure 4.9.

Any trace of table structure disappears with the borders off, creating a clean, fresh layout.

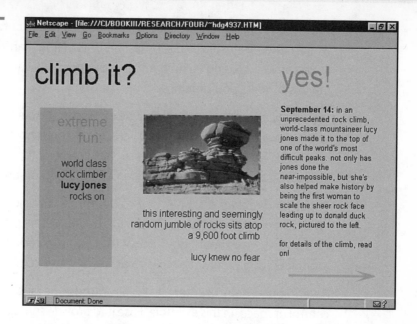

TIP: If you'd like the combined elements within a table cell to determine the width of the cell, simply don't use the width attribute in the `<td>` tag. This will result in what is known as dynamic formatting, and can be used to great success if—and here's the rub—the designer is absolutely sure that the total width of all of the page's attributes does not exceed 640 pixels at the widest. Once again, should that occur, a horizontal scrollbar will appear. This will force people using standard 640x480 resolution monitors to have to scroll to catch the data, which is uncomfortable at best and highly annoying at worst. To further ensure that this problem is avoided, be sure that your main table width is no more than 640. It is even wiser to drop width totals down to 600 pixels to neutralize any possibility of the problem occurring at all.

Stacking Tables

Just as side-by-side tables can offer interesting visual textures, stacking tables can be very useful as a layout tool. By placing tables on top of one another, you can create practical and interesting design opportunities.

In the following example, the focus is to build a bridge between practical and visually interesting table-based design. This will be carried out by stacking tables, as well as using techniques already employed in this chapter, including the use of fonts and graphics.

The practical needs of the task will be offered in the development of multiple columns via the top table, which creates a sophisticated solution for text layout. However, I'm going to use the columns for a series of graphics instead—demonstrating a visually unique method of interface design.

The second table is a simple two-column that sits below the top table and holds text potentially relevant to the top design. Although you'll only see a bit of that text, you should now know that you can continue to add text and attributes within individual cells to achieve longer columns.

As an added item of interest, I'll be introducing another method to gain control of space. In this example, I use it to provide stimulating design, but the technique is, as you will see, a practical means of creating white space between columns.

Creating a Set of Stacked Tables

To effectively stack tables, follow these steps:

1. Begin by opening a fresh editing page in your HTML editor, and then add the container syntax:

```
<html>
<head>
<title>Multiple Columns and Stacked Tables</title>
</head>
<body bgcolor="#FFCC99" text="#000000" link="#FF9966"
vlink="#999999" alink="#FFFFFF">
</body>
</html>
```

2. Construct the elements of the first table. Note that you are creating a series of six columns of specific widths. Also, make sure to include the images and color attributes I have incorporated into the syntax. I'll explain elements in greater detail as you proceed through the task.

```
<table border=1 cellpadding=0 cellspacing=0 width=600>
<tr>
<td bgcolor="#FFCC99" valign=top width=130 align=middle>
<font face=arial, helvetica size=2>
<img src="images/pic-1.gif" alt="on the trail" width=130
height=230>
on the trail
<br>
<i>day one</i>
</font>
</td>
<td bgcolor="#FF9966" background=images/tile-1.gif valign=top
width=20>
<img src="images/spacer.gif" width=18 height=1>
</td>
<td bgcolor="#FFCC99" valign=top align=middle width=130>
<font face=arial, helvetica size=2>
<img src="images/pic-2.gif" alt="sunset" width=130 height=230>
sunset spectacular
<br>
<i>day two</i>
</font>
</td>
<td bgcolor="#FF9966" background=images/tile-1.gif valign=top
width=20>
<img src="images/spacer.gif" width=18 height=1>
</td>
<td bgcolor="#FFCC99" valign=top align=middle width=130>
<font face=arial, helvetica size=2>
<img src="images/pic-3.gif" alt="vista" width=130 height=230>
impressive vista
<br>
<i>day three</i>
</font>
</td>
<td bgcolor="#FF9966" background=images/tile-1.gif valign=top
width=20>
<img src="images/spacer.gif" width=18 height=1>
</td>
<td bgcolor="#FFCC99" valign=top align=middle width=130>
<font face=arial, helvetica size=2>
<img src="images/pic-4.gif" alt="lucy" width=130 height=230>
lucy, at the top
<br>
<i>day four</i>
</font>
</td>
</tr>
</table>
```

3. Save the file as next.htm. Study the following issues before moving ahead with the task.

   Notice that within the 20 pixel-width table cells there are several intriguing attributes occurring:

❏ **Background Attribute in a Table Cell.** You're already familiar with using a background color in a table cell. The background attribute is allowed, but is only viewable by Internet Explorer 3.0+. That's why you see both the `bgcolor` and the `background=x` attributes argued. Netscape browsers will see the background color and the image will be ignored.

❏ **The Spacer GIF.** Perhaps one of the most overlooked and really useful tools in creating fixed placement within tables, the spacer GIF is a 1x1 pixel-width transparent graphic. By setting the necessary width in the image syntax, designers can call upon a spacer GIF to help control arrangement and spacing of graphics, text, and table elements.

NOTE: Another cross-browser problem is how table cell background colors are managed. In Internet Explorer 3.0+, you can use color and width to create a spacer column as I have done in this sample task. However, in Netscape Navigator 3.0+, the width will create the space, but no color is allowed until some element is introduced into the table cell. To get around this, add a spacer GIF, which will then alert the Netscape browser to load the table cell color.

CAUTION: When using spacer GIFs to create space rather than as a placement guide, set the image width to the width of the table cell, unless you are using a border, padding, or spacing value above 0. Otherwise, reduce the width to accommodate the border. You'll note in the preceding task example, I've set the spacer GIF width at 18 and the table cell width at 20. What you don't want to do is make a spacer GIF wider than the field it resides in.

4. In this step, you'll add the syntax for the next table, creating a two column table beneath the preceding seven column table. This allows for additional text, navigation, and other options to be added:

```
<table border=0 cellpadding=0 cellspacing=10 width=100%>
<tr>
<td align=left valign=top>
<font face=arial, helvetica size=2>
Duis autem vel eum iriure <a href="fp.htm">dolor in hendrerit</
a>
in vulputate velit esse molestie consequat, vel illum dolore eu
feugiat nulla facilisis at vero eros et accumsan et iusto odio
dignissim.
</font>
</td>
<td align=left valign=top>
<font face=arial, helvetica size=2>
at vero eros et accumsan et iusto odio dignissim qui blandit
praesent luptatum zzril delenit augue duis dolore te feugait
nulla facilisi.
</font>
</td>
</tr>
</table>
```

5. Save the file and view it in your browser. The results appear in
    Figure 4.10.

Figure 4.10.
*The unique end
product of a stacked,
multi-columnar table.*

Still confused by
browser inconsisten-
cies? It's the bane of
the Web designer's
existence. Look under
the Help option on
the browser's toolbar
for general informa-
tion as well as links to
specific FAQs and
browser-related
concerns.

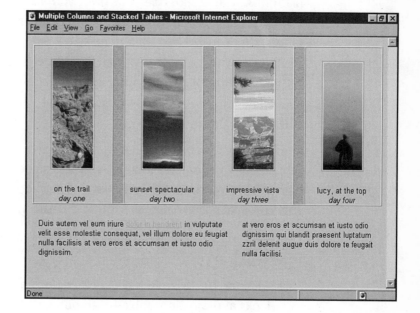

You now have a fully functional set of templates with which to play. Remove graphics, add text, and place your own graphics, color selections, font styles, and links that will help you end up with an entire Web interface based on table technology.

Workshop Wrap-Up

Working with tables can be the Web designer's entrance into high-style design. The combination of interface issues, such as consistency and visual texture with an introduction to a variety of table styles, is an excellent starting point. It's also helpful to designers who want to get more proficient not only at designing with tables, but understanding how the underlying technology operates, independently as well as across browsers. This will give the designer the most effective tools available for his or her daily site creation.

As ever, be sure to test your work with a range of browsers, as well as across platforms, if at all possible. This gives you a better look at how different computers and browsers handle the data you are supplying; you will see differences. You will also learn to make decisions on personal style development and syntax choices as you familiarize yourself with not only the techniques, but the end products they produce.

Next Steps

The following chapter continues with the discussion of interface, but this time using frames as the layout tool with which to guide a site. With the knowledge gained from this current chapter, you will find yourself easily moving into the conceptual direction Chapter 5, "Frame-Based Interface Design," takes.

Designers excited about more applications of table technology can look at the following chapters:

❏ Chapter 10, "Margin Navigation Using Tables and Frames," which looks at navigation. Table-based options are included.

❏ Chapter 16, "Using Tables for Graphic Control," has a discussion on the use of tables for multiple color and graphic controls.

❏ In Chapter 18, "Combining Tables, Frames, and Style Sheets," a combination of tables and style sheets for practical applications is covered.

❏ Appendix C, "Current HTML Standards," contains a list of all currently available table tags.

Q&A

Q: I keep seeing extra space where I didn't code for it. What's going on?

A: You're probably viewing your work in Netscape Navigator, which has an unfortunate oddity that may add extra white space on the vertical if you have line returns between your table cell tags. In most cases, this isn't a problem but a nagging annoyance. Should you require better control, try moving the beginning and ending information onto a single line and see if that doesn't solve the problem.

Q: You used a paragraph tag to separate the two stacked tables in the final task example. I'd like to create a stacked table that fits snugly beneath another. How do I do this?

A: There is an easy answer: you can't, at least not with stacking. But you can do it with nesting. Go back to the nesting example and see if you can't create a table that achieves the results you're after.

Q: I like the way you've gotten images to appear as though they are floating, such as in the second and third task examples in this chapter. How did you do that?

A: I aligned the image within the table cell, but did not place any break or paragraph tagging after the image. This allows the text to wrap dynamically around the image. More control over white space can be achieved by making sure you include it in your graphic or use the hspace and vspace attributes—the better choice in terms of optimization and speed. Set values by number until you get the look and feel you like. For more control in placement of graphics, use nested tables and individual table cells to get a custom fit. The final task in this chapter is a good example of that approach.

five

Frame-Based Interface Design

Frames are becoming one of the most used HTML tools for the creation of successful interfaces. Some might suggest that a statement like that weighs heavily on the side of opinion rather than fact. However, top Web designers working in today's competitive field are sure to agree that frames— particularly when used sensibly—are a driving force in current efforts.

In order to get a feel for how to build successful interfaces using frames, I'll begin with a simple frame-based site example. This example draws from the familiar early frame designs. It is demonstrative of a very sensible, simple inter- face. Beginning with a table-based splash page that offers users the option to see the site with or without frames, I'll move forward into demonstrating a simple system that quickly and intelligently brings visitors to the critical information. Although the focus is on interface and usability, a hint of navigation elements will be introduced to show the relation- ship between navigation and interface.

Power of Choice

Part of the rationale of providing a frames/no frames option for site visitors has grown out of the demand of Web designers to address cross-browser problems. Another part comes from the issue mentioned in Part I, "Quick Start: Elements of Tables, Frames, and Style Sheets," of this book: why frames are disliked by many people. This especially relates to frames that are visible. The issue has become relatively moot as frame interfaces are being built with the trendy no-border style.

Practically speaking, the no-border options for frames are part of what make them the powerful layout tool they are, and highlight my earlier statement regarding the scope of their current use. However, many people still want to design frames with borders, particularly in terms of interface. You will see more in-depth navigation in later chapters.

As your work advances toward sophisticated frame applications, the need for cross-browser provisions becomes less important. This is because, at that point, the work you are doing is advanced enough to focus on designing for top-of-the line, current browser technology. That begs the question: Why even bother to provide a frames/no frames option? I honestly can't answer that question other than to say the choice is individualistic, based on your company's style and the nature of a given project. However, because visible frames have caused a rift among Web visitors and designers alike, when designing for the broadest audience, it's wise to put the choice into the hands of the site's visitor.

DESIGN NOTE: Choice is more than just a way to appease Web surfers, it also happens to be the central basis of interactivity. The Web is an interactive medium largely because of the fact that there are so many options, and so many avenues of exploration based on the choice of the individual. Web designers must be savvy to the nature of interactivity, and base designs on the Web's choice-driven environment as much as they do on technical and aesthetic ideals.

Working with visible frames is also a practical place to begin, even if the trend has its sights on other design options. Much as the `border=1` option in tables assists the designer in visualizing the borders and boundaries of the layout tool he or she is applying to a design, learning frames from the visual perspective will aid you by providing strong foundations and multiple solutions for various assignments.

TASK A No Frames/Frames Splash Page

In order to achieve a successful interface built on visible frames, the splash page ideally offers two routes to the visitor. The first is the framed route, which will be built in this lesson. The second is the route with no frames. Designers can opt to design full sites with no frames if they prefer; however, because each framed page requires its own HTML page, you can simply point to those pages, which you'll equip with navigation and enough layout sense to make them usable.

1. Begin by creating a Chapter 5 folder on your computer, with a companion image subfolder. Copy the images for the chapter over from the CD-ROM.

2. In your HTML editor, open a fresh editing page.

3. Create the HTML page using "container" method syntax as follows:

    ```
    <head>
    <title>Welcome to Spoon River B&B</title>
    </head>
    <body bgcolor="#CCCCCC" text="#336699" link="#669999"
    vlink="#999999" alink="#FFFFFF">
    <center>
    </center>
    </body>
    </html>
    ```

4. Build the following simple table, noticing the use of column span (`colspan`) in the second row:

    ```
    <table border=0 cellpadding=10 cellspacing=10 width=600>
    <tr>
    <td valign=top width=207>
    </td>
    <td valign=middle width=174>
    </td>
    ```

```
</tr>
<tr>
<td valign=top align=middle colspan=2>
</td>
</tr>
</table>
```

TIP: If you want individual table cells to hold an image firmly in place, set a width within the `<td>` argument that matches the width of the image.

5. Now add the images arguments, font arguments, and text. You'll notice the `frames` and `no frames` written in text:

```
<html>
<head>
<title>Welcome to Spoon River B&B</title>
</head>
<body bgcolor="#CCCCCC" text="#336699" link="#669999"
vlink="#999999" alink="#FFFFFF">
<center>
<table border=0 cellpadding=10 cellspacing=10 width=600>
<tr>
<td valign=top width=207>
<img src="images/sr-bab.gif" width=207 height=137>
</td>
<td valign=middle width=174>
<img src="images/menu-hed.gif" alt="Welcome to Spoon River"
width=174 height=93>
</td>
</tr>
<tr>
<td valign=top align=middle colspan=2>
<font face=arial, helvetica>
Welcome to the Spoon River Bed and Breakfast!
<br>
Please select:
<p>
Frames
<br>
No Frames
</font>
</td>
</tr>
</table>
</center>
</font>
</body>
</html>
```

6. Now add the links to the respective pages:

```
<a href="frames.htm">Frames</a>
<p>
<a href="sr-wel.htm">No Frames</a>
```

NOTE: By linking the "no frames" option directly to the HTML page that you'll be targeting later, you've simply assigned the link to follow each of the HTML pages you're using for the framed site. It's a quick and clever way to keep your workload streamlined, as well as saving space. It's still a valid choice to create unique pages for a non-framed selection. It all depends on the designer's preferences and the project's needs.

7. Save the file as `index.htm` and view. The results are shown in Figure 5.1.

Figure 5.1.
A table-based splash page with frames and no frames options.

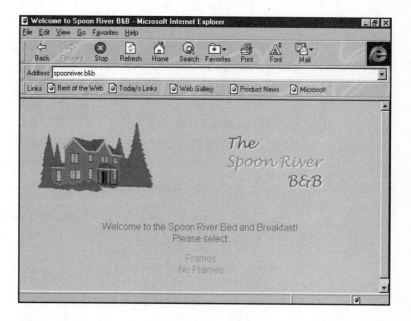

The next step will be to build the frameset, which controls the placement of HTML pages within the frame you design.

Building the Frameset

The frameset will be the `frames.htm` page that you've pointed to from the splash page. The frameset, as mentioned in Chapter 2, "Strong Foundations: The Basics of Frame Technology," is the HTML file that controls what information goes where within a framed page. In this case, I'm going to create a static left menu with options targeted to the right frame.

1. Open a fresh page in your HTML editor.

2. Add the following syntax:

   ```
   <html>
   <head>
   <title>Frameset One</title>
   </head>
   </html>
   ```

3. Now add the argument for two columns, one fixed at 215, the remainder dynamic:

   ```
   <frameset cols="215, *">
   ```

4. Below the frameset columns, add the first frame's HTML page. This creates the left, fixed menu. Note that I've named the frame menu:

   ```
   <frame src="menu.htm" name="menu" noresize scrolling=auto>
   ```

5. Now add the syntax for the right frame, immediately below the left frame syntax. You'll see that in both instances of the `<frame>`, I've argued for no resizing using the `noresize` attribute:

   ```
   <frame src="sr-wel.htm" name="right" noresize scrolling=auto>
   ```

6. The final syntax for the entire frameset should look like this:

   ```
   <html>
   <head>
   <title>Frameset One</title>
   </head>
   <frameset cols="215, *">
   <frame src="menu.htm" name="menu" noresize scrolling=auto>
   <frame src="sr-wel.htm" name="right" noresize scrolling=auto>
   </frameset>
   </html>
   ```

Looking to check your syntax? Visit http://www.columbia.edu/~daviss/work/htmlchek.html for a select list of HTML syntax tools.

> **TIP:** Make sure that frame columns and rows that will contain graphics are slightly larger in width (or height) than the graphic. This ensures that the layout differences between Netscape Navigator and Internet Explorer will be handled with ease.

Creating the Menu Page

This task will focus on building the static right-frame menu. I'll use a series of linked graphics to accomplish this.

1. In a fresh instance of an HTML page, type the following shell:

```
<html>
<head>
<title> Spoon River B&B: Welcome! </title>
</head>
<body bgcolor="#CCCCCC" text="#336699" link="#669999"
vlink="#999999" alink="#FFFFFF">
</body>
</html>
```

2. Now add the image syntax for the header:

```
<img src="images/menu-hed.gif" alt="spoon river header"
width=174 height=93>
<p>
```

3. Follow it up with the syntax for each menu option, as shown in the following code:

```
<div align=right>
<a href="sr-wel.htm" target="right">
<img src="images/menu-wel.gif" alt="welcome" width=125 height=50
border=0></a>
<br>
<a href="sr-his.htm" target="right">
<img src="images/menu-his.gif" alt="go to history" width=125
height=50 border=0></a>
<br>
<a href="sr-amn.htm" target="right">
<img src="images/menu-amn.gif" alt="go to ammenities" width=125
height=50 border=0></a>
<br>
```

```
<a href="sr-rar.htm" target="right">
<img src="images/menu-rar.gif"
alt="go to r and r" width=125 height=50 border=0></a>
<br>
<a href="sr-con.htm" target="right">
<img src="images/menu-con.gif"
alt="go to contact page" width=125 height=50 border=0></a>
<div>
```

Note the use of the `<div>` tag to flush the graphics to the right of the column.

DESIGN NOTE: When designing graphics that are to be used mostly for font and color attributes, it is wise to design like graphics to the same dimensions. In other words, each of the menu options in this chapter's example was designed on the same background. Some designers would argue that this could add up to extra, unnecessary kilobytes of data. My feelings are that the images, which contain few colors, can be optimized. Disregarding the header graphic, which is 4 kilobytes, the largest file is 2 kilobytes—very small!

4. The resulting syntax should match this example:

```
<html>
<head>
<title> Spoon River B&B: Welcome! </title>
</head>
<body bgcolor="#CCCCCC" text="#336699" link="#669999"
vlink="#999999" alink="#FFFFFF">
<img src="images/menu-hed.gif" alt="spoon river header"
width=174 height=93>
<p>
<div align=right>
<a href="sr-wel.htm" target="right">
<img src="images/menu-wel.gif"
alt="welcome" width=125 height=50 border=0></a>
<br>
<a href="sr-his.htm" target="right">
<img src="images/menu-his.gif"
alt="go to history" width=125 height=50 border=0></a>
<br>
<a href="sr-amn.htm" target="right">
<img src="images/menu-amn.gif"
alt="go to amenities" width=125 height=50 border=0></a>
<br>
<a href="sr-rar.htm" target="right">
<img src="images/menu-rar.gif"
alt="go to r and r" width=125 height=50 border=0></a>
<br>
```

```
<a href="sr-con.htm" target="right">
<img src="images/menu-con.gif"
alt="go to contact page" width=125 height=50 border=0></a>
</div>
</body>
</html>
```

5. Save the file as menu.htm and view it in a browser. For now it will look like Figure 5.2, which does look a bit strange. However, this is the fixed menu and will not be viewed outside of a frame.

Figure 5.2.

The menu as viewed without the frame container.

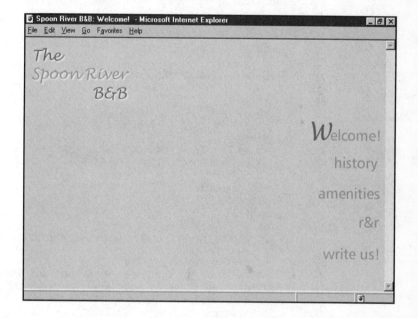

TIP: Sometimes you've seen me include alt tag arguments and descriptions, sometimes not. When is it wise to do this? Well, although you may decide it's always wise to add them, it's most critical to do so when the graphic in question is a hyperlink to another page. Use descriptions that are clearly descriptive not only of the graphic, but of the graphic's function.

For a framed site that offers up some wit and wisdom for Web designers, visit The Home for Wayward Webpage Designers at http:// chatlink.com/ ~ccubed/ html.html.

It is critical to note that I have targeted all of the image URLs to the right frame. This ensures that each will load into that frame when called upon.

In order to make the menu options actually work, you'll need to provide the individual pages. I'll begin with the welcome page, which also serves as the first no-frames page after the splash page.

A Right-Frame Welcome Page

Bearing in mind that this page will serve as a stand-alone HTML page and also a page within a frame, I've added some layout necessities. One important one is the `<blockquote>` tag, which helps create margins (and the white space margins naturally induce) on the pages.

1. Open your HTML editor

2. Begin with the following shell:

```
<html>
<head>
<title>Welcome to Spoon River B&B</title>
</head>
<body bgcolor="#CCCCCC" text="#336699" link="#669999"
vlink="#999999" alink="#FFFFFF">
<blockquote>
</blockquote>
</body>
</html>
```

3. Now add the text and images between the blockquotes:

```
<font face=arial, helvetica>
<h3>Welcome to the Spoon River Bed and Breakfast!</h3>
I hope you'll enjoy your stay. Located in the beautiful, dense
forest lands of the Upper Peninsula, the Spoon River B&B offers
a quiet getaway in a fabulous, natural setting.
<img src="images/azalea.gif" alt="azaleas" width=175 height=131
hspace=10 vspace=10 align=right>
Tired of computers and cell phones and answering machines?
A visit to Spoon River B&B is just the thing to soothe the
jangled nerves from the workaday world. While the building takes
full advantage of modern offerings such as modems and fax
machines … the point is to encourage you to focus on the sound
of nature's bounty.
<p>
</font>
```

4. Below the body text, I'll add text-based navigation. You can opt to create a graphical navigation bar or buttons, but I liked the simple look of text for this page:

```
<font face=arial, helvetica size=1>
<center>
<a href="sr-wel.htm">welcome!</a> |
<a href="sr-his.htm">history</a> |
<a href="sr-amn.htm">amenities</a> |
<a href="sr-rar.htm">rest and relax</a> |
<a href="sr-con.htm">write us!</a>
</font>
</center>
<p>
```

5. The final syntax for the welcome page should match this example:

```
<html>
<head>
<title>Welcome to Spoon River B&B</title>
</head>
<body bgcolor="#CCCCCC" text="#336699" link="#669999"
vlink="#999999" alink="#FFFFFF">
<blockquote>
<font face=arial, helvetica>
<h3>Welcome to the Spoon River Bed and Breakfast!</h3>

I hope you'll enjoy your stay. Located in the beautiful, dense
forest lands of the Upper Peninsula, the Spoon River B&B offers
a quiet getaway in a fabulous, natural setting.

<img src="images/azalea.gif" alt="azaleas" width=175 height=131
hspace=20 vspace=20 align=right>
Tired of computers and cell phones and answering machines?
A visit to Spoon River B&B is just the thing to soothe
the jangled nerves from the workaday world. While the building
takes full advantage of modern offerings such as modems and fax
machines … the point is to encourage you to focus on the sound
of nature's bounty.

<p>
</font>
<font face=arial, helvetica size=1>
<center>
<a href="sr-wel.htm">welcome!</a> |
<a href="sr-his.htm">history</a> |
<a href="sr-amn.htm">amenities</a> |
<a href="sr-rar.htm">rest and relax</a> |
<a href="sr-con.htm">write us!</a>
```

```
</font>
</center>
<p>
</blockquote>
</body>
</html>
```

6. Save the file as `sr-wel.htm` and view the page in the browser by itself. The results, which will be without the frames, should match Figure 5.3.

Figure 5.3.
The welcome page without frames.

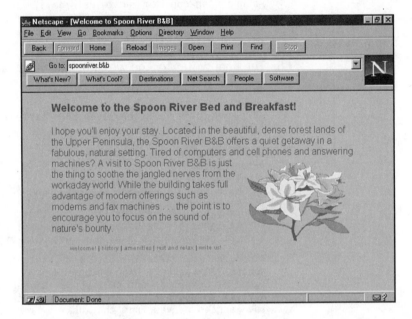

7. Open the splash page in your browser. Use the "frames" option to link to the frameset page, which will allow you to see both the left-menu and right-sided welcome page, as shown in Figure 5.4. To achieve the no-scroll effect, you may want to edit or rearrange text.

You've now successfully built the first part of an option-oriented, frames-based interface. Visitors to the splash page can select either a framed route or one without; you've set the pace with a simple and attractive solution.

The next step is to make the navigation work. This is easy for a straightforward, static framed site. And, again, every HTML page you create for the framed site will simply fall into its natural place within the non-framed option.

Figure 5.4.
The welcome page and menu in full view after selecting the "frames" option.

DESIGN NOTE: Frames are ideally used as an interface tool, not just for the sake of having them because they look cool. This means that when designing with frames, you must carefully consider how you will use them to create framed sections that ultimately make up a whole. Each section must interact with others, and each space must be used intelligently.

Adding a Subsequent Right-Frame HTML Page

This task will show you how to add a right-frame HTML page.

1. In your HTML editor, begin with the following shell syntax, including the `<blockquote>` :

```
<html>
<head>
<title>History of Spoon River B&B</title>
</head>
<body bgcolor="#CCCCCC" text="#336699" link="#669999"
vlink="#999999" alink="#FFFFFF">
<blockquote>
```

```
</blockquote>
</body>
</html>
```

2. Now add the images and text within the `blockquote` area:

```
<font face=arial, helvetica>
<h4>History of Spoon River B&B</h4>

Built originally in 1894 by early settlers to the Upper
Peninsula, Spoon River B&B originally served as the main house
Duis autem vel eum iriure dolor dolore in hendrerit in vulputate
velit esse molestie consequat, vel illum eu feugiat nulla
facilisis at vero eros et accumsan et iusto odio dignissim qui
blandit praesent luptatum zzril delenit augue duis dolore te
feugait nulla facilisi.

<img src="images/sr-blue.gif" alt="bluejay" width=100 height=75
hspace=10 vspace=10 align=left>
Dignissim qui blandit praesent luptatum zzril delenit augue duis
dolore te feugait nulla facilisi. Duis autem vel eum iriure
dolor in hendrerit in vulputate velit esse molestie consequat.
</font>
<p>
```

Now add the navigation section directly under the body text:

```
<font face=arial, helvetica size=1>
<center>
<a href="sr-wel.htm">welcome!</a> |
<a href="sr-his.htm">history</a> |
<a href="sr-amn.htm">amenities</a> |
<a href="sr-rar.htm">rest and relax</a> |
<a href="sr-con.htm">write us!</a>
</font>
</center>
<p>
```

4. Save the file as `sr-his.htm`.

5. View the file by itself to see if it looks good on its own. As Figure 5.5 shows, it does!

6. Now view the file within the framed page. Figure 5.6 demonstrates the nice results.

Figure 5.5.
The history page without frames has a clean and attractive look.

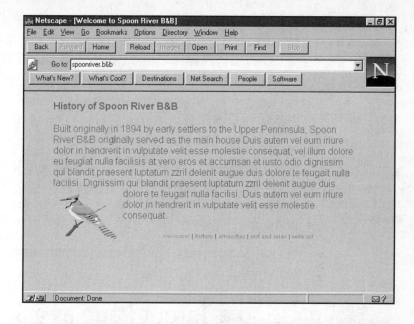

Figure 5.6.
The history page with frames— sophisticated.

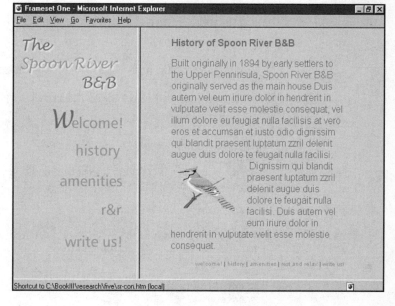

To get a taste for just how radical frame haters can be, visit The International Frame Haters Club, `http://www.wwwvoice.com/morefrm.html`. There are actually some useful insights between the rants—some sensible design comments that point to frame problems.

CAUTION: Always keep in mind that frames break up space. In order to counterbalance the visual breakup of the viewing field, be very careful to ensure that each space you create is used wisely. If you have a lot of information stuffed into a smaller frame, and not much information in a larger frame, the results will be less than desirable.

Now that you've created splash, frameset, and target pages for the frame-based site in this chapter, you have the foundation of an entire site. You can add or subtract pages as you desire, as long as you follow the basic structure of the site.

In fact, a target page can be used as a template upon which to build the remaining pages.

TASK

Using a Target Page as a Site Template

Creating templates can be helpful and speed up the coding process. This task will help you learn how to set up a template.

1. Open the `sr-his.htm` page in your HTML editor.

2. Strip the text, but leave all of the HTML tags intact:

```
<html>
<head>
<title> </title>
</head>
<body bgcolor="#CCCCCC" text="#336699" link="#669999"
vlink="#999999" alink="#FFFFFF">
<blockquote>
<font face=arial, helvetica>
<h4> </h4>
<img src="images/sr-blue.gif" alt="bluejay" width=100 height=75
hspace=10 vspace=10 align=left>
</font>
<p>
<font face=arial, helvetica size=1>
<center>
<a href="sr-wel.htm">welcome!</a> |
<a href="sr-his.htm">history</a> |
<a href="sr-amn.htm">amenities</a> |
<a href="sr-rar.htm">rest and relax</a> |
<a href="sr-con.htm">write us!</a>
</center>
```

```
</font>
<p>
</blockquote>
</body>
</html>
```

3. Replace any images with a comment tag:

```
<!-- insert image here -->
```

NOTE: Comment tagging is a very effective way to help locate elements in an HTML page. As your pages get more complicated, you'll find them especially helpful. Any information that you don't want to be visible outside of the editing environment can be placed between a `<!-- -->`. The exclamation point tells the browser to ignore everything within that tag.

4. Save the file as `sr-tpl.htm`. Figure 5.7 shows the template in an HTML editing environment. Note that some HTML editors allow for the creation of HTML pages with a distinct extension, such as `.tpl`, for creation and implementation of templates.

Figure 5.7.

A site template created from a target page.

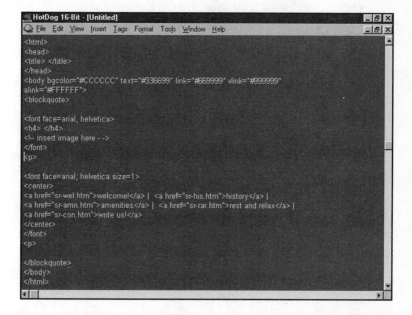

TIP: When naming files, it's a good idea to find a convention and stick to it. Each individual will have his or her own method of naming. I like to find a two- or three-letter prefix relating to the project's name, follow it with a dash, and then a descriptive short name such as `hed` for header or `tpl` for template. This assists me in quickly getting to the files I need. Furthermore, keeping filenames neat (and short—I follow the old DOS convention of no more than eight total characters in the prefix) assists in keeping the URL short, something your Web visitors will appreciate.

Do you like music? Visit `http://www.musicintheair.com/` for a nice example of a site using a similar setup to what you're creating in this chapter.

The advantage of a template file for site building is primarily speed. Another positive aspect is that you'll maintain design consistency, something that will strengthen the look and feel of your work. Certainly, as your skills become stronger, you'll want to deviate from a standard design such as the one you are currently designing. However, as many people in the design field know, deviating from consistent style can rarely be done successfully without a significant amount of skill and experience. Therefore, the template is a powerful tool for designing at all times, but especially in the early stages of building your design portfolio.

Employing the Template

Now that you have a template, it's simple to flesh out the rest of your site with the content available to you.

1. Open the template in your HTML editor.

2. Type in text for the next page in the defined areas:

```
<html>
<head>
<title>Amenities at Spoon River</title>
</head>
```

```
<body bgcolor="#CCCCCC" text="#336699" link="#669999"
vlink="#999999" alink="#FFFFFF">
<blockquote>
<font face=arial, helvetica>
<h4>Amenities at Spoon River</h4>
Duis autem vel eum iriure dolor in hendrerit in vulputate velit
esse molestie consequat, vel illum dolore eu feugiat nulla
facilisis at vero eros et accumsan et iusto odio dignissim qui
blandit praesent luptatum zzril delenit augue duis dolore te
feugait nulla facilisi.
<!-- insert image here -- >
Duis autem vel eum iriure dolor in hendrerit in vulputate velit
esse molestie consequat, vel illum dolore eu feugiat nulla
facilisis at vero eros et accumsan et iusto odio dignissim qui
blandit praesent luptatum zzril delenit augue duis dolore te
feugait nulla facilisi.
</font>
<p>
<font face=arial, helvetica size=1>
<center>
<a href="sr-wel.htm">welcome!</a> |
<a href="sr-his.htm">history</a> |
<a href="sr-amn.htm">amenities</a> |
<a href="sr-rar.htm">rest and relax</a> |
<a href="sr-con.htm">write us!</a>
</center>
</font>
<p>
</blockquote>
</body>
</html>
```

3. Now replace the image comments with any images you'd like:

```
<img src="images/sr-rwing.gif" alt="black bird" hspace=10
vspace=10 width=100 height=75 align=left>
```

4. Save the file. Here it is saved as sr-amn.htm.

5. View it in your browser, and compare the final work to Figure 5.8.

Figure 5.8.

An example of a page created with the site template. Note the highlighted box. Internet Explorer will visibly show the information within alt *tags in this fashion.*

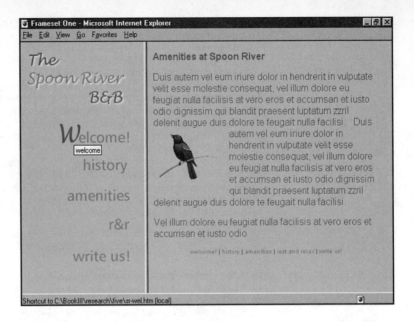

Finishing the Site Using the Template File

Now you'll get to put the template to use, and fill out the pages to create a complete site.

1. Using the original template file, repeat steps 1 through 3, filling in the information so the final HTML matches this example:

```
<html>
<head>
<title>rest and relaxation at Spoon River</title>
</head>
<body bgcolor="#CCCCCC" text="#336699" link="#669999"
vlink="#999999" alink="#FFFFFF">
<font face=arial, helvetica>
<h4>rest and relaxation at Spoon River</h4>
Duis autem vel eum iriure dolor in hendrerit in vulputate velit
esse molestie consequat, vel illum dolore eu feugiat nulla
facilisis at vero eros et accumsan et iusto odio dignissim qui
blandit praesent luptatum zzril delenit augue duis dolore te
feugait nulla facilisi. Duis autem vel eum iriure dolor in
hendrerit in vulputate velit esse molestie consequat, vel illum
```

```
dolore eu feugiat nulla facilisis at vero eros et accumsan et
iusto odio dignissim qui blandit praesent luptatum zzril delenit
augue duis dolore te feugait nulla facilisi.
<img src="images/sr-rac.gif" alt="raccoon" width=75 height=56
hspace=10 vspace=10 align=right>
Duis autem vel eum iriure dolor in hendrerit in vulputate velit
esse molestie consequat, vel illum dolore eu feugiat nulla
facilisis at vero eros et accumsan et iusto odio dignissim qui
blandit praesent luptatum zzril delenit augue duis dolore te
feugait nulla facilisi.

<p>
<font face=arial, helvetica size=1>
<center>
<a href="sr-wel.htm">welcome!</a> |
<a href="sr-his.htm">history</a> |
<a href="sr-amn.htm">amenities</a> |
<a href="sr-rar.htm">rest and relax</a> |
<a href="sr-con.htm">write us!</a>
</center>
<p>
</font>
</body>
</html>
```

2. Save this file as `sr-rar.htm`.

3. Compare your work in the browser to Figure 5.9.

Figure 5.9.
Another page example using the site's template.

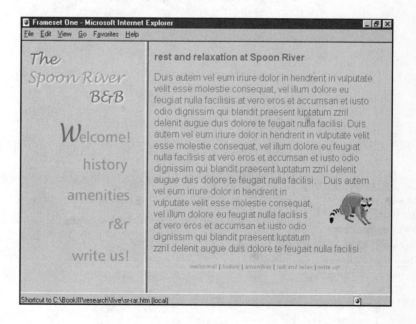

4. Using a fresh instance of the template, repeat steps 1-3 for the final page. Your syntax should match the following:

```
<html>
<head>
<title>Welcome to Spoon River B&B</title>
</head>
<body bgcolor="#CCCCCC" text="#336699" link="#669999"
vlink="#999999" alink="#FFFFFF">
<font face=arial, helvetica>
<h4>Get in Touch with Spoon River</h4>
Duis autem vel eum iriure dolor in hendrerit in vulputate velit
esse molestie consequat, vel illum dolore eu feugiat nulla
facilisis at vero eros et accumsanet iusto odio dignissim qui
blandit praesent luptatum zzril delenit augue duis dolore te
feugait nulla facilisi.
<img src="images/sr-duck.gif" alt="duck" width=150 height=113
hspace=10 vspace=10 align=left>
Duis autem vel eum iriure dolor in hendrerit in vulputate velit
esse molestie consequat, vel illum dolore eu feugiat nulla
facilisis at vero eros et accumsan et iusto odio dignissim qui
blandit praesent luptatum zzril delenit augue duis dolore te
feugait nulla facilisi.
<p>
<font face=arial, helvetica size=1>
<center>
<a href="sr-wel.htm">welcome!</a> |
<a href="sr-his.htm">history</a> |
<a href="sr-amn.htm">amenities</a> |
<a href="sr-rar.htm">rest and relax</a> |
<a href="sr-con.htm">write us!</a>
</center>
<p>
</font>
</body>
</html>
```

5. Save the file as `sr-con.htm`.

6. The results in Figure 5.10 should compare to your own.

Now I'd like you to run through the site, testing it from start to finish. Begin at the splash page, select a no frames option, and then move back and go through the framed version of the site. It should work smoothly.

For a site example that works just like this one, *including* the splash page, check out Utah County's Home Page at `http://www.valleylink.org/`.

Figure 5.10.

The final page of the site.

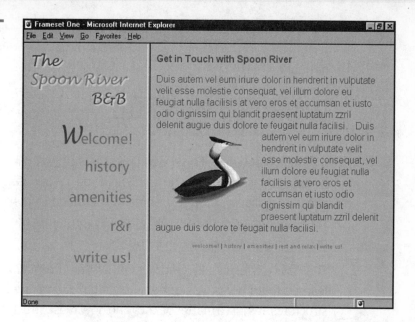

If you run into any snags while testing your pages, go back and check your syntax carefully.

DESIGN NOTE: An important design consideration regarding consistency is use of color and texture from frame to frame. If you're going to use different colors or backgrounds in the target pages, be sure that you've done so with a refined sense of palette and texture aesthetics. In other words, if you have a shocking pink background next to a blue marble target, the results will look sloppy. Each page, frame, color, and texture should be carefully considered before applying to the site. Mixing colors and textures is a technique best left in the hands of someone with significant design experience; otherwise, you run the risk of creating nice code with bad graphics.

You've now created a very useful and attractive frame-based interface. It offers flexibility through its frames/no frames option, as well as simple but effective navigation in both of the frames. This navigation is, in fact, part of the conceptual move into sophisticated Web design—combining a layout technique such as frames, with an organizational, interactive one such as navigation.

Workshop Wrap-Up

Although to some this chapter might have addressed old information, to many it's brand new. Either way, the straightforward introduction to frame-based interfaces provided here will help you in your design. For the designer already familiar with frames, some of the rationale behind frame use might strengthen your decision-making process in terms of when, and why, you decide to use frames in a given project.

The novice is especially empowered by the information here. First, you've learned that frames, while seemingly intimidating, are built on fairly simple structures. It's just a matter of knowing how these structures work that makes a difference. Seeing the relationship between a splash page, a frameset, and a target page is the pivot point from which you will learn how to employ even more complicated frame-based designs.

Furthermore, you now have a site template to add to your portfolio. By using the HTML coding within this chapter and adding your own graphics, navigation, and content, you have a framed site ready for the Web.

Remember that it's always a good idea to play with attributes; you might want to take away resizing or change scroll options to yes or no. In general, explore the various alternatives open to you. With each experimentation, you will find new opportunities and ideas to bring a fresh expression to your Web design work.

Next Steps

In the following chapter, I'll explain how the trendy borderless technique is applied. There are other chapters throughout the book that you can visit immediately to work on other types of frame-based designs. They include

❑ Chapter 7, "Designing Interfaces Combining Tables and Frames"

❑ Chapter 8, "Progressive Interfaces with Floating Frames"

❑ Part III, "Navigation that Leads the Way,"—A series of chapters dedicated to navigation

❑ Appendix B, "HTML Quick Reference"

❑ Appendix C, "Current HTML Standards" (the "Frames" section)

Of course, you can always refer back to Chapter 2, which offers up the fundamentals of frame syntax and usage.

Q&A

Q: I built a site using the information in this chapter, but I'm getting a horizontal scrollbar along the bottom right of the frame. What did I do wrong?

A: Horizontal scrollbars appear when the width of some element is wider than the pixel width of the space in which you are working. Let's say you designed a target page with a 400 pixel-wide header. Your frameset has a right column width of 250 pixels. The total amount of pixels is then 650, which does not include the frame's pixel width. Regardless, you've exceeded the limits and a horizontal scrollbar has been forced, at least on monitors that are 640x480. To avoid this problem, always make sure to keep an eye on your total widths.

Q: I placed a graphic in a frame and the frame is cutting the graphic off. I'm not even getting a scrollbar. What happened?

A: Your first problem, as mentioned in the last answer, is that you haven't anticipated the pixel limitations. Therefore, you created a graphic too wide or too tall for the column or row you've created. Following that rule alone will solve the problem. However, the second issue is that you've got your scrolling set to no when it should be set to yes or auto; in any case, it is set where you have, for some reason, chosen to design for higher resolution monitors only.

Q: As I was working on the site, I began to click the navigation and it acted strangely, loading pages into the left rather than right frames. Why did this happen?

A: Oddly enough, it seems that a frameset wants to have all of the required elements before it runs smoothly. If this problem is occurring after you've gotten all of the pages in the tasks completed, make sure you read through your syntax and check it rigorously against the examples here in the text, paying close attention to the magic target, `_right`, that occurs in the menu section of the frame.

six

Borderless Frames for High-Style Interfaces

The true power of frames lies in the structural abilities they possess. Designers who want to design interfaces that are visually appealing and also practical will appreciate the lessons available in this chapter.

The primary objective here is not just to teach a trend, which borderless frames have recently become, but to examine the practical applications of the borderless technique.

Borderless frames allow the designer to lay out a page with the ability to have certain parts remain fixed, or *static*. This creates significant opportunities for a major aspect of interface design: navigation. Furthermore, navigation has the additional advantage of allowing designers to designate fixed areas for other important uses, such as advertisement banners.

Ad banners are becoming a primary way for Web content providers to make revenue, so they're important to consider in terms of preparing to incorporate them into your design work. This chapter will provide an introduction to advertising banners, and provide a simple method of employing one within a borderless, framed site.

Another consideration in this chapter is when, and how, to use the `_blank` magic target. As you probably remember from the magic target naming discussion in Chapter 2, "Strong Foundations: The Basics of Frame Technology," this attribute spawns a new browser window. It should be used very carefully—I'll demonstrate and discuss an instance where its use is justified. Finally, another magic target name, `_top`, will be examined within the context of a complete Web site.

Borderless Frameset Pages: Considerations

As with all framed sites, the frameset page is the page that controls the layout of the frames. In the previous chapter, you learned how to build a frame with two columns. This frameset will use a combination of columns and rows to get the desired layout effect.

You've already become familiar with how to use the `<noframes>` option for browsers that don't support frames, and I've mentioned the critical element of choice when creating interactive media. However, now I want you to consider whether having a `<noframes>` option is really that useful if you're using borderless frames as a tool for layout and design rather than pure interface structure. In a sense, the work you're doing at this point requires a frames-enabled browser to be viewed properly. Because of this, you may choose not to offer options for people without such browsers.

The true consideration really lies within your knowledge of audience and the reasons why you've chosen to design a site using borderless frames. Only your awareness of a given project's goals are going to guide you. The following tasks do not include the `<noframes>` tag; however, you are encouraged to use the option, which I demonstrated in Chapter 4, "Table Controls and Site Interfaces," as your desires and needs demand.

NOTE: Before you begin any of the tasks in this chapter, please be sure to create a work folder on your computer, with a subfolder named images. Then, copy all of the Chapter 6 material from the CD-ROM (see Appendix D, "What's on the CD-ROM," for more information) into the appropriate directories on your computer.

TASK | # Creating the Index (Frameset) Page

The following task will create the frameset page. The frameset defines the way your frames will be arranged.

1. Open a fresh page in your HTML editor.

2. Copy the following shell syntax. Remember, there is no need for a body tag in the frameset; the body attributes will be taken care of within the individual pages.

```
<html>
<head>
<title>The Acoustic Cafe</title>
</head>
</html>
```

3. Now add the frameset tag for the columns. You're going to set up a total of two, with the left being a total width of 100, and the remainder left up to the browser:

```
<frameset frameborder=0 framespacing=0 border=0 cols=100,*>
```

4. Add the frame syntax for the left frame only, because you're going to break the right column into rows. The frame syntax for the left frame is

```
<frame src=menu.htm noresize scrolling=no>
```

Note that I've selected a noresize and no attribute for scrolling.

5. Now you'll break the second column into two rows. This is done by adding *another* frameset, specifying rows:

```
<frameset frameborder=0 framespacing=0 border=0 rows=*,80>
```

You'll see that I've set the *top* row at a *, or dynamic, value. I've anticipated that I'll need about 80 pixels for the bottom frame, so I've argued that numerically.

6. Now place the frame syntax for both the upper and lower frame rows:

```
<frame src=right.htm name=right noresize scrolling=auto>
<frame src=ad.htm name=bottom noresize scrolling=no>
```

Notice that the top row has a value of `auto` for scrolling. I've set this because that is going to be the mutable row. The other frames—the right column and bottom row—are both fixed.

7. Close both framesets. The final syntax is as follows:

```
<html>
<head>
<title>The Acoustic Cafe</title>
</head>
<frameset frameborder=0 framespacing=0 border=0 cols=100,*>
<frame src=menu.htm noresize scrolling=no>
<frameset frameborder=0 framespacing=0 border=0 rows=*,80>
<frame src=right.htm name=right noresize scrolling=auto>
<frame src=ad.htm name=bottom noresize scrolling=no>
</frameset>
</frameset>
</html>
```

CAUTION: If you're arguing a frameset for rows and another for columns, you must include separate framesets along with the closing `</frameset>` tag. This means one for each. Otherwise, your frameset won't work properly, and, depending on the browser you're using, it may not work at all.

8. Save the frameset as `index.htm`.

The next step is to create the fixed, or static, menu page.

 ## Creating the Static Menu

The interface you're designing in this chapter calls for a static right-margin frame. In future exercises, you'll create nonfixed, mutable menus. Each has its place in design. The power of a fixed menu is found in the advantage of speed; only one frame page is loading as opposed to one HTML page for each frame. Another strength is the creation of a visually interesting interface, with some parts moving and others staying still.

1. In your HTML editor, set up the following shell syntax:

```
<html>
<head>
<title>The Acoustic Cafe</title>
</head>
<body bgcolor="#00CC33" text="#FF6600" link="#FFFFFF"
vlink="#0033FF">
<pre>
</pre>
<center>
</center>
</font>
</body>
<             /           h         t         m         l         >
```

2. Now add the actual menu options. Obviously, I'm anticipating a number of HTML pages, plus two types of frame targets:

```
<font size=6>Menu</font>
<p>
<i>
<a href="food.htm" target="right">Eat</a>
<p>
<a href="drink.htm" target="right">Drink</a>
<p>
<a href="music.htm" target="right">Live Music</a>
<p>
<a href="res.htm" target="_top">Reservations</a>
<p>
<a href="loc.htm" target="right">Location</a>
</i>
```

The majority of the pages, as you can see, will be loaded into the right frame. However, one page, `res.htm`, uses a magic target name to load into a full page. This will be examined with more detail later in the chapter.

3. Save the file as `menu.htm`.

Now you'll create the right frame "intro" page.

The Data Section

Although I've chosen to demonstrate, in this case, a mutable data section in the upper-right portion of the interface, where the dominant frame for data is created is up to the designer. My preference with framed (bordered or borderless) sites is to keep areas of data toward the top, either the right or left, or the entire top row of a framed site.

My reason for this has more to do with comfort and practicality than style. Most people are accustomed to reading along the horizon line. Eyes will naturally fall to the most comfortable and natural area within a screen, and that's going to be within the top ¾ of the page. Placing the most critical data in a place that falls within that range is a good idea, but this isn't a hard and fast rule.

Highly experienced interface designers are finding ways of tricking the eye into feeling that there's plenty of space on a page, and they are using lower areas that serve well as data areas. Nevertheless, having a sense of what people automatically do with their line of sight can help you make strong decisions in designing interfaces.

Moreover, this area, because it will be used for the majority of interactive content and data, is, in a sense, the actual Web site, with the fixed sections providing the toolbars of the interface. Therefore, I like to think of the first HTML page to load in that section as a splash page, and treat it as such.

This page will appear in the upper portion of the right column. It's the first row, and you've ascertained, by setting the row's height dynamically and adding an automatic scroll, that the page can hold as much vertical information as necessary. In other words, if you have a full page of text, links, and graphics, it will fit into the dimensions of this section and offer scrolling, if necessary.

Preparing the Right-Frame Introductory Splash Page

This task will show you how to create the page that will fit into the right frame. In this instance, the page serves as a splash, or introduction, to the site.

1. Prepare a shell construct in your HTML editor:

```
<html>
<head>
<title>The Acoustic Cafe</title>
</head>
```

```
<body bgcolor="#FF6600" text="#FFFFFF" link="#00CC33"
vlink="#0033FF">
</body>
</html>
```

2. Add the following syntax and text, including the image from the group you've saved in your Chapter 6 folder:

```
<img src="images/ac-gui.gif" alt="acoustic guitar" width=175
height=131>
<div align=right>
<font size=6><i>The Acoustic Cafe</i></font>
<br>

where legends are made

</div>
<p>
```

3. Save the file as `right.htm`.

Looking for clip art images? Visit `http://clipart.thelinks.com/`, a well-organized list of sites that offer clip art and other graphics for the Web.

DESIGN NOTE:

You'll notice I've chosen to place text in italics. This adds to the style, but using italics for body text is dangerous if you're using more than a few lines. Part of the problem is that italics are hard to read and appear very small in certain browsers. If you are going to use italicized text, do so only for specific grammatical reasons. Or, in the case of design, use it for short bursts of text.

Advertising Banners

Web sites are rapidly becoming commercialized. Some people are upset by this because they feel it deviates from freedom of information, and they fear that advertisers will have quiet control over content in the long run. While this is seen to some degree with television and radio, advertising on the Web is currently very important to Webmasters as a source of revenue as well as getting their site the best exposure and visits possible.

Advertising banners can be offered in conjunction with a major Internet banner agency, such as Doubleclick or the Internet Banner Network. Another approach is finding individual sponsors to support your pages. This very often occurs when you're a large content provider and interested in supporting your community with advertising.

A typical advertising banner sizes in at 468×60 (see Figure 6.1). This is the standard size, and is most commonly seen in conjunction with major banner networks. Other nonstandard sizes are also seen, usually when in context of a sponsored site, as demonstrated in Figure 6.2.

Figure 6.1.
A standard size banner on a major site.

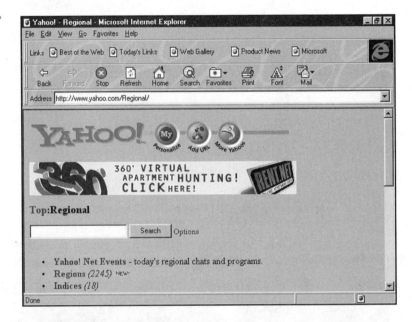

Figure 6.2.
A nonstandard banner on a sponsored site (image is 375×50).

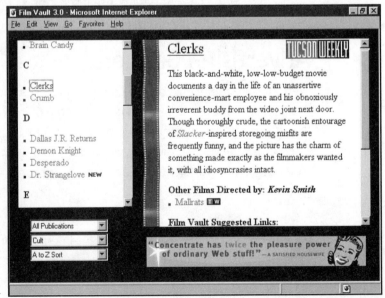

The Internet Banner Network offers targeted, flexible advertising options. Visit `http://www.banner-net.com/` for more information.

In the following task, you'll prepare the HTML page for an ad banner of standard dimensions.

Making a Bottom-Static Advertising Frame

In order to create a static frame for advertising, you'll want to follow these steps:

1. Build the following shell in your HTML editor:

```
<html>
<head>
<title> Ad HTML </title>
</head>
<body bgcolor="#FF6600" text="#000000" link="#0033FF"
vlink="#00CC33" alink="#FF6600">
<center>
</center>
</body>
</html>
```

2. Add the banner provided:

```
<img src="images/ad2.gif" border=1 width=468 height=60 align=right>
```

NOTE: You'll notice that there is a border value placed around this image. Ad banners typically require a border in order to distinguish them from other graphic elements, such as headers.

3. Save the file as ad.htm.

4. Now view the index.htm file in your browser. The results should match Figure 6.3.

Figure 6.3.

The front page of your borderless frames interface.

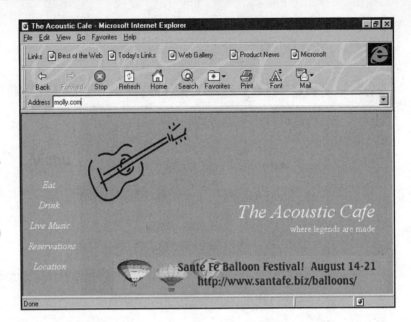

Doubleclick is considered the premier Internet advertising network. For a wealth of information on major banner advertising and how to become involved, visit http://www. doubleclick.net/.

Now that you've created the interface, you can move on to add the next content page for the site.

Adding a Content Page for the Right Frame

In this instance, the right frame is where your site contents will go. Here's how to create a content page for this frame.

1. Place the following syntax in a fresh HTML editing page:

```
<html>
<head>
<title>The Acoustic Cafe</title>
</head>
<body bgcolor="#FF6600" text="#FFFFFF" link="#00CC33"
vlink="#0033FF">
</body>
</html>
```

2. Add the image and text:

```
<img src="images/ac-food.gif" alt="food header" width=125
height=94 align=right>
<font size=6 color="#0033FF">
<i>The Acoustic Cafe: Menu</i></font>
```

```
<p>
<i>
<b>Salads:</b> only the finest, freshest ingredients!
<br>
<b>Sandwiches:</b> we feature a fantastic selection of
fresh deli-style meats and cheeses.
<br>
<b>Fresh-baked bread: </b>french, sourdough, wheat and rye
rolls, all home-made!
<br>
<b>Delicious deserts:</b> Swiss chocolates, strawberry mousse,
cheesecake, daily specialties.
</i>
<p>
```

Another good Web resource for clip art is the Clip Art Review. Point your browser to `http://www.webplaces.com/html/clipart.htm`.

Figure 6.4.
The first content page in the right frame.

3. Save the page as `food.htm`.

4. View the results in a browser; the results should match Figure 6.4.

Using the _blank Magic Target Name

As mentioned in Chapter 2, this magic target name will open an entirely new instance of a Web browser. If you use this target name carelessly, you could clutter up an innocent user's desktop with multiple browsers, draining their resources and frustrating them. However, if you're only linking to a few external sites within your own, it makes good sense to allow the site to appear in its own browser window.

Some designers think that it's wise to force external sites into the frames on the home site. The reasoning seems to be that if the visitor moves around the external site from within the home site, they won't leave. Well, my bets are placed on the fact that, between the space crunch and appearance of horizontal scrollbars, the visitor will become frustrated and may in fact leave both sites. Also, imagine what happens if the site you're linking to also has frames. You end up with a nightmare.

Therefore, I always think it's a wise rule to keep the majority of links on a framed site internal, and use external links sparingly. Create full page access for long lists of links. Be willing to allow external links to leave your site behind completely, instead of forcing the site into your interface or using the `_blank` magic target name; or, don't use frame-based environments for sites with extensive links.

TASK   Using a Magic Target for External Linking

In this task, you'll use the `_blank` magic target name as a means of opening an external site in a new Web browser.

1. Build the site in your HTML editor, beginning with the shell syntax:

   ```
   <html>
   <head>
   <title>The Acoustic Cafe</title>
   </head>
   <body bgcolor="#FF6600" text="#FFFFFF" link="#00CC33"
   vlink="#0033FF">
   </body>
   </html>
   ```

2. Add the text and images:

   ```
   <img src="images/ac-cup.gif" alt="coffee cup" width=150
   height=113 align=left>
   <font size=6 color="#0033FF">
   <i>The Acoustic Cafe: Drinks</i></font>
   <p>
   <i>
   <b>Coffees:</b> specialty roasts from
   <a href="http://www.desert.net/wilderose/" target="_blank">
   Wilde Rose Roastery</a> brewed fresh all day.
   <br>
   <b>Coffee drinks:</b> espresso, cafe mocha, cafe panna, cafe,
   ```

```
cafe, cafe! You want it, we make it!
<br>
<b>Teas:</b> exotic and delicious teas available by the cup
or by the pot, hot or iced.
</i>
<p>
```

Note the target and magic name in the preceding link. When this is clicked, the Wilde Rose site will open up in a new instance of your Web browser.

3. Save the file as `drink.htm`.

4. Connect to your Internet Service Provider.

5. Open the `index.htm` file in your browser. Move to the Drinks selection.

6. View the page. It should match Figure 6.5.

7. Now click the link to Wilde Rose and watch how a new browser window opens to accommodate the connection.

8. Take a break and surf around. You deserve it!

Figure 6.5

The Drinks page with the magic target link.

DESIGN NOTE: Where to place links is not only a technical issue, it's a practical and aesthetic one as well. Suppose you have too many links too close together—the flow of text and text color will be compromised. Practically speaking, links too early in a site or on a page can send people off your site without a chance to enjoy it fully. Links should be planned in the early stages of a site's design.

TASK Adding Subsequent Content Pages

Now that you're back from your break, you can begin by adding another content page to the site.

1. In your HTML editor, copy the following shell syntax:

   ```
   <html>
   <head>
   <title>The Acoustic Cafe</title>
   </head>
   <body bgcolor="#FF6600" text="#FFFFFF" link="#00CC33"
   vlink="#0033FF">
   </body>
   </html>
   ```

2. Now add the images and text:

   ```
   <img src="images/ac-bon.gif" alt="bongos" width=150 height=113
   align=right>
   <font size=6 color="#0033FF"><i>The Acoustic Cafe: Live Music
   </i></font>
   <p>
   <i>
   Our claim to fame is the fantastic nightly, live, acoustic music
   that we feature. You can listen to artists such as Joe Rush,
   Milkseed, and the Courage Sisters. Sunday brunches are a little
   more laid-back, with classical-style guitar from the fantastic
   duo Fla-Men-Co! Be sure to check back for special guests and
   events.
   <i>
   <p>
   ```

3. Save the file as `music.htm`.

4. View the file from the index page within the context of the interface. It should match Figure 6.6.

Figure 6.6

The Music page fits nicely into the interface theme.

An excellent reference for forms and CGI is *The CGI Developer's Guide* by Eugene Eric Kim, by Sams.net Publishing.

Another fine resource for forms and CGI scripting and how they interact with HTML is *HTML 3.2 & CGI Unleashed, Second Edition*, also from Sams.net Publishing. Both are straight-forward, easy-to-read yet detail-oriented books that will help you use the information in this book to your best advantage.

Forms for Functionality

Many Web sites will require forms. In this example, a simple reservation form helps the visitor make online reservations for shows at this fictional café. Forms use CGI (common gateway interface) scripts in order to send collected information to a final destination.

Designing forms isn't difficult, and there's a great deal of information on how to use them both in online tutorials as well as in books. For the purposes of this chapter, you'll create a form by copying syntax. The primary idea in this section is to place the form on a full page without spawning a new browser. This is done using the _top magic target name, which will load the full HTML page, ignoring any frames called for by the frameset.

I do encourage you to use any number of the recommended guides as a means to learn more about how forms can enhance your Web sites.

TIP: How a form is processed is going to depend on the server on which your Web site resides. Check with your system administrator. He or she will know how you can implement the CGI element of forms in the context of the server type being operated.

Adding a Form

This task will show you how to add a CGI form to your Web page.

1. Begin with a shell syntax as you would with any other HTML page:

```
<html>
<head>
<title>The Acoustic Cafe</title>
</head>
<body bgcolor="#FF6600" text="#FFFFFF" link="#00CC33"
vlink="#0033FF">
<blockquote>
</blockquote>
</body>
</html>
```

2. Next, add the starting text and related formatting:

```
<font size=6 color="#0033FF"><i>The Acoustic Cafe: Reserva-
tions</i></font>
<p>
<i>
We're happy to take your reservations right online for special
seating and concert events.
Your reservation will be confirmed by phone, FAX, or email.
<i>
<p>
```

3. Now add the form shell:

```
<form method="post"
action="http://your.server/htbin/suggest/(FN=555-
5555@fax.your.server/">
</form>
```

NOTE: In this case, form syntax will be guided by the server on which you are preparing your site. Although this example is close to what you'll be using, it isn't going to result in an operational form.

A good primer on CGI resides at `http://hoohoo.ncsa.uiuc.edu/cgi/overview.html`.

4. Within the form shell, add the following values. Again, this is an example. Examine the syntax, but you'll need to know the server requirements in order to make such a form functional:

```
<input name="user" type="hidden" value="RandomUser@your.server">
<input name="version" type="hidden" value="Reservation via
```

```
Cafe">
<input name="success" type="hidden" value="Thank You!
We will call to confirm when we receive your reservation.">
<input name="subject" type="hidden" value="Reservation via
Cafe">
Name: <input size=32 name="Name"><p>
Number of Guests: <input size=3 name="Guests">
Date: <input size=8 name="Date">
Time: <select name="Time">
 <option>5:30 pm
 <option>6:00 pm
 <option>6:30 pm
 <option>7:00 pm
 <option>7:30 pm
 <option>8:00 pm
 <option>8:30 pm
</select><p>
Phone: <input size=15 name="Phone">
FAX:  <input size=15name="FAX">
e-mail: <input size=15 name="email">
<p>
Which of the above is your preferred method for reservation
confirmation? <br>
<input size=45 name="method"><p>
<input type="submit" value="Make Your Reservation">
<input type="reset" value=" Clear">
<p>
<br>
</form>
<p>

Thank you for using this convenient online reservation form.
We look forward to your visit!

<center>
<font size=4>
<a href="index.htm">Return to Home</a>
</font>
</center>
```

5. Save the file as res.htm.

6. View the file. It should match Figure 6.7.

7. Click the Return Home link. The index page should load.

8. Now click the Reservations link. Notice the smooth loading within the same browser window? This is the result of a properly used _top magic target name.

Figure 6.7.
The Reservations page loads into a full window, using the _top magic target name.

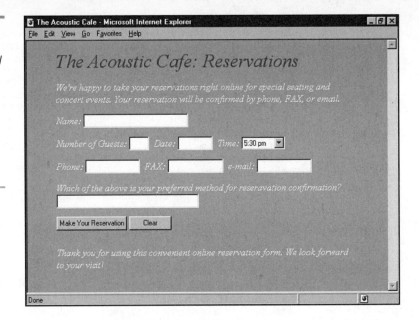

A helpful Web site for creating forms can be found at `http://www. incontext.com/ support/spider/ userguid/ editing/ forms.htm`.

TIP: When designing forms, it's always a good idea to think carefully about the type and size of fields necessary. Then, design the fields to look attractive on a page. If you have a list of fields, this can be achieved by justifying the right margin of the fields so they stack up neatly—without a ragged edge. There is no cut-and-dry method to do this other than to test and view your pages carefully.

Now, all that's necessary is to wrap up the site by adding the final page.

 ## Adding the Final Page

This task adds the final site page. In this case, you'll provide location and contact information. Even though you will benefit from having mail links and phone numbers throughout a site, it's often wise to place the complete details on a final page. Visitors can then easily decide which way they'd best like to get in touch.

1. Begin with a fresh editing environment.

2. Add the following shell syntax:

```
<html>
<head>
<title>The Acoustic Cafe</title>
</head>
<body bgcolor="#FF6600" text="#FFFFFF" link="#00CC33"
vlink="#0033FF">
</body>
</html>
```

3. Now add the image and text:

```
<img src="images/ac-tamb.gif" alt="tamborine" width=125
height=94 align=right>
<font size=6 color="#0033FF">
<i>The Acoustic Cafe: Location</i></font>
<p>
<i>
We're located downtown in the Plaza. We have outdoor seating by
the fountain, and our indoor seating surrounds our stage-in-the
round.
<p>
The Cafe is 1 mile east of the freeway, exit 450. Follow the
signs to Main Street, take the first right off of Main on to
Courthouse Drive. For more information please call 555-555-5555
8 a.m. to 10 p.m. any day of the week!
<i>
<p>
```

4. Save the file as `loc.htm`.

5. Open the `index.htm` file in a browser and move through the site. The final page should resemble Figure 6.8.

Figure 6.8.

The Location page returns to the original interface format.

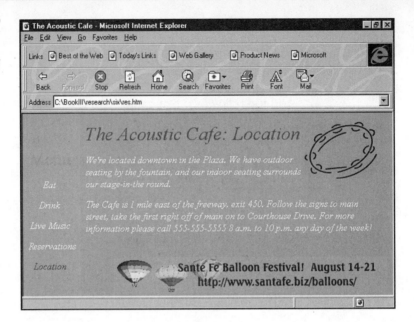

TIP: You'll note that I didn't use a lot of images in this design and it's still very bright and colorful, as you can see from the examples on the CD-ROM. Part of intelligent design is to exploit browser colors, or *client-sided* color information. This means that all of the sorting out is done on the side of the browser rather than on the server, saving a lot of time. Not only can this be done with background colors, but also to create headers as I've done by using a large font size and italics.

Testing Your Work

As you progress further into this book, it becomes more and more imperative to test all your work. This means not only trying out your work in one browser, but also Netscape 3.0 and above and Internet Explorer 3.0 and above. Go through each page on each browser, looking for how the site appears in each.

If you have the means, check out other platforms. Look at the site on a Macintosh and a PC. See if you can switch screen resolutions. The look will change, but does it change so dramatically that your basic design is mangled? If so, you'll need to go back and change things until you've achieved some balance in design.

Workshop Wrap-Up

With borderless frames, you've entered a much more sophisticated level of design and layout with HTML. You can begin experimenting with color, graphics, and columns and rows to develop your own ideas as to how to create borderless frame interfaces.

Even if you began this book with some trepidation as to the difficulty of using frames, you should now feel fairly confident that although it is, in fact, somewhat complex, the step-by-step workshops have led you to creating framed sites with relative ease.

Adding a few techniques with magic target names has also prepared you for some more complicated tricks that you'll learn as you progress throughout the book. However, it is always important to remember that the basics are just that—basic. You can always come back to these early chapters to practice your skills.

Each chapter gives you the added benefit of providing a template that you can now add to your own list of available site types.

Again, experiment! Play with attributes. Add resizing or scrolls where I've not done so. See what happens. Do you like the results? Always explore the various opportunities that HTML, which is often very flexible despite its inconsistencies, can offer as you build your own unique style as a Web site designer.

Next Steps

Chapter 7, "Designing Interfaces Combining Tables and Frames," expands on what you've just learned in this chapter by adding tables into the picture. This will give you powerful layout options. You'll see how tables control white space, graphic layout, and text alignment within the context of frames. If you have frame fever, you might want to also look at the following chapters:

❏ Chapter 8, "Progressive Interfaces with Floating Frames."

❏ Part III, "Navigation that Leads the Way,"— All of the chapters within this section discuss some element of frames, particularly advanced usage.

And don't forget the appendixes! Appendix B, "HTML Quick Reference," offers a quick HTML reference, and Appendix C, "Current HTML Standards," offers all of the available frames syntax in an easy-to-use table.

Q&A

Q: As I was checking my pages, the page I was working on loaded into the left frame, not the target frame. What happened?

A: This could actually be the result of one of several things. First, always check that your target syntax is correct. If it is, it's possible that you're trying to check a site with pages and links that haven't been coded yet—in Netscape Navigator. For some reason, if all of your menu link options have not been completed, Navigator may opt to not load your pages. Finish up all of the required HTML pages and complete all of the links within the menu pages. This should solve the problem.

Q: I'm viewing my pages and there's a thin line between each frame. Shouldn't each frame in a borderless environment be snug up against the other?

A: Yes. Borderless frames load snug up against each other with no breaks. If you are experiencing a thin break, it's highly likely you left out a closing frameset tag (`</frameset>`). Remember, you must have one for each frameset you are arguing for. If you've got a set of columns and a set of rows, you must have two closing framesets.

Q: I notice you haven't placed any navigation within the HTML pages. Why not?

A: As I mentioned earlier in the chapter, your audience and personal preference will determine how you go about offering options to site visitors. This includes a full splash page, frames and no frames options, and alternative navigation options. You must use your own design sense to determine if adding these options is right for the project you're working on. Here is a hint: In most cases, it is extremely wise to offer as many options as possible!

seven

Designing Interfaces Combining Tables and Frames

To get maximum power from today's HTML-based layout options, you can combine tables and frames for interface design. This means having the availability of static and borderless control from frames and internal, fixed-placement advantages of tables. The combination, as you will see as you move through the tasks within this chapter, enables you to design with a variety of powerful components. Your virtual toolbox is getting jam-packed with options, and the opportunities that come with those options.

As is always the case where tables and frames are concerned, how you choose to break up the space is critical. Instead of using frames to make the design areas smaller, you can maximize your space by delegating specific areas, as you have in other chapters, as static. These areas can be used for linked navigation, advertising space, whatever your individual project requires. The bottom line is to plan carefully, and it may even

Netscape-centric beginning frames designers can find help on planning and using frames from Charlton Rose's Netscape Frame Tutorial at `http://www.newbie.net/frames/`.

benefit you to sketch out your ideas on paper first. Which areas are going to be fixed? Which areas require scrolling?

Similar issues are involved when adding frames to the mix. You'll want to carefully use the frames to place graphics, align text, and create that ever-important white space. Tables should not constrain. In fact, they are best used to organize data so that it appears wide open. It's akin to painting a small room white and using mirrors to give the illusion that it's really bigger. In fact, that's a great way to think about it. Your Web pages are virtual rooms, and you can choose to arrange elements with tables and frames to open up, rather than close off, the Web space.

Graphic Treatments to Enhance Design

Many Web enthusiasts have a tendency to constrain that space by blocking off graphics with tables. Tables can effectively control the placement of graphics and, as you will see in Chapter 12, "Multiple Menus and Non-Linear Navigation," they actually work in tangent with graphics to create powerful and quick-loading graphic design. However, it's dangerous to think that placing a graphic within a border is going to enhance that graphic. In fact, it usually causes that area of the page to appear constrained and tight.

Because our desire is to free up those constraints and make the Web space appear clean, it's a good idea, unless your skills are very advanced, to avoid placing images inside table borders. In fact, there are techniques to provide context for graphics. These are called "treatments" and are often a stylized way of working with the image to add to rather than detract from the overall design of the Web site.

In the example in this chapter, you'll see I've employed a "Polaroid" style treatment (see Figure 7.1). Then, I've used a drop shadow to add dimension to the look and feel. The results are interesting: The graphics accentuate the page, and the added white space in the treatment itself gives the site a very clean yet colorful look.

Figure 7.1.
A "Polaroid" style photo treatment.

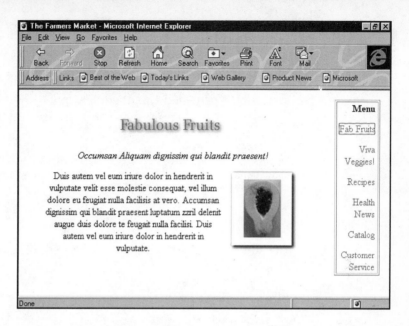

Photodisc (http://www.photodisc.com/) offers some of the best royalty-free digital stock photography and graphic treatments available. You can actually order and automatically download what you want on their Web site, which, incidentally, is designed using tables. Some of their products are expensive, but they are invaluable for the professional Web designer.

Interestingly, I use a bordered table within the right frame to visually offset the navigation. Try it without the border and see which you prefer.

Designing the "Farmer's Market"—a Frameset

The following code will set up the frames for this site's design.

1. In your HTML editor, create the following shell:

```
<html>
<head>
<title>The Farmers Market</title>
</head>

</html>
```

2. Now, add the frameset syntax. Observe that you are arguing for two columns, and are actually defining the pixel width of each. This helps define the width of your workspaces very clearly:

```
<frameset frameborder=0 framespacing=0 border=0 cols=500,100>

<frame src=left.htm name=left noresize scrolling="no">
<frame src=menu.htm noresize scrolling=no>

</frameset>
```

3. Save the file as index.htm.

Creating the Menu

This next step, as you probably guessed, is to create the menu page.

1. Open a fresh page and type the following:

```
<html>
<head>
<title>Farmers Market Menu </title>
</head>
<body bgcolor="#FFFFFF" text="#000000" link="#CC3300"
vlink="#339900" alink="#FFFFFF">

</body>
</html>
```

2. Now add this straightforward table. Note the `border=1` attribute and value:

```
<table border=1 width=75>
<tr>
<td align=right>

</td>
</tr>
</table>
```

3. Within the table cell, place the following menu text and syntax:

```
<b>Menu</b>
<p>

<a href="fruits.htm" target=left>Fab Fruits</a>
<p>

<a href="veggies.htm" target=left>Viva Veggies!</a>
<p>

<a href="rec.htm" target=left>Recipes</a>
<p>

<a href="news.htm" target=left>Health News</a>
<p>

<a href="cat.htm" target=left>Catalog</a>
<p>

<a href="cust.htm" target=left>Customer Service</a>
```

Note that all the options are targeted to the left frame, making the interface extremely easy to use and understand.

4. Save the file as menu.htm.

5. View your work in a browser and compare it to Figure 7.2.

Figure 7.2.

This menu will appear in the right field of your browser once the frameset HTML pages are complete.

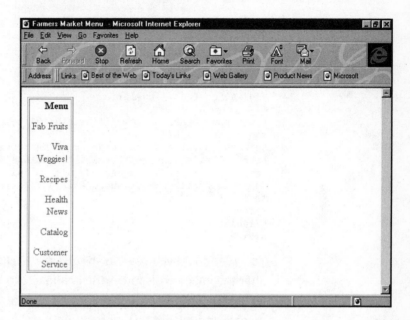

TASK Creating the Main Target Page

This task will show you how to design the main page of the site.

1. Start off with the following code:

```
<html>
<head>
<title>The Farmers Market</title>
</head>
<body bgcolor="#FFFFFF" text="#000000" link="#CC3300"
vlink="#339900" alink="#FFFFFF">

</body>
</html>
```

2. Add the table, text, and image. You'll see that I've centered it with the <div align=center> tag:

```
<div align=center>
<table border=0 cellpadding =10 cellspacing=10 width=470>
<tr>
```

```
<td valign=top align=middle width=300 colspan=2>
<img src="images/fm-hed.gif" alt="FM Header" width=300
height=50>
<p>

<i>Occumsan Aliquam dignissim qui blandit praesent!</i>
</td>
</tr>

<tr>

<td valign=top align=left>

<img src="images/fm-vg1.gif" width=120 height=131 align=left>
<br clear="right">
Duis autem vel eum iriure dolor in hendrerit in vulputate velit
esse molestie consequat, vel illum dolore eu feugiat nulla
facilisis at vero. Accumsan dignissim qui blandit praesent
luptatum zzril delenit augue duis dolore te feugait nulla
facilisi.
</tr>
</table>
</div>
```

You'll see that I've used the `<br clear="right">` tag and attribute after the image. This forces the image to align on the left and the text to the right. Although you could control the placement of this graphic and related text with individual table cells, I chose not to do so, opting to demonstrate that images can be controlled with tags other than table-related ones—even if they appear within a table.

3. Save the file as `left.htm`.

4. Open the `index.htm` file in a browser. Your results should match Figure 7.3.

NOTE: If your figure doesn't quite match, it may not be a syntax problem. See if you're using the same browser that I am to demonstrate the site. Browsers, as I've mentioned earlier, treat HTML differently. This particular site looks best in Internet Explorer, but is easily viewed in Netscape, although the layout is somewhat different. Try these sites in both browsers. It's a good habit to get into.

Figure 7.3.

The foundational interface layout is complete. Note that I'm using Internet Explorer 3.0 to view this site.

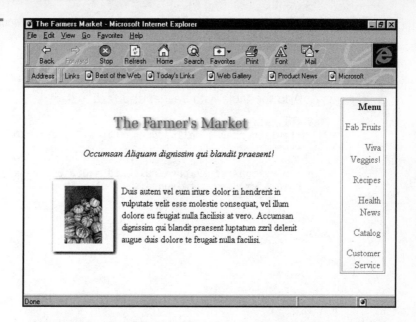

DESIGN NOTE: Although there may be differences in the way your pages appear in browsers, there still is little rationale for immediately announcing to every Web visitor that this is an "enhanced" page. Create good code to begin with and you can avoid obvious endorsements. If you do have a strong personal preference, choose to place commentary and links to your browser of choice somewhere other than on the main page of your site.

Now you'll add a content page that uses centered text alignment and a floating image.

 ## Adding a Content Page

This task shows you how to create a content page. The focus of this page is on text alignment and image placement.

1. Begin with the basics:

```
<html>
<head>
<title>The Farmers Market</title>
</head>
```

```
<body bgcolor="#FFFFFF" text="#000000" link="#CC3300"
vlink="#339900" alink="#FFFFFF">

</body>
</html>
```

2. Add the table with images and text:

```
<div align=center>
<table border=0 cellpadding =10 cellspacing=10 width=470>
<tr>

<td valign=top align=middle width=300 colspan=2>
<img src="images/fm-vghed.gif" alt="FM Header" width=300
height=50>
<p>

</td>
</tr>

<tr>

<td valign=top align=right>

<img src="images/fm-vg2.gif" alt="veggies!" width=165 height=117
hspace=10 align=right>
ccumsan dignissim qui blandit praesent luptatum zzril delenit
augue duis dolore te feugait nulla facilisi. Duis autem vel eum
iriure dolor in hendrerit in vulputate.
</td>
</tr>
</table>
</div>
```

3. Save the file as veggies.htm.

The image fm-bg2.gif has an alignment attribute, but no following break. Because I've aligned the text to the right and added a horizontal space (hspace) with a value of 10, the text appears flush right to the image, as shown in Figure 7.4. However, if I add more text, this attribute allows the text to wrap around the graphic. With the right-alignment, the results are visually unusual (and, therefore, interesting), as seen in Figure 7.5. Often referred to as "floating" images, the technique is one I often like to use to give my Web site text a more natural, flowing look.

Figure 7.4.

The text is flush right and aligned with the graphic.

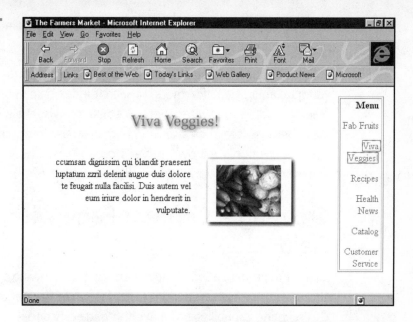

Figure 7.5.

Add more text and the image floats, creating an interesting look.

For a wealth of information on image attributes, visit The Web Developer's Virtual Library Inline Images page at `http:// WWW.Stars.com/ Authoring/HTML/ Body/img.html`.

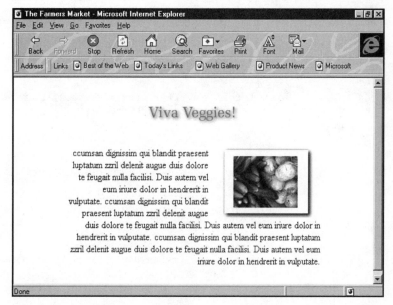

Searchable Indexes

Searchable indexes are a popular—and powerful—means of getting information that Web visitors want. If this example were a real-life produce and specialty goods shop, one thing it might offer are recipes. After all, food is one of life's pleasures, and the Web is filled with gourmets, dieters, and food lovers seeking out fun ways of serving up meals.

So, from a business perspective, it's wise to offer information that will keep visitors coming back for more. A search index helps find that information quickly. Adding the syntax that will create the visual element of a search is easy. Because searches use CGI and database programs, using them is dependent upon your own server's capabilities. Check with your systems administrator if you don't know what's available to you.

Creating a Content Page with a Search Field

HTML & CGI Un-leashed is a popular title that can assist you in learning CGI-based searches. Another good resource is *Web Programming Unleashed*. Both are texts with significant resources for the Web publisher, and both are available from Sams.net Publishing.

In order to prepare a search field, perform the following steps. Remember to check with your systems administrator for more information on setting up the CGI scripting capabilities to make this page functional.

1. Type the following shell syntax into your HTML editor:

```
<html>
<head>
<title>The Farmers Market</title>
</head>
<body bgcolor="#FFFFFF" text="#000000" link="#CC3300"
vlink="#339900" alink="#FFFFFF">

</body>
</html>
```

2. In the body, place the table, images, and text:

```
<div align=center>
<table border=0 cellpadding =10 cellspacing=10 width=470>
<tr>

<td valign=top align=middle width=300 colspan=2>
<img src="images/fm-rehed.gif" alt="FM Header" width=300
height=50> <p>

</td>

</tr>

<tr>

<td valign=top align=right>
```

```
<img src="images/fm-rp1.gif" alt="food and wine" width=175
height=124 hspace=5 align=right>

Duis autem vel eum iriure. Accumsan dignissim qui blandit
praesent luptatum zzril delenit augue duis dolore te feugait
nulla facilisi. Duis autem vel eum iriure dolor in hendrerit in
 vulputate.
<pre>

</pre>

</td>
</tr>
</table>
</div>
```

3. Between the `<pre>` tags, place the following form:

```
<form method="post" action="http://your.server/htbin/search-or">
<input name="index" type="hidden"
value="your.server:[www]searchfulltext">
<input name="show_size" type="hidden" value="no">
<input name="sort" type="hidden" value="yes">
<input name="show_score" type="hidden" value="yes">
<input name="maximum_hits" type="hidden" value="500">
<input type="text" size=15 maxlength=100 name="Query" value="">
<input type=submit value="search!">
</form>
```

Note how the different name attributes ask for a variety of values. This search, when implemented, will do a full-text search that will provide results that are sorted. Again, this is only an example, one that was based on a text-search CGI program running on the servers that I use. You must find out what search services are available to you, and your syntax will vary depending upon those services. This example serves to give you a visual idea of how such elements can be placed within a Web page, anticipating your needs as a Web designer.

4. Save the file as `rec.htm` and view it in your browser (see Figure 7.6). Although this page contains a graphic header, text, a treated photograph, a search field, and a frame layout, it doesn't seem squeezed together at all.

Figure 7.6.
Even with five elements, this page looks open and fresh.

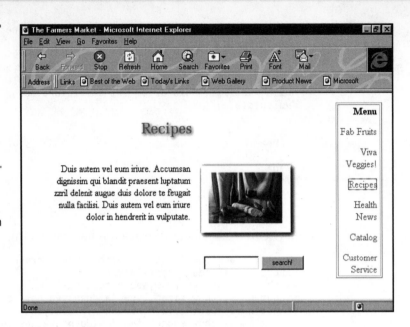

CGI information on the Web is vast and varied. One good jumping-off place can be found at the ever-helpful Web Developer's Virtual Library at http://www.Stars.com/Software/CGI/.

Adding a Columnar Content Page

Another element that many Web designers will require within a site is a newsletter or news area. In this example, a multicolumn treatment is incorporated.

1. In your HTML editor, begin with the shell syntax that follows:

```
<html>
<head>
<title>The Farmers Market</title>
</head>
<body bgcolor="#FFFFFF" text="#000000" link="#CC3300"
vlink="#339900" alink="#FFFFFF">

</body>
</html>
```

2. Now add the table shell:

```
<div align=center>
<table border=0 cellpadding =5 cellspacing=5 width=470>

</table>
```

3. Add a row and table cell to contain and control the graphic header's placement. Note the use of the `colspan` attribute. I've set the numeric value to 3, anticipating three columns.

```
<tr>

<td valign=top align=middle width=300 colspan=3>
<img src="images/fm-hnhed.gif" alt="FM Header" width=300
➥height=50>
</td>

</tr>
```

4. Now place a row and the three table data cells, with text, that will make up the three columns:

```
<tr>

<td valign=top align=left width=100>
Duis autem vel eum iriure dolor in hendrerit in vulputate velit
esse molestie consequat.
<b>Accumsan dignissim</b> qui te feugait nulla facilisi.
</td>

<td valign=top align=left width=100>

Accumsan dignissim qui blandit praesent luptatum zzril delenit
augue <i>duis dolore te</i>
feugait nulla facilisi. Duis autem vel eum iriure dolor!

</td>

<td valign=top align=left width=100>

Accumsan <b>dignissim qui blandit</b> praesent luptatum zzril
delenit augue duis dolore feugait nulla facilisi. Duis autem vel …
</td>
</tr>
```

5. Save the file as news.htm and view it in your browser. The results should match Figure 7.7.

DESIGN NOTE: In the newsletter example, you'll see I've selected several small sections of text to treat with text styles such as bold and italic. This helps draw the eye to critical information, and also lends to a stylish visual look. Although I've used basic HTML tags to create text styles in this example, you may also consider using style sheets to do this. Visit Chapter 3, "In Vogue: Cascading Style Sheets," and Part IV, "Sophisticated Pages Using Format Control," to find out the variety of ways style sheets can be used to enhance text.

Figure 7.7.
A multicolumn table example within a borderless frame.

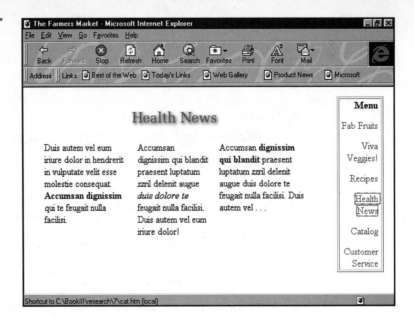

Creating a Content Page with a Sub-Menu

As you will learn in Part II, "Designing a Welcoming Interface," navigation plays a significant role in the creation of successful Web sites. In this task, you will implement a simple sub-menu, anticipating a catalog service. I've treated this page as though it were an internal splash page, emphasizing the title, which is an attractive graphic that entices the visitor.

1. Begin with the shell syntax:

```
<html>
<head>
<title>The Farmers Market</title>
</head>
<body bgcolor="#FFFFFF" text="#000000" link="#CC3300"
vlink="#339900" alink="#FFFFFF">

</body>
</html>
```

2. Add the table and graphic:

```
<div align=center>
<table border=0 cellpadding =10 cellspacing=10 width=470>
<tr>

<td valign=top align=middle width=300 colspan=2>
<img src="images/fm-cahed.gif" alt="FM Header" width=300
height=50>
<p>

<img src="images/fm-fr2.gif" alt="strawberries" width=222
height=157 align=middle>
<p>

</tr>
</table>
</div>
```

3. Beneath the strawberry image, place the text navigation:

```
<a href="fresh.htm">fresh produce</a> |
<a href="health.htm">health supplements</a> |
<a href="beauty.htm">natural beauty products</a>
```

4. Save the file as cat.htm.

5. View it in your Web browser. As Figure 7.8 shows, this is an attractive and alluring page.

Figure 7.8.
An internal catalog page made to resemble a standard splash page.

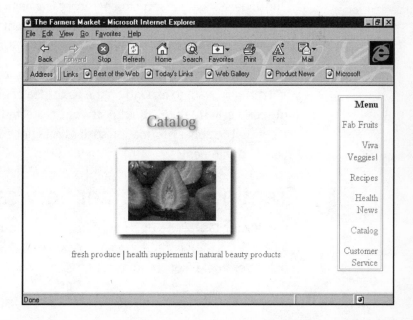

TIP: As you may have noticed, I like to employ the | symbol to use as a break between text-based navigation elements. I also will use a double dash on occasion, but on the whole, I prefer the vertical line. It creates an attractive visual division between text, making each title easy to read yet contained within its own environment.

An excellent example of customer service on the Web can be found at MCI's home page located at http://www.mci.com/.

Want to find out what happened to that FedEx package that was supposed to be on your desk this morning? Visit http://www.fedex.com/ for a complete customer-service tracking center. Another excellent example of a similar service is United Parcel Service (UPS), which has an information and package-tracking site at http://www.ups.com/.

Customer Service on the Web

The Web environment is a natural medium for the provision of customer service. As long as the company has the human power to answer e-mail, process forms and orders, respond to global queries by phone and fax, or use other communication methods, providing customer service online is one of the best ways to employ a Web site. The primary reason is because it makes the site useful, and a useful site is one that brings people back to it. This enables a commercial entity to promote its product as well as provide information, 24 hours a day, seven days a week, to anyone with Web access anywhere in the world.

Those readers who are commercial Web designers are sure to be empowered by the understanding that customer service is a major selling point to potential clients, as well as a major selling point from the client to the customer. A well-designed customer service center is a key step in Web site success.

For the purposes of this next example, I'll keep the form very short. However, you'll certainly want to expand on the basic idea of providing client feedback forms, and even to think about password protected areas where customers can get vital personal information such as account balances, or track product orders and shipments.

 TASK

Creating a Customer Service Page

The following task serves up a mini-form that you can expand upon to create a full-service customer questionnaire. As with all CGI forms, the syntax here is only an example. Your requirements will rely on what is available to you via your Internet Service Provider.

This example will use a stack of two tables.

1. Begin with the basics:

```
<html>
<head>
<title>The Farmers Market</title>
</head>
<body bgcolor="#FFFFFF" text="#000000" link="#CC3300"
vlink="#339900" alink="#FFFFFF">

</body>
</html>
```

2. Add your first table, which contains the header graphic:

```
<div align=center>
<table border=0 cellpadding =10 cellspacing=10 width=470>
<tr>

<td valign=top align=middle width=300 colspan=2>
<img src="images/fm-cshed.gif" alt="FM Header" width=300
height=50>
</td>
</tr>
</table>
```

3. Add the second table, which lays out the form:

```
<table border=0 cellpadding=5 cellspacing=5 width=400>
<tr>
<td valign=top width=200>

</td>

<td valign=top width=200>

</td>
</tr>
</table>

</div>
```

4. In the first data cell, place the form:

```
<form method="post" action="http://your.server/htbin/mailto">
<input name="from" type="hidden" value="freshfood@fm.biz">
<input name="subject" type="hidden" value="Orders">
<input name="version" type="hidden" value="Form version is 2.0">
<input name="to" type="hidden" value="orders@fm.biz">

<pre>
Name:    <input type="text" name="Name" size="15">
Phone:   <input type="text" name="Phone" size="15">
Fax:     <input type="text" name="Fax" size="15">
```

```
email:   <input type="text" name="email" size="15">
</pre>
```

5. In the second data cell, place the remainder of the form:

```
<pre>
Feedback:
<textarea name="Message" rows=3 cols=25></textarea>
<input type="submit" value="Send your Request">
<input type="reset" value="Clear">
</pre>

</form>
```

6. The final syntax should match this:

```
<html>
<head>
<title>The Farmers Market</title>
</head>
<body bgcolor="#FFFFFF" text="#000000" link="#CC3300"
vlink="#339900" alink="#FFFFFF">

<div align=center>
<table border=0 cellpadding =10 cellspacing=10 width=470>
<tr>

<td valign=top align=middle width=300 colspan=2>
<img src="images/fm-cshed.gif" alt="FM Header" width=300
height=50>
</td>
</tr>
</table>

<table border=0 cellpadding=5 cellspacing=5 width=400>
<tr>

<td valign=top width=200>

<pre>
Name:    <input type="text" name="Name" size="15">
Phone:   <input type="text" name="Phone" size="15">
Fax:     <input type="text" name="Fax" size="15">
email:   <input type="text" name="email" size="15">
</pre>

</td>

<td valign=top width=200>

<pre>
Feedback:
<textarea name="Message" rows=3 cols=25></textarea>

<input type="submit" value="Send your Request">
<input type="reset" value="Clear">
```

```
</pre>
</form>

</td>
</tr>
</table>

</div>
</body>
</html>
```

7. Save the file as `cust.htm`.

8. View it in your browser and see if your work matches the results in Figure 7.9.

Figure 7.9.

A simple customer service form.

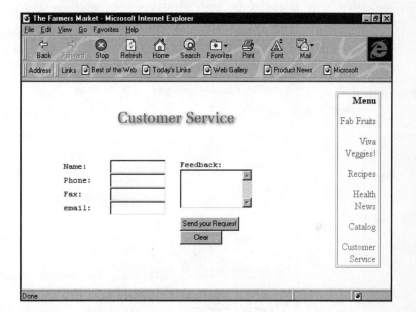

CAUTION: Although button values can be set to any name, using conventional naming, such as Submit and Clear, helps provide a Web visitor with a quick frame of reference in terms of what each button is supposed to do. He or she can quickly make selections. It's a good idea to stick to the convention, unless you are certain that the names you are using make sense and are quickly processed visually.

As always, test your work. I mentioned earlier that results viewed through different browsers can vary. Figure 7.10 shows the way Netscape aligns the same page compared to Figure 7.9. Notice, however, that both pages are readable and engaging. If you don't get readable results in a variety of browsers, you must go back and check your syntax. You may find that simple alignment changes, table and table cell widths, image attributes, and font sizes will all affect the way your pages are viewed. Also, be sure to check frame pages by opening the frameset page and moving to that page. This ensures the integrity of the site.

Figure 7.10.

The customer service form as viewed in Netscape Navigator 3.0. Note the shift in alignment and treatment of the form. But, the page is still accessible and attractive.

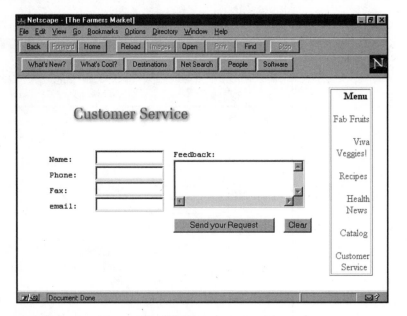

Workshop Wrap-Up

As you become more adept at using both tables and frames, you will discover numerous ways to employ the combination of the two. As an experiment, try switching this entire site around, placing the menu frame and the table-based content pages on the right. You're on your own with this one, with no help from me. I bet you'll get it right.

Even if you choose to not apply a frame-and-table combination to a given site, the functional and design elements introduced in this chapter will enable you to dramatically alter the way your sites appear visually and perform mechanically. First and foremost, start building a library of royalty-free graphics and graphic treatments. Those tools alone will move your design to the forefront.

The next step is to begin examining a variety of CGI scripting and database management tools. Research vigorously. Begin with the Internet Service Provider where you purchase server space, or if you're running your own shop, check with the systems administrator as to what your server is capable of. If you're on your own, don't be proud—read the manual. It's a good place to start. You then can begin enhancing your scripting and database knowledge, empowered by an understanding of the specific tools with which you are creating your own, unique brand of Web site design.

Next Steps

The next chapter examines interface design with floating frames, also known as "I-frames." Although there are the usual browser issues to jump over with this type of interface, the chapter will provide a look into an unusual and potent method of organizing data.

Specific chapters of interest to fans of the previous lessons should be sure to check out:

❏ Atomic Media's beautiful use of tables and frames as demonstrated in Chapter 9, "Real-Time Example: Atomic Media—A Real-Life Interface Using Tables and Frames"

❏ Chapter 10, "Margin Navigation Using Tables and Frames"

❏ Chapter 16, "Using Tables for Graphic Control"

Q&A

Q: I've created a frame and table combination, making sure that my width is contained to 600 pixels. Yet, while viewing it at a 640x480 screen resolution, I still get a horizontal scrollbar. What's wrong?

A: Check your syntax carefully. What are your individual table cell widths? Are you using values for cellspacing and cellpadding?

Perhaps you have a graphic element or text attribute that is too wide. Remember that you must total up the sum of your parts, including the width of a frame's scrollbar or a table's border.

Q: I've implemented the customer service form you've described in this chapter. I checked with my systems administrator, and she tells me I've done everything properly. Why isn't it working?

A: It's possible that breaking up the form between table cells is choking the form. Try placing the form by itself into one table cell and see if that solves the problem.

Q: The idea of graphic treatments really excites me. I like high-quality graphics, but I don't know much about how to work with them. What do I need?

A: Any Web designer worth his or her weight will purchase a recent copy of Photoshop. I've heard groans from students and small Web design companies that it's expensive. Well, because it is the state-of-the-art design tool for Web graphics, being without it is tantamount to losing your design edge. Spend the money; you'll be glad you did. Visit `http://www.adobe.com/` for all the information available on their suite of design tools. There are also many shareware or low-cost programs that you'll need for graphic optimization as well; a few are available on the enclosed CD-ROM. Finally, don't forget about the valuable Photodisc reference early in this chapter. Begin building a good resource library of royalty-free images, clip art, and graphic elements and treatments.

eight
Progressive Interfaces with Floating Frames

Why progressive you might ask? Well, the main reason is because floating frames are extremely powerful as an interface tool, but, unfortunately, not well supported. Much like cascading style sheets, floating frames were initiated by Microsoft's Internet Explorer browser, and have been Internet Explorer-centric ever since. So, although they are really useful from a design standpoint, the practical nature of their use is limited.

Then, why teach them? Well, hopefully they will be widely implemented "real soon now," as the old computer saying goes. Another reason is to further demonstrate the power of frames in general and, specifically, to offer you yet another design approach.

However, unless you are absolutely sure of your client base, or you're willing to develop a site that has an option to bypass the floating frames interface, I wouldn't recommend using them for most commercial site applications. If you're working in an intranet situation where the browser of choice is Internet Explorer 3.0, you will find them to be a powerful option for a variety of applications.

What Are Floating Frames?

Floating frames, also referred to as "I-frames," are frame extensions that creates frames anywhere on a page. As with standard frames, the I-frame is a window into another HTML page. Unlike frames, I-frames do not require a frameset page; rather, the syntax goes right into a standard HTML page. This means that you can literally put a frame within a frame within a frame, ad infinitum. Of course, that's not entirely practical, but playing with the concept can certainly help you come up with some very creative applications for the technology.

For a technical overview of Internet Explorer extensions such as floating frames, visit `http:// www.microsoft .com/ie/support/ docs/tech30/ html.ht`.

A good way to think of I-frames is as an image. This means that wherever you place an image on a Web page, you can place an I-frame. It also means that you can horizontally and vertically control the I-frame placement with standard `hspace` and `vspace` attributes. Unlike an image, I-frames allow for any elements that you can place within an HTML page to be placed within that space—links, color, text, even interactive media.

I-Frame Syntax

I-frame syntax is a bit unusual. Because of some changes between browser versions, to successfully define I-frames across Internet Explorer browser versions requires a doubling of attributes in both the initiating tag and the frame tag. It begins with a standard concept, a closing and opening tag, placed within the body of a standard HTML document:

```
<iframe>
```

```
</iframe>
```

Within the I-frame tags, a `<frame>` tag is required:

```
<frame>
```

The bare-bones results look like this:

```
<iframe>
```

```
<frame>
```

```
</iframe>
```

The syntax must be fleshed out from there. Begin with the initial I-frame tag, including values for width and height, and the URL that provides the information that will appear in the frame window:

```
<iframe width=400 height=400 src="inside.htm">
```

The oddity with I-frame syntax is that you must repeat whatever syntax you include in the I-frame tag in the frame tag as well:

```
<frame width=400 height=400 src="inside.htm">
```

The resulting syntax of this I-frame set is as follows:

```
<iframe width=400 height=400 src="inside.htm">
```

```
<frame width=400 height=400 src="inside.htm">
```

```
</iframe>
```

Scrolling and Borders

As with standard frames, scrolling and border attributes can be defined. I-frames have a standard border and scroll. If you want to create a borderless, scroll-less I-frame, you must place the standard syntax into both the I-frame and frame tags:

```
<iframe width=400 height=400 scrolling=no frameborder=0
src="inside.htm">
```

```
<frame width=400 height=400 scrolling=no frameborder=0
src="inside.htm">
```

```
</iframe>
```

CAUTION: Adding a value of no to the scrolling option can be a very dangerous thing to do. Consider that the I-frame is basically a window through which you will view another HTML page. Then consider the disparity between platforms and monitor resolutions and types. The danger comes when you have an HTML page that ends up too big for the window area: Critical data might be cut off. To avoid this, leave in the scroll. If you have the opportunity to thoroughly test the results of your work on a variety of systems, you can use no scroll options as you see fit.

Alignment and Spacing

Just as you can align and space an image, you can align and space an I-frame. Simply place the desired standard attributes within the I-frame and frame source code:

```
<iframe width=400 height=400 hspace=10 vspace=10 align=right
src="inside.htm">

<frame width=400 height=400 hspace=10 vspace=10 align=right
src="inside.htm">

</iframe>
```

The results of this I-frame will be a 400x400 pixel frame, aligned to the right of the page and spaced 10 pixels on the horizon line and 10 pixels on the vertical from any surrounding elements.

And, just as with the tasks in Chapter 7, "Designing Interfaces Combining Tables and Frames," you can use a <br> tag with the clear attributes in order to clear the frame. If your frame aligns to the left, clear to the right:

```
<br clear="right">
```

If you'd like your right-aligned frame to clear to the left, set the attribute as follows:

```
<br clear="left">
```

If you'd like to clear completely, set the attribute to all.

```
<br clear="all">
```

DESIGN NOTE: If you want to keep the "float" in floating frames, don't set a break at all. Allow text to dynamically wrap around the frame. This isn't always attractive or practical, so use breaks where necessary and logical.

Naming Conventions

I-frames follow the frames convention of naming, with magic target names allowed. Again, the only absolute is that to be fully compliant, you must use the naming convention within both the I-frame and frame tags, as well as within the link:

```
<iframe width=400 height=400 hspace=10 vspace=10 align=right
src="inside.htm" name="coolframe">

<frame width=400 height=400 hspace=10 vspace=10 align=right
src="inside.htm" name="coolframe">

</iframe>
```

Files linking to this frame will have the following syntax:

```
<a href="menu.htm" target="coolframe">You're one click away from the
cool link of the day!</a>
```

Similarly, magic targets can be employed:

```
<iframe width=400 height=400 hspace=10 vspace=10 align=right
src="inside.htm" name="_blank">

<frame width=400 height=400 hspace=10 vspace=10 align=right
src="inside.htm" name="_blank">

</iframe>
```

If you have a link with this target, the page will load in a new browser window:

```
<a href="review.htm" target="_blank">Just click for our Reviews!</a>
```

The following tasks will help you put these concepts into practice.

Creating an I-Frame

The following HTML page will link to your first I-frame.

1. In your browser, type the following shell code:

```
<html>
<head>
<title> Soul Sailin'</title>
</head>
<body bgcolor="#FFFFFF" text="#000000" link="#00CC99"
vlink="663300" alink="FFFFFF">

</body>
</html>
```

2. Go ahead and set up a table to lay out the page:

```
<table border=0 cellpadding=5 cellspacing=5 width=600>
<tr>


<td valign=top width=190>
</td>

<td valign=top width=400>

</td>

</tr>
</table>
```

3. Fill the first table cell with the titles, text, and menu options:

```
<font size=6 color="#663300">Soul Sailin'</font>
<p>

<center>
<b>The Internet Guide to Sailing and Recreational Boating</b>
</center>
<p>

Select from the following:
<p>

<center>

<font size=4>
<a href="boats.htm" target=left>Boats</a> --
<a href="treks.htm" target=left>Treks</a>
<br>
<a href="news.htm" target=_top>Newsletter</a> --
```

```
<a href="links.htm" target=_top>Links</a>
</font>
<p>

<img src="images/ss-sl4.gif" alt="sailboat" width=100 height=75>

</center>
```

4. Add the I-frame syntax to the second table cell:

```
<iframe width=400 height=300 name="left" src="ss-int.htm">
<frame width=400 height=300 name="left" src="ss-int.htm">
</iframe>
```

This creates a 400x300 pixel I-frame with a name of `left`. Note the HTML source `ss-int.htm`. This will be the page that actually fills the I-frame.

5. Save the page as `index.htm`.

6. View the page in the Internet Explorer browser. You'll see that the I-frame has not rendered yet, as shown in Figure 8.1. This is because the HTML page that fits into the frame hasn't been constructed. After you've done that, you'll be able to view the I-frame.

Figure 8.1.
An HTML page without I-frame content.

A wealth of frame information and browser "peculiarities" reside at `http://www.eskimo.com/~bloo/html/tagpages/f/frame.htm`.

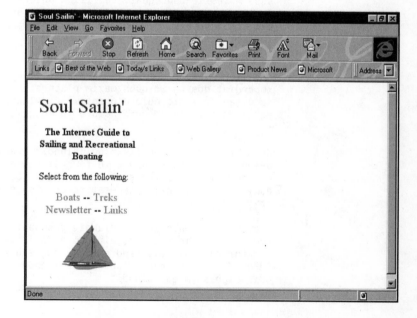

Creating the Main I-Frame Page

In order to view the first I-frame, complete the following syntax.

1. Construct a Web page beginning with the following HTML:

```
<html>
<head>
<title> Soul Sailin'</title>
</head>
<body bgcolor="#CCFFFF" text="#000000" link="#00CC99"
vlink="663300" alink="FFFFFF">

<blockquote>


</blockquote>
</body>
</html>
```

2. Add a header and some filler text:

```
<font size=4 color="#00cc99">Soul Sailin'</font>
<p>

Duis autem vel eum iriure dolor in hendrerit in vulputate velit
esse molestie consequat, vel illum dolore eu feugiat nulla
facilisis at vero eros et accumsan et iusto odio dignissim qui
blandit praesent luptatum zzril delenit augue duis dolore te
feugait nulla facilisi.
<p>

Nam liber tempor cum soluta nobis eleifend option congue nihil
imperdiet doming id quod mazim placerat facer possim assum.
Accumsan et iusto odio dignissim qui blandit praesent luptatum
zzril delenit augue duis dolore te feugait nulla facilisi.
<p>

Eros Et Accumsan dignissim qui blandit praesent luptatum zzril
delenit augue duis dolore te feugait nulla facilisi. Nam liber
tempor cum soluta nobis eleifend option congue nihil imperdiet
doming id quod mazim placerat facer possim assum.
<p>

Lusto odio dignissim qui blandit praesent luptatum zzril delenit
augue duis dolore te feugait nulla facilisi! Nam liber tempor
cum soluta nobis eleifend option congue nihil imperdiet doming
id quod mazim placerat facer possim assum. Accumsan et iusto
odio dignissim qui blandit
```

3. Save the file as `ss-int.htm`.

4. Now view the index file in Internet Explorer. You should see your first I-frame, as demonstrated in Figure 8.2.

Figure 8.2.

Your first I-frame.

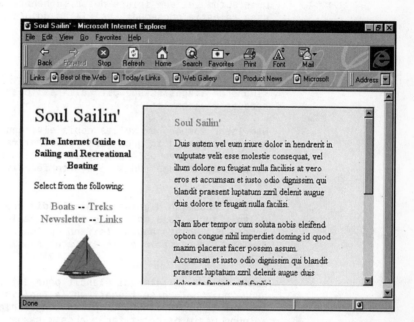

TASK Designing the First I-Frame Target Page

Now you'll create a target page for the first link off of the main menu.

1. Begin with the following syntax:

```
<html>
<head>
<title> Soul Sailin': Boats</title>
</head>
<body bgcolor="#CCFFFF" text="#000000" link="#00CC99"
vlink="663300" alink="FFFFFF">

<blockquote>

</blockquote>
</body>
</html>
```

2. Add a header, text, and a floating image as follows:

```
<font size=4 color="#00cc99">Soul Sailin': Boats</font>
<p>

Duis autem vel eum iriure dolor in hendrerit in vulputate velit
esse molestie consequat, vel illum dolore eu feugiat nulla
facilisis at vero eros et accumsan et iusto odio dignissim qui
blandit praesent luptatum zzril delenit augue duis dolore te
feugait nulla facilisi.
<p>

<img src="images/ss-sb2.gif" alt="sailboat" width=125 height=94
hspace=10 align=left>

Nam liber tempor cum soluta nobis eleifend option congue nihil
imperdiet doming id quod mazim placerat facer possim assum.
Accumsan et iusto odio dignissim qui blandit praesent luptatum
zzril delenit augue duis dolore te feugait nulla facilisi.
<p>

Eros Et Accumsan dignissim qui blandit praesent luptatum zzril
delenit augue duis dolore te feugait nulla facilisi. Nam liber
tempor cum soluta nobis eleifend option congue nihil imperdiet
doming id quod mazim placerat facer possim assum.
<p>

Lusto odio dignissim qui blandit praesent luptatum zzril delenit
augue duis dolore te feugait nulla facilisi! Nam liber tempor
cum soluta nobis eleifend option congue nihil imperdiet doming
id quod mazim placerat facer possim assum.
Accumsan et iusto odio dignissim qui blandit
```

3. Save the file as boats.htm.

4. Now, open the index file again and select the first link. Note how the page you created loads into the I-frame, just as with a regular target frame.

5. Your results should match Figure 8.3. If they do not, check your syntax carefully and try again.

Figure 8.3.

The I-frame with a targeted link.

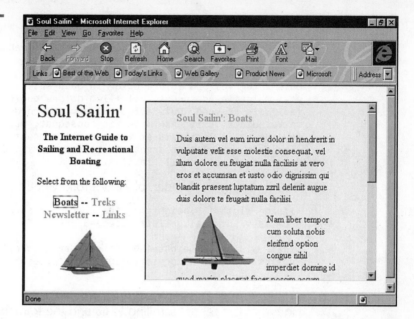

 Adding a Target Page with a Borderless I-Frame Page

In this task, you'll create an I-frame within an I-frame.

1. Start with the basics:

```
<html>
<head>
<title> Soul Sailin': Treks</title>
</head>
<body bgcolor="#CCFFFF" text="#000000" link="#00CC99"
vlink="663300" alink="FFFFFF">

<blockquote>

</blockquote>
</body>
</html>
```

2. Add a header and body text:

```
<font size=4 color="#00cc99">Soul Sailin': Treks</font>
<p>

Duis autem vel eum iriure dolor in hendrerit in vulputate velit
esse molestie consequat, vel illum dolore eu feugiat nulla
facilisis at vero. Duis autem vel eum iriure dolor in hendrerit
in vulputate velit esse molestie consequat, vel illum dolore eu
feugiat nulla facilisis at vero eros et accumsan et iusto odio
dignissim qui blandit praesent luptatum zzril delenit augue duis
dolore te feugait nulla facilisi.
```

3. Directly below the header, place the following I-frame syntax:

```
<iframe width=135 height=140 frameborder=0 scrolling="no"
src="ss-tr.htm" align=left hspace=5 vspace=5>

<frame width=135 height=140 frameborder=0 scrolling="no"
src="ss-tr.htm"  align=left hspace=5 vspace=5>

</iframe>
```

Note that I've set the scrolling to no and the frameborder to 0. As I
mentioned in a Caution box early in the chapter, this can be a
dangerous thing to do! I've kept this particular example very small so
as not to run into a problem. The caution remains an important one.

4. Save this file as `treks.htm`.

Before viewing, make the sub-page for the included I-frame.

 # Making the I-Frame Sub-Page

This page will be a very simple page so as to fit within the small I-frame I've
created for it.

1. Begin with the shell syntax:

```
<html>
<head>
<title> Soul Sailin'</title>
</head>
<body bgcolor="#FFFFFF" text="#00CC99" link="#CCFFFF"
vlink="663300"
alink="FFFFFF">
```

```
<blockquote>

</blockquote>
</body>
</html>
```

2. Add a short ordered list with dummy text:

```
<ol>
<li>Duis
<li>Iriure
<li>Hendrerit
<li>Vulputate
<li>Consequat
</ol>
```

3. Save the file as ss-tr.htm.

4. Open the index page in Internet Explorer and click treks. Watch the page load with the small I-frame. You now have created an I-frame within an I-frame.

5. Check your results against Figure 8.4. Do they match? If not, check your work carefully for any errors.

Figure 8.4.

An I-frame within an I-frame.

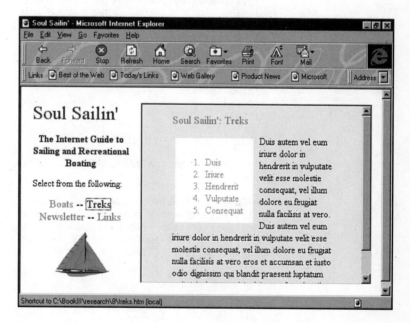

The next step is to add a page for the magic target menu link.

TIP: Ordered and bulleted lists are an easy way to organize information. And, by the virtue of the indent elements naturally contained within their construct, they provide white space to boot. The ordered list begins with the <ol> tag and ends with the related </ol>. Using the <li> at the beginning of each line will automatically place numbers in ascending order as the list progresses. An unordered list is a list with bullets and is created with the <ul> and </ul> tags, respectively.

TASK Magic Targeting a Non-Framed Page

In the first task, you created two links to pages with the magic target _top. Build the first of those target pages by completing the following exercise:

1. Begin with the following syntax:

```
<html>
<head>
<title> Soul Sailin'</title>
</head>
<body bgcolor="#CCFFFF" text="#000000" link="#00CC99"
vlink="663300"  alink="FFFFFF">

<blockquote>

</blockquote>
</body>
</html>
```

2. Add a header, text, and image:

```
<font size=4 color="#00cc99">Soul Sailin':News</font>
<p>

<b>Duis autem vel</b> eum iriure dolor in hendrerit in vulputate
velit esse molestie consequat, vel illum dolore eu feugiat nulla
facilisis at vero eros et accumsan et iusto odio dignissim qui
blandit praesent luptatum zzril delenit augue duis dolore te
feugait nulla facilisi.
<p>
```

```
<img src="images/ss-pl.gif" alt="pilings" width=125 height=94
hspace=10 vspace=5 align=left>

Nam liber tempor cum soluta nobis eleifend option congue nihil
imperdiet doming id quod mazim placerat facer possim assum.
Accumsan et iusto odio dignissim qui blandit praesent luptatum
zzril delenit augue duis dolore te feugait nulla facilisi. Eros
Et Accumsan dignissim qui blandit praesent luptatum zzril
delenit augue duis dolore te feugait nulla facilisi. Nam liber
tempor cum soluta nobis eleifend option congue nihil imperdiet
doming id quod mazim placerat facer possim assum.
<p>

<div align=center>
<a href="index.htm"><i>Return Home</i></a>
</div>
```

Note that the link to return home simply returns to the index page.

3. Save the file as news.htm.

4. Compare your work to Figure 8.5.

Figure 8.5.
*A magic target name
forces the news page
to load in the full
window.*

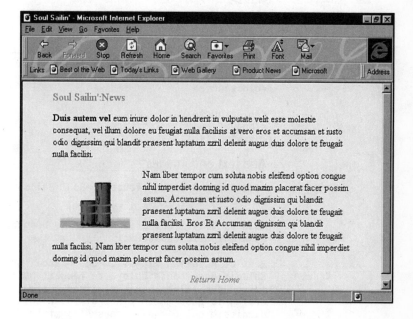

5. Open the index page and click the newsletter link. Does the target page load in the full window, overriding any of the I-frames? If so, good work. If not, go back and check your syntax carefully.

6. Check the link from the newsletter page back to Home. It should load the index page with the original I-frame smoothly into the same window.

 ## Designing a Page with Multiple I-Frames

You can have as many I-frames on a page as you want. Here's an example of an HTML page that calls for three.

1. Begin with the following:

```
<html>
<head>
<title> Soul Sailin'</title>
</head>
<body bgcolor="#CCFFFF" text="#000000" link="#00CC99"
vlink="663300" alink="FFFFFF">

<blockquote>

</blockquote>
</body>
</html>
```

2. Add text and images:

```
<font size=4 color="#00cc99">Soul Sailin': Cool Links!</font>
<p>

Duis autem vel eum iriure dolor in hendrerit in vulputate velit
esse molestie consequat!

Eros Et Accumsan dignissim qui blandit praesent luptatum zzril
delenit augue duis dolore te feugait nulla facilisi. Nam liber
tempor cum soluta nobis eleifend option congue nihil imperdiet
doming id quod mazim placerat facer possim assum. Lusto odio
dignissim qui blandit praesent luptatum zzril delenit augue duis
dolore te feugait nulla facilisi! Nam liber tempor cum
soluta nobis eleifend option congue nihil imperdiet doming id
quod mazim placerat facer possim assum. Accumsan et iusto odio
dignissim qui blandit!
```

Lusto odio dignissim qui blandit praesent luptatum zzril delenit augue duis dolore te feugait nulla facilisi! Nam liber tempor cum soluta nobis eleifend option congue nihil imperdiet doming id quod mazim placerat facer possim assum. Accumsan et iusto odio dignissim qui blandit! Lusto odio dignissim qui blandit praesent luptatum zzril delenit augue duis dolore te feugait nulla facilisi! Nam liber tempor cum soluta nobis eleifend option congue nihil imperdiet doming id quod mazim placerat facer possim assum. Accumsan et iusto odio dignissim qui blandit!
```
<p>

<b>Please visit our sponsor:</b>

<div align=center>
<a href="index.htm"><i>Return Home</i></a>
</div>
```

3. Place the first I-frame under the first line of text in the initial paragraph and use the `<br>` tag to clear:

```
<iframe width=150 height=200 src="ss-li1.htm" hspace=10
vspace=10 align=right>
<frame width=150 height=200 src="ss-li1.htm" hspace=10 vspace=10
align=right>
</iframe>
<br clear="left">
```

4. Now put the second I-frame between the two main paragraphs, again employing the `<br>` tag:

```
<iframe width=150 height=200 src="ss-li2.htm" hspace=10
vspace=10 align=left>
<frame width=150 height=200 src="ss-li2.htm" hspace=10 vspace=10
align=left>
</iframe>
<br clear="right">
```

5. Add the final I-frame beneath the Visit our Sponsor section:

```
<iframe width=500 height=100 src="ss-sp.htm" frameborder=0
scrolling=no>
<frame width=500 height=100 src="ss-sp.htm" frameborder=0
scrolling=no>
</iframe>
```

6. Save the file as `links.htm`.

Before you can view the file, you must create the sub-pages.

Creating the First I-Frame Sub-Page

This task will show you how to create a sub-page for an I-frame.

1. Begin by creating the following shell syntax:

```
<html>
<head>
<title> Soul Sailin'</title>
</head>
<body bgcolor="#FFFFFF" text="#00CC99" link="#CCFFFF"
vlink="663300" alink="FFFFFF">

</blockquote>
</body>
</html>
```

2. Add this simple but lengthy ordered list:

```
<ol>
<li>Duis
<li>Iriure
<li>Hendrerit
<li>Vulputate
<li>Consequat
<li>Duis
<li>Iriure
<li>Hendrerit
<li>Vulputate
<li>Consequat
<li>Duis
<li>Iriure
<li>Hendrerit
<li>Vulputate
<li>Consequat
<li>Duis
<li>Iriure
<li>Hendrerit
<li>Vulputate
<li>Consequat
</ol>
```

3. Save the file as ss-li1.htm.

Now move on to create the second I-frame.

Adding the Second I-Frame Incident

This is the second I-frame task, which enables you to add the next incident of a floating frame.

1. Use the following shell:

```
<html>
<head>
<title> Soul Sailin'</title>
</head>
<body bgcolor="#00CC99" text="#FFFFFF" link="#CCFFFF"
vlink="663300" alink="FFFFFF">

</body>
</html>
```

2. Add another ordered list:

```
<ol>
<li>Duis
<li>Iriure
<li>Hendrerit
<li>Vulputate
<li>Consequat
<li>Duis
<li>Iriure
<li>Hendrerit
<li>Vulputate
<li>Consequat
<li>Duis
<li>Iriure
<li>Hendrerit
<li>Vulputate
<li>Consequat
<li>Duis
<li>Iriure
<li>Hendrerit
<li>Vulputate
<li>Consequat
</ol>
```

3. Save the file as ss-1i2.htm.

Now you'll create the final content page.

Adding the Advertisement I-Frame

This content page will contain an advertisement. Note that I-frames are a great way of presenting interactive media such as server-push animation, live cameras, and virtual reality applications. You can use the I-frame as a viewing box. The strength of this is that you can easily manage data because you only need to make changes and updates to the HTML content page, not the master HTML page that carries more text and information.

1. Build the following shell syntax in your HTML editor:

```
<html>
<head>
<title> Soul Sailin'</title>
</head>
<body bgcolor="#FFFFFF" text="#000000" link="#00CC99"
vlink="663300" alink="FFFFFF">

</body>
</html>
```

2. Add the image:

```
<img src="images/ad1.gif" alt="sponsor ad" width=468 height=60
border=1>
```

3. Save the file as `ss-sp.htm`.

4. Now view the `links.htm` file in your browser. Compare the results to Figures 8.6 and 8.7.

5. Return to the index page using the Return to Home link.

6. Run through the site, testing your page links as you go. Each page should load smoothly. You will be able to see how the I-frames load into the page, first creating a gray square, and then filling that area with the content HTML.

For more information on adding interactivity to your pages, be sure to check out Chapter 14, "Adding Interactive and Dynamic Content."

Figure 8.6.

The first I-frame link.

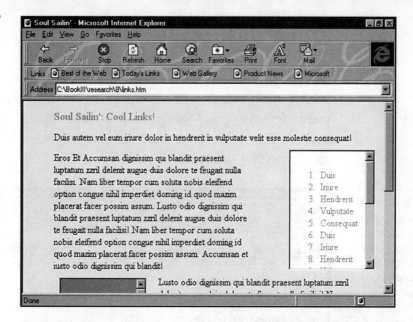

Figure 8.7.

A second and third instance of multiple I-frames on the same page.

Workshop Wrap-Up

Because Netscape Navigator 3.0 does not support I-frames, your results will be less than ideal. Figure 8.8 shows how the index page looks. If you click the links, you will get to the associated page, as shown in Figure 8.9. Interestingly, these links are opened in a new browser, which displays the page. However, any data within an I-frame won't be visible. Notice in Figure 8.10 how the sponsor section just appears blank.

Figure 8.8.

The index page as viewed through Netscape Navigator 3.0. Note how the I-frame simply does not appear.

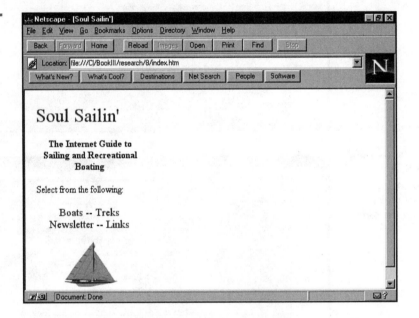

Again, if you plan on using I-frames, do so with complete knowledge of your audience and the browser they use. The other route to take is to provide a "non–I-frame" interface option. You might want to give this a try and see if you like the results.

It's a challenge knowing that there is a method, such as I-frames, that can be used to create clever interfaces and interesting, dynamic treatments for Web site design but not be able to freely implement those methods. One day, browser technology will come to some kind of better balance, and Web designers will enjoy the freedom to use a variety of the tools that are already available to them. But, then again, I said that a year ago, and although many cross-browser and platform problems have been solved, new ones have rushed in to take their place.

Figure 8.9.

Click a link and Netscape Navigator 3.0 will load the page in a new browser window.

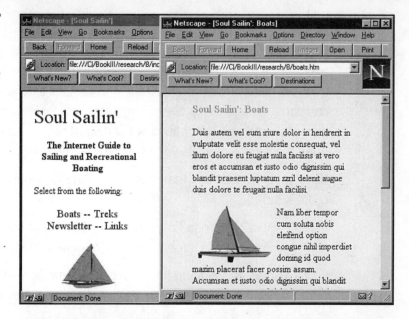

Figure 8.10.

Notice how the information where the I-frame should go doesn't appear when viewed through Netscape Navigator 3.0.

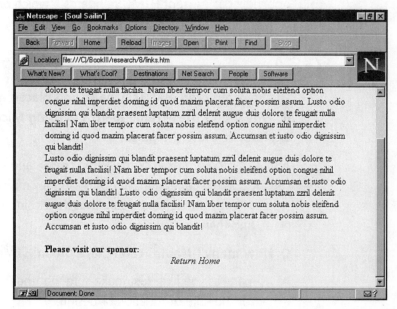

The great consolation with working in such instability is that you are constantly in step with the pulse of progress, if not actually helping to force it along. You are forced to be creative, to come up with innovative solutions, and to figure out ways to incorporate technologies such as I-frames so that your audiences can enjoy the content you're out to provide.

Next Steps

You've worked so hard in these past chapters that I'm going to give you a pleasant treat. Chapter 9, "Real-Time Example: Atomic Media—A Real-Life Interface Using Tables and Frames," is a real-time example of a media design company. Atomic Media uses a combination of tables and frames to create a beautiful interface. The chapter will show just how this interface was created using the very techniques you've already learned.

Other areas of the book that you'll find relate well to the lessons within this chapter include

- ❏ Chapter 2, "Strong Foundations: The Basics of Frame Technology," which provides a strong overview of general frame syntax

- ❏ Chapter 14, "Adding Interactive and Dynamic Content," where you can learn how to add interactive content to tables and frames

- ❏ Appendix C, "Current HTML Standards," which provides a table of current tags and which browsers support them

Q&A

Q: I've completed an HTML page and placed an I-frame within it. Why won't the I-frame load? I'm using Microsoft's Internet Explorer to view the page.

A: Look at the syntax in both your `<iframe>` *and* `<frame>` strings. Did you include the commands in both? Do they match exactly? Any typos? Fix any problems, be sure that the closing `</iframe>` tag is in place, and then view again.

Q: How many I-frames can I place on an HTML page?

A: As many as you like. Just make sure that they serve a purpose— either for the sake of function or design.

Q: I wish I could put the scrollbar on the left, not the right, of the I-frame. Can this be done?

A: I wish it could be done, too. I've searched the literature and can't come up with a solution. It appears as if the default scroll always falls to the right of the I-frame.

nine

Real-Time Example: Atomic Media—A Real-Life Interface Using Tables and Frames

Now that you've spent hard hours cutting and pasting, typing and erasing, adjusting and viewing, you're going to get a treat. Sit back and enjoy this visual guided tour through a real-life example of how one design company has used many of the elements you've just learned to create a high-style, superbly crafted interface.

Atomic Media is a media design company specializing in multimedia, Web design, print, and typography. Its designs are numerous and sophisticated. Be sure to check out the links to various sample sites throughout the margin notes in this chapter.

As you move through the site, keep the word "interface" in mind. What does it really mean? How does this site achieve it? Be especially aware of what parts of the site are fixed, or static, and what areas move.

Atomic Media has created many award winning Web sites, print media, multimedia designs and contributions to typography. Although the experience and talent of lead designer Matthew Bardram ring loud throughout these pages, there is little here technically that you cannot now do. In fact, you've already put most of the HTML elements together; throughout this chapter I'll show you exactly how. Using code samples from the Atomic Media site, I'll go ahead and show, with each screen shot, just how the site was assembled and what creative methods were employed to create the sophisticated look and feel found within its pages.

Some of the elements you'll see put into real-time operation are

❏ An effective, intriguing splash page using tables for layout control

❏ A frame with multiple rows and columns for the interface

❏ Borderless frames

❏ Borderless tables

❏ Bordered tables for enhanced areas

❏ No Scroll and Auto Scrolling frames

❏ Frame naming

❏ Targeted linking

❏ Use of background color within table cells

❏ Stacked tables

❏ Table width, cellpadding, and cellspacing attributes

❏ Forms and interactive content

❏ Choice options for Web site visitors

The Splash Page in Action

Think back about the first element I discussed regarding Interface. "The first part of interface design," I said, "is deciding what the virtual front door of your site is going to look like." Atomic media has chosen a splash page, seen in Figure 9.1, that defies the complex, yet intrigues nonetheless. Using an unusual font for the header, which simply says "Atomic," and a clever catch phrase, "Enter the Atomic Age," the visitor is compelled to look beyond this deceptively simple door into whatever awaits beyond.

Figure 9.1.

The Atomic Media splash page.

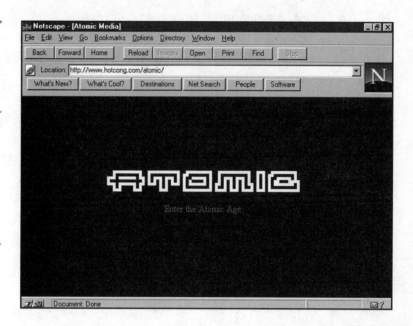

To visit Atomic Media on the Web, point your Web browser to `http://www.hotcong.com/atomic/`.

Atomic Media incorporates lots of JavaScript. More on where to find JavaScript and how to employ it in your Web page can be found in Chapter 14, "Adding Interactive and Dynamic Content."

And although the visual is simple, the underlying code is more complex. The designer uses JavaScript to spawn a special browsing window, as you'll discover if you visit the site. More pertinent to our discussion is the use of a table to lay out the design you see.

Exploring the Atomic Media Splash Page

You can create the Atomic Media splash page by copying the corresponding chapter directories (9 and `images`, respectively) from the CD-ROM onto your hard drive.

1. In your HTML editor, begin with the following shell:

```
<html>
<head>
<title>Atomic Media</title>
</head>
<body bgcolor="000000" link="#996600" vlink="#996600">

<center>
```

```
</center>
</body>
</html>
```

2. Add the table and graphics:

```
<table border=0>
<tr valign="middle">

<td>

<a href="index.htm">

<center>

<img width=330 height=35 border=0 src="images/atomic.gif">
<p>
Enter the Atomic Age

</center>

</a>

</td>
</tr>
</table>
```

3. Save the file as index.htm.

4. View the file in your browser and compare it with Figure 9.1.

The Atomic Media Interface

The next step in interface design is to achieve a system that quickly and intelligently brings visitors to the critical information. Atomic Media has done this by creating a right-margin, borderless frame; a bottom frame with additional navigation; and a main content section that is used in a variety of flexible ways (see Figure 9.2).

Interestingly, the interface all fits within a single screen shot. This treatment reminds me of the way a CD-ROM interface might be designed. The necessary elements are contained within a specific space. Without a studied approach to interface design, it could be very easy for someone to make the mistake of putting too many elements onto the page, giving it a cramped feeling, much like that windowless, tiny room I spoke of in Chapter 8, "Progressive Interfaces with Floating Frames." Instead, the elements are placed very carefully, and this creates an interactive experience that communicates as being contained but not constrained.

Figure 9.2.
Atomic Media's interface.

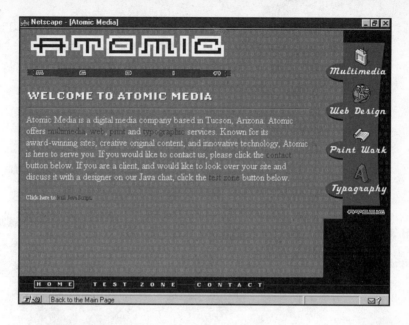

Web designers should take heed from graphic artists and learn to work with color palettes. There are three colors used in this interface—black, deep red, and caramel. Other colors are used to accentuate, but these three colors dominate the site's design and reinforce that ever-important consistency.

Note that the complete page space is treated as an entirety. In a well-built interface, the eye always knows where to go.

DESIGN NOTE: Interface design is undeniably a complex area of study. More information can be sought by Web designers by doing searches for "interface" or "multimedia" at your favorite search engine. Classes in interface design and multimedia tend to be regularly available—certainly more so than Web design classes—at community colleges and art schools; there may be one in your area worth auditing. I know that studying the theory, as well as the practice of interface, has given me some credible insights into how to effectively create them for the Web, and I see that this carries through with other designers who have studied something of the concepts.

The Frameset and Contents

The frameset syntax for Atomic Media calls for two rows and two columns:

```
<frameset rows=370,24 border=0 frameborder=0 framespacing=0>
<frameset cols=*,118 border=0 frameborder=0 framespacing=0>
```

Note that the border, frameborder, and framespacing are set to 0.

This frameset creates four areas. There are two rows, the top running down the vertical axis 370 pixels, allowing 24 pixels below. The column areas are the right column, which runs along the horizontal for a dynamic * amount of pixels, but demands a right frame of 118 pixels.

The frame tag calls for the content page, as follows:

```
<frame src="filling3.htm" scrolling="auto" name="main">
```

You'll see that there's an auto scroll set, and that the name for the frame is "main". The main content page matches Figure 9.3.

Figure 9.3.
The Content Page as viewed without the frameset.

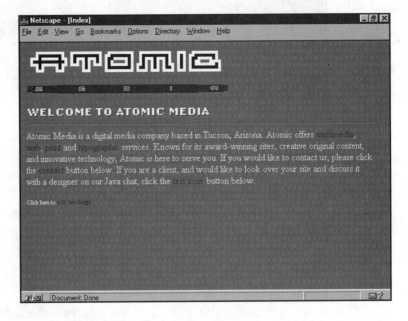

The Navigation

The next frame calls for the right-frame navigation:

```
<frame src="nav3.htm" scrolling="NO" name="navigation">
```

One element that you do not need to add into your total sum for frame definition is a background graphic. Background graphics will size to the field that you determine.

Here you'll see that the designer called for a value of no for the scrolling attribute, and he has named the area "navigation". As you learned in the various frame-based tasks, a value of no fixes the scroll, and designers have to be very careful to be sure that the contents within that area are dimensionally fixed as well. In other words, the total some of your graphics, text, and other elements within the HTML page must be equal to or smaller in total width and height than the defined frame area.

Atomic Media has achieved this perfectly, although it's interesting to look at the way the HTML page looks without frames (see Figure 9.4), because you see the background image taking up the remainder of the visual field. However, once viewed through the frameset, as you will soon see, the background image matches up with the dimensions of the defined frame.

Figure 9.4.
The actual HTML page and corresponding graphics for the right frame navigation.

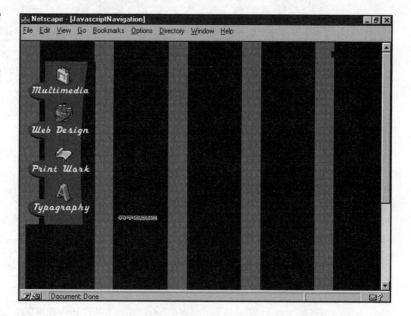

NOTE: The background texture pattern takes up the remainder of the page when not viewed through the frameset.

Another navigation area has been defined within the frameset. The syntax is as follows:

```
<frame src="bottom3.htm" scrolling="NO" name="bottom">
```

Again, you'll notice that the designer has named the frame "bottom" and that scrolling has been set to a value of no. The results without the frameset can be seen in Figure 9.5.

Figure 9.5.
Atomic Media's bottom navigation.

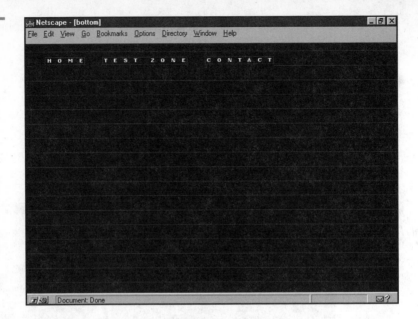

Auto Scroll in Action

The first page of Atomic Media's Multimedia section demonstrates how the auto attribute for scrolling is important. When you select the auto scroll option, a scrollbar will appear only if necessary. Because I'm viewing this site at 640x480, and the screen captures are shot at that resolution, a scrollbar appears in order to accommodate the content information (see Figure 9.6).

When viewed at higher resolutions, it's likely that this page will not require a scroll, because it is only slightly longer than the viewing frame. However, the designer was very specific in selecting an auto value for this page. He knew that at lower resolutions, the screen might require scrolling, but at higher resolutions, it wouldn't. If he selected no, the information would be cut off at 640x480 resolution. Similarly, if he had placed a yes attribute, the scrollbar would have appeared even at high resolution. The auto attribute makes it so the scrollbar appears when it's needed, and doesn't when it's not, keeping the design flexible yet as visually clean as possible.

The QTVR example shown here can also be viewed on the home site, the Club Congress, at http://www.hotcong.com/congo/club/.

Figure 9.6.
At 640x480, a scroll-bar appears in this page to accommodate the content.

Want more practice with magic target names? Return to Chapter 2, "Strong Foundations: The Basics of Frame Technology," and experiment with the various target names offered.

Accommodating an External Link

Because QTVR requires a plug-in to work successfully on most machines, and because the multimedia page is one of the first in Atomic Media's example, the designer chose to create a link to the download site *without* incorporating magic frames (see Figure 9.7). In other words, he's done something I've generally recommended you not do: contain external sites within your interface. My recommendation has been to use the magic target name `_top` to load the new site over your current window, or to use (with caution) the magic target name `_blank`, which would allow the visitor to get the external link information in a new browser window.

But in this case, Atomic Media actually made a good choice in going against using a magic target name, because linking within the interface is appropriate. The idea is to get you to download the software to view the movie, but not to leave the site. It's not a frivolity in this case; it's a very specific need to empower the visitor, not confuse or anger them.

Figure 9.7.
Don't have the QTVR plug-in? Atomic Media offers a site link for download, but keeps that link within the interface.

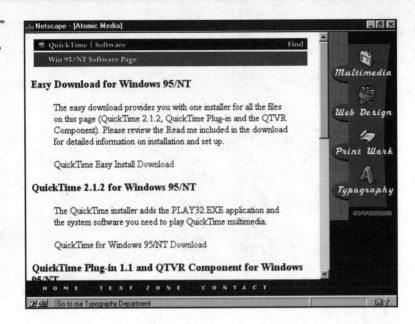

Bordered Tables for Internal Layout

The use of background color in table cells adds to overall look and feel and expands the interface's design. Atomic Media has used a black table cell background to override the page's background graphic.

In order to lay out the internal content pages, Atomic Media has chosen to use a bordered table with cellpadding and cellspacing to control the immediate data (see Figure 9.8). The background color is achieved by using the `bgcolor=` attribute within the table cells. This overrides the background graphic and adds to the visual interest of the page.

The shell syntax used to create the table follows. Note the border value, the table cell background color, and the cellpadding and cellspacing attributes.

```
<table width=400 cellpadding=5 cellspacing=1 border=1>
<tr>

<td valign=top bgcolor="000000">

</td>

<td valign=top bgcolor="000000">

</td>
</tr>

</table>
```

Figure 9.8.

This page shows a bordered table with two table cells containing the data.

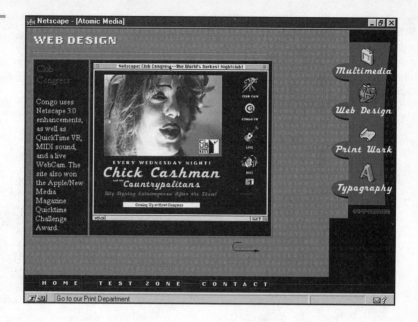

A small, borderless table resides underneath this one, in order to hold the "next" arrow and link to the next content page within Atomic Media's Web section. Here is the syntax used to achieve this seemingly "floating" graphic:

```
<table width=400 border=0>
<tr>

<td valign=top>

<a href="web3.htm"><img border=0 align="right" src="images/
next.gif"></a>

</td>
</tr>
</table>
```

Bordered Table with Mixed Background Styles

To add diversity to the general look and feel, Atomic Media chose to use the same table syntax as it did for the Web example on this Print example page (see Figure 9.9). However, one table cell uses the black background while the other allows the page's background graphic through.

Figure 9.9.
Notice the difference between the left black cell and the right cell, which uses the page's background?

The Hotel Congress Web site can be reached by visiting `http:// www.hotcong.com/ congo/`.

Here is the shell syntax used to create the look:

```
<table width=400 cellpadding=5 cellspacing=1 border=1>
<tr>

<td valign=top bgcolor="000000">

</td>

<td valign=top>

</td>
</tr>

</table>
```

You'll notice in this example that the designer alternates backgrounds between rows. The center row uses background color in the table cell.

Studying a Table with Multiple Rows

Atomic Media's contact page features a table incorporating both a combination of background attributes as well as the use of multiple rows to lay out the form it contains.

1. Examine how the table for the form was created using the following syntax:

```
<table border=1 cellpadding=5 cellspacing=1 width=400>
<tr>

<td valign=top>

</td>

<td valign=top>

</td>

</tr>
<tr>

<td bgcolor="000000" valign=middle>


</td>

<td bgcolor="000000" valign=middle>


</td>

</tr>
<tr>
```

2. Note the `colspan` attribute:

```
<td colspan=2>

</td>
</tr>
</table>
```

The results can be seen in Figure 9.10.

Figure 9.10.
Multiple table rows are used to lay out the form on Atomic Media's Contact page.

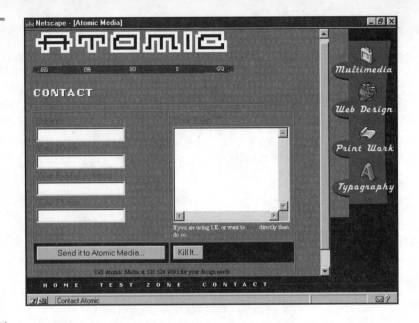

TASK

A selection of Atomic Media's contribution to designing Web-based newspapers includes such prestigious papers as *The Phoenix New Times* at `http://www.phoenixnewtimes.com/`, *The Tucson Weekly* (in a team effort with DesertNet, `http://www.desert.net/`) at `http://www.tucsonweekly.com/tw/`, and the *Denver Westword* at `http://www.westword.com`.

Examining a Form

Atomic Media's feedback form fits nicely into the table just defined. I'm going to show the overall syntax for the form as one piece. This serves as an example of a form in action; you get to see the actual syntax used to converse with the server. This is CGI in action.

1. Create the following shell:

```
<table border=1 cellpadding=5 cellspacing=1 width=400>
<tr>

<td valign=top>

</td>

<td valign=top>

</td>

</tr>
<tr>

<td bgcolor="000000" valign=middle>


</td>

<td bgcolor="000000" valign=middle>
```

```
</td>

</tr>
<tr>

<td colspan=2>

</td>
</tr>
</table>
```

2. Use the following syntax and see if you can't place it within the table—on your own—to get the correct layout.

```
<form method=post name="mailme"
action="mailto:congo36@mail.opus1.com"
enctype = "text/plain">
<font size=3 color="#aa0000"
face="OaklandSix, Espy Sans Bold">Subject:
<br>
<input name = "subject" cols=22>
<br>Your Name:
<br><input name = "name" cols=22>
<br>Your E-Mail Address:
<br><input name = "email" cols=22>
<br>Your Phone:
<br><input name = "phone" cols=22>

<font size=3 color="#aa0000" face="OaklandSix, Espy Sans Bold">
Your Rant:</font>

<br><textarea name="content" rows=8 cols=22></textarea>
<font size=1>
<br clear=all>If you are using I.E. or want to
<a href="mailto:matthew@libcong.com">mail</a> directly then do
so.

<input type = "submit" value = "Send it to Atomic Media...">
<input type = "reset" value = "Kill It...">

<font size=1 color="#000000">
<center>Call Atomic Media at 520.624.9891 for your design
needs.</center>
```

3. Match your results to the following syntax:

```
<html>
<table border=1 cellpadding=5 cellspacing=1 width=400>
<tr>
<td valign=top>
<form method=post name="mailme"
action="mailto:congo36@mail.opus1.com"
enctype = "text/plain">
<font size=3 color="#aa0000" face="OaklandSix, Espy Sans Bold">
Subject:
<br><input name = "subject" cols=22>
```

```
<br>Your Name:
<br><input name = "name" cols=22>
<br>Your E-Mail Address:
<br><input name = "email" cols=22>
<br>Your Phone:
<br><input name = "phone" cols=22>
</td><td valign=top><font size=3 color="#aa0000"
face="OaklandSix, Espy Sans Bold">Your Rant:</font>
<!--text box for response-->
<br><textarea name="content" rows=8 cols=22>
</textarea><font size=1>
<br clear=all>If you are using I.E. or want to
<a href="mailto:matthew@libcong.com">mail</a>
directly then do so.
</td>
</tr>
<tr>
<td bgcolor="000000" valign=middle>
<input type = "submit" value = "Send it to Atomic Media...">
</td><td bgcolor="000000" valign=middle>
<input type = "reset"  value = "Kill It...">
</td>
</tr>
<tr>
<td colspan=2>
<font size=1 color="#000000">
<center>
Call Atomic Media at 520.624.9891 for your design needs.
</center>
</td>
</tr>
</table>
</form>
</body>
</html>
```

Interactive Chat

Web sites truly come alive with interactivity. You've already seen evidence of this when examining QTVR earlier in this chapter and the form just discussed. Another exciting interactive option that Atomic Media incorporates is a real-time chat for the client to discuss issues with the designer. This chat uses JavaScript, which will be described in greater detail in Chapter 14, "Adding Interactive and Dynamic Content."

Remember that interactivity begins with providing visitors with a choice.

Now this page is actually laid out in two ways: One is using frames, the other isn't. If you have Java (not JavaScript) turned off on your browser, this page will tell you (see Figure 9.11). The information in this instance uses a frame.

Figure 9.11.
*Java off? Here's a
table-based option
that lets you know.*

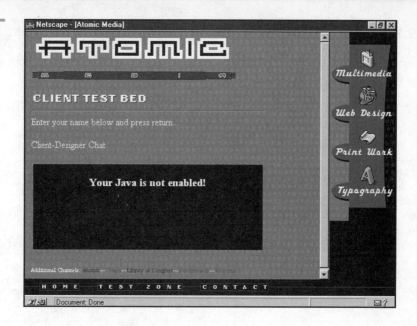

The syntax used to achieve this is as follows:

```
<table width=400>
<tr>

<td bgcolor="#000000" valign=center align=middle>

<font color=white size=4>

<b>Your Java is not enabled!</b>

</font>

</td>
</tr>
</table>
```

Now, if you have Java on, the chat room will appear in place of the Java message (see Figure 9.12). The chat room is arranged with standard HTML.

Figure 9.12.
With Java turned on, you can see the chat interface.

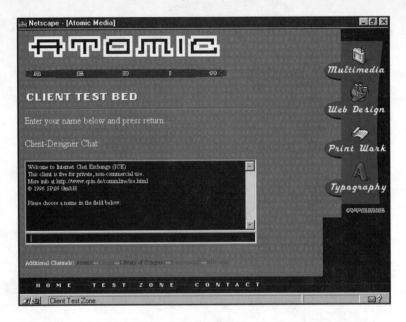

The chat that Atomic Media is using is from Spin Communication. The Internet Chat Exchange can be found by visiting `http:// www.spin.de/ commline/ ice.html`.

Studying a Java On/Java Off Option

This task examines the option created by Atomic Media for browsers that don't support or don't care to use the Java chat interface.

1. Examine the following syntax:

```
<html>
<head>
<title>Client Test Zone</title>
</head>

<body bgcolor="#996600" text="#ffffff" link="#aa0000"
vlink="#660000" alink="#996600" background="art/background.gif">

<img hspace=8 width=330 height=35 src="art/atomic.gif">
<p>

<img hspace=2 width=348 height=18 src="art/media.gif">
<p>

<img width=330 height=21 vspace=0 hspace=0 src="art/
testbed.gif">

<hr align=left width=400>

<font size=3 color="#ffffff"
face="oaklandsix, espy sans bold">enter your name below and
press return...</b>
```

```
</font>
<p>

<font size=3 color="#ffffff" face="oaklandsix, espy sans bold">
client-designer chat
</font>
<p>
```

2. If the visitor's browser is Java-enabled, the following applet will run:

```
<applet code="embryoclient.class"
codebase="http://www.spin.de/classes/" width=400 height=140>
<param name="bgcolor" value="000000">
<param name="fgcolor" value="ffffff">
<param name="fontsize" value="10">
<param name="channel" value="atomic">

<table width=400>
<tr valign=center>
<td bgcolor=black valign=center align=middle>
<spacer type=block align=left width=1 height=140>
<br>
<font color=white size=4>
```

3. If the browser does not have Java enabled, the following comment is seen:

```
<b>your java is not enabled!</b>
</font>
</td>
</tr>
</table>
</applet>
<p>
<font size=1>additional channels:
<a href="test.html">atomic</a>---
<a href="test2.html">congo</a>---
<a href="test4.html">library of congress</a>---
<a href="test5.html">bandersnatch</a>---
<a href="test3.html">welcome</a>
</font>
</b>
</body>
</html>
```

Client Choice

Giving clients a choice as to how much of a given technology to view is a decision Web designers often make. Many times in these chapters, I've referred to the importance of making that decision for yourself, based on your knowledge of the individual project on which you are working.

Other Web sites incorporating Atomic Media's distinct design include The New Times, Inc. corporate page at `http://www.newtimes.com/` and the Ruxton Group at `http://www.ruxton.com/`.

Atomic Media knows that its clients are going to be looking for high-end design, and takes pride in being able to show off how it incorporates a number of current technologies. However, because the site is heavily JavaScript enhanced, the designer did put in a "switch" to take the Java Script off; it uses a magic target name:

```
Click here to <a href="index2.htm" target="_top">kill JavaScript</a>
```

This example then loads another version of the site—JavaScript-free—over the entire viewing window. By employing the `"target="_top"` magic target name, the new version simply takes over the pre-existing Java-heavy one, as shown in Figure 9.13.

Figure 9.13.
The site with Java turned off.

The site looks pretty much the same as with the JavaScript on, at least at first glance. Run the mouse over the right and bottom navigation bars and you get no hot-spot animation. So, if this bores you, you're welcome to switch back to the JavaScript-enhanced version—with one click of a magic target button:

```
Click here to <a href="index3.html" target="_top">add JavaScript</a>
```

Workshop Wrap-Up

Atomic Media provides a colorful and strong example of interface. Beyond that, you took a tour through the site and saw just how the designer put it together. I'd like to take this opportunity to thank Atomic Media and lead designer Matthew Bardram for letting me deconstruct his site so that you may benefit. If you like his work, let him know.

Because of the vast span of skills, different people using this book are going to be experiencing a range of responses after seeing how a top-line professional has employed the same techniques you've been learning. I hope that most of you are able to immediately see how you either have already been or can soon begin employing your skills to create interesting sites. For those of you who are still a little unsteady with the materials, don't hesitate to repeat the chapters and tasks that have given you trouble. Repetition is very often what helps you to increase not only your knowledge base, but the speed at which you ultimately can work.

Next Steps

Chapter 10, "Margin Navigation Using Tables and Frames," begins the third part of the book, which is dedicated to looking primarily at navigation. There are other topics you might wish to jump to immediately after this chapter, however. They include

❏ A discussion of multiple menus and non-linear navigation in Chapter 12, "Multiple Menus and Non-Linear Navigation"

❏ Chapter 14, "Adding Interactive and Dynamic Content," which discusses adding interactive content to your pages

❏ An overview of how to control graphics with tables, found in Chapter 16, "Using Tables for Graphic Control"

❏ Helpful charts for table and frame syntax in Appendix C, "Current HTML Standards"

Q&A

Q: Although I am beginning to understand the HTML fundamentals of using tables and frames, I'm no graphic designer. What can I do to make my sites have as much design savvy as Atomic Media?

A: This is a good question, and one that probably concerns many Web designers who come from a technical or other non-artistic field. If you feel you have the talent, consider taking graphic design courses at your local art school, university, or community college. You can often audit classes. There are many books and Web graphic resources on the Web itself. Go to your favorite search engine and see what you can find. Another option is to hire a professional graphic designer to work with you. You can do this by contacting any number of existing Web and graphic design firms in your area or from your Web search resources.

Q: I like the JavaScript animation on the navigation bars. Is this easy to do?

A: There's a lot of free JavaScript running around on the Web, so the answer is yes. You needn't be an author to employ some really fun script code, providing that the place you get it from is amenable to your using it. Chapter 14 of this book covers interactive media, and there are some good references available within that chapter.

Q: I hear you talk about client choice rather frequently. Doesn't trying to bridge the gap between every audience make more work for the designer?

A: The answer here is simply, yes. There's an easy way to avoid that, and that's to use very simple HTML and graphics for your client pages. If that's what they want, great. But in the long run, learning the technologies and putting in the extra work will pay off, not only in the quality of the sites you make, but the type of client base you'll be able to attract. So, not only is there this pervasive idea of client choice, but designer choice as well. You are the only one who can determine what is best and most appropriate for you, your audiences, and your clients.

III

Navigation that Leads the Way

ten

Margin Navigation Using Tables and Frames

Navigation is as critical to a site's design as interface. It's the way people get to the content you're providing. If a Web visitor can't do that, you may as well not even have a Web site. Navigation should be considered early in the planning stages of your sites, along with interface. When the two are successful, the combination creates the groundwork for the most effective sites around, and, as a result, the most desirable site designers in the business.

In fact, designers who have made groundbreaking discoveries in how to use the Web's non-linear, interactive potential as a basis for navigation techniques have gotten significant attention for those efforts.

You'll see examples of some of those contributions in the next chapters, and descriptions of why such navigation is unusual or significant.

But why is navigation so important, you might be asking? Isn't it just a matter of offering up site section options and allowing people to go to those areas with links? Well, that's true, but there are two complications—perhaps the better word is opportunities—involved in creating navigation for the Web.

A good, Web-based frames tutorial is "Framing the Web" by Dan Brown. Visit `http://www.webreference.com/dev/frames/` to find out more.

The first is pretty straightforward and involves the fact that many Web sites are enormous. Web sites hold thousands, if not tens or even hundreds of thousands of individual pages of data. If you aren't convinced, look at a site such as Microsoft (`http://www.microsoft.com/`). Another example, and one you'll see deconstructed and closely examined in Chapter 12, "Multiple Menus and Non-Linear Navigation," is the *Tucson Weekly*. Newspapers, in general, are challenged by how to manage back issues. And, as the content pages add up, so does the need to find a way to manage all of that data, behind the scenes as well as in front of them.

The second issue is the non-linear environment of the Web. With the opportunities that are available to a Web designer via hypermedia, linking, and multiple forms of navigation, the choices for both the designer and the end user become diverse. A Web site isn't a book—you don't page forward and occasionally turn back a page to get to the information. Well, you can present information that way, and numerous other ways as well. A detailed discussion of non-linear navigation continues in Chapter 12. For the time being, bear in mind these considerations as you begin to work with navigation concepts.

Elements of Navigation

Navigation on the Web can be broken down into a number of elements. Some of the most common involving HTML include

❏ **Text menus.** This is the use of text linking in some consolidated form that creates a navigation menu. You've already seen examples of this in earlier tasks. A closer look at how and where to use them will come into play in this chapter.

❏ **Hypermedia.** By linking graphic elements, you can create another addition to the navigation tool box. Originally, the Web was based on *hypertext* (as in Hypertext Markup Language—HTML). This linked text quickly became linked media, such as graphics.

❑ **Linking.** This is hypertext in its original form. It allows for a variety of flexible opportunities, particularly when used along with other forms of navigation.

❑ **Image maps.** Image maps are actually hypermedia with a twist. You can add multiple links to one piece of graphic data by applying simple HTML techniques.

Placement and Organization

Another significant element in navigation is where the elements go. For example, you can run navigation along the top, bottom, or either side margin, as well as within a page itself. In the following chapters, you'll look at a variety of placement. In this chapter, you'll focus on left and right styles, and how to accommodate their implementation.

An excellent, online style guide is published by Sun Microsystems. "Guide to Web Style" can be found at `http:// www.sun.com/ styleguide/`.

Organization of your HTML page is becoming a critical issue. Up to this point in the book, the examples have been relatively short and straightforward. At this point, it's imperative to introduce a method of organizing your HTML so that details are easy for you to find. As your sites become more complex, this organization will be appreciated.

You may have already noticed that I'm in the habit of flushing most of my HTML tags to the right of a page. I think that's a really strong way of getting to the tag I need to edit quickly. I've seen some very good coders keep all of their code crunched together. This is, for me, like a really messy room. Sure, you might know where things are, but if you sent someone else in there to find your right boot under the piles of clothing, they might not be as successful.

As long as you are the only one working on your code, and you are comfortable with a free-form presentation, it really boils down only to pride in ownership. When someone looks at that code (and you never know who is going to do just that), he or she might pass your work over for someone else's because they can't figure it out. Another perhaps more critical point is that as you add people to your staff, you must have some kind of system by which they can go into that virtual room and find the missing element, fix the problem, and make the critical change.

There is a simple way to handle this situation and that is the use of *comment tagging.* This is simply placing comments within syntax that the browsers will ignore and not project onto the HTML page. By using comment tagging, the coder is empowered because he or she can work on long documents and find sections without any trouble. In fact, if you use comment standards, your coders can simply do a search for the comment words and get to the area ready for a repair or a change immediately. Comment tagging uses the opening `<!--` and closing `-->` to hold the comment information. Here's an example:

```
<!-- this page built by molly media, contact molly@molly.com -->

<!-- begin header -->

<html>
<head>
<title>Comment Tag Example</title>
</head>

<!-- begin body -->
<body>

<!-- begin footer -->

</body>

</html>
```

You'll see comment tagging in action. I recommend you begin using it in your own work. Again, as the pages you create become more detailed, it is in your best interest to have well-organized code.

Backgrounds for Table-Based Margin Navigation

Before moving into the actual HTML, it's important to look at one of the most common Web conventions, and that is margin backgrounds. You've seen this a great deal: a strip to the left or right margin of color and design followed by a solid color or textured field that holds the body of text (see Figure 10.1).

Before you begin tasks that will instruct you how to put this type of navigation together, there are several considerations regarding the backgrounds. As mentioned many times in this book, there are issues regarding screen resolutions, monitor sizes, and the like. In order to create margin-based navigation that doesn't repeat, you must build the backgrounds appropriately. If your margins are too short, they will repeat (see Figure 10.2).

Figure 10.1.
A standard margin background.

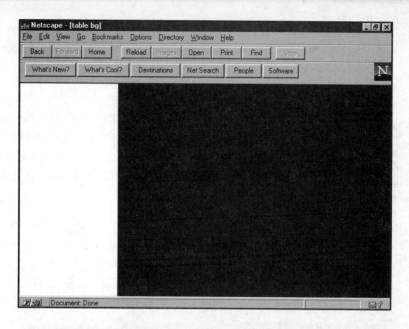

Figure 10.2.
A too-short background will repeat.

I recommend building all of your backgrounds to a pixel width of 1,024 or higher. Consider that most computer users are using a 640 pixel width; the next common on the Web is probably 800 pixels wide. The higher resolutions, such as 1,280 or above, aren't that common. Although, if you want to make your graphics that wide, that's fine. Just remember size issues. It's fairly standard to build background graphics for this purpose at 1,024. With the limited number of colors and graphics techniques required to create margin backgrounds, the ultimate file size in kilobytes will be small when properly compressed.

Then, place your margin within a field you can control. For a left margin, this means starting at the extreme left and ending where you've left enough natural space for content at low resolution. The total margin will then usually be no wider than 200 pixels, with 400 or so remaining for the text and content in the right field.

Conversely, a background created for a right margin must allow for the text and content field to run the appropriate width (approximately 400–450 pixels). The right margin design begins at that point, continuing on for the remaining amount of the total 1,024. By doing this, you've solved part of the contributory problems to horizontal scrollbars, and avoided repeating background designs.

Want to know more about backgrounds? "The Background FAQ," an online resource maintained by Mark Koenen, is available at `http://www.sci.kun.nl/thalia/guide/color/faq.html`.

Left-Margin Table Layout and Navigation

Now I'll show you how to create a table-based layout over such a background, with the focus on left-margin navigation.

1. Begin in your HTML editor, typing in the following shell. Pay special attention to the comment tags:

```
<html>

<!-- begin header -->

<head>
<title>Station X</title>
</head>

<body text="#FFFFFF" bgcolor="#000000" vlink="#0000FF"
alink="#FFFF00" link="FF0000" background="images/bkgrd.gif">

<!-- end header -->


<!-- begin table -->
```

```
<table valign=top cellspacing=10 cellpadding=10 border=0>
<tr>

<td width=125 valign=top>

<!-- begin navigation -->


<!-- end navigation -->
</td>

<!-- begin gutter -->

<td width=20>

</td>

<!-- end gutter -->

<td valign=top width=425>

<!-- begin content -->


<!-- end content -->


<!-- begin footer -->


<!--end footer -->

</td>
</tr>

</table>

<!-- end table -->
</body>
</html>
```

DESIGN NOTE: You'll notice the use of a table cell set to 20 pixels for a "gutter" or spacing effect. Many designers also like to add a transparent, single-pixel GIF and stretch it to the 20 pixels, securing the fixed, defined distance. It's not completely necessary, particularly as browsers become more table stable. The GIF trick is also used to push graphics to a specific distance. More on this will be discussed in Chapter 12.

2. Next, add the header image and text-based navigation to the navigation section:

```
<font face=arial, helvetica size=4>

<img src="images/sx-hed.gif" alt="station x header" width=95
height=100>
<p>

<a href="music.htm">m u s i c</a>
<p>

<a href="film.htm">f i l m </a>
<p>

<a href="art.htm">a r t </a>
<p>

<a href="thea.htm">t h e a t r e</a>
<p>

<a href="poli.htm">p o l i t i c s</a>
<p>

<a href="live.htm">l i v i n g</a>
```

3. In the content section, place the content images, text, and syntax:

```
<img src="images/sx-mhed.gif" alt="culture hed" width=250
height=100
align=right>
<br clear="all">
<p>

<font face=arial,helvetica size=6>S i c K?</font>
<p>

<font face=arial, helvetica>
of hearing how X'ers have no culture, no drive? Well, so are we.
So Duis autem vel eum iriure dolor in hendrerit in vulputate
velit esse molestie consequat, vel illum dolore eu feugiat nulla
facilisis at vero eros et accumsan et iusto odio dignissim qui
blandit praesent luptatum zzril delenit augue duis dolore te
feugait nulla facilisi.
</font>
<p>
```

4. Place the footer information within the comment tags for that section:

```
<center>

<font size=-1>
```

```
<a href="music.htm">m u s i c</a> | <a href="film.htm">
f i l m </a> |
<a href="art.htm">a r t </a> | <a href="thea.htm">
t h e a t r e</a> |
<a href="poli.htm">p o l i t i c s</a> | <a href="live.htm">
l i v i n g</a>
<p>

&copy; 1997
</font>
</center>
```

NOTE: This bottom navigation is a secondary form of navigation; it repeats the left-margin navigation exactly. This provides a natural frame of reference, as many people are used to bottom-navigation options. Also, if your pages are very long, having navigation on the bottom enables them to move through the site without having to scroll back to the top again, which is inconvenient.

5. Save the file as `left.htm`.

6. View it in the browser of your choice. The results should match Figure 10.3.

Figure 10.3.

A left-margin table-based design.

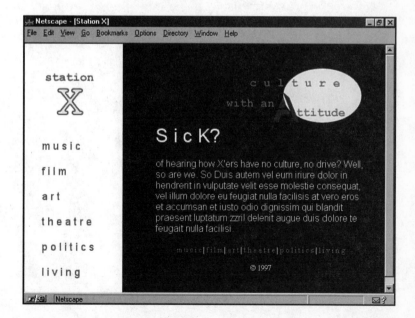

TASK ## Creating a Right-Margin Table Layout

Now, with the same images and content, except for the background image (viewable in the Chapter 10 "image" section on the CD-ROM), you will create a right-margin treatment for the design. Notice how the syntax is reversed. You begin the table with the content area, follow it up with the footer, the gutter, and then the navigation.

1. Begin as before with the "shell." I want you to get used to using the comment tagging, so pay close attention:

```
<html>

<!-- begin header -->

<head>
<title>Station X</title>
</head>

<body text="#FFFFFF" bgcolor="#000000" vlink="#0000FF"
alink="#FFFF00" link="FF0000" background="images/rbkgrd.gif">

<!-- end header -->

<!-- begin table -->

<table valign=top cellspacing=10 cellpadding=10 border=0>
<tr>

<td valign=top width=425>

<!-- begin content -->


<!-- end content -->


<!-- begin footer -->


<!--end footer -->

</td>

<!-- begin gutter -->

<td width=20>

</td>

<!-- end gutter -->
```

```
<td width=125 valign=top>

<!-- begin navigation -->

<!-- end navigation -->

</td>

</tr>
</table>

<!-- end table -->

</body>
</html>
```

2. Now add the content elements to the content section:

```
<img src="images/sx-mhed.gif" alt="culture hed" width=250
height=100 align=right>
<br clear="all">
<p>

<font face=arial,helvetica size=6>S i c K?</font>
<p>

<font face=arial, helvetica>
of hearing how X'ers have no culture, no drive? Well, so are we.
So Duis autem vel eum iriure dolor in hendrerit in vulputate
velit esse molestie consequat, vel illum dolore eu feugiat nulla
facilisis at vero eros et accumsan et iusto odio dignissim qui
blandit praesent luptatum zzril delenit augue duis dolore te
feugait nulla facilisi.
</font>
<p>
```

3. In the footer section, add the footer information:

```
<center>

<font size=-1>
<a href="music.htm">m u s i c</a> | <a href="film.htm">
f i l m </a> |
<a href="art.htm">a r t </a> | <a href="thea.htm">
t h e a t r e</a> |
<a href="poli.htm">p o l i t i c s</a> | <a href="live.htm">
l i v i n g</a>
<p>

&copy; 1997
</font>
</center>
```

4. In the final table cell, place the navigation:

```
<font face=arial, helvetica size=4>

<img src="images/sx-hed.gif" alt="station x header" width=95
height=100>
<p>

<a href="music.htm">m u s i c</a>
<p>

<a href="film.htm">f i l m </a>
<p>

<a href="art.htm">a r t </a>
<p>

<a href="thea.htm">t h e a t r e</a>
<p>

<a href="poli.htm">p o l i t i c s</a>
<p>

<a href="live.htm">l i v i n g</a>
```

5. Save the file as `right.htm`.

6. View it in your browser. You should have a design, shown in Figure 10.4, that is a reverse of the first one.

Figure 10.4.
A right-margin table-based design.

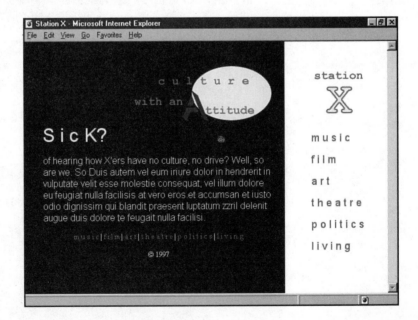

Remember back in earlier chapters the discussions pertaining to multiple tables, stacked tables, nested tables, and table row, cell, columns, and spanning? All of these attributes can begin to be employed to create even more diversity for your table design. Be sure to take a look at Chapter 15, "Real-Time Example: Interactivity in Action—Core Wave's Glass Bead Game," which demonstrates more complex table techniques in action.

Nevertheless, with these two simple exercises, you've covered the basics for creating right- and left-margin navigation layouts with tables.

DESIGN NOTE: Where you've used text in these examples, you can easily trade out for images, creating hypermedia links. Examples have already been used in this book. Check back in Chapter 5, "Frame-Based Interface Design," to see an example of hypermedia in action.

Image Maps

For details on server-sided mapping, check with your systems administrator for the components necessary to create your server maps. `http://curry.edschool.virginia.edu/go/WebTools/Imagemap/home.html` offers a nice overview of maps, their differences, advantages, and how to make them.

You'll now get to graduate to developing a hypermedia element for navigation: the image map. There are two types of image maps, client-sided and server-sided. Server-sided maps are rapidly becoming a thing of the past because they are more time-consuming than client maps. The difference between them is that the server maps rely on a CGI script to process them, meaning that the server and the browser have to communicate more data, which slows down the process.

Client-map data is handled by the browser, which means faster and easier implementation. Most common browsers are now image-map–compliant. However, to avoid problems, you can include text navigation or double up on your mapping so that the browser will default to whichever is immediately available. For the purposes of this discussion, I'm going to stick to client-sided mapping.

The other advantage of client mapping is that it is included in your HTML. This makes it part of the coding process, just as if you were to code links for text-based navigation. The syntax is relatively simple, and will be demonstrated as I walk you through the following task.

Creating a Client-Sided Image Map

The first step in this process is opening up the graphic you want to map with the appropriate software package on the CD-ROM for your computer platform. Because I do my coding on a PC, I'm going to demonstrate how to complete this process using a wonderful shareware program called MapEdit.

The image I've selected to map is shown in Figure 10.5. If you run your cursor over the map currently, nothing happens. Click it? Nothing happens. This changes once you add the mapping syntax.

Figure 10.5.

The rose is the header graphic, and the individual section areas are to be mapped.

DESIGN NOTE: When selecting or creating images for mapping, be sure to use one that logically makes sense to map. These would include graphics with very specifically defined areas, shapes, or graphic elements such as text in a font style. This helps to visually distinguish that element as a distinct section.

1. Open the image with the mapping tool.

2. Select the appropriate area shape, in this case a rectangle.

3. Select the first area you want "hot," or linked.

4. Input the corresponding URL.

5. Continue doing this until each area you want mapped is complete.

6. Save the file using the "client-sided map" option. MapEdit allows you to save this data into your already existing HTML file.

7. The resulting syntax will look like this:

```
<img src="images/gb-hed.gif" alt="Image Map for Gabrielles"
width="125" height="325" border="0" usemap="#gb-hed">
<p>

<map name="gb-hed">
<area shape="rect" coords="10,154,113,187" href="skin.htm"
target="top">
<area shape="rect" coords="11,189,113,210" href="hair.htm"
target="top">
<area shape="rect" coords="12,212,113,239" href="body.htm"
target="top">
<area shape="rect" coords="12,241,113,266" href="prods.htm"
target="top">
<area shape="rect" coords="13,268,113,304" href="loc.htm"
target="top">
<area shape="rect" href="index.htm" coords="0,0,124,324">
</map>
```

8. Save the file as map.htm and view it in a browser.

9. Pass the cursor over the hot sections, noticing how now there is every indication that this will be linked, or hot, media—hypermedia (see Figure 10.6).

10. Set the file aside. You'll need it in just a bit.

Now let's incorporate the map into a left-margin navigation design using frames.

Figure 10.6.

Note the little white box, which shows that the browser understands the map is now "hot."

Frame Navigation for Right and Left Margins

Realistically, you already know exactly how to do either one of these layouts. Chapters 5, 6, and 7 each covered methods of using frames that called for navigation sets on the left or right. The only difference at this point is expanding your options by understanding how to incorporate image mapping into the frame.

The other necessity is to build an even stronger foundation for creating powerful interfaces and navigation devices as you move through the following tasks. You'll need to start focusing more intensely on how to incorporate multiple instances of linking, hypermedia, and navigation.

Look at the simple designs I've used so far to demonstrate how to create interfaces, and begin using them in different ways. Create an image map and place it in the example, add text navigation where there isn't any—that sort of thing. How can you expand on and improve the interfaces I've provided? The more you experiment and think about these issues, the more your own native talent will have an opportunity to develop and shine.

Designing a Left-Margin Frameset

This task will teach you to design a left-margin navigation option with frames.

1. As with all frame-based layouts, you'll begin by designing the frameset. Start with the shell syntax and comment tags:

```
<html>

<!-- begin header -->

<head>
<title>Gabrielle's Frameset</title>
</head>

<!-- end header -->

<!-- begin frameset -->

<!-- end frameset -->

</html>
```

2. Inside the frameset comments, add the following syntax, which sets up the frame:

```
<frameset frameborder=0 framespacing=0 border=0 cols=150,*>

<frame src=menu.htm noresize scrolling=no>

<frameset frameborder=0 framespacing=0 border=0 rows=*,100>

<frame src=top.htm name=top noresize scrolling="auto">
<frame src=ad.htm name=bottom noresize scrolling="no">

</frameset>
</frameset>
```

Note that this frame is borderless, has a right column of 150 pixels, a dynamic left column. The frame contains two rows: the first being dynamic, with the bottom row being 100 pixels in height.

3. Save the frameset as `index.htm`.

 ## Adding the Menu Frame and Image Map

Now you'll create the Menu Frame, and add the image map.

1. Begin with the following syntax:

```
<html>

<!-- begin header -->
```

```
<head>
<title>Gabrielle's Home Page</title>
</head>

<body bgcolor="#FFFFFF" text="#000000" link="#0033FF"
vlink="#00CC33" alink="#FF6600">

<!-- end header -->

<!-- begin map data -->

<center>

<!-- end map data -->

</body>
</html>
```

2. Open the file map.htm.

3. Copy the syntax.

4. Paste the syntax into the map data area.

5. The following code is the final result:

```
<html>

<!-- begin header -->

<head>
<title>Gabrielle's Home Page</title>
</head>

<body bgcolor="#FFFFFF" text="#000000" link="#0033FF"
vlink="#00CC33" alink="#FF6600">

<!-- end header -->

<!-- begin map data -->

<center>

<img src="images/gb-hed.gif" alt="Image Map for Gabrielles"
width="125" height="325" border="0" usemap="#gb-hed">

</center>
<p>

<map name="gb-hed">
```

```
<area shape="rect" coords="10,154,113,187" href="skin.htm"
target="top">
<area shape="rect" coords="11,189,113,210" href="hair.htm"
target="top">
<area shape="rect" coords="12,212,113,239" href="body.htm"
target="top">
<area shape="rect" coords="12,241,113,266" href="prods.htm"
target="top">
<area shape="rect" coords="13,268,113,304" href="loc.htm"
target="top">
<area shape="rect" href="index.htm" coords="0,0,124,324">
</map>

<!-- end map data -->

</body>
</html>
```

6. Save the file as menu.htm.

Before viewing the page, go on to build the bottom and right-sided frame.

TASK   Adding a Bottom Advertisement Frame

Follow these steps to create the bottom, right-sided frame.

1. Copy the simple syntax:

```
<html>

<!-- begin header -->

<head>
<title> Ad HTML </title>
</head>
<body bgcolor="#FFFFFF" text="#000000" link="#0033FF"
vlink="#00CC33" alink="#FF6600" >

<! -- end header -->

<!-- begin ad -->
<img src="images/ad2.gif" width=468 height=60>

<!-- end ad -->

</body>
</html>
```

2. Save the file as ad.htm.

Adding a Content Page

Now, you'll add the content for the frameset.

1. Copy the following shell syntax:

```
<html>

<!-- begin header -->

<head>
<title> Gabrielle's</title>
</head>

<body bgcolor="#FFFFFF" text="#000000" link="#0033FF"
vlink="#00CC33" alink="#FF6600" >

<!-- end header -->

<!-- begin contents -->

<!-- end contents -->

</body>
</html>
```

2. Place the following contents within the content tagging:

```
<img src="images/gb-skin.gif" alt="picture of woman" width=133
height=168 hspace=10 border=0 align=right>

Occumsan Aliquam dignissim qui blandit praesent luptatum zzril
delenit augue duis dolorete feugait nulla facilisi. Nam liber
tempor cum soluta nobis eleifend option congue nihil imperdiet
doming id quod mazim placerat facer possim assum. Iusto odio
dignissim qui blandit.Duis autem vel eum iriure dolor in
hendrerit in vulputate velit esse molestie consequat, vel illum
dolore eu feugiat nulla facilisis at vero eros et accumsan et
iusto odio.
<p>
```

3. Save the file as top.htm.

4. Open the frameset, index.htm, in your browser.

5. View the results, which should match Figure 10.7.

Figure 10.7.
A left-margin, frame-based, navigation layout.

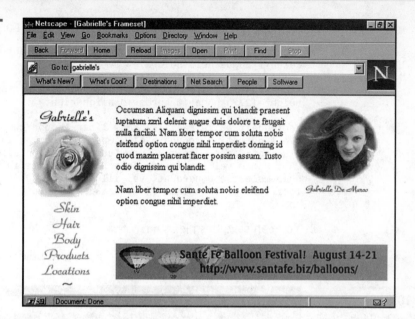

TASK Adding Additional Content Pages

In order to see the image map fully functional, you'll need to complete the HTML pages required for the site. All of the images you'll need are on the CD-ROM. Use the following syntax as a template to create the remaining pages on your own.

1. To build the template, begin with the following:

```
<html>

<!-- begin header -->

<head>
<title> Gabrielle's</title>
</head>

<body bgcolor="#FFFFFF" text="#000000" link="#0033FF"
vlink="#00CC33" alink="#FF6600" >

<!-- end header -->

<!-- begin content -->

<!-- end content -->

</body>
</html>
```

2. Add dummy text and images to the shell content area.

```
Occumsan Aliquam dignissim qui blandit praesent luptatum zzril
delenit augue duis dolore

<img src="images/gb-hair.gif" alt="Picture of Woman" width=105
height=127 hspace=10 border=0 align=right>

te feugait nulla facilisi. Nam liber tempor cum soluta nobis
eleifend option congue nihil imperdiet doming id quod mazim
placerat facer possim assum. Iusto odio dignissim qui blandit.
Duis autem vel eum iriure dolor in hendrerit in vulputate velit
esse molestie consequat, vel illum dolore eu feugiat nulla
facilisis at vero eros et accumsan et iusto odio.
<p>
```

3. You can save this file as `hair.htm`.

4. View the page from within the frameset, as I did in Figure 10.8.

Figure 10.8.

A content page in the left-frame navigation example.

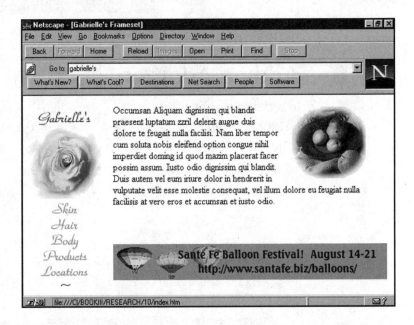

5. Continue creating content pages and complete the site. Figure 10.9 demonstrates the results as you move through the image map.

Figure 10.9.
Another view of the left-frame example.

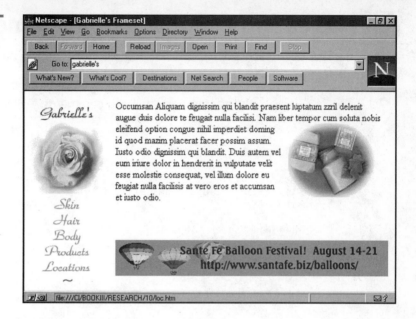

Right Margin Frame-Based Navigation

At this point, your task should be pretty clear. The idea is to simply reverse what you just created already. However, with right-frame navigation there is an additional instance of the frameset required. The reason for this is that when you are with rows and columns, and want to ensure that the row is contained within the space of the browser, you must argue for the frame's total width. This is done using a column argument. The frameset syntax for a right, borderless frame navigation with two rows and two columns would resemble this:

```
<frameset frameborder=0 framespacing=0 border=0 cols=450,150>
<frameset frameborder=0 framespacing=0 border=0 rows=300,100>

</frameset>

<frameset frameborder=0 framespacing=0 border=0 cols="600">

</frameset>
</frameset>
```

Note how the one closing frameset appears before the additional syntax. This ensures cross-browser compatibility. As always, the amount of framesets equals the amount of closing `</frameset>` incidents.

Creating a Right-Margin Frame

This task teaches you how to create a right-margin navigation set using frames.

1. Begin with the frameset shell and comments:

```
<html>

<!-- begin header -->

<head>
<title>Gabrielle's Frameset</title>
</head>

<!-- end header -->

<!-- begin frameset -->

<!-- end frameset -->

</html>
```

2. Add the frameset structure. Note the size of the additional column used to accommodate the area of the frame has been set to 600.

```
<frameset frameborder=0 framespacing=0 border=0 cols=450,150>
<frameset frameborder=0 framespacing=0 border=0 rows=300,100>

<frame src=top.htm name=top noresize scrolling="auto">
<frame src=ad.htm name=bottom noresize scrolling="no">
</frameset>

<frameset frameborder=0 framespacing=0 border=0 cols="600">
<frame src=menu.htm noresize scrolling=no>

</frameset>
</frameset>
```

3. Save the file as index2.htm in the same folder as the previous frameset.

4. View the index file in your browser.

Everything should work! This is because all of the naming remains the same; the browser understands where to put each file called upon in this example. Figure 10.10 shows the locations page.

Figure 10.10.
The same site treated with a right-margin frameset.

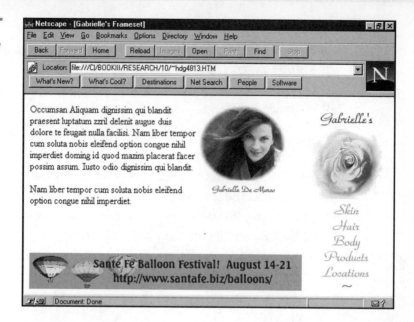

DESIGN NOTE: Obviously you'll be developing sites individually and not reusing data as I have, unless you decide to change a site's look for freshness' sake. You'll want to adjust content page information so that it looks its best within the frame. For example, I would move the content page images in Figure 10.10 around so that they don't bump up against the menu.

Workshop Wrap-Up

Along with the navigation discussion, the examples in this chapter should help you get started on the creation of popular navigation options for the Web. As you proceed through this book, and throughout your own site-building experiences, you will find that the simple concepts learned here provide an excellent foundation for more complicated table- and frame-based design.

Of equal importance is learning more about HTML style. Although the language is in itself not difficult, there are many pitfalls that can easily be remedied by understanding not only style, but developing your own management system for documents. Beyond that, having an idea of the idiosyncratic nature of browsers and browser-based HTML tags challenges you to design your own methods for managing the sites that you design. This rings true in the study of image mapping, which can be either server- or browser-dependent. It's up to you to develop strategies to deal with these complicated Web design issues.

Always at question is your audience, the browser that audience prefers, and the logic behind selecting a particular presentation style. The left margin navigation solution isn't as widely popular as it is just by accident. On the other hand, just because something is logical doesn't mean it's best. Your audience might be very Web-savvy, and possibly tired of left-margin navigation treatments. Consider working with right-margin approaches for some diversity. Or, continue on and learn other methods, and combinations of methods, that will further empower your design efforts.

Next Steps

Chapter 11, "Top and Bottom Navigation Options," covers top and bottom navigation options using tables and frames. It's a good next step, but you may also be interested in looking at these other chapters as well:

❏ Chapter 12, "Multiple Menus and Non-Linear Navigation," expands on some of the navigation theory introduced in this chapter.

❏ Chapter 13, "Non-Static and Multi-Framed Navigation," looks closely at navigation for targeting multiple frames.

❏ Chapter 15, "Real-Time Example: Interactivity in Action—Core-Wave's Glass Bead Game," is an intriguing look at the use of tables and non-linear navigation techniques.

Q&A

Q: Do I have to use a background margin to employ the table-based techniques in this chapter?

A: Not at all. You can use the layouts as you want. In fact, you might try using background color for table cells rather than a background image—experiment!

Q: Are image maps better than individual, hot-linked graphics?

A: That's totally a designer's call. It will depend on your preferences and the needs of your audience. Some designers prefer using individual graphics and controlling their layout with tables. One advantage to that is that you don't always have to have fixed options, but can switch between the navigation options you need at that particular point in the site.

Q: Is there a standard way of comment tagging? I've seen it done differently from how you do it here.

A: As long as you follow the correct syntax to hide the comments from the viewable HTML page, you can use any kind of comments that you feel comfortable with. Some coders place start tags only where a certain part of the information begins; others place their comments before or after certain syntax sequences. It's a person thing. Remember, its major use is to help you and those who work with you to locate and navigate the internal workings of a site.

Q: Why do you consider placement so important? Doesn't flushing tags to the right and separating them with spaces make your HTML file sizes larger?

A: Placement is important for me because I find that without a logical frame of reference, working on long documents takes an equally long time. Yes, my technique does add to file size, but remember that HTML files tend to be very small, usually only 1 or 2 kilobytes. As a result, you do have some freedom in terms of how you like to code. This doesn't give license for lots of empty space, however, and conservative coding is a good choice. Ultimately, you must find an organizational style that suits you.

eleven

Top and Bottom Navigation Options

In this chapter, the focus will be on navigation at the top and bottom of the Web page space. Navigation is a critical aspect of design: It helps a Web visitor know where to go, and what to do once he or she gets there.

As you move forward in the study of navigation and how it fits in to the general layout of a Web site, you'll notice that the demands on you as a coder and designer become more complex. You'll see code getting longer, tables multiplying, and, more specific to upcoming discussions, the amount of data you are planning to work with getting larger.

Part of the reason you begin to add navigation elements to multiple sections of a Web page is that you're working with larger amounts of content information, and, therefore, require more logical ways of getting people to that content. You want to add navigation quickly and accurately, never losing the style and design that is equally critical to the final, successful results of a site.

Top Navigation: The Why and How

For some great reading about the Internet from those who live and work with it daily, visit Start Reading (`http://home.microsoft.com/reading/voices.asp`). Not only do the articles span a number of visionary and vocal topics, but the page is a prime example of top navigation that doesn't interfere with other page elements.

Why use top navigation? The reason is to create navigable interfaces by using more than one area for navigation without cutting into precious content space. However, top-aligned navigation must always be approached with care. This is because the top area is one of the first places the eye naturally falls. If you have elements there that distract the visitor from the main intent of the site, you run the risk of losing that visitor's interest.

This doesn't mean you shouldn't use top-aligned navigation. However, you should do so carefully, so as not to interfere with other important information that could be placed at the top of the page. Be sure the navigation is easy to use and integrated well into the architecture of the site. If you integrate elements and have other, immediate items that do not focus on your top-aligned navigation, you'll bring a better balance between your navigation and your page's content-related items.

The "how" aspect of top-aligned navigation is straightforward. It can be accomplished, as shown by this book, using frames or tables. Each will bring with it unique potential and the usual package of quirks. You'll see these come to life in the following tasks.

To keep your tasks concise, I've chosen to use elements more than once. In this chapter, you'll be using the same navigation bar for both the top and bottom menu. It's a single, image-mapped graphic. The repetition of using this piece in several ways is intended to get you comfortable with the concept of why top and bottom navigation can be important for the Web designer.

Bear in mind that just because I use a single, mapped image for the navigation doesn't mean you shouldn't try other methods. Use individual graphics, plain text links, or try a combination of styles. Once you feel comfortable with the general structure and how-to, you can, and should, experiment freely.

Mapping the Image

I'll map the image first, as it will be a consistent element in each of the tasks to come.

1. From the Chapter 11 `images` directory on the CD-ROM, copy the `menu.jpg` into a Chapter 11 `images` subfolder on your computer.

2. Open the image using the appropriate mapping tool, which can also be found on the CD-ROM. For Windows machines, this will be Mapedit (see Figure 11.1).

Figure 11.1.
The Mapedit editing environment.

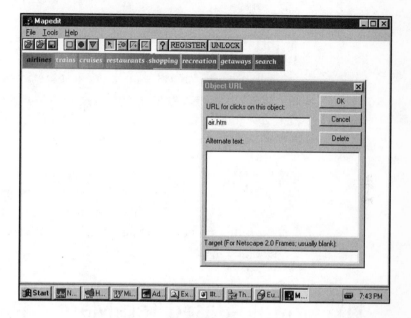

3. Select the appropriate area shape (in this case, a rectangle).

4. Draw the cursor over the area to be hot-linked. Here, each individual word on the image has been hot-linked.

5. Input a corresponding URL.

6. Continue doing this until each area is mapped.

7. Save the file using the Client-Side Map option. MapEdit allows you to save this data into your already existing HTML file.

The following is the resulting syntax:

```
<center>
<img src="images/menu.jpg" width="450" height="27" border="0"
usemap="#menu">
</center>
<map name="menu">
<area shape="rect" coords="0,0,52,25" href="air.htm">
<area shape="rect" coords="54,0,93,25" href="train.htm">
<area shape="rect" coords="95,0,139,25" href="cruise.htm">
<area shape="rect" coords="141,0,212,25" href="food.htm">
```

```
<area shape="rect" coords="214,0,270,25" href="shop.htm">
<area shape="rect" coords="272,0,334,25" href="rec.htm">
<area shape="rect" coords="336,0,394,25" href="get.htm">
<area shape="rect" coords="396,0,448,25" href="search.htm">
<area shape="default" nohref>
</map>
```

NOTE: If your coordinates differ slightly from those I've created, it's probably not a critical issue. If you test the areas and they work logically, the reason for the difference is that you've mapped your area in a slightly different place than I have.

CAUTION: Be careful that you don't overlap when mapping. This can cause problems, such as the browser not pulling up the correct link. Although not a difficult task, image mapping does take a steady hand and eye.

TASK   Table-Based Top-Margin Navigation

This task shows you how to create top-margin navigation using tables.

1. In your HTML editor, prepare the following shell syntax:

```
<html>
<!-- begin header -->
<head>
<title> Tour de Force</title>
</head>
<body bgcolor="#FFFFFF" text="#000000" link="#333399"
vlink="#00CCFF" alink="FFFFFF">
<!-- end header -->
<!-- begin main table -->
<table width=600 border=0>
<tr>
<td valign=top width=450>
</td>
</tr>
<td valign=top width=150>
</td>
</table>
<p>
</body>
</html>
```

2. Now add the primary data for the first cell, creating the top menu and the map data:

```
<img src="images/menu.jpg" width=450 height=27>
<p>
<!-- begin map -->
<map name="menu">
<area shape="rect" coords="0,0,52,25" href="air.htm">
<area shape="rect" coords="54,0,93,25" href="train.htm">
<area shape="rect" coords="95,0,139,25" href="cruise.htm">
<area shape="rect" coords="141,0,212,25" href="food.htm">
<area shape="rect" coords="214,0,270,25" href="shop.htm">
<area shape="rect" coords="272,0,334,25" href="rec.htm">
<area shape="rect" coords="336,0,394,25" href="get.htm">
<area shape="rect" coords="396,0,448,25" href="search.htm">
<area shape="default" nohref>
</map>
<!-- end map -->
```

3. Beneath that, in the same table cell, you'll lay out a secondary table to manage the content area text and graphics:

```
<!-- begin text table -->
<table border=1 width=430 cellpadding=5 cellspacing=0>
<tr>
<td>
<font face=arial,helvetica color="#333399" size=5><b>Full
<i>Force</i> Travel!</b></font>
</td>
</tr>
<tr>
<td valign=left>
<img src="images/tn-eur.gif" width=125 height=121 border=0>
</td>
<td>
<font face=arial,helvetica>
Europe in focus! Duis autem vel eum iriure dolor in hendrerit in
vulputate velit esse molestie consequat. Accumsan et iusto odio
dignissim qui blandit praesent luptatum zzril. Accumsan et
iusto odio dignissim.
</td>
</font>
</tr>
</table>
<p>
<!-- end text table -->
```

4. Now you'll add another table to the content area, a bordered table to add color and break up space:

```
<!-- begin sub-table -->
<table border=1 cellpadding=5 cellspacing=0 width=445>
```

```
<tr>
<td bgcolor="#00CCFF" width=200>
<font face=arial,helvetica>
Nam liber tempor cum soluta nobis eleifend option congue nihil.
Accumsan et iusto odio dignissim qui blandit!
</font>
</td>
<td bgcolor="#FFFFFF" width=200 align=middle>
<font face=arial,helvetica>
<i>Accumsan et iusto odio dignissim qui blandit! Nam liber
tempor!</i>
</td>
</tr>
</table>
<!-- end sub-table -->
```

5. In the following cell of the main table, add the right navigation as follows:

```
<!-- begin right navigation -->
<img src="images/tn-logo.gif" width=125 height=94>
<p>
<img src="images/tn-slog.gif" width=125 height=50>
<p>
<a href="about.htm">
<img src="images/tn-abt.gif" width=125 height=25 border=0></a>
<p>
<a href="news.htm">
<img src="images/tn-news.gif" width=125 height=25 border=0></a>
<p>
<a href="fares.htm">
<img src="images/tn-fare.gif" width=125 height=25 border=0></a>
<p>
<a href="res.htm">
<img src="images/tn-res.gif" width=125 height=25 border=0></a>
<!-- end right navigation -->
```

6. Check your work against the full page of code:

```
<html>
<!-- begin header -->
<head>
<title> Tour de Force</title>
</head>
<body bgcolor="#FFFFFF" text="#000000" link="#333399"
vlink="#00CCFF" alink="FFFFFF">
<!-- end header -->
<!-- begin main table -->
<table width=600 border=0>
<tr>
<td valign=top width=450>
<img src="images/menu.jpg" width="450" height="27" border="0"
usemap="#menu">
<p>
```

```
<map name="menu">
<area shape="rect" coords="0,0,52,25" href="air.htm">
<area shape="rect" coords="54,0,93,25" href="train.htm">
<area shape="rect" coords="95,0,139,25" href="cruise.htm">
<area shape="rect" coords="141,0,212,25" href="food.htm">
<area shape="rect" coords="214,0,270,25" href="shop.htm">
<area shape="rect" coords="272,0,334,25" href="rec.htm">
<area shape="rect" coords="336,0,394,25" href="get.htm">
<area shape="rect" coords="396,0,448,25" href="search.htm">
<area shape="default" nohref>
</map>
<!-- begin text table -->
<table border=0 width=430 cellpadding=5 cellspacing=0>
<tr>
<td>
<font face=arial,helvetica color="#333399" size=5>
<b>Full <i>Force</i> Travel!</b></font>
</td>
</tr>
<tr>
<td valign=left>
<img src="images/tn-eur.gif" width=125 height=121 border=0>
</td>
<td>
<font face=arial,helvetica>
Europe in focus! Duis autem vel eum iriure dolor in hendrerit in
vulputate velit esse molestie consequat. Accumsan et iusto odio
dignissim qui blandit praesent luptatum zzril. Accumsan et
iusto odio dignissim.
</td>
</font>
</tr>
</table>
<p>
<!-- end text table -->
<!-- begin sub-table -->
<table border=1 cellpadding=5 cellspacing=0 width=445>
<tr>
<td bgcolor="#00CCFF" width=200>
<font face=arial,helvetica>
Nam liber tempor cum soluta nobis eleifend option congue nihil.
Accumsan et iusto odio dignissim qui blandit!
</font>
</td>
<td bgcolor="#FFFFFF" width=200 align=middle>
<font face=arial,helvetica>
<i>Accumsan et iusto odio dignissim qui blandit! Nam liber
tempor!</i>
</td>
</tr>
</table>
```

```
<!-- end sub-table -->
</td>
<td valign=top width=150>
<!-- begin right navigation -->
<img src="images/tn-logo.gif" width=125 height=94>
<p>
<img src="images/tn-slog.gif" width=125 height=50>
<p>
<a href="about.htm">
<img src="images/tn-abt.gif" width=125 height=25 border=0></a>
<p>
<a href="news.htm">
<img src="images/tn-news.gif" width=125 height=25 border=0></a>
<p>
<a href="fares.htm">
<img src="images/tn-fare.gif" width=125 height=25 border=0></a>
<p>
<a href="res.htm">
<img src="images/tn-res.gif" width=125 height=25 border=0></a>
<!-- end right navigation -->
</td>
</tr>
</table>
</body>
</html>
```

7. Save the file as index.htm.

8. View the file in your browser. The results should match Figure 11.2.

Figure 11.2.

*Top-margin naviga-
tion created with
table layout.*

As you work on more
complex tables, the
need for comment
tagging becomes
more important.
There is more code,
the pages can appear
confusing, and the
comment tags assist
you as guides to
finding your way to
specific areas quickly.

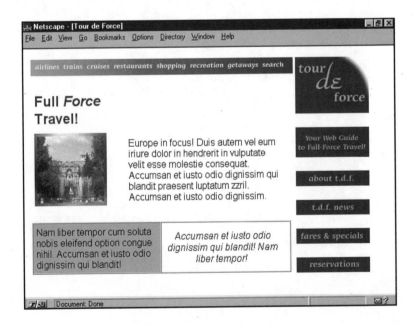

DESIGN NOTE: Client-side maps tend to be more user-friendly because the URL appears in the browser status bar as opposed to only the map's coordinates.

Top Navigation: Frames

In the following task, you'll learn how to complete a similar layout using frames. The advantage in this case is to create a navigation area that remains static throughout a visit to the Web site. Instead of pages reloading information, the top frame stays in place. Not only does this allow for a constant reference point, but it also increases load-times of pages because the focus is now on loading only content, and not navigation.

CAUTION: Don't make the mistake of creating a small frame for a lot of information. In other words, if you're making a frame that's only 75 pixels in height, make sure your content fits inside that restriction with some white space to cushion it. Otherwise, you end up forcing people to read data in a tiny space. Not only is this unattractive from a design standpoint, but it's also impractical and inconvenient for your Web site visitors.

DESIGN NOTE: White space is a design fundamental and a serious necessity. The eye needs the freedom to relax and absorb information without clutter and noise. White space offers the eye respite; otherwise, the site feels cramped and encourages the viewer to leave.

 Creating the Top-Navigation Frameset

In this case, the focus is on a frame-based, top-navigation interface.

1. Begin with the following syntax:

```
<html>
<head>
<title>TDF Frame top</title>
</head>
</html>
```

2. Add the frameset syntax, giving enough room for the graphic and additional white space. I've chosen a total of 75 pixels:

```
<frameset rows=75,*>
</frameset>
```

3. Now add the frame files:

```
<frame src="menu.htm" name=menu>
<frame src="content.htm" name=contents>
```

4. Save the frameset as frame-t.htm.

NOTE: In this frameset, I've not used any attributes to control scrolling or resize. This allows for a scroll to appear, if necessary. I can also resize the page to a full screen, hiding the menu and providing maximum viewing area on the page.

TASK Creating the Menu Page

Now that you have created the frame, the first step is to create the navigation, or menu page.

1. The following forms the shell for the menu page:

```
<html>
<head>
<title>TDF top menu</title>
</head>
<body bgcolor="#FFFFFF" text="#000000" link="#333399"
vlink="#00CCFF" alink="FFFFFF">
</body>
</html>
```

2. Add the map image and the coordinates just as you did in the top-margin navigation table example:

```
<center>
<img src="images/menu.jpg" width="450" height="27" border="0"
usemap="#menu">
</center>
```

```
<map name="menu">
<area shape="rect" coords="0,0,52,25" href="air.htm">
<area shape="rect" coords="54,0,93,25" href="train.htm">
<area shape="rect" coords="95,0,139,25" href="cruise.htm">
<area shape="rect" coords="141,0,212,25" href="food.htm">
<area shape="rect" coords="214,0,270,25" href="shop.htm">
<area shape="rect" coords="272,0,334,25" href="rec.htm">
<area shape="rect" coords="336,0,394,25" href="get.htm">
<area shape="rect" coords="396,0,448,25" href="search.htm">
<area shape="default" nohref>
</map>
```

3. Save the results as `menu.htm`.

TASK Creating the Content Page

The next step in creating a fully visible framed interface is to add the content page, as follows:

1. To create the actual content page, begin with the following:

```
<!-- begin header -->
<head>
<title> Tour de Force</title>
</head>
<body bgcolor="#FFFFFF" text="#000000" link="#333399"
vlink="#00CCFF" alink="FFFFFF">
<!-- end header -->
</body>
</html>
```

2. I've chosen to use a straightforward (non-table) layout for the content page. To ensure that I create margins, I've included blockquotes:

```
<blockquote>
</blockquote>
```

3. Now you can add the images and dummy text between the blockquoted areas:

```
<blockquote>
<font face=arial,helvetica color="#333399" size=5>
<b>Full <i>Force</i> Travel!</b></font>
<p>
<img src="images/tn-eur.gif" width=125 height=121 border=0
hspace=10  align=left>
<font face=arial,helvetica>
Europe in focus! Duis autem vel eum iriure dolor in hendrerit in
vulputate velit esse molestie consequat. Accumsan et iusto odio
dignissim qui blandit praesent luptatum zzril. Accumsan et
iusto odio dignissim.
<p>
```

```
Nam liber tempor cum soluta nobis eleifend option congue nihil.
Accumsan et iusto odio dignissim qui blandit!  ccumsan et iusto
odio dignissim qui blandit praesent luptatum zzril. Accumsan et
iusto odio dignissim.
<p>
</blockquote>
```

4. Now save the file as content.htm.

5. Open the frame-t.htm file in your browser and view the results.

6. Match your work to Figure 11.3.

Figure 11.3.

*Top-margin layout
created with a
bordered frame.*

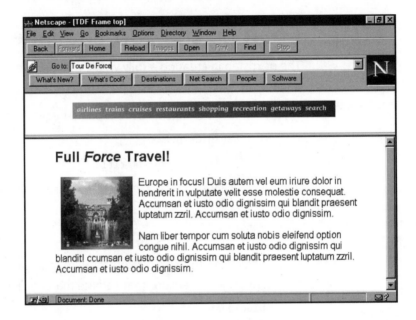

7. With your cursor, grab the frame's horizontal bar and move it up. Notice that you now have hidden the navigation and allowed for maximum viewing area, as shown in Figure 11.4.

Figure 11.4.

The frame bar can be moved to hide the navigation for maximum page viewing space.

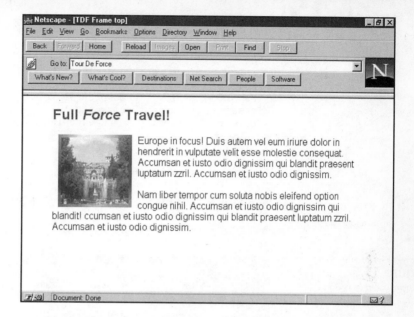

TASK

Creating a Borderless Top-Navigation Frame

In order to accomplish a borderless effect, simply change the frameset attributes. There is no need to revise the content and menu pages; they will serve perfectly in the borderless design.

1. Begin with the shell:

```
<html>
<head>
<title>TDF Frame top: Borderless</title>
</head>
</html>
```

2. Add the frameset, with borderless attributes:

```
<frameset rows=75,* frameborder=0 framespacing=0 border=0>
</frameset>
```

3. Include the frame syntax:

```
<frame src="menu.htm" name=menu>
<frame src="content.htm" name=contents>
```

4. The final frameset looks like this:

```
<html>
<head>
<title>TDF Frame top: Borderless</title>
</head>
<frameset rows=75,* frameborder=0 framespacing=0 border=0>
<frame src="menu.htm" name=menu>
<frame src="content.htm" name=contents>
</frameset>
</html>
```

5. Save the file as frame-tb.htm.

6. View the borderless frame design in your browser.

7. Match the results to Figure 11.5.

Figure 11.5.
Borderless top-frame navigation.

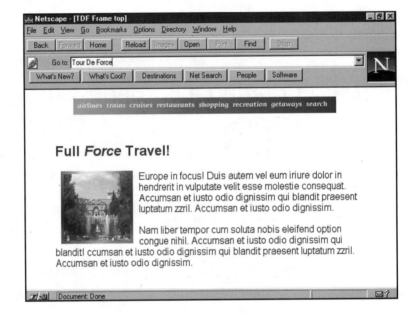

Bottom-Based Navigation

Bottom-based options are perhaps the most common navigation system. In this section, you'll learn to create them using tables and frames, instead of standard HTML methods. This gives you maximum flexibility when deciding how to approach a given Web project.

When using tables to control bottom navigation, I like to remember the lessons learned regarding interface. How can you best achieve an attractive design? Tables give you a lot of control over individual elements, such as graphics, text, and navigation. Therefore, think of the entire page as an integrated whole. A good example that clarifies this is Atomic Media's site featured in Chapter 9, "Real-Time Example: Atomic Media—A Real-Life Interface Using Tables and Frames." The bottom navigation works in concert with the other page elements to create a true interface.

For the frame-based option, the advantages are similar to top-based navigation. First, your navigation is fixed. It can be on any page you want it to be without reloading, and it maintains a consistent presence even as you switch from content page to content page. Then, you also have the flexibility of creating visually available *or* borderless frames. And, as with a frame-based, top alternative, a visually available frame gives you the option of offering resizing for maximum screen control.

Bottom-Margin Table-Based Navigation

An alternative to the top-margin navigation is a bottom-margin option. This task shows you how.

1. Begin with the shell syntax:

```
<html>
<head>
<title>Tour De Force Bottom Navigation</title>
</head>
<body bgcolor="#FFFFFF" text="#000000" link="#333399"
vlink="#00CCFF" alink="FFFFFF">
</body>
</html>
```

2. Add the main table:

```
<!-- begin main table -->
<table border=0 width=600>
<tr>
<td width=150>
</td>
<td valign=top>
</td>
</table>
```

3. Starting with the first table cell, add the right-based navigation:

```
<img src="images/tn-logo.gif" width=125 height=94>
<p>
<img src="images/tn-slog.gif" width=125 height=50>
<p>
<a href="about.htm">
<img src="images/tn-abt.gif" width=125 height=25 border=0></a>
<p>
<a href="news.htm">
<img src="images/tn-news.gif" width=125 height=25 border=0></a>
<p>
<a href="fares.htm">
<img src="images/tn-fare.gif" width=125 height=25 border=0></a>
<p>
<a href="res.htm">
<img src="images/tn-res.gif" width=125 height=25 border=0></a>
```

4. In the second cell, you'll nest a table:

```
<!-- begin text table -->
<table border=0 width=430 cellpadding=5 cellspacing=0>
<tr>
<td valign=top width=430>
</td>
</tr>
<tr>
<td align=left>
</td>
</tr>
</table>
<!-- end text table -->
```

5. Then add the data for the individual cells within that table:

```
<!-- begin text table -->
<table border=0 width=430 cellpadding=5 cellspacing=0>
<tr>
<td valign=top width=430>
<font face=arial,helvetica color="#333399" size=5>
<b>Full <i>Force</i> Travel!</b></font>
</td>
</tr>
<tr>
<td align=left>
<img src="images/tn-eur.gif" width=125 height=121 border=0
hspace=10 align=right>
<font face=arial,helvetica>
Europe in focus! Duis autem vel eum iriure dolor in hendrerit in
vulputate velit esse molestie consequat. Accumsan et iusto odio
dignissim qui blandit praesent luptatum zzril. Accumsan et
iusto odio dignissim. Nam liber tempor cum soluta nobis eleifend
option congue nihil imperdiet doming id quod mazim placerat
```

```
facer possim assum. Accumsan et iusto odio dignissim qui blandit
praesent luptatum zzril delenit augue duis dolore te feugait
nulla facilisi.
<p>
Ccumsan et iusto odio dignissim. Nam liber tempor cum soluta
nobis eleifend option congue nihil imperdiet doming id quod
mazim placerat facer possim assum. Accumsan et iusto odio
dignissim qui blandit praesent luptatum zzril
</td>
</font>
</tr>
</table>
<!-- end text table -->
```

6. Now add another table, this time for the navigation:

```
<!-- begin bottom navigation -->
<table>
<tr>
<td valign=top width=450>
<img src="images/menu.jpg" width=450 height=27 border=0>
</td>
</tr>
</table>
<!-- end bottom navigation -->
```

7. Close the main table. The full code is as follows:

```
<html>
<!-- begin header -->
<head>
<title>Tour De Force Bottom Navigation</title>
</head>
<body bgcolor="#FFFFFF" text="#000000" link="#333399"
vlink="#00CCFF" alink="FFFFFF">
<!-- end header -->
<!-- begin main table -->
<table border=0 width=600>
<tr>
<td width=150>
<img src="images/tn-logo.gif" width=125 height=94>
<p>
<img src="images/tn-slog.gif" width=125 height=50>
<p>
<a href="about.htm">
<img src="images/tn-abt.gif" width=125 height=25 border=0></a>
<p>
<a href="news.htm">
<img src="images/tn-news.gif" width=125 height=25 border=0></a>
<p>
<a href="fares.htm">
<img src="images/tn-fare.gif" width=125 height=25 border=0></a>
<p>
<a href="res.htm">
```

```
<img src="images/tn-res.gif" width=125 height=25 border=0></a>
</td>
<td valign=top>
<!-- begin text table -->
<table border=0 width=430 cellpadding=5 cellspacing=0>
<tr>
<td valign=top width=430>
<font face=arial,helvetica color="#333399" size=5>
<b>Full <i>Force</i> Travel!</b></font>
</td>
</tr>
<tr>
<td align=left>
<img src="images/tn-eur.gif" width=125 height=121 border=0
hspace=10 align=right>
<font face=arial,helvetica>
Europe in focus! Duis autem vel eum iriure dolor in hendrerit in
vulputate velit esse molestie consequat. Accumsan et iusto odio
dignissim qui blandit praesent luptatum zzril. Accumsan et iusto
odio dignissim. Nam liber tempor cum soluta nobis eleifend
option conguenihil imperdiet doming id quod mazim
placerat facer possim assum. ccumsan et iusto odio dignissim qui
blandit praesent luptatum zzril delenit augue duis dolore te
feugait nulla facilisi.
<p>
Ccumsan et iusto odio dignissim. Nam liber tempor cum soluta
nobis eleifend option congue nihil imperdiet doming id quod
mazim placerat facer possim assum. Accumsan et iusto odio
dignissim qui blandit praesent luptatum zzril
</td>
</font>
</tr>
</table>
<!-- end text table -->
<!-- begin bottom navigation -->
<table>
<tr>
<td valign=top width=450>
<img src="images/menu.jpg" width=450 height=27 border=0>
</td>
</tr>
</table>
<!-- end bottom navigation -->
</table>
</body>
</html>
```

8. Save the file as `index2.htm`.

9. View the file in your browser. Your work should match Figure 11.6.

Figure 11.6.

A bottom-based table layout. Note the symbiotic relationship of graphics, text, and navigation.

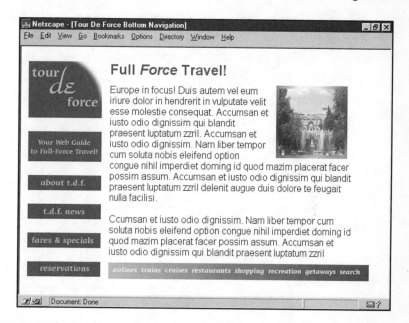

> **NOTE:** Although I'm using nested tables to achieve my design, there are many other ways to lay out interface and control navigation. You can choose to stack tables, or arrange information within individual table cells. As always, I encourage you to venture out on your own—as you feel comfortable—and try a variety of different techniques.

Creating Frame-Based Bottom Navigation

The following tasks focus on creating frame-based bottom navigation. The most important thing to remember is to control the overall size of the layout. This can be done using dynamic or fixed values for row attributes. Bear in mind that if you're going to fix the row heights to achieve a single-screen design, you take into account all of your elements so as not to overstep the 480 pixel-height absolute maximum.

 ## The Bottom-Based Navigation Frameset

To create bottom navigation using frames, start with a frameset.

1. Begin with the shell:

```
<html>
<head>
<title>TDF Frame bottom</title>
</head>
</html>
```

2. Add the frameset. Note that I've used a dynamic attribute for the top row, and a specified pixel width for the bottom:

```
<frameset rows=*,75>
</frameset>
```

3. Place the frame links inside the frameset:

```
<frame src="content.htm" name=contents>
<frame src="menu.htm" name=menu>
```

4. Save the file as frame-b.htm.

   Because the file calls for the same menu and contents you've already created, there's no need to add additional files to complete the example.

5. View the file in your browser.

6. The results should match Figure 11.7. Because there's resizing available, you can resize the frame to occlude the navigation and achieve maximum viewing space results, as shown in Figure 11.8.

Figure 11.7.

Frame-based bottom navigation.

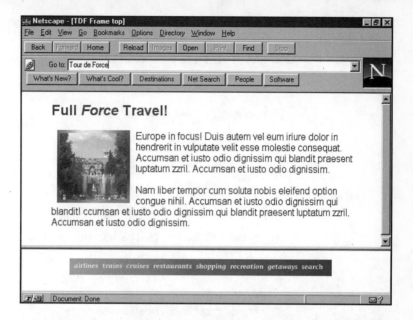

Figure 11.8.

Move the frame border down to obscure the navigation; maximum viewing space is achieved.

Creating a Borderless Frameset for Bottom Navigation

In this case, you'll simply argue for borderless attributes in the frameset.

1. Begin with the shell:

```
<html>
<head>
<title>TDF Frame bottom</title>
</head>
</html>
```

2. Add the frameset with borderless syntax:

```
<frameset rows=*,75 frameborder=0 framespacing=0 border=0>
</frameset>
```

3. Place the frame tags and attributes within the frameset tags:

```
<frame src="content.htm" name=contents>
<frame src="menu.htm" name=menu>
```

4. Save the file as frame-bb.htm.

5. View the file.

6. Enjoy the borderless results, as shown in Figure 11.9.

Figure 11.9.

Borderless bottom-based navigation. The navigation bar remains static as you move through the site.

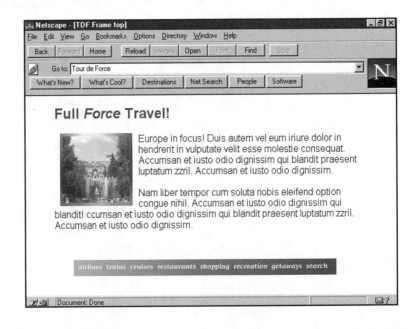

NOTE: At first glance, the borderless bottom-based frame example looks just like a standard HTML page with no frames. However, should you build content for the rest of the site and test the navigation, you'll see that it remains static while the upper portion changes. It's an interesting new treatment for a standard look.

Workshop Wrap-Up

I've tried to subtly sneak in the fact that the code you've been working on, particularly code related to tables, has become more complex in the last two chapters. My sense is that you've probably already noticed this. My hopes are that it hasn't made the tasks and understanding of the concepts harder, but rather a bit more challenging as you move toward advanced layout design.

You now have skills to allow you to code navigation for all margins and create a variety of interfaces with navigation for small or large sites; there is also a significant amount of design sense beginning to accumulate in your personal base of knowledge.

Because the advancement of your skills is about to be tested, I highly recommend going back over those areas that might have been trouble spots for you. Redo the tasks, visit any tutorial sites given, refer to the appendixes for examples of legal tags. The stronger your skills, the easier it will be to understand the advanced application of table layout and navigation that will be offered in Chapter 12, "Multiple Menus and Non-Linear Navigation."

Next Steps

In the next chapter, you're going to examine multiple menus and non-linear navigation. In order to learn these advanced techniques, I'm going to deconstruct the interface and layout of a real-life site. You'll see many of the skills you've already learned put into action, be asked to learn some concepts and techniques that break traditional thinking, and move into one of the most challenging aspects of designing for the Web: working in a non-linear environment.

Other chapters of immediate interest include

❏ Chapter 13, "Non-Static and Multi-Framed Navigation"

❏ Chapter 14, "Adding Interactive and Dynamic Content"

❏ Chapter 15, "Real-Time Example: Interactivity in Action—Core-Wave's Glass Bead Game"

Q&A

Q: I notice that you place the menu coordinates immediately below the image used for the map. Is that where the coordinate information must be?

A: Not at all. In fact, you can place the coordinate information anywhere you like. Two good choices for this are directly under the mapped image, as I have used, or in a distinct section at the bottom of the page.

Q: Can I use tables to lay out multiple images or text options in a framed menu section?

A: Yes, that's an excellent method for controlling graphic alignment within a framed section. The issue to be concerned with is to leave plenty of white space and plan carefully to not have the graphic and text elements in your small frames overlap. If you're designing at high-screen resolution, you may think everything just fits fine. Drop down to 640x480, and guess what? The design is cramped and a scrollbar is forced to accommodate the data that doesn't fit into your frame. Check your work carefully.

Q: Do I have to use these areas for navigation? I've seen bottom and top frames used for advertising—and just for fun, too.

A: Use the areas any way you'd like; you're not limited to what you've learned here. The prominent theme in this section is navigation; use what you've learned in any way you see fit.

Q: I've seen top-aligned navigation fit snugly against the top border of the browser. How can I do this?

A: Microsoft's Internet Explorer allows you to control top margins, and, as you've already read in Chapter 3, " In Vogue: Cascading Style Sheets," style sheets enable you to do this, as well. For standard HTML top margin control in Internet Explorer, place the attribute and numeric value `topmargin=0` in the `<body>` syntax. This will force your page to the topmost margin. Unfortunately, Netscape Navigator 3.0 and earlier browsers do not support this feature.

twelve
Multiple Menus and Non-Linear Navigation

One of the most potent aspects of the Web is that it is a non-linear, interactive medium. Unlike newspapers, radio, and television, the Web isn't built on a page-forward, page-back delivery system. A newspaper is read left to right. Radio and TV provide information in a package and serve it to you with little involvement from you. Your only current, interactive choices with radio and TV are to turn them on, change the volume, switch the channel, and turn them off.

As the Web and related technologies converge, there will probably be a change in this dominant, non-linear arrangement. But for now, instead of the limitation of choice, there are many choices, as you've seen with navigation. And, with the hypertextual basis of the Web, there is the non-linear aspect.

From a conceptual standpoint, linearity is like your morning drive to work. Usually you take the same road, because you know it gets you there quickly, the traffic is lighter than another route, and its rhythms are familiar to you. Non-linearity would be taking a different route to work every day: turning down an unfamiliar road just for the heck of it, maybe even going in a completely different direction for a while because the scenery is so attractive.

This example helps you see how linearity and non-linearity both have advantages and disadvantages. It's no accident that Western society has been based on the linear. In order to survive and thrive, the straightest, most effective route has been necessary. It's worked to an advantage in many ways; almost everything in this culture is done quickly, and often quite efficiently. But what is often lost is the opportunity for new vistas and possibilities that can be found when that side road is explored.

Philosophically, this points to the possibility that a combination of linear and non-linear methods might be the strongest way to approach a problem. If you have a bit of extra time, you might just take a different route to work that morning. Who knows what the results will be?

Because all of us have been accustomed to the linear, the non-linear tangents that exist on the Web provide a challenge to the Web designer, through hyperlinks that take us off one site and drop us in the middle of another one, or multiple choice navigation options that make each drive down the information highway a different experience. Each user must harness the tangential nature of the Web in order to express a given site's intent and logic to the visitor. However, making a Web site linear is denying the possibilities of the Web, and the unusual places and experiences it can offer.

A Case in Point

In this chapter, I'm going to show you a highly successful method of harnessing and taking advantage of the opportunities of non-linear structures and interactivity. It may be a familiar example to those of you who have followed my work because I use it often to demonstrate non-linear, choice-driven design.

The Tucson Weekly remains the best example on the Web regarding non-linear navigation. In fact, the online publication has actually expanded its interactivity as time has progressed. Perhaps this publication's early entrance into the Web medium, combined with the innovative mind of its designer, Wil Gerken, have given it the edge over other publications and Web sites that have attempted (but have difficulty in achieving) non-linearity. The intention is to offer the inner workings to you, walk you through the task of building one of the Tucson's Weekly's pages, and showing you why the navigation is so extraordinary in providing the Web visitor with an effective site that captures, but does not control, the underlying tangential environment of the Web.

Multiple Navigation

The primary way the Tucson Weekly has achieved this "capture without control" concept is by providing numerous methods of navigating the site, as well as offering ways of jumping off to other related, but out-of-house sites.

Here's an overview of the paper's structure and navigation and what it accomplishes:

❏ **The home page.** The home page, which rests "above" the splash page, offers detailed graphic and text media links to past issues, information for new users, advertisers, staff pages, feedback, and its online parent, DesertNet. This page can be reached from the internal section page via a hyperlinked graphic (see Figure 12.1).

Figure 12.1.
The Tucson Weekly home page.

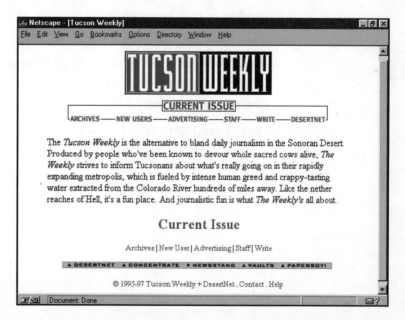

❏ **Splash page entrance.** The splash page is the main access to the paper and its sections. It changes each week to accommodate the current cover (see Figure 12.2).

Figure 12.2.
A Tucson Weekly splash page.

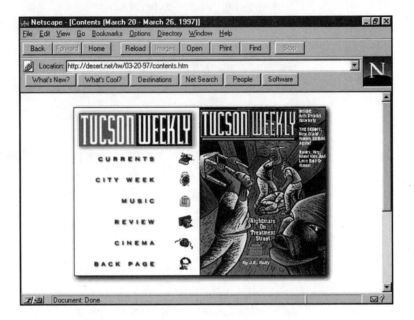

❏ **Table-based right-margin navigation.** The primary sections of the paper are offered up in a right-margin image map, so no matter what section of the paper you are in, you can jump to another section (see Figure 12.3).

❏ **Bottom-based text option of right-margin navigation.** The primary sections are reachable through a text option at the bottom of the page (see Figure 12.4).

❏ **Text-based links to internal pages.** Sections are broken down into links to articles and related online forums within the Weekly site (see Figure 12.5).

Figure 12.3.
The right-margin image map.

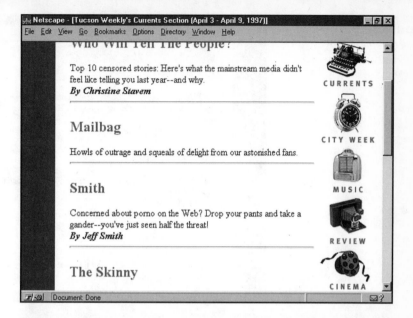

Figure 12.4.
Bottom-based text options.

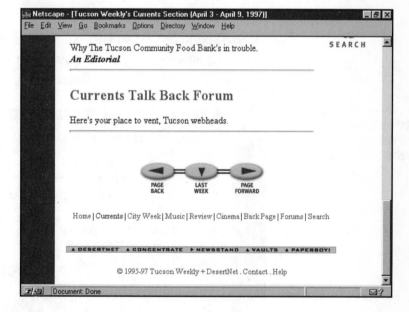

Figure 12.5.

A section page with hypertext links to articles.

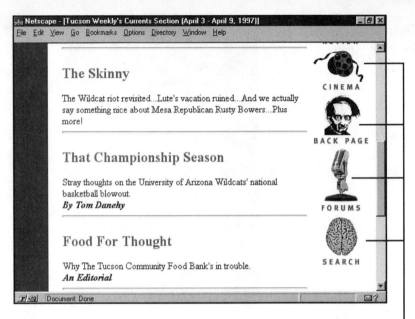

Text-based links to internal pages

❏ **Internal page links.** Text links within articles offer doorways to the rest of the Internet. This offers related information on a given subject discussed with the article (see Figure 12.6).

Figure 12.6.

An article with hypertext links to the rest of the Net.

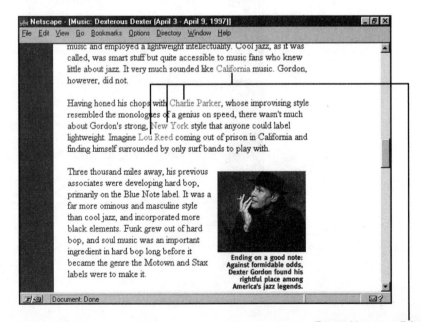

External hypertext links

❏ **Internal page main menu.** This menu is the shining glory of the Weekly's navigation. It offers a linear option in the guise of page-forward and page-back. It adds non-linear tangents to last week's issue and next week's issue (if you're in an archived section of the paper), as well as a "jump" to the current week's edition. No matter where you are in terms of time and space, the date of the publication, or the place of the publication, you can get to any other place in the paper within a few clicks of the mouse (see Figure 12.7).

❏ **Hypertext links of interest.** Several rotating links of interest are provided at the bottom of each page. For example, in the Cinema section, you'll find links to the Cinema Forum and the Film Vault—a searchable index of films (see Chapter 16, "Using Tables for Graphic Control"). The Music section provides similar links to music areas of interest (see Figure 12.7).

❏ **DesertNet's menu.** This is a side-by-side graphic menu to take you to other offerings of this unparalleled online publishing company, including DesertNet's home page and sister projects (see Figure 12.7).

Figure 12.7.
The main menu, links of interest, and DesertNet menu combo.

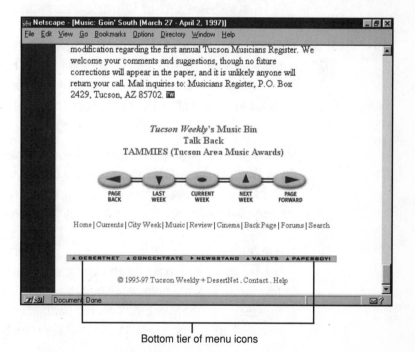

Bottom tier of menu icons

❏ **Advertising.** At the top of Tucson Weekly pages local as well as national advertisers are provided with ad space (see Figure 12.8).

Figure 12.8.
Advertising on the Tucson Weekly.

Advertising at the top of the page

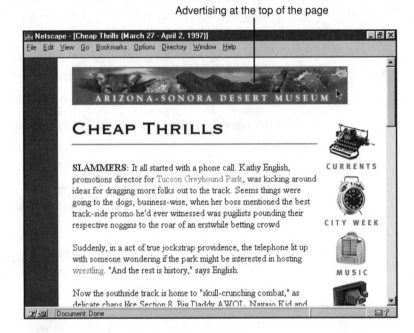

This may seem like a lot to absorb. However, there is little here that you have not already worked on if you've completed this book in a linear fashion. In other words, if you've followed the book chapter by chapter, you've been exposed to almost all of the techniques to pull off working on these pages, which is exactly what you're about to do.

Splash pages, table-based layouts, image maps, standard navigation, advertising, and comment tagging are already under your belt. You'll be learning to think about navigation for large amounts of data, maximizing options, and putting together pages that are not only functional, but also attractive.

NOTE: For the purposes of this book, I've taken the liberty of removing JavaScript and other elements that relate specifically to the mechanical processing of the Weekly. I've also changed code to accommodate this book's learning structure. The focus here is on building the pages and accommodating the multiple, non-linear navigation in a mock-up fashion. Therefore, some links and functionality won't work or do the same things that the live version of the publication do. Please visit the Weekly in its full glory at http://www.tucsonweekly.com/tw/.

TASK A Multiple Menu Splash Page

I'll begin by demonstrating the Weekly's splash page.

1. Begin with the familiar shell syntax:

```
<html>
<head>
<title>Contents (April 3 - April 9, 1997)</title>
</head>
<body bgcolor="#ffffff" link="#d60017" vlink="#29295a"
alink="#000000" text="#000000">
</body>
</html>
```

2. Add the splash images, noting that the one on the left is an image map.

```
<center>
<img src="images/contents.gif" border=0 usemap="#ContentsMap"
alt="Contents Image Map" width=225 height=302></a>
<a href="cover.htm">
<img src="images/cover.gif" border=0 alt="Cover" width=227
height=302></a>
<p>
</center>
```

3. Add the map coordinates:

```
<map name="ContentsMap">
<area shape="rect" coords="0,0,224,77" href="../twhome.htm">
<area shape="rect" coords="0,78,224,107" href="currents.htm">
<area shape="rect" coords="0,108,224,144" href="cityweek.htm">
<area shape="rect" coords="0,145,224,178" href="music.htm">
<area shape="rect" coords="0,179,224,213" href="review.htm">
<area shape="rect" coords="0,214,224,249" href="cinema.htm">
<area shape="rect" coords="0,250,224,301" href="backpage.htm">
<area shape="rect" coords="0,629,97,718" href="search.htm">
</map>
```

4. Now you'll add the Last Week navigation:

```
<center>
<img src="images/last3.gif" width=74 height=60>
<p>
```

5. Next, place the text-based navigation within your HTML:

```
<font size=2>
<a href="../twhome.htm">Home</a> |
<a href="currents.htm">Currents</a> |
<a href="cityweek.htm">City Week</a> |
<a href="music.htm">Music</a> |
<a href="review.htm">Review</a> |
<a href="cinema.htm">Cinema</a> |
<a href="backpage.htm">Back Page</a> |
<a href="http://bbs.desert.net">Forums</a> |
<a href="search.htm">Search</a>
</font>
<p>
<br>
```

6. Now you'll add DesertNet's main menu:

```
<nobr>
<a href="http://desert.net/">
<img src="images/desnet1.gif" alt="DesertNet" border=0 width=95
height=11></a>
<a href="http://desert.net/concentrate/">
<img src="images/concentrate1.gif" alt=" Concentrate" border=0
width=110 height=11></a>
<a href="http://desert.net/newsstand/">
<img src="images/newsstand2.gif" alt=" Newsstand" border=0
width=97 height=11></a>
<a href="http://desert.net/vaults/">
<img src="http://desert.net/images/vaults1.gif" alt=" Vaults"
border=0 width=67 height=11></a>
<a href="http://desert.net/htbin/buildindex.pl">
<img src="http://desert.net/images/paperboy1.gif" alt="
Paperboy!" border=0 width=95 height=11></a>
</nobr>
<p>
```

DESIGN NOTE: The no-break tag <nobr> is a powerful HTML tag that keeps graphics and text elements next to one another without breaking the row. In this example, there are five graphics placed snugly next to one another. The no-break tag keeps them on the same horizon line. Even if someone resizes the browser, the graphic line will not break. It's an effective design tool for maintaining the integrity of a layout. More information on the <nobr> tag is available in Appendix B, "HTML Quick Reference."

DesertNet can be visited at http:// www.desert.net/.

7. Finish the code with the copyright, contact, and help information:

```
<font size=-1>
<a href="http://desert.net/">&#169; 1995-97 Tucson Weekly +
DesertNet</a> .
<a href="http://desert.net/contact_publications.htmlx">Contact
</a> .
<a href="http://desert.net/faq_publications.htmlx">Help</a>
<br>
</font>
</center>
<!-- End Footer -->
```

8. Compare your work to the final code. I've included the entire stretch of code so you can get a good sense of how a fully designed page appears.

```
<html>
<head>
<title>Contents (April 3 - April 9, 1997)</title>
</head>
<body bgcolor="#ffffff" link="#d60017" vlink="#29295a"
alink="#000000" text="#000000">
<center>
<img src="images/contents.gif" border=0 usemap="#ContentsMap"
alt="Contents Image Map" width=225 height=302></a><a
href="cover.htm"> <img src="images/cover.gif" border=0
alt="Cover" width=227 height=302></a>
<p>
</center>
<map name="ContentsMap">
<area shape="rect" coords="0,0,224,77" href="../twhome.htm">
<area shape="rect" coords="0,78,224,107" href="currents.htm">
<area shape="rect" coords="0,108,224,144" href="cityweek.htm">
<area shape="rect" coords="0,145,224,178" href="music.htm">
<area shape="rect" coords="0,179,224,213" href="review.htm">
<area shape="rect" coords="0,214,224,249" href="cinema.htm">
<area shape="rect" coords="0,250,224,301" href="backpage.htm">
<area shape="rect" coords="0,629,97,718" href="search.htm">
</map>
<!-- begin footer -->
<center>
```

```
<img src="images/last3.gif" width=74 height=60>
<p>
<font size=2>
<a href="../twhome.htm">Home</a> |
<a href="currents.htm">Currents</a> |
<a href="cityweek.htm">City Week</a> |
<a href="music.htm">Music</a> |
<a href="review.htm">Review</a> |
<a href="cinema.htm">Cinema</a> |
<a href="backpage.htm">Back Page</a> |
<a href="http://bbs.desert.net">Forums</a> |
<a href="search.htm">Search</a>
</font>
<p>
<br>
<nobr>
<a href="http://desert.net/">
<img src="images/desnet1.gif" alt="DesertNet" border=0 width=95
height=11></a>
<a href="http://desert.net/concentrate/">
<img src="images/concentrate1.gif" alt=" Concentrate" border=0
width=110 height=11></a>
<a href="http://desert.net/newsstand/">
<img src="images/newsstand2.gif" alt=" Newsstand" border=0
width=97 height=11></a>
<a href="http://desert.net/vaults/">
<img src="http://desert.net/images/vaults1.gif" alt=" Vaults"
border=0 width=67 height=11></a>
<a href="http://desert.net/htbin/buildindex.pl">
<img src="http://desert.net/images/paperboy1.gif"
alt=" Paperboy!" border=0 width=95 height=11></a>
</nobr>
<p>
<font size=-1>
<a href="http://desert.net/">&#169; 1995-97 Tucson Weekly +
DesertNet</a> .
<a href="http://desert.net/contact_publications.htmlx">Contact
</a> .
<a href="http://desert.net/faq_publications.htmlx">Help</a>
<br>
</font>
</center>
<!-- End Footer -->
```

9. Save the file as `tw-sp.htm`.

10. View the results in your browser. They should match Figure 12.9.

Figure 12.9.

The "mock" results of the splash page.

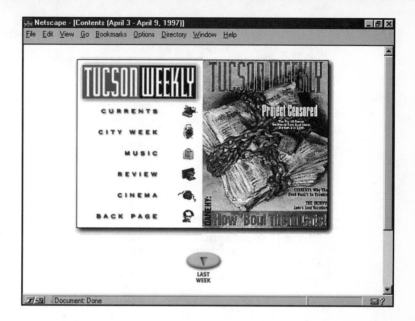

TASK

Building the Table and Navigation for a Section Page

This task will walk you through a standard Tucson Weekly section page. The layout uses stacked tables. You'll add them one by one along with the comment tagging, text, and images.

1. Begin with the shell HTML:

```
<html>
<head>
<title>Tucson Weekly's Currents Section (April 3 - April 9,
1997)</title>
</head>
<body background="images/twback.gif" bgcolor="#ffffff"
link="#d60017" vlink="#29295a" alink="#000000" text="#000000">
</body>
</html>
```

2. Add the date header. This includes the graphic hyperlink to the Weekly's home page and the date of the publication:

```
<!-- Begin Date Header -->
<table border=0 width=100% cellspacing=0 cellpadding=0
<tr>
<td valign=top align=left>
```

```
<a href="../twhome.htm">
<img src="images/twlogo3.gif" border=0 width=108 height=31
alt=""></a>
</td>
<td valign=top align=right>
<b>April 3 - April 9, 1997</b>
</td>
</tr>
</table>
<p>
<!-- End Date Header -->
```

3. Add the section header, referred to as Contents Bar in this example. This includes the graphic icon image and graphic name header of the section:

```
<!-- Begin Contents Bar -->
<table border=0 width=100% cellspacing=0 cellpadding=0>
<tr>
<td valign=top align=left>
<img src="images/type.gif" width=45 height=50 alt="">
<img src="images/currbar.gif" hspace=30 width=437 height=38
alt="Currents">
</td>
</tr>
</table>
<p>
<!-- End Contents Bar -->
```

4. Add the contents table:

```
<!-- Begin Contents -->
<table border=0 width=100% cellspacing=0 cellpadding=0>
<tr>
<td align=left>
<img src="images/filler.gif" width=72 height=1 alt="">
</td>
<td valign=top>
<h2><a href="cover.htm">Who Will Tell The People?</a></h2>
Top 10 censored stories: Here's what the mainstream media didn't
feel like telling you last year--and why.
<br>
<b><i>By Christine Stavem</i></b>
<br>
<hr><p>
<h2><a href="mailbag.htm">Mailbag</a></h2>
Howls of outrage and squeals of delight from our astonished
fans.
<br>
<hr><p>
<h2><a href="smith.htm">Smith</a></h2>
Concerned about porno on the Web? Drop your pants and take a
gander--you've just seen half the threat!
```

```
<br>
<i><b>By Jeff Smith</b></i>
<br>
<hr><p>
<h2><a href="skinny.htm">The Skinny</a></h2>
The Wildcat riot revisited...Lute's vacation ruined...And we
actually say something nice about Mesa Republican Rusty
Bowers...Plus more!
<br>
<hr><p>
<h2><a href="curr1.htm">That Championship Season</a></h2>
Stray thoughts on the University of Arizona Wildcats' national
basketball blowout.
<br>
<b><i>By Tom Danehy</i></b>
<br>
<hr><p>
<h2><a href="curr2.htm">Food For Thought</a></h2>
Why The Tucson Community Food Bank's in trouble.
<br>
<b><i>An Editorial</i></b>
<br>
<hr><p>
<h2><a href="http://bbs.desert.net">Currents Talk Back Forum
</a></h2>
Here's your place to vent, Tucson webheads.
<br>
<hr><p>
```

NOTE: In the following section, "Creating a Content Page," you'll add the menu navigation image and map coordinates.

```
<!-- Begin Menu -->
</td>
<td valign=top align=center width=110>
<img src="images/menu2.gif" hspace=10 border=0 width=98
height=719 usemap="#MenuMap" alt="Image Map - Alternate Text is
at bottom of Page">
</a></td>
<map name="MenuMap">
<area shape="rect" coords="0,0,97,90" href="currents.htm">
<area shape="rect" coords="0,91,97,182" href="cityweek.htm">
<area shape="rect" coords="0,183,97,264" href="music.htm">
<area shape="rect" coords="0,265,97,350" href="review.htm">
<area shape="rect" coords="0,351,97,428" href="cinema.htm">
<area shape="rect" coords="0,429,97,514" href="backpage.htm">
<area shape="rect" coords="0,515,97,628" href="http://
bbs.desert.net/">
<area shape="rect" coords="0,629,97,718" href="search.htm">
```

```
</map>
<!-- End Menu -->
</tr>
</table>
<p>
<!-- End Contents -->
```

5. Add the footer information, including the Page Back and Forward navigation. Note that this is a current issue, so it doesn't provide the Next Week option. You'll go through an example of that in the next task.

```
<!-- Begin Footer -->
<center>
<a href="contents.htm">
<img src="../images/pback2.gif" name="pback" width=74 height=60
border=0 alt=" Page Back "></a>
<a href="../03-27-97/currents.htm">
<img src="../images/last3.gif" name="last" width=74 height=60
border=0 alt=" Last Week "></a>
<a href="cover.htm">
<img src="../images2/pforw3.gif" name="pforw" width=74 height=60
border=0 alt=" Page Forward "></a>
<p>
```

6. Add the text-based section links:

```
<font size=2>
<a href="../twhome.htm">Home</a> |
<a href="currents.htm">Currents</a> |
<a href="cityweek.htm">City Week</a> |
<a href="music.htm">Music</a> |
<a href="review.htm">Review</a> |
<a href="cinema.htm">Cinema</a> |
<a href="backpage.htm">Back Page</a> |
<a href="http://bbs.desert.net">Forums</a> |
<a href="search.htm">Search</a>
</font>
<p>
<br>
```

7. Now place the DesertNet graphic links:

```
<nobr>
<a href="http://desert.net/">
<img src="images/desnet1.gif" alt="DesertNet" border=0 width=95
height=11></a>
<a href="http://desert.net/concentrate/">
<img src="images/concentrate1.gif" alt=" Concentrate" border=0
width=110 height=11></a>
<a href="http://desert.net/newsstand/">
<img src="images/newsstand2.gif" alt=" Newsstand" border=0
```

```
width=97 height=11></a>
<a href="http://desert.net/vaults/">
<img src="http://desert.net/images/vaults1.gif" alt=" Vaults"
border=0 width=67 height=11></a>
<a href="http://desert.net/htbin/buildindex.pl">
<img src="http://desert.net/images/paperboy1.gif"
alt=" Paperboy!" border=0 width=95 height=11></a>
</nobr>
<p>
```

8. And the copyright, contact, and help info:

```
<font size=-1>
<a href="http://desert.net/">&#169; 1995-97 Tucson Weekly +
DesertNet</a> .
<a href="http://desert.net/contact_publications.htmlx">Contact
</a> .
<a href="http://desert.net/faq_publications.htmlx">Help</a>
<br>
</font>
</center>
<!-- End Footer -->
```

9. Save the file as `tw-sec.htm`.

10. View the file in your browser. Note the top navigation options (link to TW home page and right-margin navigation) and how they are integrated into the page layout (see Figure 12.10).

Figure 12.10.

The mock results of a section page.

For another look at non-linear navigation created by the same designers, for another paper, visit the Albuquerque Alibi at `http://www.desert.net/alibi/`.

Creating a Content Page

The Tucson Weekly content page is similar to the layout, look and feel, and navigation of a section page. I'll point out the subtle differences as you work through this task, intended to confirm your understanding of how the table layout and navigation work together to create a whole. Because this content page was taken directly from a live page on the Web, I've shown the page's text in bold in the following code examples. Again, the code sections and full text have been left intact so you can see the way complex code is managed.

1. Begin with the shell code:

```
<html>
<head>
<title>Cinema: Free In Par&iacute;s (March 20 - March 26,
1997)</title>
</head>
<body background="images/twback.gif" bgcolor="#ffffff"
link="#d60017" vlink="#29295a" alink="#000000" text="#000000">
</body>
</html>
```

2. Add the advertisement table, image, and link:

```
<!-- begin advertisement -->
<table border=0 width=100% cellspacing=0 cellpadding=0>
<tr>
<td valign=top align=left>
<img src="images/filler.gif" width=72 height=1 alt="">
<a href="http://www.hotcong.com/congo">
<img src="images/clubcam.gif" width=468 height=60></a>
</td>
</tr>
</table>
<p>
<!-- end advertisement -->
```

3. Begin the main table, concentrating on the header information and graphics:

```
<table border=0 width=100% cellspacing=0 cellpadding=0>
<tr>
<td align=left>
<img src="images/filler.gif" width=72 height=1 alt="">
</td>
<td valign=top>
<img src="images/hedcin.gif" alt="Free In París" width=400
height=33>
<br>
<hr noshade>
<font size=4><b><i>
```

```
Filmmaker Greta Schiller Captures The Magic Of Paris In The'20s.
</i></b></font><br>
<pre><b><b>By Stacey Richter</b></i></b></pre>
<p>
```

4. Add the story. Note the use of graphics and, especially, external links. Pay specific attention to the way the text is formatted with HTML. I'll point out interesting uses of syntax along the way.

```
<!-- begin story -->

<b>THE PRIMAVERA FILM</b> Festival continues this weekend with a
presentation of the 1996 documentary
<i><a href="http://desert.net/filmvault/alibi/p/
ParisWasaWoman.html" target="_self">
```

NOTE: A magic target name without a frame? What's this? Well, in this case, the target name ensures that the link loads in the current browser window.

```
Paris Was A Woman</a></i>, downtown at The Screening Room.
It's hard to think of a more apt selection to celebrate the
participation of women in the arts than this documentary,
mostly assembled from archival footage, that chronicles the
ground-breaking achievements of artists and writers in Paris
between the wars. The work and lives of Gertrude Stein, Colette,
and Romaine Brooks, among others, are described through photo-
graphs and by people who knew them. Interviews with surviving
friends (including Berthe Cleyrergue, housekeeper to poet
Natalie Barney, who reports that Alice B. Toklas was &quot;very
pleasant&quot;) are intercut with archival footage and the stray
comment from an academic or two to produce an affectionate,
thoughtful fanletter to a spirited bunch of free-thinkers in a
time when women were not encouraged to think much at all.
<p>
```

NOTE: Instead of actual quotation marks, the Tucson Weekly designer uses ", which is known as a character entity. For more information on the usage of character entities, check out *Laura Lemay's Teach Yourself Web Publishing with HTML 3.2 in 14 Days*.

```
<img src="images/cinema.gif" alt="Cinema" align=left hspace=10
vspace=5 width=117 height=64>
```

Director Greta Schiller has been interested, throughout her career, in making documentaries composed of archival footage that investigate lost or overlooked aspects of history (her other films include <i>Before Stonewall</i> and <I>Sweethearts of Rhythm</i>, the story of an all-female, interracial jazz band from the '40s). Together with writer and historian Andrea Weiss, she'sproduced a film about one of the most discussed and inves-tigated periods of literary history--the '20s, the period of " the lost generation. " ("They didn't seem lost at all," comments Janet Flanner, for years the <i>New Yorker's</i> Paris corespondent. "They knew exactly where they were going--straight to Paris.") By focusing on the work and lives of the female artists and intellectuals drawn to Paris in the '20s, Schiller and Weiss have produced a film that seriously considers the contribution of women to Modernism, a movement mostly dominated by men.

<p>

American artists, male and female, were drawn to Paris by the strength of the dollar between the wars, the availability of good food and wine (especially alluring during Prohibition), and by its reputation as a haven for artists. But women, in particular, were attracted to Paris because they believed it was a place where they could live in whatever way they wished. Parisians were tolerant (Gertrude Stein said they were busy living their lives so that she was free to live hers), and those women who wished to live in a free and unconventional manner seemed to find the place irresistible. Most of the women Schiller tracks in her documentary were lesbians; most were also displaced Americans. Though Schiller may be guilty of skewing her history a bit in favor of expatriate lesbians, it's hard to fault her, since their stories are so interesting, and their motivation for emigration to the Left Bank of Paris, where unconventionality seems to have flourished in conservative times, seems so clear.

<p>
<img src="images/cin.gif" alt="" align=right hspace=10 vspace=10width=150 height=227>

Most famous of these expatriates was Gertrude Stein, who was known at the time for her collection of modern art and weekly salons. Stein served as mentor for <a href="http://www.yahoo.com/Arts/Art_History/Artists/Picasso__Pablo__1881_1973_/">Picasso</a>, Hemingway and Sherwood Anderson, influencing their work heavily even as her own writing remained unknown. If Gertrude Stein were alive today, she would probably be some sort of major media figure--her presence, even on the scratchy home movies that Schiller unearthed, is mag-netic. With her cropped hair, deep voice and matronly dresses, Stein is the most seductive presence in the film, spinning off quotable lines and tramping through the countryside with her "great companion," Alice B. Toklas.

<p>

Also featured in the film is Sylvia Beach, owner of Shakespeare and Co., a bookstore that became the center of expatriate intellectual culture at the time. Schiller has located some great black-and-white footage of Beach taken in the '60s, where she breezily recounts her early literary adventures, including befriending the young Hemingway, who insisted on taking her to sporting events. Beach championed the work of James Joyce and published <i>Ulysses</i> when no one else would touch it. (It was considered obscene.) Later, Joyce broke their contract and sold the rights to Random House without giving Beach a penny.

<p>

Other, lesser-known artists like the tortured Djuna Barnes and the heiress/poet Natalie Clifford Barney are given serious attention in this film, along with photographer Gisele Freund and painter Marie Laurencin.

<p>

The coming of World War II quashed the spirit of Paris' community of artists, but Greta Schiller's film presents a fine chronicle of those who once considered the city neither a mistress nor a muse, but a haven where they were free to think and work.

<p>

<a href="http://desert.net/filmvault/alibi/p/
ParisWasaWoman.html" target="_self">
Paris Was A Woman</a>

continues through Sunday, March 23, at The Screening Room
(622-2262).
<!-- end story -->

<a href="../twstaff.htm">
<img src="images/twend.gif" alt="TW" align=bottom width=14
height=11 border=0>
</a>
<p>

NOTE: The little TW symbol after the review links back to the staff page so you can view credits and write to article authors if they have e-mail accounts.

5. Add the right-margin menu syntax and map coordinates:

```
<!-- begin menu -->
</td>
<td valign=top align=center width=110>
<img src="images/menu2.gif" hspace=10 border=0 width=98
height=719 usemap="#MenuMap" alt="Image Map - Alternate Text is
at bottom of Page">
```

```
</a>
</td>
<map name="MenuMap">
<area shape="rect" coords="0,0,97,90" href="currents.htm">
<area shape="rect" coords="0,91,97,182" href="cityweek.htm">
<area shape="rect" coords="0,183,97,264" href="music.htm">
<area shape="rect" coords="0,265,97,350" href="review.htm">
<area shape="rect" coords="0,351,97,428" href="cinema.htm">
<area shape="rect" coords="0,429,97,514" href="backpage.htm">
<area shape="rect" coords="0,515,97,628" href="../forums/
index.htm">
<area shape="rect" coords="0,629,97,718" href="search.htm">
</map>
<!-- end menu -->
</tr>
</table>
<p>
```

6. Now add the top section of the footer. The links here represent an example of the Links of Interest navigation option:

```
<!-- begin footer -->
<center>
<a href="../forums/cinema/cin.htm">
<b>Write your own reviews in the Cinema Forum</a></b>
<br>
<a href="http://desert.net/filmvault/">
<b><i>DesertNet</i>'s Film Vault</b></a>
<br>
<p>
```

7. Complete the non-linear navigation, noting the additional elements for Next Week and Current Issue:

```
<a href="cinema.htm">
<img src="images/pback2.gif" name="pback" width=74 height=60
border=0 alt=" Page Back ">
</a><a href="../03-13-97/cin.htm">
<img src="images/last2.gif" name="last" width=74 height=60
border=0 alt=" Last Week "></a>
<a href="../current/cin.htm">
<img src="images/current2.gif" name="current" width=74 height=60
border=0 alt=" Current Week "></a>
<a href="../03-27-97/cin.htm">
<img src="images/next2.gif" name="next" width=74 height=60
border=0 alt=" Next Week "></a>
<a href="filmclip.htm">
<img src="images/pforw2.gif" name="pforw" width=74 height=60
border=0 alt=" Page Forward "></a>
<p>
```

8. Place the bottom-based text options for publication sections:

```
<font size=2>
<a href="../twhome.htm">Home</a> |
<a href="currents.htm">Currents</a> |
<a href="cityweek.htm">City Week</a> |
<a href="music.htm">Music</a> |
<a href="review.htm">Review</a> |
<a href="cinema.htm">Cinema</a> |
<a href="backpage.htm">Back Page</a> |
<a href="../forums/index.htm">Forums</a> |
<a href="search.htm">Search</a>
</font>
<p>
<br>
```

9. Add the DesertNet graphic link options:

```
<nobr>
<a href="http://desert.net/">
<img src="images/desnet1.gif" alt="DesertNet" border=0 width=95
height=11></a>
<a href="http://desert.net/concentrate/">
<img src="images/concentrate1.gif" alt=" Concentrate" border=0
width=110 height=11></a>
<a href="http://desert.net/newsstand/">
<img src="images/newsstand2.gif" alt=" Newsstand" border=0
width=97 height=11></a>
<a href="http://desert.net/vaults/">
<img src="http://desert.net/images/vaults1.gif" alt=" Vaults"
border=0 width=67 height=11></a>
<a href="http://desert.net/htbin/buildindex.pl">
<img src="http://desert.net/images/paperboy1.gif"
alt=" Paperboy!" border=0 width=95 height=11></a>
</nobr>
<p>
```

10. Finish the footer data with the Copyright, Contact, and Help links:

```
<font size=-1>
<a href="http://desert.net/">&#169; 1995-97 Tucson Weekly +
DesertNet</a> .
<a href="http://desert.net/contact_publications.htmlx">Contact
</a> .
<a href="http://desert.net/faq_publications.htmlx">Help</a>
<br>
</font>
</center>
<!-- end footer -->
```

11. Save the file as `tw-con.htm`.

12. View it in your browser, noting specifically the text formatting results (see Figure 12.11) and the bottom non-linear navigation additions (see Figure 12.12).

Figure 12.11.
Text and graphic formatting from your mockup.

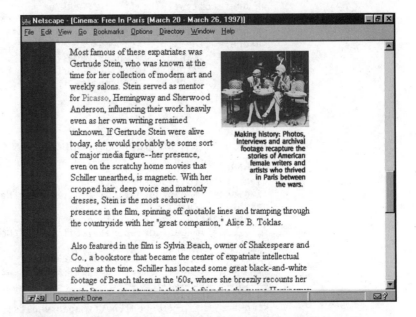

Figure 12.12.
The complete view of your mockup's bottom navigation options.

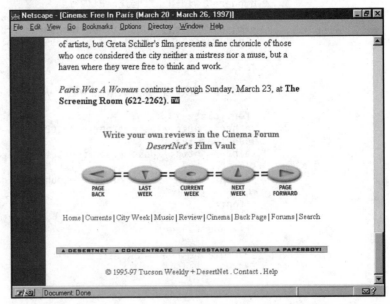

Workshop Wrap-Up

Exhausted yet? I am! The Tucson Weekly is processed every week, delivered to the Web site the Wednesday evening before the print paper is available, and (here's the magic) takes only several hours per week to accomplish. The way that is done remains a trade secret, but should serve to inspire you to think big, and think originally. Use the example of layout and imaginative navigation in this chapter to push yourself into new levels of design.

Focus intently on how multiple navigation options can serve to enhance, or confuse, the Web visitor. In the case of the Tucson Weekly, the reason so many options achieve a balance between the non-linear environment of the Web and the linear thought process most of us are accustomed to is because the fundamental design doesn't deviate from the familiar.

Standard elements such as a right navigation menu, bottom menus, text and graphical links, and the blue margin background, serve as visual grounding because they are familiar aspects of Web pages They aren't foreign to you. However, it is the *way* in which these are combined and used that is unusual and even visionary. The main thing to remember is that none of this is beyond your talents, and in fact may inspire fresh and unique ways of approaching Web design.

Next Steps

The following chapter looks at non-static frame navigation, a technique that deviates from standard frame technology and creates interesting opportunities in design. You may also be interested in

❏ Chapter 14, "Adding Interactive and Dynamic Content," which examines how to add interactivity to your site

❏ Chapter 15, "Real-Time Example: Interactivity in Action—Core-Wave's Glass Bead Game"

❏ Chapter 16, "Using Tables for Graphic Control," where you'll see more of DesertNet's interesting work applied to table layouts for color and graphic control

Q&A

Q: I've followed the code for the side-by-side DesertNet graphics, yet my images aren't fitting snug up against one another, even though I'm using the `<nobr>` tag. What's wrong?

A: Make sure that the image syntax is snug up against the next image's syntax. Because of the 70 character line breaks, code printed in this book sometimes deviates from the exact way it should appear. This will solve the problem.

Q: I see that the Weekly uses the `alt=` attribute in all of its images. How is this attribute best used?

A: The `alt=` attribute allows you to offer a description of the graphic for nongraphic browsers as well as for the pop-up graphic identification available in Internet Explorer and Netscape 4.0. In DesertNet's code, you'll often find the argument written out with no description, `alt=""`. This is reserved for graphics that don't require a description, such as a spacer.

Q: Speaking of spacers, I see they are used frequently in these examples. What do they do, exactly?

A: Spacer graphics assist in fixing placement of graphics and text within tables. For example, if you want to be certain that your text and graphics land in just the right spot from the left margin, you can take a spacer graphic, made of a single-pixel transparent image, and stretch it to the width you require. As I've mentioned elsewhere in the book, this also can assist in fixing the width of gutter cells in tables. As browsers become more sophisticated and stable, and cascading style sheets (see Chapter 3, "In Vogue: Cascading Style Sheets") are fully embraced, the need for this clever workaround becomes less important.

thirteen

Non-Static and Multi-Framed Navigation

From time to time, you'll be faced with the need to have an entire frameset replace itself with another. To do this is fairly easy, and uses a magic target name not previously discussed: `target=_parent`. This target name, when activated, tells the browser to load pages into the master frameset.

In previous chapters, you've created only one frameset per site. Even if you left the site using a magic target name, the originating site still had only one frameset. Because a frameset calls for the layout of frames and related HTML documents, if you had more than one frameset, you could conceivably have limitless frame designs within a single site.

In this chapter's example, you will work through a site example that uses the parent magic target name, and replaces the same frame design with a new frameset each time. Think of the frameset as the "parent," and the placement of the individual HTML pages within it the "children."

Sedgwick China was after a menu that changed to reflect the location of the visitor. Although this could also be done with JavaScript or another interactive application, the challenge to the designers involved was to come up with a way to simultaneously reload the images that the client liked with the content pages.

This simultaneous changing removes the static nature of frames as you have studied them so far, introducing the "non-static" aspect of the teaching. The existence of two frames and multiple framesets creates a multi-frame navigation option.

Visit Sedgwick China's home page at `http://www.insworld.com/sedgwick/china/`.

Bear in mind that you can create a site with any number of framesets. You can create sets with only rows, or a mixture of columns and rows. In fact, at the end of the chapter, you'll create a "switching" frame game based on the `target=_parent` magic name. But first, I'll get you comfortable using the convention.

 ## Creating the Splash Page

You'll begin with a traditional splash page for the example:

1. Build the shell syntax:

```
<html>
<head>
<title>Sedgwick</title>
</head>
<body background="images/bg.jpg" bgcolor=#ffffff link="#06067E"
vlink="#992d32">
</body>
</html>
```

2. Add the main image:

```
<center>
<a href="main.map"><img src="images/main.jpg"
width=523 height=262 border = 0 usemap="#mainmap"></a>
<p>
```

3. Now, you'll add the map coordinates:

```
<map name="mainmap">
<area shape="rect" coords= "0,239,138,262"
href="overhisf.htm">
<area shape="circle" coords= "63,227,10"
href="overhisf.htm">
<area shape="rect" coords= "138,239,279,262"
href="growthf.htm">
```

```
<area shape="circle" coords= "208,228,10"
href="growthf.htm">
<area shape="rect" coords= "279,239,344,262"
href="servicef.htm">
<area shape="circle" coords= "307,227,10"
href="servicef.htm">
<area shape="rect" coords= "344,239,456,262"
href="aboutf.htm">
<area shape="circle" coords= "394,228,10"
href="aboutf.htm">

<area shape="rect" coords= "456,239,522,262"
href="contactf.htm">
<area shape="circle" coords= "481,227,10"
href="contactf.htm">
<area shape="polygon" coords= "258,0,184,91,326,91"
href="aboutf.htm">
<area shape="rect" coords= "184,91,341,142"
href="overhisf.htm">
<area shape="rect" coords= "0,0,522,261" nohref>
</map>
```

4. Add text options for the map:

```
<font size=1>
<a href="index.htm">Welcome</a> |
<a href="overhisf.htm">Overview and History</a> |
<a href="growthf.htm">Growth and Direction</a> |
<a href="servicef.htm">Services</a> |
<a href="aboutf.htm">About Sedgwick</a> |
<a href="contactf.htm">Contact</a>
<br>
</font>
```

5. Finish with the copyright information:

```
<font size=1>&#169; 1996 Sedgwick</font>
</center>
```

6. Save the file as `index.htm`.

7. View it in your browser.

8. Match the results to Figure 13.1.

DESIGN NOTE: By now, you've seen several instances of copyright information placed at the bottom of a page. Copyrighting pages is always a good thing to do, and how to manage the copyright in a visual design sense is important, too. It's critical information, but in order to not detract from design, it's a good idea to make the copyright notice small and in a familiar place—typically the bottom of a content page. If you have extensive copyright and trademark information to include, you can hyperlink the copyright notation to a main copyright page that discusses all the details. This way, you've included all the legal information without compromising your design and navigation. Be sure to check with an attorney for the appropriate language and presentation of the data within copyright references.

Figure 13.1.
The Sedgwick China home page.

The First Frameset

Because the first frame called for is the Overview and History page, I'll show you how to build the frameset for this page, and then how to add the menu and content. Note that the `<noframes>` option has been employed in this example.

1. Create the shell syntax:

```
<html>
<head>
<title>Sedgwick</title>
</head>
</html>
```

2. Add the frameset:

```
<frameset cols="125,*">
</frameset>
```

3. Now place the target HTML pages (the children) for this frameset (the parent) within the frameset:

```
<frame src="menu1.htm" scrolling="no" marginwidth="0"
marginheight="0" name="menu" noresize>
<frame src="overhist.htm" scrolling="auto" marginwidth="10"
marginheight="10" name="right" noresize>
```

4. Beneath this information, begin the <noframe> container:

```
<noframe>
</noframe>
```

5. Because this section will be viewable by browsers that don't support frames, you must add body attributes:

```
<body background="images/bg3.jpg" bgcolor=#ffffff link="#06067E"
vlink="#992d32" alink="#06067E"></body>
```

6. Within the body, place the images and formatted text as follows. Note that the text in bold is the actual site's text.

```
<center><img src="graphics/overvhd.jpg"></center><br>
<blockquote>
```

Sedgwick is proud to have been the first broker opening a representative office in China. We have maintained a continuous presence there since 1981, and are excited by our increasing involvement in the arranging of insurance for foreign joint venture and wholly foreign-owned companies.

```
<p>
```

```
<img src="graphics/write.jpg" alt="Chinese Writing" width=57
```

```
height=162 hspace=25 border=0 align=left>
```

In 1988, two new Chinese insurance companies were formed, China Pacific in Shanghai, and Ping An in Shenzhen. They commenced soliciting business from Sedgwick. This solicitation created competition with the only original Chinese insurance company, PICC. PICC's major branches were equally interested in maintaining their existing clients and winning new business.

<p>

We approached the regulatory authority, the People's Bank of China, and explained that in addition to making insurance arrangements for foreign investors, we were being asked to recommend an insurance company. This meant that we were expected to perform the duties of an insurance broker. We felt that the time had come for us to change our status in China from a representative office to a company fully authorized to carry out the business of insurance broking.

<p>

We explained that this change in our status would enable us to respond to changes in the Chinese insurance market and support future development. The People's Bank of China was very interested in Sedgwick's ability to introduce technical expertise to China.

<p>

On May 23, 1993, after two years of negotiations and nine months of document submissions and approval, Sedgwick received authorization from the Governor of the People's Bank of China to be the first insurance broker in China.

<img src="graphics/hkright.jpg" alt="Hong Kong View !" width=200 height=hspace=25 vspace=5 border=0 align=right>

Subsequently, Sedgwick Insurance and Risk Management Consultants (China) Limited was formed. This company is registered in China and is wholly owned by Sedgwick. The license granted is unrestricted in that we may act for local indigenous Chinese companies, foreign joint venture companies, and wholly-owned foreign companies anywhere in China.

<p>

</blockquote>

7. Place text navigation and copyright options below the closing blockquote:

```
<center>
<font size=2>
<a href="index.html">Welcome</a> |
<a href="overhisf.html">Overview and History</a> |
<a href="growthf.html">Growth and Direction</a> |
<a href="servicef.html">Services</a> |
<a href="aboutf.html">About Sedgwick</a> |
<a href="contactf.html">Contact</a>
<p>
</font>
<font size=1>&#169; 1996 Sedgwick</font>
</center>
```

Netscape offers frame information, particularly as it relates to Netscape-centric design, at `http://home.mcom.com/comprod/products/navigator/version_2.0/frames/index.html`.

8. Save the file as `overhisf.htm`. This is your frameset and the "parent" target for the corresponding menu and content pages, respectively.

Creating the Menu Template

Because the menu is going to change each time, you'll need to create as many menus as necessary to accomplish the non-static options. This example can be used as a template. Simply replace the name of the image and name the file appropriately for all subsequent menu files. Remember that a different one will be called for in each frameset. Each is essentially identical, except for a slight change in the menu graphic. The coordinates for mapping remain the same.

1. Begin with the standard HTML:

```
<html>
<head>
<title>Sedgwick</title>
</head>
<body background="images/bg.jpg">
</body>
</html>
```

2. Add the logo and map image:

```
<center>
<img src="images/logo.jpg">
<p>
<a href="menu1.map"><img src="images/menu1.gif"
width=111 height=154 border = 0 usmap="#sedgmap"></a>
</center>
```

3. Add the map coordinates. Pay special attention to the use of magic target names. Each of the linked HTML files is an individual frameset.

```
<map name="sedgmap">
<area shape="rect" coords= "0,0,111,19"
href="index.htm" target="_parent">
<area shape="rect" coords= "0,19,111,56"
href="overhisf.htm" target="_parent">
<area shape="rect" coords= "0,56,111,91"
href="growthf.htm" target="_parent">
<area shape="rect" coords= "0,91,111,109"
href="servicef.htm" target="_parent">
<area shape="rect" coords= "0,109,111,135"
href="aboutf.htm" target="_parent">
<area shape="rect" coords= "0,135,111,153"
href="contactf.htm" target="_parent">
<area shape="rect" coords= "0,0,110,153" nohref>
</map>
```

4. Save the file as menu1.htm.

DESIGN NOTE: Creating area identification by using change in color, graphics, or adding an interactive component that helps differentiate the page you are on versus other pages in a menu is a common design trick. Notice how Sedgwick China uses a red dot to indicate where you are in the site. This kind of identification is very helpful to site visitors, particularly if your site is extensive.

Adding the Contents to the Sedgwick Home Page

In this case, you'll modify the contents of the previous example. The contents are basically identical to those in the `<noframes>` options, with the one exception being the navigation syntax at the bottom of the page. Because this content page is within the frameset, the parent targets must remain intact.

1. Copy all of the contents from between the `<noframes>` tags and place between a standard HTML denotation:

```
<html>
<!--add contents here- ->
</html>
```

2. Replace the text navigation at the bottom of the page with the following, paying close attention to the parent targets and frameset HTML (ending with "f"):

```
<font size=1>
<a href="index.htm" target="_parent">Welcome</a> |
<a href="overhisf.htm" target="_parent">Overview and History</a> |
<a href="growthf.htm" target="_parent">Growth and Direction</a> |
<a href="servicef.htm" target="_parent">Services</a> |
<a href="aboutf.htm" target="_parent">About Sedgwick</a> |
<a href="contactf.htm" target="_parent">Contact</a>
<p>
</font>
```

3. Save the file as `overhist.htm`.

4. Open the index file and move to the Overview and History link.

5. View the results and match them to Figure 13.2.

To complete the site, you'll need to create menu, content, and frameset pages for each of the subsequent sections. I'll walk you through the modified syntax, allowing you to create the full site from the materials on the CD-ROM.

Figure 13.2.

The Overview and History Page, with related map.

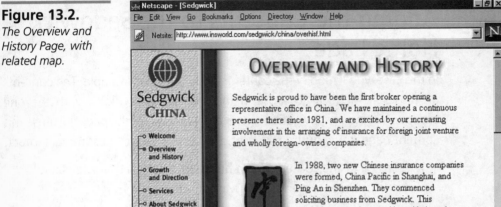

TASK   The Subsequent Frameset

This task will create the next frameset, controlling the layout for the next framed page.

1. The next frameset, or parent, is to control the "Growth and Direction" page layout. Begin with the frameset shell:

```
<html>
<head>
<title>Sedgwick</title>
</head>
<frameset cols="125,*">
</frameset>
</body>
```

2. Add the frames:

```
<frame src="menu2.html" scrolling="no" marginwidth="0"
marginheight="0" name="menu" noresize>
<frame src="growth.html" scrolling="auto" marginwidth="10"
marginheight="10" name="right" noresize>
```

3. You can copy the `<noframes>` section from the associated content page, remembering to strip the parent targets out, and change the links to the content HTML pages rather than the frameset pages.

4. Save the file as `growthf.htm`.

Now create the adjoining menu page:

5. Copy the syntax from the template into a fresh instance of your HTML editor.

6 Replace the map image name with the next image in the sequence, in this case, `menu2.gif`.

7. Save the file as `menu2.htm`.

Adding the Related Content

Now you'll add the actual content for the pages just created.

1. Start with the standard HTML shell and body attributes for this site:

```
<html>
<head>
<title>Sedgwick</title>
</head>
<body background="graphics/bg3.jpg" bgcolor=#ffffff
link="#06067E" vlink="#992d32" alink="#06067E">
</body>
</html>
```

2. Add the header images, graphics, and text. Note the table. In this case, the table is used as a bona-fide table rather than a layout or design tool. You'll see the `<th>` tags used; these are for "table header" and define a table section as a header rather than a cell:

```
<center><img src="graphics/growthhd.jpg"></center>
<br>
<blockquote>
<h2>The Economy</h2>
```

In the early 1980's the Chinese government opened its industry to the rest of the world. Fourteen coastal cities were designated open cities, and foreign companies were offered financial incentives to invest in them.

```
<img src="graphics/harbor.jpg" alt="Chinese Harbor" width=170
height=171 hspace=25 border=0 align=right>
<p>
```

As a result, the Chinese economy has boomed. For example, one of the coastal cities, Shenzhen, has grown from a small farming community of 20,000 people to a bustling city of more than 2 million. The labor force is competitive, educated, and is China's greatest asset.

```
<p>
```

The Chinese economy is growing at a year-on-year rate of more than 10 percent; with some provinces growing at more than 20 percent per year. China is rapidly becoming the economic powerhouse of the Asian Pacific and presents excellent opportunities for Western companies to participate in what is considered to be the world's largest market.

```
<p>
<h2>Sedgwick: Expansion in China</h2>
```

Currently, we have three offices — in Beijing, Shanghai, and Shenzhen, with a total staff of 23. We anticipate that we will have 32 local employees by the end of 1996. Our business plan calls for us to open, within the next couple of years, three more offices. They will be located in Shenyang, to the north; Chengdu in the central part of China; and Xiamen, on the coast opposite Taiwan.

```
<p>
<img src="graphics/hkleft.jpg" width=213 height=76 hspace=25
border=0 align=left>
```

China has 30 provinces. The largest, Sichuan, has a population of 107 million. Geographic distance and diverse cultures in the various provinces mandates the establishment of strategically located offices. Companies with local presence provide easy and comfortable access to clients, thereby increasing opportunities.

```
<p>
<h2>Current Insurers in China</h2>
```

The Chinese market is growing rapidly. Currently, there are seven licensed insurers in China. The classes of insurance offered by these groups are quickly growing in number. Insurers are keen to learn and will often be guided by brokers and supporting markets on the rating and use of wording for more unusual classes.

```
<p>
<center>
<table border=5>
<tr><th>PICC</th><td><A HREF="http://www.gy.com/trade/invest/
invest/tpi.htm">
People's Insurance Company of China</A></td><td>1949</td></tr>
<tr><th>CPIC</th><td>China Pacific Insurance Company</
td><td>1988</td></tr>
<tr><th>PAIC</th><td>Ping An Insurance Company</td>
<td>1988</td></tr>
<tr><th>AIG</th><td>Restricted to Shanghai</td>
<td>1992</td></tr>
<tr><th>TF&M</th><td>Tokio Fire and Marine</td>
<td>1994</td></tr>
<tr><th>TAIC</th><td>Tian An Insurance Company</td>
<td>1995</td></tr>
<tr><th>DZIC</th><td>Da Zhong Insurance</td><td>1995</td>
</tr></table>
<p>
</center>
```

These seven insurers openly compete with one another, and individual branches of the same company are commonly in competition. These branches are enabled by the fact that some branches under one company have their own treaty reinsurance arrangements. This is unlike many companies, which are centrally controlled and subject to Head Office treaties. In addition, some branches offer different products. It is therefore important to be associated with a locally established broker who can efficiently track the rapidly changing environment.

```
<p>
```

It is of interest to note that today, Sedgwick is`<i>` still`</i>` the only licensed foreign insurance broker in China.

```
<p>
<h2>Other China Business Links:</h2>
<ul>
<li><a href="http://www.mediawhse.com/csp/csp.html">China Re-
source Online Directory:</a> providing companies access to
services and direct contacts in China for import/export or
market analysis.
<li><A HREF="http://preston-management.com/cbc/welcome.htm">
China Business Corner:</A> a directory of business opportunities
and contacts.
<li><A HREF="http://darkwing.uoregon.edu/~felsing/cstuff/
cmaps.html">
Maps of China</A>
</ul>
</blockquote>
```

3. Add the navigation. For the content page, the parent and "f" (frameset) HTML pages must be called upon.

```
<center>
<font size=1>
<a href="index.html" target="_parent">Welcome</a> |
<a href="overhisf.html" target="_parent">Overview and History</a> |
<a href="growthf.html" target="_parent">Growth and Direction</a> |
<a href="servicef.html" target="_parent">Services</a> |
<a href="aboutf.html" target="_parent">About Sedgwick</a> |
<a href="contactf.html" target="_parent">Contact</a>
<p>
</font>
<font size=1>&#169; 1996 Sedgwick</font>
</center>
```

4. Save the file as `growth.htm`.

5. Open the index file.

6. Move to the Overview and History section. Watch the frames fill.

7. Using the menu navigation, move to the Growth section (see Figure 13.3). Watch how both the menu and content area fills. This is non-static navigation in action.

Figure 13.3.
The Growth section and related menu.

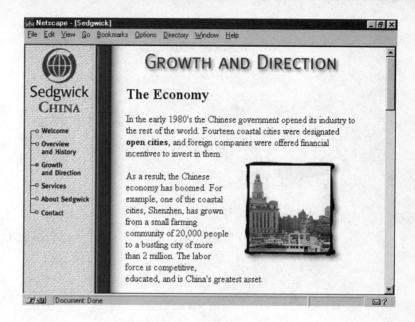

Multi-Frame Targeting

Now I'm going to show you use of the _parent target attribute using borderless frames. Remember, the objective is to create a frameset for each in order to maximize the power of the magic target name. You'll begin with the content pages, and then move on to the individual parent framesets.

Making the Content Pages

For the purposes of this simple experiment, you'll create four content pages, each one a different color and with a different link.

1. Begin with the following syntax, paying close attention to the name of the linked HTML document and the target name:

```
<html>
<head>
<title> blue </title>
</head>
<body bgcolor="#0099CC" link="FFFFFF">
<center>
<h1><a href="two.htm" target=_parent>Switch</a></h1>
</center>
</body>
</html>
```

2. Save the file as blue.htm.

3. Using the same template, change the color, the link color, and the link:

```
<html>
<head>
<title>yellow</title>
</head>
<body bgcolor="#FFFF33" link="#0099CC">
<center>
<h1><a href="three.htm" target=_parent>Switch Again</a></h1>
</center>
</body>
</html>
```

4. Save the file as yellow.htm.

5. Repeat the same steps for a green page:

```
<html>
<head>
<title>green</title>
</head>
<body bgcolor="#009933" link="#FFFFFF">
<center>
<h1><a href="four.htm" target=_parent>Switch Yet Again!</a></h1>
</center>
</body>
</html>
```

6. Save the file as green.htm.

7. And, finally, repeat the preceding steps for a red page. You'll note that this page has no link:

```
<html>
<head>
<title>red</title>
</head>
```

```
<body bgcolor="#FF0000">
</body>
</html>
```

8. Save the file as `red.htm`.

TASK Build the First Frameset

This task shows you how to build a frameset for multiple frames.

1. Create the shell:

```
<html>
<head>
<title> first parent frameset </title>
</head>
</html>
```

2. Add the frameset rows and columns:

```
<frameset cols="300,300" frameborder=0 framespacing=0 border=0>
<frameset rows="200,*" frameborder=0 framespacing=0 border=0>
```

3. Finish with the frames and closing frameset tags:

```
<frame src="green.htm" name=green>
<frame src="yellow.htm" name=yellow>
</frameset>
<frame src="blue.htm" name=blue>
</frameset>
```

4. Save the file as `index-g.htm`.

TASK Create the Second Frameset in the Series

The next step in creating multiple frames is to create a second parent, as follows:

1. Begin with the shell HTML tags:

```
<html>
<head>
<title> second parent frameset </title>
</head>
</html>
```

2. Add the frameset and frame data:

```
<frameset cols="300,300" frameborder=0 framespacing=0 border=0>
<frameset rows="100,100" frameborder=0 framespacing=0 border=0>
<frame src="blue.htm" name=blue>
<frame src="green.htm" name=green>
```

```
</frameset>
<frame src="yellow.htm" name=yellow>
</frameset>
```

3. Save the file as `two.htm`.

TASK Make the Third Frameset

Now you'll add another frameset.

1. Begin as usual:

```
<html>
<head>
<title> third parent frameset </title>
</head>
</html>
```

2. Add the frameset and frame data:

```
<frameset cols="300,300" frameborder=0 framespacing=0 border=0>
<frameset rows="100,*" frameborder=0 framespacing=0 border=0>
<frame src="blue.htm" name=blue>
<frame src="yellow.htm" name=yellow>
</frameset>
<frame src="green.htm" name=green>
</frameset>
```

3. Save the file as `three.htm`.

TASK The Final Frameset in the Series

This task shows you how to create the last frameset necessary for the exercise.

1. Start with the shell:

```
<html>
<head>
<title> fourth frameset </title>
</head>
</head>
```

2. Add the frameset and frame information:

```
<frameset cols="300,300" frameborder=0 framespacing=0 border=0>
<frameset rows="200,*" frameborder=0 framespacing=0 border=0>
<frame src="red.htm" name=red>
<frame src="yellow.htm" name=yellow>
</frameset>
<frame src="blue.htm" name=blue>
</frameset>
```

3. Save the file as `four.htm`.

Multi-Frame Navigation in Action

To reward you for your patience, now you get to play. I'll take you through a series of navigation moves to see just how the targets you've created work.

1. Open index-g.htm in your browser.

2. Compare the results to Figure 13.4.

Figure 13.4.

The first frameset results.

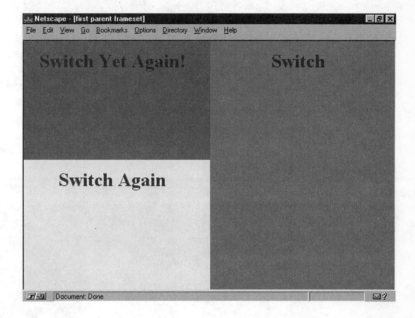

3. Click the Switch link and watch how the target links to the new frameset, as shown in Figure 13.5.

4. Now, click the Switch Again link.

5. See the results? They are guided by the "parent" frameset.

6. Match the results to Figure 13.6. If they are correct, continue. If not, go back and check your syntax.

7. If your results are correct, click the Switch Yet Again! link.

8. Note how a new frameset appears, as shown in Figure 13.7.

Figure 13.5.
A new frameset appears when clicking on the Switch link.

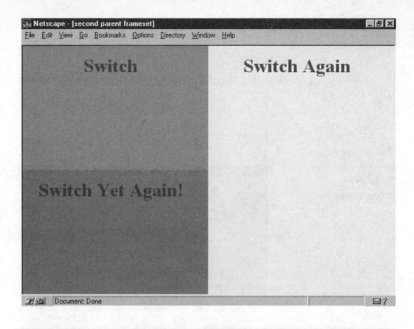

Figure 13.6.
The Switch Again link.

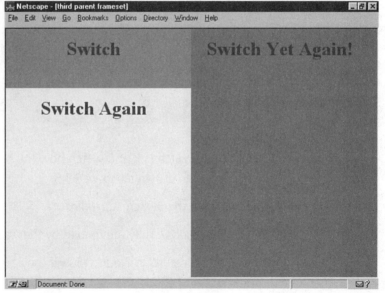

9. Now, to prove how a link only loads its parent, open `two.htm` in your browser.

10. Click the Switch link. The page reloads, but everything remains static. This is because the link calls on the parent, which orders it to recall the same HTML file (see Figure 13.8).

Figure 13.7.
The results after switching again.

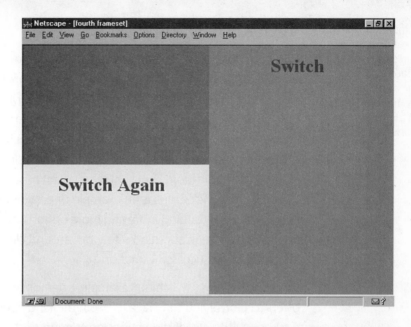

Figure 13.8.
The switch page reloads the first frameset again.

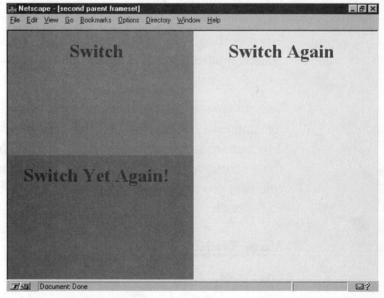

As you can imagine, this type of linking can offer some interesting options when targeting frames. Keep in mind that you don't have to stick to the parent model; you can break out of it at any time and use another target, or another magic target.

Use your imagination, and have some fun!

For more fun with frames, visit Harley Hahn's Amazing Multiplying Frames page at `http://www.harley.com/multiply/index.html`.

Workshop Wrap-Up

Non-static design offers opportunities to create a lot of movement with frame-based sites. You'll notice that I gave a real-life example in order to show one treatment of non-static frames. Part of my intent is to exemplify client-specific solutions. This example used bordered frames, and is a very attractive design over-all. The technique serves the client well, but here is a case where the same effect could have been handled using JavaScript or another multimedia application. The client didn't want that, so the frame solution does the trick. Sedgwick China is an example of providing the client with what he or she is after. By adding more and more options to your design bag of tricks, you can often think about how to work around client needs and still provide interesting and successful solutions.

In the subsequent "switching" example, a demonstration of multiple framesets offers a colorful and fun place to begin thinking about ways to apply targets. Go back to the earlier discussions on frames, particularly the introduction in Chapter 2, "Strong Foundations: The Basics of Frame Technology," and begin experimenting with target combinations. Combine static and non-static options, multiple frames, and create bordered as well as borderless options in order to come up with design opportunities that you like.

One note of caution is to avoid too much switching. There's a lot to be said for continuity, and keeping a certain visual consistency from page to page is an important part of sophisticated design. There are times to break free from those constraints, however, and the stronger your skills become, the more confident you will feel about when and how to break from the consistency you've built.

Next Steps

Chapter 14, "Adding Interactive and Dynamic Content," is an overview of a variety of interactive options that you can use to enhance not only your site's navigation, but look and feel as well. There are tasks to give you a taste of some of the common and available interactive techniques, as well as references as to where to find more information about current interactive opportunities.

Other sections in this book of interest include

❏ Chapter 2, "Strong Foundations: The Basics of Frame Technology," provides information to strengthen your understanding of magic target names and frame essentials.

❏ Appendix B, "HTML Quick Reference," is a quick-reference guide to HTML. Visit to learn some basic syntax as well as more advanced techniques that can assist your frame-based design.

❏ Appendix C, "Current HTML Standards," has a chart defining frame tags and browser support. It's an essential resource for anyone interested in frame-based design.

Q&A

Q: I notice you didn't use tables to lay out any of the actual graphics and text. Can I do that in non-static design?

A: Absolutely. Tables can be used wherever you like in terms of layout. For example, if you wanted to place the Sedgwick logo and site menus in a table-based design, that's fine. Also, if you wanted to lay out the content pages using tables, simply use techniques taught elsewhere in this book to do so. The only place in frame design that tables are not relevant is in the frameset itself. You can place tables within the <noframes> section; however, bear in mind that non-frame browsers may not support tables either.

Q: It seems like creating all of these framesets and related content pages makes for a lot of work—and for an organizational nightmare. Isn't there an easier way?

A: It is a lot of work, and the way to know if it's appropriate for a given project is by asking, "Does this method achieve what I set out to achieve in the most effective way?" Only you can decide the answer to that question, and I've already addressed the issue of organization. Because organization is essential to timeliness, and timeliness may or may not be an issue for a given project, you must weigh the approach to the results. The most important thing is having as much in your HTML knowledge base as possible so you can make truly informed decisions about how to approach a project, from interface to navigation, to organization and project management—all the way through the final product.

fourteen

Adding Interactive and Dynamic Content

The days of inactive front-line Web pages are coming to an end. This doesn't mean that there isn't room on the Web for data and information that is stationary or elegant in design, but that, particularly in the commercial realm, Web sites on the Internet are going to demand more and more technical know-how from designers than just simple HTML.

Certainly, intranet, informational databases, and other document-heavy sites will need some stability, both in function and form. But even these types of sites can be perked up a bit to take advantage of the technologies available. In fact, you'll see in Chapters 17, 18, and 19 exactly how to do just that. But, as you wrap up your lessons in interface and navigation, it is only wise that I introduce methods to help make your sites come to life with the latest and greatest of interactive, dynamic technologies.

Because the focus of this book is layout, and the specific applications you've been working with involve interface and navigation, my intentions in this chapter are to not only familiarize you with what options are out there that can be added to your bag of tricks, but also specifically to aid you in investigating some of these options for navigation and interface design. Therefore, I will begin with an introduction to the concepts of interactive and dynamic content, move into an overview of available technologies used to achieve that content, and include link and book references to get you to the detailed information you'll require to put these technologies to work.

Interactivity

Interactivity is tossed about by Web designers and surfers casually, without a great deal of understanding of what interactivity really means. I've already touched upon the critical element of interactivity, and that is user choice.

So how is this applied to a Web page? What makes a Web site interactive? On the most immediate level, you already know the answer to these questions if you read and worked through the tasks in Chapter 12, "Multiple Menus and Non-Linear Navigation." The harnessing of hypermedia is the basis of Web interactivity. By putting the hyperlinked, non-linear structure of the Web to work, you are beginning to achieve interactivity.

The first place this is most obvious is in linking, which fits into the broader issue of navigation. Any time a choice is given to a visitor, whether it's to stay and read the information on that site, leave the site for another, or navigate the site in any way desired, interactivity is achieved.

But user choice is only the most overt aspect of interactive design. The ensuing element that is attached to user choice is the content that the user receives upon exercising that choice. In other words, if I click on a link, that link gives me something back. The delivery of some content is the second feature of interactivity.

Now you click on that link, and content is delivered to you. You will naturally respond to this content, and this is the third feature of interactivity. Not only have you exercised choice, and have had something delivered to you, but you've responded in some fashion to the content of that delivery.

NOTE: You'll notice that interactivity is used loosely and doesn't strictly adhere to the true relationship I've just described. One example is the animated GIF. In and of itself, this type of animation is active but not interactive unless it's hyperlinked to something else. The important point is that you learn the true meaning of interactivity in order to achieve it when you wish to do so. Figure 14.1 shows the cycle of interactivity.

Figure 14.1.
The cycle of interactivity.

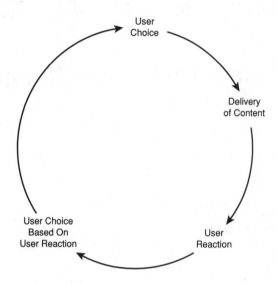

Leave it to clever Web application designers who spend time researching and developing ways of getting around technology's limitations to lay a groundwork for a fully interactive future on the Web. The technologies available now may sometimes appear limited and rudimentary; however, they are in fact genius in that they function as well as they do in spite of the limitations of the Web environment. That you can learn to use some of these applications with relative speed is even more encouraging. The future of interactivity is filled with possibilities that you and I can only enjoy in the speculative sense.

Dynamic Content

As with the word interactive, the word *dynamic* often all-too-easily spills off the tongues of Web enthusiasts. I've been guilty of it myself, and am learning to pace my use of the words to the applications being created specifically for the Web.

Dynamic, in Web-speak, refers to change or movement. You've heard me use the word many times, both in terms of this main definition or of "dynamic" in its secondary Web meaning—intuitive. So, when speaking of Web-based content, the most explicit use of the word means an intuitive change or movement.

Two examples of this definition that have become familiar to you in the course of this book are the dynamic wrapping of text around floating images or frames, and the dynamic ability of a frameset.

 # Creating Dynamically Wrapped Text

This task will help demonstrate the concept of "dynamic." The text herein intuitively wraps around the graphic; it's not forced into a specific placement.

1. In your HTML editor, build the shell syntax:

```
<html>
<head>
<title> wrapping text </title>
</head>
<body bgcolor=#FFFFFF>

</body>
</html>
```

2. Place the image link above your dummy text and align it. Do not follow it with any breaks or paragraph marks:

```
<img src="critter.gif" border=0 hspace=10 vspace=5 align=right>
```

3. Place the dummy text immediately below it:

```
Eros Et Accumsan dignissim qui blandit praesent luptatum zzril
delenit augue duis dolore te feugait nulla facilisi. Nam liber
tempor cum soluta nobis eleifend option congue nihil imperdiet
doming id quod mazim placerat facer possim assum. Iusto odio
dignissim qui blandit praesent luptatum zzril delenit augue duis
dolore te feugait nulla facilisi. Nam liber tempor cum soluta
nobis eleifend option congue nihil imperdiet doming id quod
mazim placerat facer possim assum. Accumsan et iusto odio
dignissim qui blandit
<p>
```

4. Save the file as `critter.htm`.

5. View it in your browser. See how the text wraps around the figure?

Figure 14.2 shows the results of this dynamic text example.

Figure 14.2.
This text wraps dynamically around the graphic.

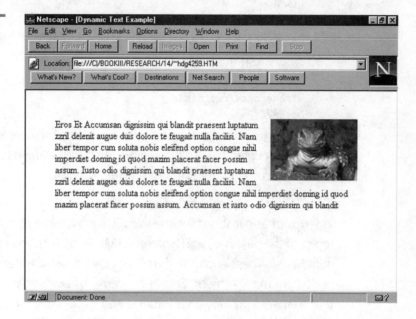

The outcome of this combination is dynamic. The image is given an alignment as well as a horizontal and vertical control, but it does not ask for a break between its parameters and the text. This means that the browser must intuitively move the text around the graphic. The results are referred to as "floating." The same event occurs with independent, or floating frames, as discussed in Chapter 8, "Progressive Interfaces with Floating Frames."

Creating a Frameset for Dynamic Control

Now think about a frameset. Remember that when setting up columns and rows, you can use an * in place of a numeric option to define the space? This creates an intuitive result on the browser's part.

1. Begin with the shell:

```
<html>
<head>
<title> frameset dynamics </title>
</head>

</html>
```

2. Add the frameset columns, noting how an * is used in the first instance:

```
<frameset cols="*,122" frameborder=0 framespacing=0 border=0>
```

3. Now finish the frame:

```
<frame src="blue.htm">
<frame src="red.htm">
</frameset>
```

Depending upon the environment in which the browser loads this information, the left column will dynamically contract or expand (change or move) in order to accommodate the very specific, fixed numeric right column of 122 pixels.

In terms of applications for the Web, three types of dynamic media are hot topics of the day. They are Dynamic HTML, Push Technology, and Interdependent Media. These applications move away from strict internal HTML methods of content management. Each is concerned, however, with creating content that changes and moves via intuitive applications that rely less on the hands-on management of data. These technologies allow for the focus of individuals to create rather than shepherd content.

Current Interactive Web Technologies

This area is quite involved and no single chapter can do detailed justice to the subject. What I will provide instead is a brief overview of the most commonly employed technologies and some information on how they are used. Also included are examples and references as to where to find more information regarding these technologies.

I like to think of interactivity on the Web as being compartmentalized into three main areas. The first is client-server interactivity. Two examples of this are the common gateway interface (CGI) and preprocessing. The next is Web programming. This area relies on specific languages, scripts, and active applications such as Java, JavaScript, Visual Basic, VBScript, ActiveX, and the Virtual Reality Modeling Language, or VRML (pronounced ver-mull). Finally, there's multimedia, which encompasses a variety of simple as well as complex applications ranging from animated GIFs to completely interactive design packages such as Macromedia's Shockwave.

The next sections will focus on the most popular interactive technologies within these groups, and offer visual as well as referenced examples so you can access more information on any individual item that impresses or inspires you.

Client-Server Interactivity

The name is a bit nebulous because a Web page relies on the client-server relationship in order to appear on your virtual doorstep in the first place. However, the mere appearance of a page doesn't necessarily make it interactive, so I like to take a closer look at the way that clients and servers interact in order to deliver a variety of media.

Server-Sided Image Maps

One form of interactivity that you've been exposed to in this book is the image map. Although I've chosen to focus on the popular client-sided map, which very purposely does not rely on the server for data, the server-sided map has also been discussed. With a server-sided map, the map coordinates are placed in a file on the server, and a string within your HTML points to that file in order to interpret the image. Figure 14.3 shows a server-sided map in action. You'll notice that in the status bar, the navigation shows coordinates rather than URLs. The server map process is a form of CGI, which is in and of itself a major component of interactive abilities on the Web.

Figure 14.3.
A server-sided map. Look closely at the status bar to see the coordinates of the map rather than URLs.

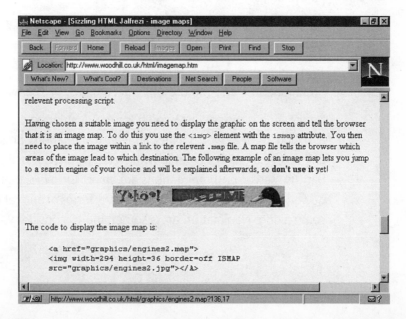

Interactive Forms

Another very common interactive method that you've had a taste of is the interactive form. These are also CGI-based. Although they are mainly used for gathering demographic data or as a point-of-contact, truly innovative and fun games have been created using them, as shown in The Love Test in Figure 14.4. Forms, like other client-server methods, are among the oldest available interactive Web technologies.

Figure 14.4.

Romance abounds in this interactive form, The Love Test.

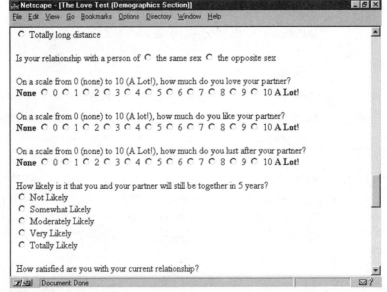

Take The Love Test at `http:// world.topchoice. com/~psyche/ lovetest/` and find out how you rate in the world of romance.

Server Push

Two primary uses for server push include a type of animation called "Nanimation," and the use of Web cameras, or "cams" for short.

Nanimation is the earliest known form of animation on the Web. The term is a hybrid of the words Netscape and animation, and to this day these animations are only viewable with Netscape browsers. It's unfortunate, truly, because server-push animations are an art form (see Figure 14.5). Although newer, and perhaps even more effective, forms of animation technology have come along, Nanimation art is something to consider when you know your audience, or you need to have alternative options available for Internet Explorer users.

Figure 14.5.
A Nanimation.

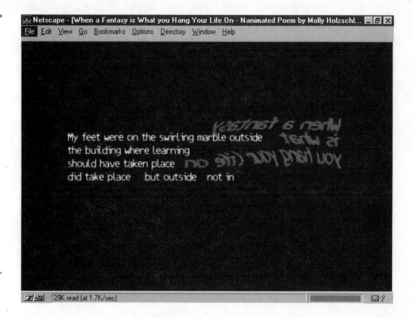

Figure 14.5.
A Nanimation.

The Nanimation in Figure 14.5 can be viewed at `http://www.molly.com/poetry/fant.html`. Three commercial Nanimations that I enjoyed creating are viewable at `http://www.desert.net/loft/`. Please remember to use Netscape to see these examples of server-push animation.

For a list of Web cameras, visit `http://www.intertain.net/~cameras/` and see (literally) where the action is.

Cameras are the way the Web peeks into people's lives, places, fish-tanks, you name it; there's a video camera out there delivering information to the Web via server push. Talk about appealing to the reaction aspect of interactivity! Basically, video cameras are set up to interact with a server that can interpret the visual data and pass it along to the browser via a CGI style script. That might seem frivolous, but there are some very sincere applications of cameras. The World Famous Club Cam serves up images of concerts and live activities at the Club Congress (`http://www.hotcong.com/congo/burn/cam.html`) and a variety of weather cameras in a number of world locations are available.

Preprocessing Randomization

This is one of my favorite techniques. By exploiting a server's preprocessing capabilities, you can actually randomize individual images and text, text and image combinations, or an entire HTML page.

In simple terms, this means every time a page loads, areas (or the full page) will change randomly. The random process is set up by the designer, who must provide the images, text, and pages that will be called upon. It's a relatively easy way to get interactivity and dynamic processes on your site.

TASK Creating a Randomized Page

Typically, randomization requires two core components: an HTML page and the random data.

For this task, I've selected to randomize a series of quotes.

1. Create an HTML page:

```
<html>
<head>
<title>Molly's Random Quote Page</title>
</head>
<body bgcolor="#FFFFFF">
<center>
</center>
</body>
</html>
```

2. Put this page aside.

3. Build a list of quotes. I have actually collected 100, but here are two for this example's purpose. Note that I have formatted the examples with italics, but that I haven't used any other HTML tags:

```
<i>Happiness belongs to those who are sufficient unto
themselves. For all external sources of happiness are, by their
very nature, highly uncertain, precarious, ephemeral, and sub-
ject to chance. Arthur Schopenhauer</i>

<i>May you live in interesting times. Old Chinese Curse</i>
```

4. Save this file as `quotes.txt` in ASCII text format.

5. Reopen your HTML and include the syntax to call the random quote file. In my server's case, the syntax structure looks like this:

```
<!--#include file="quotes.txt" random="100"-->
```

CAUTION: To avoid problems with your server, be sure that the random number equals the total number of items to be randomized.

6. Save the HTML file with the random extension. In the case of my server, HTMLX denotes a random file. I'm saving this file as `quotes.htmlx`.

7. Place both of the files on your server and enjoy.

Figures 14.6 and 14.7 demonstrate the same URL with different results on each individual visit.

To see a random process with graphics instead of text, visit the Fodor's site, http://www.fodors.com/.

Figure 14.6.
The first visit.

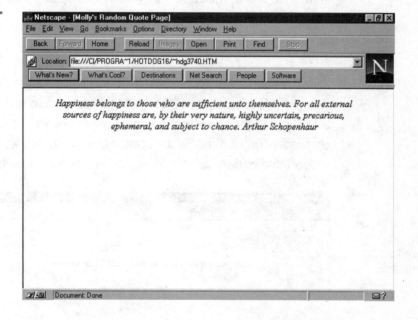

For more information on how you can add randomization, find out what your systems administrator has to say about your server's capabilities. The syntax and setup will determine how you can employ this almost magical client-server-related technique.

Randomization will be looked at in more detail in Chapter 15, "Real-Time Example: Interactivity in Action—CoreWave's Glass Bead Game," where it's used to drive an entire site.

Web Programming

The rapidly advancing area of Web programming offers up some of the most exciting potential for program-based interactivity. The disadvantage of

Web-based programming is that it can be very challenging for nonprogrammers to learn and employ. Fortunately, developers are savvy to this fact, and because they have a vested interest in promoting their products, a great deal of headway has been made in offering simple applications that designers can quickly integrate into their sites, without spending the time to learn how to program themselves.

Also, with the Internet still proclaiming its freedom despite the commercialism that is beginning to drive it financially, there are many human resources. Programmers and enthusiasts who come up with applications often make them available to you for free. The only caution with free products from individuals is that the code may or may not be bug-free, so use it carefully, especially on professional sites.

Java

Java has been a hot topic since its introduction to the Web by Sun Microsystems in 1996. Despite a history that threatened to spill Java off the Net on a few occasions, Java has not only maintained its position as a serious contender for multimedia applications, but also has actually gained more support and enthusiasm for its capabilities as time goes on.

Figure 14.7.
A second visit shows the results of a randomized process: another quote.

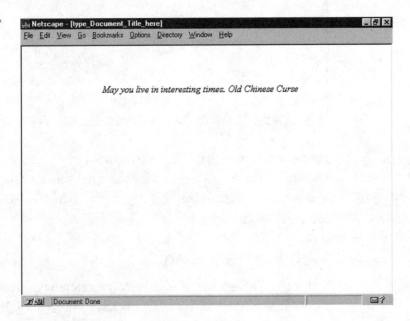

For more information on Java and JavaScript, visit Sun Microsystem's home site at http://www.sun.com/.

Java, at its core, is a programming language that resembles C++. The language allows programmers to create a package of objects with a stream-lined, platform-independent piece of programming code. The package is sent to a browser where it will then run completely client-side—not having to query the server again. This allows for quick delivery of an application, or "applet," which can include animations, audio, and interactive graphics.

Creating a Java Ticker-Tape Banner with Applet Ace

Applet Ace is a Macromedia package that makes programming Java applets a breeze; the programming is done for you.

Download Applet Ace from Macromedia's Web site at http://www.macromedia.com/.

1. Open the dialog box for Applet Ace.

2. Fill out the various attributes that you'd like the banner to have, such as background color, text font and color, and speed and size.

3. Select any HTML file you'd like to add the applet to and input the information into the dialog box.

4. Applet Ace will generate the code into a dialog window; here's mine:

```
<applet code="Banners.class"  width="300" height="150"
codebase="C:/PROGRAM FILES/MACROMEDIA/APPLETACE/PowerApplets/
Banners/" >
<param name="cpf"          value="2">
<param name="fps"          value="20">
<param name="bgColor"      value="Pink">
<param name="size"         value="36">
<param name="exit"         value="scrollDown">
<param name="font"         value="Helvetica">
<param name="effect"       value="color">
<param name="style"        value="BoldItalic">
<param name="bgEnter"      value="None">
<param name="align"        value="Center">
<param name="enter"        value="scrollUp">
<param name="repeat"       value="1">
<param name="bgExit"       value="None">
<param name="pause"        value="1">
<param name="messages"     value="hey hi ho there!">
</applet>
```

5. Load the HTML file and the class (in this case, `banner.class`) file onto your server.

6. Test the page.

The results are shown in Figure 14.8.

Figure 14.8.
Java applet banner.

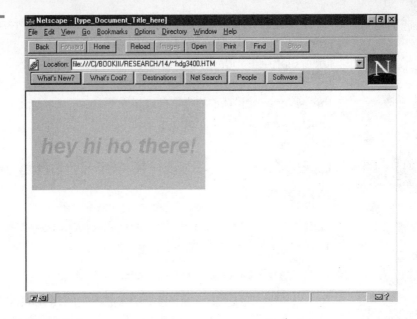

JavaScript

JavaScript is used a great deal to create interactive and dynamic navigation. Max Cannon's Red Meat comic site uses clever JavaScript to create interesting mouse-over navigation, as shown in Figure 14.9.

Figure 14.9.
JavaScript navigation. Note the reverse coloration of the icon next to the cursor.

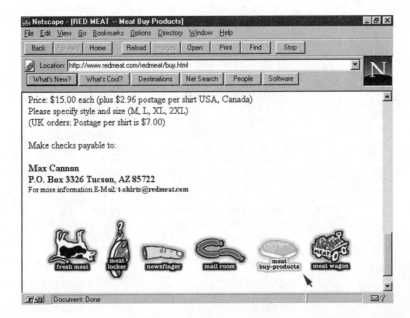

You'll notice that the designer uses a comment tag, expressing his offering of free use of the code as long as the author and copyright lines are kept intact:

```
<script language="JavaScript">

<!-- JavaScript (c) 1996-97 DesertNet . http://desert.net/ -->
<!-- Author: Wil Gerken . wil@desert.net -->
<!-- Note: You are welcome to use this code, but we require that -->
<!-- you keep the copyright and author lines intact and that you -->
<!-- email us so we can view your site also. Thanks.

// Define Browser Version (c) 1996-97 DesertNet
ver = "";
bName = navigator.appName;
bVer = parseInt(navigator.appVersion);
if (bName == "Netscape" && bVer >= 3) ver = "n3";

function imgToggle(imgObjectName, imgObjectState) {
 if (ver == "n3") {
  imgObject = new Object();
  imgObject = imgObjectName;
  imgObject.src = imgObjectState;
 }
}

function imgPreLoad(i, img) {
 if (ver == "n3") {
  cacheImg[i] = new Image();
  cacheImg[i].src = img;
 }
}

// Declare and Load Images
fresh = "images/rm_nav1b.gif";
locker = "images/rm_nav2b.gif";
prime = "images/rm_nav3b.gif";
smokey = "images/rm_nav4b.gif";
buy = "images/rm_nav5b.gif";
fun = "images/rm_nav6b.gif";
cacheImg = new Array();
imgPreLoad(0,fresh);
imgPreLoad(1,locker);
imgPreLoad(2,prime);
imgPreLoad(3,smokey);
imgPreLoad(4,buy);
imgPreLoad(5,fun);

// End Script -->

</script>
```

Here's the actual navigation:

```
<a href="fresh.html" onMouseover="imgToggle(fresh,'images/
rm_nav1b.gif')"
onMouseOut="imgToggle(fresh,'images/rm_nav1a.gif')">
```

```
<img src="images/rm_nav1a.gif" name="fresh" border=0 width=97
height=108 alt="fresh meat"></a>

<a href="locker.html" onMouseover="imgToggle(locker,'images/
rm_nav2b.gif')" onMouseOut="imgToggle(locker,'images/
rm_nav2a.gif')"><img src="images/rm_
nav2a.gif" name="locker" border=0 width=57 height=108 alt="meat
locker"></a>

<a href="prime.html" onMouseover="imgToggle(prime,'images/
rm_nav3b.gif')" onMouseOut="imgToggle(prime,'images/
rm_nav3a.gif')"><img src="images/rm_
nav3a.gif" name="prime" border=0 width=85 height=108 alt="prime
cuts"></a>
<img src="images/rm_nav4c.gif" name="smokey" width=106 height=108
alt="smokey links">

<a href="buy.html" onMouseover="imgToggle(buy,'images/rm_nav5b.gif')"
onMouseOut="imgToggle(buy,'images/rm_nav5a.gif')">
<img src="images/rm_
nav5a.gif" name="buy" border=0 width=85 height=108 alt="meat-buy
products"></a>
```

View Max Cannon's site at http://www.redmeat.com/redmeat/.

```
<a href="fun.html" onMouseover="imgToggle(fun,'images/rm_nav6b.gif')"
onMouseOut="imgToggle(fun,'images/rm_nav6a.gif')"><img src="images/rm
nav6a.gif" name="fun" border=0 width=89 height=108 alt="fun with
meat"></a>
<p>
```

NOTE: More information and actual examples of Java are available on the CD-ROM accompanying this book.

Visual Basic and VBScript

Microsoft offers up the popular Visual Basic program and its related script for Web interactivity. Especially good for form authentication, customization, and multimedia events that run on the client-side, Visual Basic and VBScript are stable and sensible additions to the Web programming family.

VBScript has occasionally been referred to as the "Java Killer," but time isn't proving that to be even remotely true. With cross-browser implementation from Netscape and Microsoft's native Internet Explorer, there's little reason to consider the two in competition. It really boils down to a matter of personal choice and program flexibility.

Figure 14.10 demonstrates an interesting use of VBScript. The Explorer (Windows 95 file management system) style frame hierarchy is actually live. Click a + sign to get the subdirectories available.

Figure 14.10.
VBScript in action.

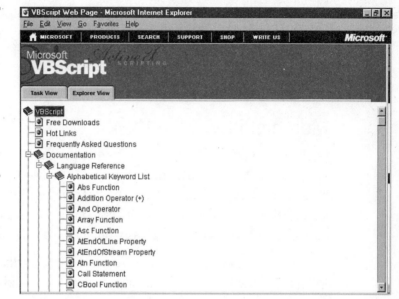

See Microsoft's VBScript site in action at `http://www.microsoft.com/vbscript/` and get more information on Visual Basic and VBScript to boot.

For complete information on ActiveX and a link to examples, visit the SiteBuilder Network's Programming page at `http://www.microsoft.com/workshop/prog/default.asp`.

ActiveX

Another entry into the Microsoft realm of program-style offerings is ActiveX. ActiveX seeks to incorporate components for objects built in any language and make them viewable via the Internet Explorer Web browser. This technology is extremely potent because it can control everything from the way navigation is managed to interactive objects such as marquees and tickers, right up to plugging in entire applications programmed in Visual Basic or other languages.

Virtual Reality Modeling Language (VRML)

A visionary programming language that has yet to find its true purpose in Web technology is the Virtual Reality Modeling Language, or VRML. VRML creates virtual environments and objects, and associated plug-in controls allow for visitors to spin the image, back up, and fly through virtual space.

The application is truly interactive, but its professional use is still limited. Because of its capabilities, it does hold a lot of promise for the future. Those capabilities and the fact that sound can now be added to VRML bring the language to an entirely new level.

A great site to look at VRML images and codes can be found at `http://vrml.sgi.com/worlds/index.html`.

VRML allows for linking from one place in the object to another, or even to another Web page. I could literally create doorway after doorway of VRML-based pages. The VRML code is in its second version, and continues to fascinate some of the Web's foremost programmers.

Multimedia

Multimedia on the Web takes many forms. It's as simple as an animated GIF, or as complex as a full multimedia package such as Macromedia's Shockwave. In between there are a variety of multimedia delivery systems, including individual video and audio clips, streaming video and audio, and animation packages such as Macromedia Flash (originally called FutureSplash).

How to deliver multiple forms of media over bandwidth that varies from house to house, office to office, city to city, state to state, and country to country proves no easy challenge. Media developers are continually looking to find ways of minimizing file sizes by optimizing technology. Some have succeeded quite gracefully, but often at a loss in quality. A good example of this is "streaming" media such as RealAudio or Video. Although both provide relatively fast delivery of data, there may be jumps and starts, and the medium is not ideal for high-fidelity or high-resolution products.

Advanced multimedia integration in Web sites is therefore recommended only when a good knowledge of audience and site intent are in order. If you're out to have fun, or dazzle your visitors, or have a very specific reason for delivering such media, fantastic! However, if your aim is to reach a broad audience that may or may not have the capabilities or desire to view advanced applications, stick to simple active media events such as animated GIFs.

Animation and Multimedia Packages

The most common animation and multimedia packages in use today on the Web are

Looking for the latest animation tools? Check out the CD-ROM for starters. To read all about GIF animation technology, visit Royale Frazier's Animated GIF site at `http://members.aol.com/royalef/index.html`.

❑ **GIF animation.** Taking advantage of certain aspects of the GIF89a technology, GIF animations are a clever and useful way of adding active content to Web pages. They are very compact, run independently of the server (as all the data is contained in the GIF), and are supported by Netscape Navigator 2.0b4 and above, Internet Explorer 3.0 and above, as well as other browsers. Another advantage is that they are terrifically simple to make. All that is required is a simple graphic animating tool such as the GIF Construction Set for Windows, or GIFBuilder for the Macintosh. The animator creates a series of GIF graphics that will be placed in sequential order. These graphics are much like the typical "cells" used in standard animation. Then, using the construction tool, the animator places the cells in sequence and adds a loop value. GIF animations can loop indefinitely, loop once and stop, and have different time sequences between cells.

Download the current demo version of Flash at `http://www.macromedia.com/software/flash/`.

❑ **Animation using Macromedia Flash.** Just a few months ago, a small software company named FutureWave came out with a terrific product, FutureSplash. It is a compact animation tool with powerful options. Macromedia quickly bought the product and introduced it as part of Shockwave under the name "Flash."

Macromedia has added several new features in the new version of Flash, including the addition of audio. The interface is extremely user friendly, and available for Windows 95, Windows NT, Macintosh, and Power Macintosh users. A trial version is available for download right off of the site, and the product is reasonably priced. I highly recommend this product for individuals who are looking to add very attractive, interactive content to Web pages with very little learning curve. In fact, the tutorials in the software are really easy to use, and help you get a quick start on putting the product to work.

❑ **Animation, audio, and interactive presentations with Macromedia Shockwave.** Shockwave has been around for several years now, and a steady following of enthusiasts have made it the option when it comes to inline presentations from a complete multimedia package.

Get all the latest on Shockwave from Macromedia's Shockzone at `http://www.macromedia.com/shockzone/`.

Supported by a plug-in for Netscape and an ActiveX control for Internet Explorer, Shockwave is exciting because it allows multimedia designers to use familiar tools such as Director in order to accomplish the end goal of a Web-based presentation. Recently, an exciting addition was made to the Shockwave package: streaming data. This means the information reaches your computer faster than ever.

QTVR is made by Apple. For software and support, point your browser to `http://qtvr.quicktime.apple.com/`.

❏ **QuickTime Virtual Reality.** Known as QTVR for short, this is an effective tool for virtual panoramas and objects. Using still photography that is "sewn" together with QTVR applications panoramic views of rooms, products, or whatever you require for close viewing can be created. The viewer allows the visitor to zoom in, move up, down, and side to side.

To decide for yourself the better package, visit Black Diamond at `http://www.bdiamond.com/`.

❏ **Surround Video.** Based on similar "seaming" technology, Black Diamond's Surround Video accomplishes the same panoramic, virtually real vistas as QTVR. The differences appear to be better stability and cross-platform compatibility.

Audio

Audio on the Web can be handled in the following ways:

Visit RealAudio's Web site at `http://www.realaudio.com/`.

❏ **Streaming Audio.** The best and most popular example of streaming audio is RealAudio. Streaming data is an effective solution to large data transfers, because its underlying technology works to deliver the results quickly, allowing people almost instantaneous access to the media.

Many sites are employing RealAudio into their long-term plans. An interesting and very logical application of RealAudio can be found at National Public Radio's Web site at `http://www.npr.org/`.

❏ **Inline Audio.** It's possible to add small MIDI or WAV files right onto a page. IE 2.0 introduced the option via the `<embed>` tag. Netscape 3.0 caught up quickly to enable the feature.

Size is the critical element here: Large sound files take time to load and a person might be off the page by the time the sound file has been delivered from the server.

CAUTION: Another problem with embedded audio is looping. Some people like to loop the sound to repeat over and over again. If you're spending any period of time with a Web page, this can become annoying. Multimedia should be used like makeup. Enhance, but don't detract from your site's natural style.

For an excellent discussion of audio file and file types, visit sound engineer Phil Stevens's audio page at `http://www.euphoria.org/home/help/help.html`.

❏ **Sound Files.** Downloadable sound is very handy for certain applications. For example, if you're a record label and want to demo some of your high-fidelity tunes, offering sound files can be an efficient method of media delivery. People in those circumstances are willing to wait for the files, and that should be your criteria for using any downloadable media. Ask whether the visitor will wait; if the answer leans toward the affirmative, go for it.

Video

Video on the Web works much like audio, but because of the amount of data inherent to video, it's even more difficult to manage. There are streaming and inline options as well as downloadable file types:

❏ **Streaming and inline video.** This works in the same way that streaming audio does. The results are intriguing, as shown in Figure 14.11. Some of the companies making streaming video products include Progressive Networks, the makers of RealAudio (`http://www.realaudio.com/`); Vivo Software (`http://www.vivo.com/`); Xing technologies (`http://www.streamworks.com/`); and VDO (`http://www.vdo.com/`). Visit these Web sites to get the latest on products, performance, platform, and browser compatibility.

❏ **Video files for download.** Some of the formats for downloadable, cross-browser video include `.AVI` and `.MOV` from Microsoft and Apple, respectively. MPEG is another choice for cross-platform stability. For tools and a host of information on video products, visit `http://www.realvideo.com/` (not affiliated with RealAudio).

Figure 14.11.
*Streaming Video
from Progressive
Networks and
filmmaker Spike Lee.*

TASK Creating an Animated GIF

For this task, you'll need a GIF animating program, which makes the animation process very simple. I'm going to demonstrate the exercise with Cel Assembler for Windows 95, which is located on the CD-ROM. You can use any shareware or professional animation tool that you like.

1. Open Cel Assembler or the animation program.

2. Add the images provided in the Chapter 14 `image` directory into the program. Note that each of these files is a small, optimized GIF. If you're creating your own animations, you'll want to save your files in this fashion.

3. After the images are added, you'll need to decide how many times to loop (how many times the animation will play) the animation.

CAUTION: To avoid frustrating visitors, an animation should usually run once or twice. You can run it endlessly, but make sure there's a reason to do so.

4. Save the file as a GIF.

5. View it in your browser. Notice that the end result is fun and simple, but also small—only 14 kilobytes.

Dynamic Content

Dynamic content is making headlines, and the reasons are numerous. In terms of Dynamic HTML, the general response is excitement, because this technology is a very clear-cut advancement in the way the Web and its underlying structure are used. However, dynamic forms, such as Push Technology, are creating turmoil on the ever-vocal Net.

Ideally, dynamic content enables designers to update as well as alter content in terms of style, presentation, and structure. This usually makes content both interactive and dynamic. To achieve this end, current methods used are proprietary, or are often cumbersome and time-consuming.

On the other hand, Push Technology suggests a significant change in the way that data is manipulated. The full discourse regarding what Push Technology is and why there's so much controversy surrounding it follows. I'm personally still sitting on the fence regarding the concept. I'm intrigued by the progress of what the technology could mean, but I'm concerned about taking the focus of the Web away from interactivity. In the instance of Push, as you will soon read, dynamic and interactive aren't necessarily inseparable.

Finally, there's a gray area in dynamic technologies. Proprietary platforms that interact with Web browsers have existed for some time. Some people are grouping these under Push, but actually they are not pure Push because the underlying technology demands more interaction between server and client than Push does. I call this type of media *interdependent,* because the interactivity and dependency on Net technology is equally distributed. An example of interdependent media is PointCast, which you can download and see in action at `http://www.pointcast.com/`.

Dynamic HTML

The main premise of Dynamic HTML is to add interactivity and dynamic changes to HTML pages and do this, as much as possible, on the client side.

The ultimate goal is to give Web designers maximum interactive and update control while reducing their work load.

Dynamic HTML is the result of a team effort between Microsoft (`http://www.microsoft.com`) and the World Wide Web Consortium (the standards committee governing HTML). Internet Explorer 4.0 introduces the feature, which claims to give designers the ability to dynamically alter content, style elements (text and graphic features), and a Web page's HTML structure.

Dynamic HTML controls are defined by Microsoft as allowing Web designers control of "the dynamic behavior of pages through the languages that they use today, such as JavaScript, Java, and Visual Basic, Scripting Edition."

Netscape has rushed to add Dynamic HTML compliance into its 4.0 browser. For more details on Dynamic HTML, please visit Microsoft's white sheet on the subject at `http://www.microsoft.com/workshop/prog/aplatfrm/dynhtml-f.htm`.

Push Technology

This technology runs on the premise that a server pushes data to your desktop. Another term for Push Technology is Web Broadcasting.

Simply said, Push Technology "broadcasts" information to your computer automatically. All you need to do is sign up with a given provider, much like cable television.

Supporters of the technology point to two primary defenses for the it. First is the fact that many people want information on demand. That's part of the attraction of the Web. It's especially attractive to businesses interested in reaching computer users who don't want to deal with what they perceive as a learning curve regarding the Net. Push solves that problem; the information is prepared and delivered without the individual having to go out and find it. The second, and perhaps most compelling issue, is that Push Technology is a firm step toward convergence. The strength in this argument is that the technology will itself move technology toward new levels of interactivity, which some analysts have denied will be possible for years to come. That equals progress to some thinkers.

On the other side of the fence sit those who are concerned with the problem that the Web will really end up like TV. This is perceived by some as a challenge to the free-ranges of the Internet, and nay-sayers fear the impending commercialism, censorship, and control that Push Technologies could conceivably bring along with them. A concern from my more academic perspective is that Push Technologies force attention away from the very aspects of the Web that make is compelling: the ability to connect with other people; its nonlinear environment, which encourages new ways of thinking and assists people with learning how to make choices; its promotion of individual and community expression on a global scale; and finally, the fact that it forces designers within it to work simultaneously in the realm of art and science.

Workshop Wrap-Up

There's a great deal to learn about interactive and dynamic content, and I wanted to spend some time giving you an overview of existing as well as up-and-coming technologies. After all, if you're designing Web sites using tables, frames, and style sheets, you're already advanced enough to require as much data on interactive and dynamic media as possible.

Next Steps

Chapter 15 is a real-time journey through CoreWave's Glass Bead Game. This compelling site relies on random processes in order to function. Not only is it an interesting example of dynamic and interactive content at work, it uses table-based layouts, multiple menus, and nonlinear navigation. It's colorful and intriguing, and pulls together many of the concepts introduced in this part of the book.

Other points of interest include

❏ Chapter 16, "Using Tables for Graphic Control"

❏ Chapter 17, "Creating Professional Presentations"

❏ Chapter 19, "Style Sheets at Work and Play"

Q&A

Q: There's so much talk about interactivity, but beyond animated GIFS, I don't see it used that much on the Web. How feasible is it, really?

A: In the short term, the answer to that question lies with your audience. Is this something they want? Is this something the client is going to insist on? In the long term, absolutely. Everything about the Web's current evolution suggests that interactivity, particularly multiple forms of media delivery, is going to be critical for designers to use on a regular basis. Don't get left behind. Savvy Web designers will learn everything they can about current technologies, even if they don't employ them immediately.

Q: Isn't most of this expensive and time-consuming?

A: Yes. And this is about business. There are plenty of come-and-go Internet and Web service providers. Many of them hear that the Internet is a great place to make a quick buck. That's not really true, and I have some sincere advice for you if you're looking for a future in new media. Take the time. Spend the money. Learn as much as you can, and where you can't learn something, find the people who can fill in those gaps. If you truly want to be competitive and not just what I call a "Fly-By-Nite.COM," you'll need to go into this business as you would any other long-term venture. Commitment is paramount, and that means finding the resources.

Of course, this doesn't mean run out and buy every technology right now, but do the research. There are plenty of demos, shareware products, books, and developer communities to help you at little or no cost. Take the time and find out what's going to work best for the type of business you envision. Your money will then be well-spent.

fifteen

Real-Time Example: Interactivity in Action— CoreWave's Glass Bead Game

Tasks in this Chapter

❏ Exploring Random Processes

❏ Looking at CoreWave Tables Step by Step

❏ Examining Linear and Non-Linear Structures

❏ Designing with Clarity, Color, Consistency

❏ Examining CoreWave's Contribution Form

This real-life example provides an opportunity to see active, interactive, and dynamic content used not for a commercial purpose, but an experiential and educational one. This departure from the commercial mien is meant both to provide a refreshing alternative to the business side of Web design and show an example of what can happen when the Web is used for creative purposes.

CoreWave set out to create a contemporary interpretation of author Hermann Hesse's famous novel, *A Glass Bead Game*. In this interpretation, the objectives are to create a highly

For an interesting discussion of Hermann Hesse and his works, visit `http://www.peabody.jhu.edu/~juragaga/Hesse.htm`.

Visit CoreWave's Glass Bead Game at `http://ybi.com/corewave/`.

interactive opportunity for people to make associations between human experiences and various media such as books, art, music, science, and technology.

The game has numerous rules relating to participation, which is encouraged via feedback forms and a planned interactive forum. Currently, the site is a richly colored experience that features interesting symbols, eloquent hand-drawn iconography by artist Erik Lundquist, and exceptional table-based layout. A specifically intriguing aspect of the game is that it has dynamic content. The dynamic aspect of Glass Bead Game isn't achieved through Push or Dynamic HTML. Both of those technologies are in their early stages and not immediately applicable to broad audiences. The intuitive change in this regard comes about as a result of pre-processed, randomized data used in an innovative fashion that is at the core of the game's premise.

As you experience the site, remember the lessons learned in the past chapters, especially in terms of navigation, non-linear navigation, and how interactivity is created. The joining of these functions is critical, providing a powerful example as to how they can be combined for unique results.

Some of the highlighted learning examples in this chapter are

- ❏ Standard navigation such as client-sided maps and hyperlinks
- ❏ Bottom-based navigation
- ❏ Non-linear navigation
- ❏ Text navigation
- ❏ Multiple menus
- ❏ Comment tagging
- ❏ Interactivity with:
    - ❏ JavaScript
    - ❏ GIF animations
- ❏ Dynamic content with pre-processed randomization techniques

The Core Experience

The splash page is the starting point of Glass Bead Game's experience. You are met with three visual elements: a site header graphic, a main splash graphic, and an animated GIF (see Figure 15.1). The main splash is very compelling, with stylized arrows pointing to a central eclipse.

Figure 15.1.
CoreWave's Glass Bead Games splash page.

Many others have created models of Hesse's Glass Bead Game on the Web, and there's even a mailing list for fans of the work. So much interest in applying Hesse's visionary ideas (the book was written in the 1940s) exists in fact that the Yahoo! search engine has an entire section dedicated to it at `http://www .yahoo.com/ Recreation/ Games/Glass_ Bead_Game__The/`.

Immediately apparent is that the page requires a response. It's not just a click; there are obvious although subtle choices. Should you select an intellectual path? An emotional one? Just where will these areas take you?

The visuals are intriguing, as is the code. This is especially true with regard to the random process, the first of which is introduced immediately with this page. Here's the structure of the splash page, including the graphic images and the random syntax.

Exploring Random Processes

This task will give you a feel for the way a random process is created.

1. Begin in your HTML editor with the following shell syntax:

```
<html>
<head>
```

```
<title>A Glass Bead Game</title>
</head>

</center>

</body>

</html>
```

2. Add the images and mark the section where you'll place the random process syntax:

```
<body bgcolor="#330066" text="#FFFFFF" link="#330066"
vlink="#330066" alink="#33066">

<center>

<img src="graphics/gb-head.jpg" width=400 height=46>
<br>

<!-- Begin Random Process -->
<!-- End Random Process -->

<img src="graphics/hf.gif" width=430 height=23>
```

3. Insert the random process syntax:

```
<!--#include file="hrefs.txt" random="16" -->
<br>
```

NOTE: This is a "mock-up" example, provided to give you a taste of how CoreWave created the randomization syntax. Chapter 14, "Adding Interactive and Dynamic Content," has a full example on randomization.

4. Upon closer examination of the random code, you'll see that it's really very straightforward for this particular server. The #include statement is fairly self-explanatory, meaning that the file called upon should be included in the place of the code:

```
<!-- Begin Random Process -->

<!--#include file="hrefs.txt" random="16" -->
<br>

<!-- End Random Process -->
```

NOTE: The HTMLX extension denotes a random file on this server. Other servers will control the syntax and extensions differently. Check with your systems administrator for more details on how to create random dynamic data with the hardware and software available to you.

5. But then something interesting happens. The browser calls upon a text file. This file controls the 16 currently available HTML, images, and JavaScript "mouse-over" data. This is the central "brain" of the main interface, plugging in the dynamic information to the splash page.

```
<a href="./rec/1.htmlx" onmouseover="window.status='Question
Everything'; return true"><img src="graphics/splasha.jpg"
width=400 height=253></a>

<a href="./rec/2.htmlx" onmouseover="window.status='Go here';
return true"><img src="graphics/splasha.jpg" width=400
height=253></a>

<a href="./rec/3.htmlx" onmouseover="window.status='Do This';
return true"><img src="graphics/splasha.jpg" width=400
height=253></a>

<a href="./rec/4.htmlx" onmouseover="window.status='Click Now';
return true"><img src="graphics/splasha.jpg" width=400
height=253></a>

<a href="./rec/5.htmlx" onmouseover="window.status='What do we
have Here?'; return true"><img src="graphics/splasha.jpg"
width=400 height=253></a>

<a href="./rec/6.htmlx" onmouseover="window.status='Mystery
Ensues'; return true"><img src="graphics/splasha.jpg" width=400
height=253></a>

<a href="./rec/7.htmlx" onmouseover="window.status='What is
Truth'; return true"><img src="graphics/splasha.jpg" width=400
height=253></a>

<a href="./rec/8.htmlx" onmouseover="window.status='Believe
only what you want'; return true"><img src="graphics/
splasha.jpg" width=400 height=253></a>

<a href="./rec/9.htmlx" onmouseover="window.status='Have Faith';
return true"><img src="graphics/splasha.jpg" width=400
height=253></a>
```

```
<a href="./rec/10.htmlx" onmouseover="window.status='Who am I?';
return true"><img src="graphics/splasha.jpg" width=400
height=253></a>

<a href="./rec/11.htmlx" onmouseover="window.status='Question
Faith'; return true"><img src="graphics/splasha.jpg" width=400
height=253></a>

<a href="./rec/12.htmlx" onmouseover="window.status='Have
Everything?'; return true"><img src="graphics/splasha.jpg"
width=400 height=253></a>

<a href="./rec/13.htmlx" onmouseover="window.status='You Need
This!'; return true"><img src="graphics/splasha.jpg" width=400
height=253></a>

<a href="./rec/14.htmlx" onmouseover="window.status='Click Here
for Sex!'; return true"><img src="graphics/splasha.jpg"
width=400 height=253></a>

<a href="./rec/15.htmlx" onmouseover="window.status='Wanna Shake
the Hand of God?'; return true"><img src="graphics/splasha.jpg"
width=400 height=253></a>

<a href="./pro/god-jux.htm" onmouseover="window.status='Om';
return true"><img src="graphics/splasha.jpg" width=400
height=253></a>
```

Figures 15.2 and 15.3 demonstrate what happens on two different visits to the splash page.

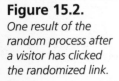

Figure 15.2.
One result of the random process after a visitor has clicked the randomized link.

Figure 15.3.

The viewer has clicked the randomized link, and yet another page appears.

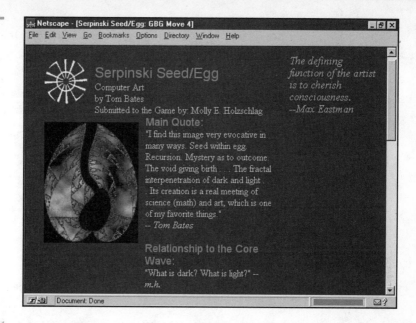

TASK   Looking at CoreWave Tables Step by Step

The content pages within the game follow a similar layout design, as you've just seen with Figures 15.2 and 15.3. Underneath the page is detailed table layouts, relying on stacked, as well as nested, tables.

The first table cell is jam-packed with details, including titles, graphics, and hypermedia options:

1. Examine the following code. You'll notice several important things about this first section of the cell. First, the section is clearly defined with comment tags. Then, you get to see another layer of randomization. The symbol link refers to a definition of the symbol: a page with the HTMLX extension, denoting that there is randomization on that level of the site. Finally, there's also a JavaScript mouse-over call. All of this is in the very first section of the layout.

   ```
   <!-- begin Highlight data table -->

   <table border="0" cellpadding="0" cellspacing="10" width="600">
   <tr>
   ```

```
<td width="420" valign="top">
<a href="http://ybi.com/corewave/symb-def.htmlx"
onmouseover="window.status='symbol definition'; return true">
<img src="../graphics/sym-ani1.gif" width="77" height="75"
border="0" align="left" hspace="10" vspace="10"></a>
<br clear="right">

<!-- update the following for each recommendation -->
```

2. The table cell continues with the following. Special emphasis should be placed on the way that breaks, particularly the `<br clear="all">`, are used to keep the information flush together.

```
<font face="arial,helvetica" size="+2" color="#cc6633">
the red line
</font><br>
paintings
<br>
by Bill Rabinovitch
<br>
submitted to the game by: Robert Carrillo Cohen
<br clear="all">
```

3. Now you'll see the introduction of a nested table. This table holds a graphic and a main quote. Look specifically at the way table cells are used to contain the graphic and the quotation:

```
<table width="400" border=0 cellspacing=0 cellpadding=0>
<tr>

<!-- insert highlight graphic here. adjust width with hspace if
needed. -->

<td valign="top">
<img src="../graphics/horse.jpg" width=125 height=159 hspace=10
vspace=20 border=0 align=left></td>
</td>

<td valign="center">
<font face="arial,helvetica" size="+1" color="#cc6633">main
quote:</font><br>
"I am fundamentally interested in conveying a sense of pain
and struggle about life, art and relationships between men and
women, tempered with my native ability to find beauty in the
ashes."<br>
<i>
-- Bill Rabinovitch
```

```
</i>
<p>

<font face="arial,helvetica" size="+1"
color="#cc6633">Relationship to the Core Wave: </font><br>
"Are we the most present when we are absent?
Does art come from inner or outer inspiration?"
<i>
-- r.c.c.
</i>

</td>
</tr>
</table>
```

Now the sub-table closes.

4. The main table continues with the following, which includes an example of a random event. In this case, a text file containing 100 quotes is called upon to deliver one each time this page is contained. This constant use of randomization makes for a very compelling site because you can conceivably visit the page 100 times and see it differently every time.

```
<!-- begin random process for quote -->

<td valign=top width=200>
<font size=+1 color="#99cc66">

<!--#include file="quotes.txt" random="100"-->

</font>

<!-- end random process -->

</td>
</tr>

</table>

<!-- end highlight data table -->
```

TASK Examining Linear and Non-Linear Structures

As you continue through the page code, both linear and non-linear navigation options begin to appear. The central bank of links, both graphical and textual, offer avenues to other sections of the site using compelling icons that symbolically represent specific areas, and mouse-over JavaScripting to identify the area section. The main division is between a "main" category, the dominant theme in which the content has been placed, and "related" categories, areas of interest linked to more content. The result is a complex Web of non-linear and dynamic relationships.

At this point in the game, a bit of linearity is introduced, with the text options beneath the iconographic ones. In this case, a link to the game rules, a main map back to the splash page, submissions, and a related catalog are offered.

Figure 15.4 shows a close-up of this intricate navigation section of the Glass Bead Game.

1. Examine the code for this section. The first table cell contains iconographic navigation as seen with the linked images in bold:

```
<!-- begin icon bank -->

<hr width="75%">

<center>

<table border=0 cellspacing=0>
<tr>

<td>
<center>
<font face="arial,helvetica" size="+1"
color="#cc6633">main category
</font>
<p>

<a href="../cat/art-cat.htmlx" onmouseover="window.status='art';
return true">
<img src="../icons/art-ico.gif" alt="icons" width="30"
height="30" border="2">
</a>

</center>
</td>
```

2. Now you'll notice the use of a spacer, with a descriptive comment to alert people maintaining the page as to what its use is for:

```
<!-- table cell with invisible pixel used for spacing between
main category and related categories -->
```

```
<td>
<img src="../graphics/dot.gif" hspace="10">
</td>
```

Figure 15.4.
*Icon and text
navigation close-up.*

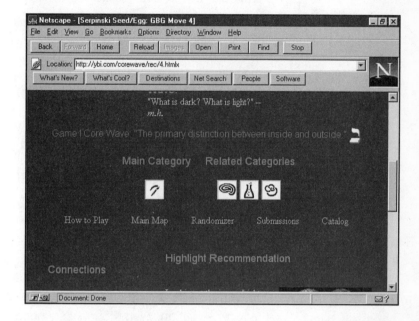

3. The following table cell holds the icon-based navigation. On each
CoreWave content page, the icons are individually selected from a
main group to match the contents of that page. Therefore, each
content page might have a different series of icons. Note how the
icons are stacked in the code. This places them side by side:

```
<td>
<center>
<font face="arial,helvetica" size="+1" color="#cc6633">related
categories
</font>
<p>

<a href="../cat/bel-cat.htmlx" onmouseover="window.status='belief';
return true"><img src="../icons/bel-ico.gif" alt="icons"
width="30" height="30" border="2"></a>

<a href="../cat/comm-cat.htmlx" onmouseover="window.status=
'communications';
return true"><img src="../icons/comm-ico.gif" alt="icons"
width="30" height="30" border="2"></a>
```

```
<a href="../cat/comu-cat.htmlx" onmouseover="window.
status='community';
return true"><img src="../icons/comu-ico.gif" alt="icons"
width="30" height="30" border="2"></a>

<a href="../cat/myth-cat.htmlx" onmouseover="window.status='myth';
return true"><img src="../icons/myth-ico.gif" alt="icons"
width="30" height="30" border="2"></a>

<a href="../cat/work-cat.htmlx" onmouseover="window.status='tools';
return true"><img src="../icons/tools-ico.gif" alt="icons"
width="30" height="30" border="2"></a>

<a href="http://ybi.com/corewave/random.htmlx"
onmouseover="window.status=
'have faith/question everything'; return true"><img src="../
icons/spir-ico.gif"
alt="icons" width="30" height="30" border=2></a>

</center>
</td>

</tr>
</table>
```

4. The comment tagging makes the logic of the syntax easy to follow. If you were updating code on this complex page, you could easily find the text navigation, even though it's embedded in so much code:

```
<!-- text navigation bar -->

<a href="../adm-main.htmlx" onmouseover="window.status=
'clarify'; return true"> how to play</a><img src="../graphics/
dot.gif" hspace="17">

<a href="../map-main.htmlx" onmouseover="window.status='find
your way';
return true"> main map</a><img src="../graphics/dot.gif"
hspace="17">

<a href="../random.htmlx" onmouseover="window.status=
'nonlinear'; return true">
randomizer</a><img src="../graphics/dot.gif" hspace="17">

<a href="../sub-main.htmlx" onmouseover="window.status='make a
move';
```

```
return true">submissions</a><img
src="../graphics/dot.gif" hspace="17">

<a href="../mtv-main.htmlx" onmouseover="window.status='corewave
catalog'; return true">catalog</a>

</center>

<hr width="75%">
<p>

<!-- end icon bank -->
```

5. After this icon bank, the table continues with content layout, including static quotes, graphics, and text. When you finally reach the bottom of the page, a linear, familiar form of navigation stabilizes the site in the mind of the visitor. Note the image mapping in this code example:

```
<!-- main navigation bar -->

<center>
<img src="../graphics/main-nav.gif" width=425 height=45 border=0
usemap="#all-map">
</center>
<br>

<!-- begin map data -->

<map name="all-map">
<area shape="rect" coords="316, 25, 395, 45"
href="../mtv-main.htmlx"
onmouseover="window.status='corewave catalog'; return true">

<area shape="rect" coords="161, 26, 269, 46" href="../sub-
main.htmlx"
onmouseover="window.status='make a move'; return true">

<area shape="rect" coords="14, 25, 127, 45" href="../adm-
main.htmlx"
onmouseover="window.status='clarify'; return true">

<area shape="rect" coords="246, 3, 356, 20" href="http://
ybi.com/corewave/
random.htmlx" onmouseover="window.status='nonlinear'; return
true">
```

```
<area shape="rect" coords="56, 2, 159, 22" href="../map-
main.htmlx"
onmouseover="window.status='find your way'; return true">

<area shape="default" nohref>
</map>

<!-- end map data -->
```

6. The coders of the site then added a footer containing the copyright and mail link for contacting CoreWave:

```
<!-- begin footer -->

<center>

<font size="-3">
&copy; <a href="mailto:corewave1@aol.com">1997 CoreWave (tm)</a>
</font>

</center>

<!-- end footer -->
```

Figure 15.5 shows a close-up of the bottom-base map navigation, which also uses JavaScript for link associations.

Figure 15.5.
This bottom-based navigation menu adds linearity.

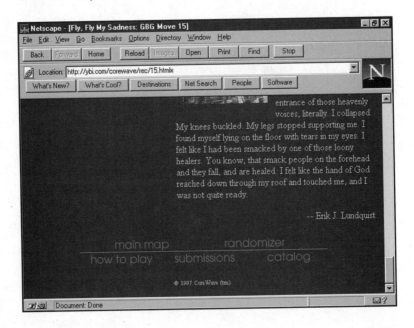

Linear Grounding

One important need that CoreWave's Glass Bead Game addresses is a centralization of data. This helps to "ground" the visitor by providing a main map of the site. All of the site areas are available from this section, as shown in Figure 15.6.

Figure 15.6.
The site's main map offers a grounding point for site visitors.

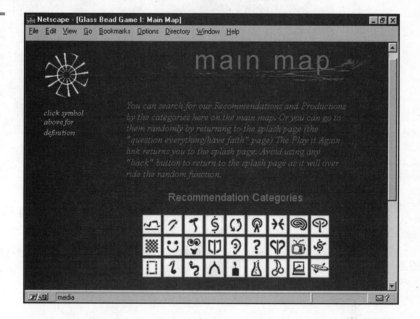

Movement

Dynamic and interactive content demands change and movement. Glass Bead Game offers this up most consistently with the continual random changes that occur.

An additional example of movement on the site is The Symbol. Inspired by Hopi Indian symbols, The Symbol required three artists to create, color, and animate the final versions. There are three animated GIF renditions of The Symbol (see Figure 15.7) on the site.

Figure 15.7.
The primary symbol animation.

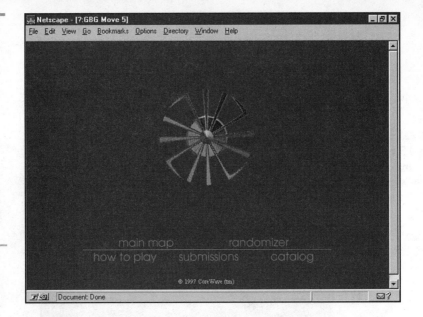

Appendix A, "Directory of Resources," offers a number of graphic design resources, including animation information. The CD-ROM accompanying this site also provides tools with which to design GIF animations.

The primary symbol is quite a hypnotic and engaging element of the total design, and adds a visual dynamic that is relatively simple to pull off. GIF animations are pretty simple to do, largely due to the fact that some terrific tools exist to assist designers in making them. One such tool is Cel Assembler, and can be found on the CD-ROM accompanying this book.

Designing with Clarity, Color, and Consistency

Why is this site so successful despite the amount of interactive, dynamic, and diverse content it contains? Through the study of its well-defined structure, as noted in the previous task, you can achieve a sense of the clear options within what might appear to be confusing amounts of code. You can achieve this in your own site work by clarifying and defining the site's intent with explanations of why the site functions in a certain way. This aids the visitor in understanding the way a site works, its purpose, and how to fully interact with the site. One example of this on the CoreWave site is the definition of The Symbol, which appears in Figure 15.8.

Figure 15.8.
*The Symbol's
definition page.*

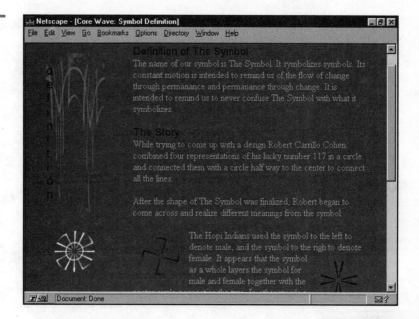

Now study this next design concept. Color helps a visitor determine where in the site he or she is. This is done with a color palette change. Anything that is strictly in the game has a violet-blue background, but CoreWave's administration sections and definitions appear with a rust background (see the CD-ROM for color details). But pay attention: The title and link colors are drawn from the Game palette.

Finally, repetition is important. Repeated symbols and variations on headers and designs carry through each section, achieving much-needed consistency (see Figure 15.9). The repetition of color, icons, and symbolic designs assist in creating order to the chaos that a very dynamic site can readily fall into. Designers are offered a very strong example of a concept discussed in Chapter

12, "Multiple Menus and Non-Linear Navigation." Capturing the Web's non-linear power without *controlling* it too dramatically can produce interesting effects.

Figure 15.9.
Note the subtle repetition of top-level elements in headers and graphics.

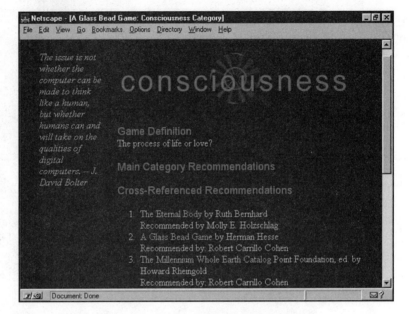

Interaction and Involvement

Visitors to the site can actually become contributors to the game. This adds another level of interactivity: the ability for an individual to react with the game and the people behind it in order to be full participants.

The interactive form (see Figure 15.10) based on CGI scripting allows the visitor to input a recommendation for the game. These recommendations will be reviewed by the Game Master for inclusion into the site.

Figure 15.10.
Want to contribute?
Fill out the form!

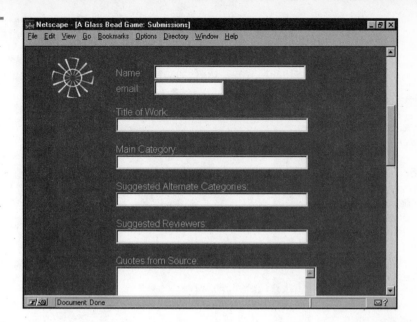

Examining CoreWave's Contribution Form

CGI form code provides a real-life example of the form calling to the `mailto` CGI function on the ybi server. Check with your system administrator for the proper syntax necessary to process forms on the server you are using.

Here's a look at CGI code in action:

1. You begin, as with all forms, using the `<form>` tag. The attributes that follow are specific to the server that CoreWave uses:

```
<form method="post" action="http://ybi.com/htbin/mailto">
<input name="from" type="hidden" value="corewave@bitbucket.opus1.com">
<input name="subject" type="hidden" value="submissions">
<input name="version" type="hidden" value="form version is 2.0">
<input name="to" type="hidden" value="corewave1@aol.com">
```

2. The code continues with the input fields for name, e-mail, and the submission you'd like to recommend. For example, if you read a great book that you think would fit in with the CoreWave experience, you can fill that information in here:

```
<pre>

<font face=arial,helvetica size=+1>
```

In the case of Glass Bead Game, participation is encouraged because that's part of the game concept. A very prominent method of gaining and increasing audience or customers for an event or product is to make them feel a part of that event, or the culture surrounding a product. There's no better example of this than television advertising, which some analysts consider to be exploitative of that phenomenon. I encourage Web designers to understand the influence of media, and how to harness that influence to make your site a successful one, always keeping a sense of ethics in mind.

```
name:   <input type="text" name="name" size="35">
email:  <input type="text" name="email" size="15">

title of work:
<input type="text" name="title" size="45">

main category:
<input type="text" name="main cat" size="45">

suggested alternate categories:
<input type="text" name="alt cats" size="45">

suggested reviewers:
<input type="text" name="suggested reviewers" size="45">

quotes from source:
<textarea name="quotes" rows=5 cols=40></textarea>

highlight review:
<textarea name="review" rows=5 cols=40></textarea>

highlight core wave:
<textarea name="core wave" rows=5 cols=40></textarea>

additional comments:
<textarea name="core wave" rows=5 cols=40></textarea>

</pre>
<p>
```

3. Now the buttons are added by using the `submit` and `reset` attributes:

```
<input type="submit" value="send submission">
<input type="reset" value="do over">
```

4. And the form is completed by closing the `font` and, of course, the `form` tags, respectively:

```
</font>
</form>
```

Simplicity Works, Too

Although very interesting visually, the site's main focus is on deep and thoughtful interactions. Humor is a part of the game of life—and of Glass Bead Game. There are several lighter sections to enjoy, including Juxtapositions and Belivertisements (see the CD-ROM accompanying this book). These two sections offer a sense of light-hearted fun to the site, but maintain the design sophistication and consistency that dominates.

These sections rely less on interactivity and more on the content's punch. This helps clarify another Web design guideline: Simplicity is sometimes the appropriate choice. In Glass Bead Game, the sections that are most heavily coded result in content-rich but intense pages. The lighter side of the game relies on less intricate but very visual pages.

Workshop Wrap-Up

Glass Bead Game is a fantastic example of combining interface, layout, navigation, interactivity, and dynamic content with refined Web design. It's colorful and engaging, which makes it popular. Although many of you aren't looking to create educational or entertainment-oriented sites, the lessons learned from this real-life example can be carried into the commercial design realm. By paying specific attention to the many elements that make this site strong, designers can be guided, and even inspired, to do some unique work.

Simply stated, the combination of graphic design and underlying technology make this site powerful. Balance is a dominant theme both literally and figuratively with CoreWave's Glass Bead Game. Designers will do well to achieve this balance.

It's worth mentioning that many individuals work to maintain that balance. This site combines the talents of many people, but the drive of the design and code was overseen by a single designer. This shows that a thriving Web site requires vision as well as participation. That's the finest example of dynamics: when a site engages and involves people on many levels—technical, artistic, and emotional.

Next Steps

The next section of the book focuses on graphic design elements and how to use tables and style sheets to master graphics, fonts, and manage large data. These seemingly elementary aspects of Web design are actually only now coming into the control of designers through the introduction of more sophisticated Web browsers and underlying code.

Check out the following topics of interest:

❏ Chapter 16, "Using Tables for Graphic Control," discusses how to control graphic layout with tables and how to move away from standard placement and sizing of graphics.

❏ Chapter 17, "Creating Professional Presentations," offers insight into graphic design fundamentals that will help you add visual refinement to your sites.

❏ Chapter 19, "Style Sheets at Work and Play," focuses on using layout tools such as tables and style sheets to manage large data, including intranet data management.

Q&A

Q: I've viewed the images on the CD-ROM and I really like the color palettes in this example. How do you go about figuring out what colors to use?

A: Many designers have books on color palettes and sources. Check around your bookstore the next time you're out. Look in the graphic arts section and you're sure to find some excellent books that will meet your needs. Most important, you'll need to reference a "Web safe" color palette in order to select your colors. A safe palette is available on the CD-ROM.

Q: The JavaScript in this example looks so easy. Is it really?

A: What you see is what you get! Copy and paste the mouse-over script into any URL and view with a supportive browser—and there you have it. Some designers don't like this particular script because it obscures the URLs that would normally appear. In the case of CoreWave's Glass Bead Game, that is part of the fun—not knowing where you're going to end up.

PART

IV

Sophisticated Pages Using Format Control

sixteen

Using Tables for Graphic Control

Tables really come into their own when applied to graphic control. By combining the innate power of borderless tables to Web graphic design, movement away from the ordinary and into the extraordinary or unusual can occur.

There are two places where this is most apparent. The first is in complexity. A page design's layout can, as you've seen in Chapter 15, "Real-Time Example: Interactivity in Action— CoreWave's Glass Bead Game," offer a great deal of control over many elements. The end design is more dramatic and detailed than the standard Web page of old, which typically would boast a header graphic, a footer menu, and a graphic or two within the page's content. This is not to say that pages of this type are no longer useful. In many cases, a standard approach is what your audience needs (see Chapter 19, "Style Sheets at Work and Play"). However, one dominant concept in this chapter is to learn how to lay out pages in order to control the way graphics are arranged.

The other obvious move from ordinary to unusual is found in the sizing of graphics. Typical Web pages use small graphics. This can be very limiting, as well as difficult to enjoy. The reason this has been so prevalent comes from the fear of making pages too graphics heavy. Long download times are a perfect way to lose visitors, and it's long been thought that graphics that are larger visually are going to be larger in size.

This is not the case, and sometimes the results are astonishing in terms of visual intrigue and remarkably small file size. Larger graphics can, and do, function very well when laid out properly and when masterful techniques to control color have been employed.

The main teaching in this chapter comes from two real-life sites that employ this technique. The first, The Film Vault, will demonstrate how tables can be used for complex layouts. The second is Paperboy, which shows how to use table layouts and graphics control to create larger visual graphics. A preliminary look at Meta-tags, which are used in both of these sites' code, will get you started.

TIP: A trade secret: Try rendering concepts in QuarkXpress or another desktop publishing application before even attempting to go to the Web. Lay out a page just as you would any other graphic job, not thinking about the constraints the Web places upon you—at first. Then look at what you've created and solve it as though it were a puzzle. Can this design fit into the Web medium? If so, what measures will you need to take in order to make that happen?

Meta-Tagging

The code in these sites also brings up an opportunity to learn the skill of Meta-tagging. The Meta tag can be used for a number of different reasons, such as assigning ownership to a page, or even to automatically refresh pages at given intervals. For the purpose of commercial and popular Web sites, Meta-tagging enables you to provide important information about your site, including descriptions and key words.

Some of you are probably familiar with search engines and Web "worms" or "crawlers." These are intelligent "bots" and databases that seek and find Internet information. Two excellent examples are Infoseek (`http://www.infoseek.com`) and AltaVista (`http://www.altavista.digital.com`). These crawlers travel the Web and document sites for search purposes. If you've set up your Meta tags properly, the crawler will grab the information and use it, giving you ultimate control over how your listings appear.

Instead of waiting for the crawlers to get to you, you can speed up the process by submitting your URLs to Infoseek and AltaVista, as well as to other search databases. By making sure your Meta tags are appropriately maintained, you will ensure maximum exposure for your site.

TASK Using the Meta Tag

Meta tags are placed in between the `<head>` tags and below the `<title>` tag. The first important attribute for search-and-find purposes is the `name="description"` and its partner, `content=`. The second item of note is the `name="keywords"` attribute and its partner, `content=`. The description allows you to write a brief description of the site (or specific page), and the keyword allows you to list words that people might use in order to search for your information. The following task will help you put the `<meta>` tag to work.

1. Open any HTML page you've created and place the cursor after the `</title>` tag and before the `</head>` tag.

2. Add the following syntax, replacing my description with one that fits your page. Note that the Meta string simply places attributes and values without requiring a `</meta>` tag:

   ```
   <meta name="description" content="Welcome to the Company Page.
   We specialize in the highest quality service available to you!">
   ```

TIP: Make sure that your Meta descriptions are succinct and clearly state what the page is about. The shorter the better, so pack as much information as possible into the first few words. This allows people to quickly understand what your site is about and why they should visit.

3. Now add the key words, replacing my sample text with top key words you would use to define your site:

   ```
   <meta name="keywords" content="business, quality, service,
   excellence, industry leaders, well-noted">
   ```

4. You may also add the page author's name:

   ```
   <meta name="author" content="my name, my assistant's name">
   ```

5. Save the changes to your file.

Now you're ready to enjoy the benefits of Meta-tagging.

Enchanted Puzzle

The dazzling solution to the challenge of complex and large visual layout is really very simple. Instead of fitting graphics into the constraints of the Web, a table is fitted to contain the design layout. This means the graphic may have to be broken up into bits and pieces and placed in different parts of a table. This solution is profoundly changing the way graphics are controlled and designed.

It's helpful to think of the process as putting together pieces of a puzzle. The pieces in this case are made of broken-up graphics and text. The table acts as a guide to how those pieces will fit together.

The first case, shown in Figure 16.1, is a sophisticated-looking page that actually has been created using a puzzle-style piecing together of content. To give you a clear-cut idea of how these pieces fit together, look at Figure 16.2, which shows the site with table borders set to 2. The following tasks will walk you through the creation of this page and show you how and why the designers solved the layout in the manner that they did.

NOTE: Pay careful attention to the use of cells versus rows. Cells are what create columns, and are, therefore, most common to the vertical, scrolling environment of a Web site. Rows are useful for layout, but try to envision sites on the vertical first.

Figure 16.1.
The Film Vault layout.

Figure 16.2.
The same layout with the borders set to 2.

 Getting a Sense of the Puzzle

In this task, you'll actually view the graphic pieces of the FilmVault page one by one in order to see how they ultimately fit together.

1. Copy the necessary files from the CD-ROM to the Chapter 16 subfolder, images.

2. Open main1.gif, now in your Chapter 16 images subdirectory, using your browser. It should match Figure 16.3. Note how this figure is vertical and how it's cut off, both to the right and at the bottom. The designers did this in order to accommodate an "attachment" to both the vertical and horizontal edges. This creates an opportunity for a right-angle design.

Figure 16.3.
The vertical puzzle piece main1.gif shows the upper-left corner of the page's design.

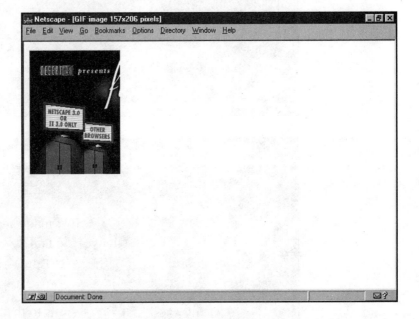

3. Open main2.gif from your images subdirectory. This is a horizontal figure, and fits snugly against the vertical piece of the graphic when placed into the table. This allows for the right angle.

DESIGN NOTE: Remember that smaller file sizes mean less load time. Another good reason to break up images, aside from the layout issue, has to do with keeping individual, and therefore total, file sizes smaller. Conceivably, this design could all be placed on one graphic, but the extra data takes up precious load time.

4. View `main3.gif` from the `images` directory. This is the bottom vertical piece, and it's animated (see Figure 16.4). Keeping this file small also helps reduce total download time.

Figure 16.4.

The bottom vertical piece `main3.gif` shows the bottom piece of the image seen in Figure 16.3.

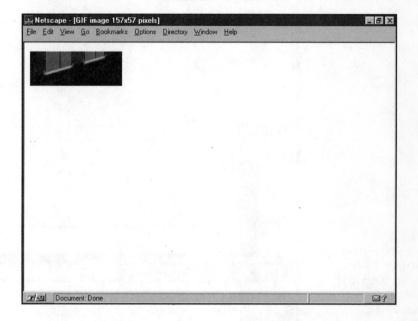

5. Take a look at `newreviews.gif`. This image appears on the page down and slightly to the right of the title. It would be impossible to place this graphic without tables (see Figure 16.5), or to place it with a graphic with a large file size.

6. Finally, view `menu3.jpg`. This menu sits to the extreme right of the page, and also relies on the vertical results of a table cell for placement (see Figure 16.6).

Visit the FilmVault at `http:// www.filmvault.com/ filmvault/`.

With these figures in mind, go to the code and create the entire page's layout, including the smaller icon graphics for the links, as well as the Internet Explorer and Netscape Navigator logos.

Figure 16.5.
The
`newreviews.gif`
sits at a central point.

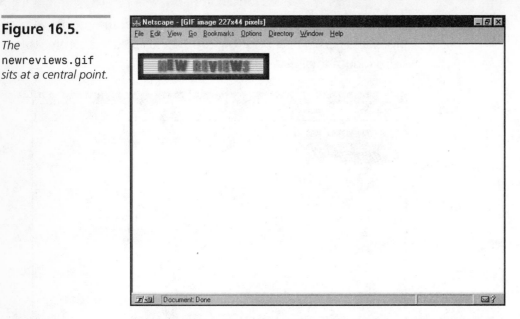

Figure 16.6.
The right-margin
navigation
menu3.jpg.

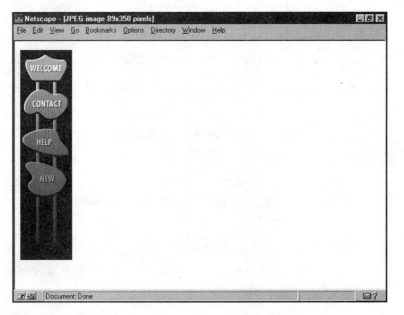

Putting the Puzzle Together with Tables

You'll put together the table step-by-step in this task. Some of the actual data has been removed from the early task activities in order to help you see the flow. The full HTML has been provided later in the task for you to check your syntax immediately, and you can always refer to the CD-ROM materials where the full source code is saved.

1. Begin as usual for a standard HTML page, setting up the shell syntax:

```
<html>

<head>
<title>DesertNet's Film Vault</title>

</head>

<body bgcolor="#000000" text="#ffffff" link="#d60017"
vlink="#d60017" alink="#d60017">

</body>
</html>
```

2. Add the meta tags, copying the prepared text as follows:

```
<meta name="keywords" content="cinema, film, film vault,
capsule, movies, movie theatre, movie theater, movie reviews,
cinema reviews, popcorn, new movies, film, video, capsules,
hollywood, actor, director, archive, actress, cult, b-movie,
independent, art, horror, sci-fi, drama, comedy, desert,
desertnet, desert net">

<meta name="author" content="wil gerken, nathan hendler,
amy burnham">
```

3. Create the table head and the first column, including images and map data. Note that the vertical pieces fit into this table, as well as any text links and comments:

```
<table border=0 width=600 cellpadding=0 cellspacing=0>
<tr>

<td valign=top align=center width=157>

<img src="images/main1.gif" width=157 height=206 border=0 alt=""
usemap="#DoorTop"><br>

<img src="images/main3.gif" width=157 height=57 border=0 alt=""
usemap="#DoorBottom">

<p>

<map name="DoorTop">
```

```
<area shape="rect" coords="15,24,75,41"
href="http://desert.net/">

<area shape="polygon" coords="25,127,92,132,92,96,26,90,26,125"
href="framed.html">

<area shape="polygon"
coords="26,146,71,156,71,205,26,205,27,144" href="framed.html">

<area shape="polygon"
coords="97,120,97,135,96,135,93,136,95,148,140,150,142,126,98,122"
href="nonframed/atoz-a.html">

<area shape="polygon"
coords="93,162,93,205,126,205,126,167,93,162"
href="nonframed/atoz-a.html">

<area shape="default" nohref>

</map>

<map name="DoorBottom">

<area shape="polygon" coords="26,37,72,24,71,0,27,0,28,37"
href="framed.html">

<area shape="polygon" coords="92,16,127,7,126,0,94,0,95,17"
href="nonframed/atoz-a.html">

<area shape="default" nohref>

</map>

<b>Enter the Vault</b>
<p>

<i>Main Feature</i><br>
<a href="framed.html">Internet Explorer 3.0<br> and Netscape 3.0
only</a>
<p>

<i>Bargain Matinee</i><br>
<a href="nonframed/atoz-a.html">Other Browsers</a>
<p>
</td>
```

NOTE: The design sophistication of this site is evident in the offering of multiple options for preferred browsers, including text access.

4. Begin the second column, including the two top images (main2.gif and newreviews.gif) and the body text:

```
<td valign=top align=left width=354><img src="images/main2.gif"
alt="" width=242 height=104>
<p><br>

<blockquote>

<img src="images/newreviews.gif" alt="New Reviews" width=227
height=44>
<p>

<!-- Begin Body -->

<a href="http://desert.net/filmvault/tw/l
LostHighway_f.html">Lost Highway</a><img src="images/twicon.gif"
valign=absmiddle width=23 height=11 alt="" hspace=5><br>

David Lynch creates a tricky&#44; troublesome&#44; ultimately
fascinating film noir experience in Lost Highway.
<p>

<a href="http://desert.net/filmvault/tw/p
PrivateParts_f.html">Private Parts </a><img src="images/
twicon.gif" valign=absmiddle width=23 height=11 alt=""
hspace=5><br>

Really now&#44; who gives a damn about Howard Stern?<p>

<a href="http://desert.net/filmvault/tw/s
subUrbia_f.html">subUrbia</a> <img src="images/twicon.gif"
valign=absmiddle width=23 height=11 alt="" hspace=5><br>

Richard Linklater&#44; director of Slacker&#44; Dazed and
Confused and the new subUrbia&#44; makes movies about the kind
of people Tucsonans know&#44; are&#44; or have produced as
offspring: Bored&#44; disaffected&#44; Suburban kids.<p>
<p>

<b>New Film Clips:</b><p>


<a href="http://desert.net/filmvault/tw/b/
BloodandWine.html">Blood and Wine</a><img src="images/
twicon.gif" valign=absmiddle width=23 height=11
```

```
alt="" hspace=5><br>

<a href="http://desert.net/filmvault/alibi/d/DonnieBrasco_
f.html">Donnie Brasco</a><img src="images/alibi_b.gif"
valign=absmiddle width=30 height=11 alt="" hspace=5><br>
<p>

<!-- End Body -->

</blockquote>

</td>
```

5. Now add the third column, including the right-border menu, map data, and browser links:

```
<td valign=top align=center width=89>
<img src="images/menu3.jpg" width=89 height=350 border=0
usemap="#Menu" alt="">
<p>

<map name="Menu">
<area shape="polygon"
coords="20,49,67,49,79,28,75,16,58,14,42,6,27,16,
10,16,9,29,21,48" href="welcome.html">

<area shape="polygon"
coords="8,90,27,66,40,66,55,73,72,73,81,84,75,103,
58,114,46,114,30,102,20,106,9,103,7,91" href="contact.html">

<area shape="polygon"
coords="5,143,38,132,58,132,68,150,80,167,80,173,
59,175,32,169,4,153,6,143" href="help.html">

<area shape="polygon"
coords="12,188,34,188,65,198,79,214,71,230,58,
240,40,243,25,240,17,233,14,224,23,215,10,195,11,190"
href="index.html">

</map>
```

NOTE: In the map data for the right-margin navigation, you'll notice the extensive coordinates. This is because the shapes are unusual: rounded rather than angular. Mapping tools allow you to accommodate this more difficult form of coordinate finding with ease, allowing for a variety of shapes, instead of just rectangles, to be mapped.

```
<a href="http://home.netscape.com/">
<img src="images/netscape.gif" width=88 height=31 border=0
alt=""></a>
<p>

<a href="http://www.microsoft.com/ie/">
<img src="images/ie.gif" width=88 height=31 border=0 alt=""></a>
<p>
</td>
</tr>
</table>
<p>
```

6. Finally, place the bottom navigation, design firm identification, and copyright information at the bottom of the page:

```
<font size=-1>
<a href="welcome.html">Welcome</a> .
<a href="contact.html">Contact</a> .
<a href="help.html">Help</a> .
<a href="index.html">New</a>
<p>
Site by <a href="http://desert.net/designs/">DesertNet Designs
</a><br>
&#169; 1995-97 <a href="http://desert.net/">DesertNet</a>
<br>
</font>
</center>

</body>
</html>
```

Paper, Anyone?

A service that is growing in popularity with Web providers and the public alike is custom delivery of news and entertainment. Web designers will do well to do the extra research and learn about how to use CGI, Perl, and other scripting and programming skills in order to offer such services to their clients and audiences.

In this example, you'll look at one such service. Paperboy delivers custom opinion and entertainment news from the southwestern United States. By filling out the form, which uses CGI and Perl to process your personal desires, you get a complete, well-designed personal paper. It's a very valuable technique, and you'll get a chance to peek at some of the code used for this particular custom provision. Also featured will be the way this form is built into the table layout.

But the most enchanting and unusual aspect to Paperboy's main page is the large, hand-drawn comic that literally splashes across the screen (see Figure 16.7). This is a real departure from the smaller, constrained graphics that dominate the Web currently. Of note is the use of multiple table rows and columns to achieve the final results.

Figure 16.7.
Paperboy's larger-than-usual image is fast loading, too.

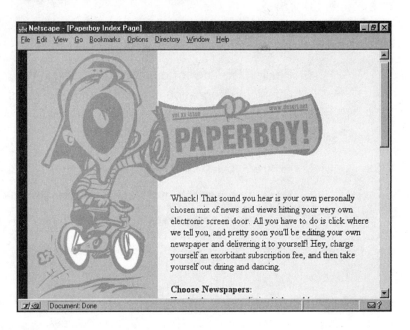

See PaperBoy in all his glory at `http://desert.net/paperboy/`.

Be sure to view the graphics on the CD-ROM to get a close look at the way color is handled on this site. Color control is a significant aspect of designing larger graphics. You'll notice there are two different blues and a bit of white in the cartoon. Keeping the number of colors down to a minimum and breaking up the graphics makes for smaller file sizes and bigger images.

 ## Examining the Parts

As you did earlier, you're going to examine the specific parts of the "puzzle."

1. In your browser, open `splash_logo1.gif`. This is the far left, top-most point of the character's head (see Figure 16.8).

2. `splash_logo2.gif` is the remaining vertical portion of the character (see Figure 16.9).

Figure 16.8.

The first piece of Paperboy.

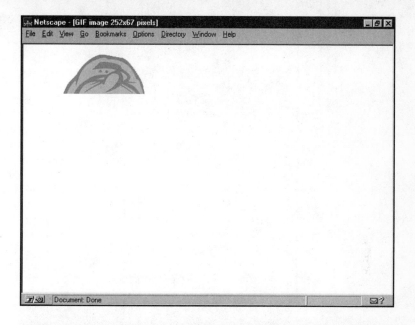

Figure 16.9.

The second vertical piece.

3. Open `splash_logo3.gif` to see the right horizontal element of the design (see Figure 16.10).

Figure 16.10.
The right horizontal element.

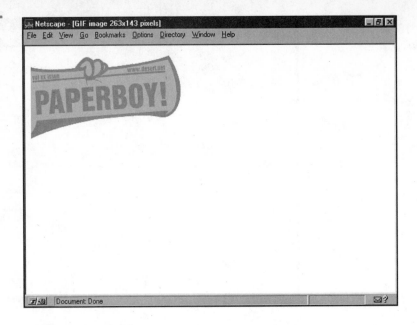

These are the primary puzzle pieces. The underlying layout with the table turned on can be seen in Figure 16.11. The only remaining graphics on the page include the background graphic and the DesertNet main navigation, which you worked with in Chapter 12, "Multiple Menus and Non-Linear Navigation."

Figure 16.11.
Paperboy's underlying layout.

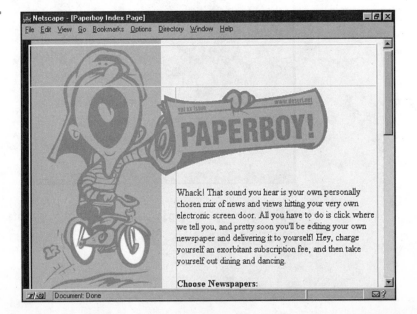

Table Control

Now you can comfortably move on to building the table for the site layout.

1. Begin with the "shell" HTML:

```
<html>
<head>

<title>paperboy index page</title>

</head>

<body bgcolor="#ffffce" background="images/splash_bkgd.gif"
vlink="#990000" link="#003399">

</body>
</html>
```

2. Add the table head and the first table cell, which contains the top-left graphic.

```
<table border=0 cellpadding=0 cellspacing=0>
<tr>

<td valign=bottom>
<img src="images/splash_logo1.gif" width=252 height=67 alt="">

</td>
```

3. The coder in this case used another cell and a paragraph mark to fill out the second empty column:

```
<td valign=bottom>

<p>

</td>

</tr>
```

NOTE: Another way to code this section and remain consistent to the dominant HTML style in this book would be to delete the preceding cell; however, be sure to include the `colspan=2` statement in the first table cell, `<td valign=bottom colspan=2>`.

4. Add the next row and the first column of the table with the second vertical graphic piece:

```
<tr>

<td valign=top width=252><img src="images/splash_logo2.gif"
width=252 height=345 alt=""><br>

</td>
```

5. Now place the following cell, which contains the final graphic part:

```
<td valign=top><img src="images/splash_logo3.gif"
width=263 height=143 alt="">

<p>
```

6. The preliminary form syntax and related text can be added as follows. Note the `.pl` (Perl) extensions in the CGI syntax, which points to a Perl script for processing.

```
<form action="http://desert.net/htbin/buildlist.pl" method=post>
<p>
Whack! That sound you hear is your own personally chosen mix of
news and views hitting your very own electronic screen door. All
you have to do is click where we tell you, and pretty soon
you'll be editing your own newspaper and delivering it to
yourself! hey, charge yourself an exorbitant subscription fee,
and then take yourself out dining and dancing.<p><b>choose
newspapers:</b><br>
Here's where you can limit which weekly newspapers you get to
choose articles from. If you are unsure, pick them all.
<p>

<input type="checkbox" name="pubs" value="tw" checked>
Tucson Weekly <input type="checkbox" name="pubs" value="alibi">
Albuquerque Alibi
<p>

<b>Choose Topics:</b><br>
Check the topics that interest you.
<p>
```

7. In the following section, a nested table provides the layout.

```
<table border=0 valign=top>
<tr>
<td width=50%>

<input type="checkbox" name="sections" value="news & opinion">
News & Opinion<br>

<input type="checkbox" name="sections" value="film & tv"
checked>
```

```
Film & TV<br>

<input type="checkbox" name="sections" value="music" checked>
Music<br>

<input type="checkbox" name="sections" value="arts & leisure"
checked> Arts & Leisure<br>
</td>

<td width=50% valign=top><input type="checkbox" name="sections"
value="food" checked> Food<br>

<input type="checkbox" name="sections" value="books" checked>
Books<br>

<input type="checkbox" name="sections" value="comics" checked>
Comics<br>

</td>

</tr>
</table>
<p>
```

8. The nested table ends, and the following information continues within the main table:

```
<b>Pre-Check Filters:</b><br>
Articles appearing on the next page will be checked or unchecked
according to the filters you pick. If this is your first visit,
just skip these options.
<p>

<input type=checkbox name="preselect" value="all" > <b>All</b> -
Checks Every Article<br>

<input type="checkbox" name="filter" value="topten" checked>
<b>Top 10% By Request</b> - Checks The Most Read Articles<br>

<input type="checkbox" name="filter" value="quality">

<b>Top 10% By Rating</b> - Checks Articles With The Highest
Users' Ratings
<p>

<b>Issue Date:</b><br>

<select name="date">
<option value="02-07-97">02-07-97
<option value="02-14-97">02-14-97
<option value="02-21-97">02-21-97
<option value="02-28-97">02-28-97
```

```
<option value="03-06-97">03-06-97
<option value="03-13-97">03-13-97
<option value="03-20-97">03-20-97
<option value="03-27-97">03-27-97
<option selected value="04-03-97">04-03-97
</select>

<input type="hidden" name="uniqueid" value="5860320603">
<p>

<input type="submit" name="give me my paper boy!" value="click
here">
</td>

</tr>
</table>

<p>
<input type="hidden" name=".cgifields" value="sections">
<input type="hidden" name=".cgifields" value="pubs">
<input type="hidden" name=".cgifields" value="filter">
</form>

<center><p><br>
<nobr>
```

9. The form ends, and the bottom navigation begins:

```
<a href="http://desert.net/">
<img src="images/desnet1.gif" alt="desertnet" border=0
width=95 height=11></a>

<a href="http://desert.net/concentrate/"><img src="images/
concentrate1.gif" alt=" concentrate" border=0 width=110
height=11></a>

<a href="http://desert.net/newsstand/">
<img src="images/newsstand1.gif" alt=" newsstand"
border=0 width=97 height=11></a>

<a href="http://desert.net/vaults/"><img src="images/
vaults1.gif"
alt=" vaults" border=0 width=67 height=11></a>

<a href="http://desert.net/htbin/buildindex.pl">
<img src="images/paperboy2.gif" alt=" paperboy!" border=0
width=95 height=11></a>
</nobr>

<p>
```

```
<font size=-1>

<a href="http://desert.net/">&#169; 1995-97 DesertNet</a> .
<a href="http://desert.net/contact_paperboy.htmlx">Contact</a> .
<a href="http://desert.net/faq_paperboy.htmlx">Help</a>
<br>

</font>

</center>
```

11. Save the file as `pboy.htm` and view it in your browser.

DESIGN NOTE: Transparent GIFs can be made with image programs, such as LView, available on the CD-ROM. They are a refined technique. For more information on how to make these with LView, check out *Laura Lemay's Guide to Sizzling Web Site Design,* published by Sams.net, which offers a step-by-step tutorial on the subject. If you're interested in creating them in Photoshop, visit `http://www.ccsr` `.uiuc.edu/~kc/kc/HTMLTools/CreateTransparent.html` for details.

Workshop Wrap-Up

The lessons encountered in this chapter are some of the most critical you can learn in terms of contemporary solutions to layout challenges. Because tables are well incorporated into most common browsers, there is little risk that your designs will fail visually. In a sense, designing with table layouts as the primary control is the least risky of all current layout tools, because it is the most stable.

This is very strengthening to the designer. Learning these techniques will put you on the forefront of creating innovative-looking designs. When you consider that you also have the ability to add frames, style sheets, or both, the possibilities become quite vast.

Tables enable the artist to first think about design without worrying about the constraints of the Web. Typically, Web designers have had to work the other way around—creating designs that will fit into the Web model. Now you can figure out ways to incorporate designs by using clever table layouts and constructs.

Next Steps

The following chapter is primarily a tutorial on some fundamental design techniques—typography, relationship of graphics and text, alignment, and white space. Chapter 17, "Creating Professional Presentations" is set up to prepare you for more detailed design tasks using style sheets.

Be sure to take some time to study:

❏ Appendix A, "Directory of Resources," which offers an abundance of resources to help you achieve your design goals

❏ Appendix B, "HTML Quick Reference," which has an HTML quick-start guide for HTML fundamentals and questions you might not otherwise have found an answer to

❏ Appendix C, "Current HTML Standards," contains a tag reference chart for style sheets, tables, and frames

Q&A

Q: Meta tags seem like a great tool for accuracy. How can I get more information on using them?

A: Visit the AltaVista engine from Digital Computers. There's a fantastic tutorial on how to use them well in the Help section. This is available from the main page at http://www.altavista.digital.com.

Q: Sometimes tables seem very complex to me. As I work through the chapters, it makes sense, but when I try to create full pages with them, I get all kinds of odd results. What am I doing wrong?

A: Well, table layouts can seem complex, but, as with most things, the more you work at it, the better you get. Go back and read the introductory section on tables. Starting simple and building from there will help you understand how table layouts are used. Honestly, it took me some time to understand how to use them well, but, then again, I didn't have the advantage of the resources that currently exist. Stay with it!

Q: I notice that the Paperboy images load right over the background. The images are square, but the results aren't. How on earth are you doing this?

A: This is the result of *transparent* GIFs. Transparency is achieved by selecting one color in the graphic to be clear. In a sense, it's like drawing a picture on a piece of clear tape. Put the tape on a piece of red paper, and the red shows through the clear sections, while the picture remains visible.

seventeen
Creating Professional Presentations

As you move forward in your Web design activities, you will benefit greatly from knowing about style. Style, in the context of this chapter, refers to the application of design attributes: fonts, color, shape, size, and spatial relationships. Style is much more than trends, but a piece of long-lasting, quality design. Trends, particularly on the Web, come and go in the blink of an eye. If you use a lot of trendy technology without style, your site might intrigue others—in the short term. For sites meant to endure, understanding elements of style is going to help you immeasurably.

This is particularly true as cascading style sheets come in to play. They are a powerful front, bearing down on the Web with significant force. But if there's nothing to back up a style sheet in terms of artistry, the technology can work against, not with, your goals.

Of course, style is often in the eye of the beholder. However, good design transcends taste as well as trends. Even is someone gets to a site that doesn't specifically appeal to his or her aesthetics, it's unlikely that a well-planned, refined communication of style is going to disturb them. In the purely artistic world, you can have the luxury of being experimental, unusual, or even offensive. In the commercial mien, that luxury is not usually available.

This doesn't mean that your commercial work can't be interesting, or even fun. It can. Doing something unique for a company, even something so seemingly insignificant as using or creating an unusual font, can actually enhance that company's identity. From a media standpoint, you want to do this. When something works for a client, he or she is going to appreciate it, and you will feel satisfaction in knowing that you've put your hard-earned skills to work.

But how does one get style? Is it something that comes naturally, or through learning? Well, truthfully, having an eye for aesthetics is an important aspect of good artistry. But, this does not mean that if you don't feel strong as an artist that you cannot have style. By learning design concepts and the related techniques to achieve them, you will certainly strengthen the look of your work. Even superb artists who work in other media come to the Web and sometimes choke. Familiar with a high-resolution environment, or the ability to use many colors, font styles, and shapes, artists can easily fail at the Web medium if they don't take the time to learn how to harness the technology.

Ultimately, that's what this book is about: finding an aesthetic and technological balance through the combined application of art and technology. This chapter will help you with the more artistic or style aspects of the field to ensure that you have a foundation on which to work with a variety of Web design demands.

Style Elements

For the purposes of this book and the learning within it, I'm going to focus on three areas of style. I'll describe the areas here, and then go into detail later, using descriptions and tasks to aid you in learning how to gain Web style.

Text Control

Text control, in Web terms, refers to how text is controlled. Graphic designers will be familiar with this area as typography. As mentioned in Chapter 3, "In Vogue: Cascading Style Sheets," the study of typography sometimes dominates individual's lives. I had a professor in graduate school who literally spent his life studying, creating, and teaching about the various aspects of typography. I've known other graphic designers who are so highly skilled at the field that they become type specialists, using and developing fonts as a living.

The Web has historically offered very little in the way of font control. This is largely due to the fact that when using fonts, even with planning, your design is still going to default to whatever fonts are available on the end user's machine. This makes your work much more difficult, because if you want to employ fonts at all, you have to ensure that you cover the standard font styles. You also want to feel confident that in the end, the viewer will see the design you worked so hard to achieve.

Dynamic HTML promises to allow for on-the-fly text variations.

Fortunately, HTML tags have allowed for a bit of font control in the past year or so, getting designers accustomed to, or at least thinking about, using fonts. The results can't be lost on Web visitors, even if they don't know what they're seeing, and certainly if they are able to view the various typographical elements that designers are introducing into their site work. Now, with Netscape seriously involved in making browsers compliant with style sheets, there will be a significant movement to use style sheets for text control.

Color and Shape

Color, and the use of it on the Web, seems to be something many Web designers face, and they meet a serious challenge. It might be that color controls on the Web, like text controls, are limited, and this is why there's so much inconsistency. Another reason color is so challenging is that Web designers, unless they have a graphic design or other artistic background, have yet to understand how color palettes work in general, and for the Web specifically. Moreover, the information on how to work with Web color is limited or buried in hard-to-find places.

Until all video monitors and computer platforms are the same, managing color on the Web will remain a specialized field of study for the Web designer. He or she must deal with cross-browser management problems, cross-platform differences, and monitor resolution issues. There are some specific guidelines that can empower the designer to make good, stable choices, both in terms of visual style and technical know-how.

Shape is another issue. The Web is filled with rectangles. Headers, footers, margins, even graphics-based designs fall prey to the misleading notion that if it's being viewed through a rectangle, it should be a rectangle. This is not so. In fact, Web sites that use shape in interesting and pleasing ways can really depart from the mundane, as you've seen with Paperboy's fun graphic in the previous chapter.

Shapes are usually created within graphics, but shapes can also be created by combining HTML-based color controls combined with graphics. Either way it's done, shape is an important element of design because different shapes express subtle but powerful meanings to us. It's true! Shapes have archetypal, historic significance. Media artists know this, and use it to entice and please people who see their work via television, print ads, and billboards.

Spatial Relationships

The way that space is treated makes an enormous difference in a Web site, both as a functional interface and a successful design. Space is regularly disregarded on the Web; or, maybe, space is feared. Remember that earlier discussion on frames and why they can be controversial? The issue is space, and how space is often broken up and constrained by too many or ill-used frames.

That message carried right through to the larger issue. Every time you place text, graphics, a programming event, or multimedia piece into the page, you take up space. So how can one successfully use that space to their advantage?

First, you should understand that space must be opened up in order to reduce the sense of containment. I've already used the small room metaphor, where mirrors are added and everything is done in a light color to give it a larger appearance. The same is true of a Web page. Being aware of a page element's location, how close to each other they are, in what direction the element lies, and what lies in-between each element, makes a difference in your design, and can help you tap into the power of the layout control that style sheets, tables, and frames offer.

Text Style and Control

Because the Web was originally a text-based environment, there are many ways of achieving certain aspects of style with text, particularly as it relates to placement. First font controls and then cascading style sheets pushed the window of opportunity wide open for new levels of text to be controlled on the Web.

I'll examine various controls one by one, introduce a technology, and, often, a task to help you get a better sense of how this is achieved.

Font Families

Fonts are the different styles of type used by designers to achieve look and readability. They are broken down into families. There are two dominant font families: Serif and Sanserif. Other fonts include decorative, script, and monospaced styles.

❏ **Serif.** These fonts are those that have strokes on the letters, and are believed to be good for readability purposes. This may be due to the fact that the strokes provide a horizontal line for the eye to follow, but no one really knows why readability tests have shown the Serif font to be superior as a body text font. And, those tests were made before the Web was around. As it stands, there's a strong trend to use the San Serif font families for body text.

❏ **Sanserif.** These fonts don't have the strokes, and are, in fact, smooth and often rounded. They are easy on the eye, and have been traditionally useful for headers rather than body text. Again, however, their use in the Web environment is causing a shift in this tradition. It's possible that the computer screen, by nature more tiring to read from because of the light and heat it emanates, softens with the smoother look of a Sanserif font.

The breaking of tradition here is exciting, because it enables designers to experiment with a variety of looks that work for them. This is best done after gaining some understanding of the way fonts work, and designers are encouraged to wait until they have studied typography a bit in order to deviate from tradition. Browsers tend to default to Serif fonts, usually Times, anyway.

❑ **Decorative.** These font families are described more by their decorative assets: added features such as dimension, unusual strokes, or calligraphic influences. These families tend to be best used as their name suggests, as decoration, or to enhance text headers. They rarely, if ever, make good body text.

❑ **Scripts**. These fonts are just that—font families that resemble script-style handwriting. They are bad choices for body text, but can make wonderful enhancements to headers and areas where text is used as a design element.

❑ **Monospaced**. These are the fonts where each individual character takes up the exact amount of space. An "M" is different than an "I" in width, but in a monospaced font, width is adjusted to be equal for every character within the font. Monospaced fonts can, and frequently are, used for body text as well as header and design artistry.

Font Mixing

Mixing fonts is something beginning designers do because they are striving to create visual interest. Unfortunately, they often fail because of a lack of familiarity with how fonts are mixed. A good rule of thumb for beginners is to avoid mixing fonts from the same family. In other words, don't mix Garmond and Times (Serif fonts), and don't mix Arial with Verdana (Sanserif fonts). They are too similar to create contrast, which is visually interesting, and too dissimilar to allow for continuity, which is necessary.

If you're going to mix fonts on a page, choose fonts from two different families. Also, consider not using more than two font styles on a page until you're familiar with the territory.

DESIGN NOTE: How do you gain contrast while using fonts? One way is to use size. A small font placed along the top of a really big font can be interesting because the look is in contrast. Another is weight. Fonts, like people, can be slim, plump, or downright broad. Mixing weight can achieve contrast without falling into the problem of losing continuity.

Font Sizing

Sizing fonts is also challenging in the Web environment. Currently, there are only positive and negative numeric values to give to a font size attribute. Style sheets change that, giving sizing values in points, pixels, centimeters, inches, and percents. This is really valuable for precision control.

The size of a font is important to style because you can treat pages with typographic repetition and continuity, or not. Typographic repetition is important for text-heavy documents, getting away from repetition and into a range of font sizes enables a designer to take numerous approaches to his or her work.

CAUTION: The day that any kind of text sizing became available, even via the header tag, people creating Web pages thought they would have some fun and make some letters in a word large and others small, creating a "wave" effect. Avoid surf-sickness. Although it was fun for the moment, it wasn't very design-savvy and, in fact, became cliché in no time.

Creating Harmonious Font Style with Tags and Style Sheets

There are two technical ways to create fonts with HTML. The first is by using the `<font>` attribute, as you've seen done throughout the book.

1. Choose two font families. I'm going to select a Serif style for my header and a Sanserif for my body text.

2. In an HTML shell file, type the following:

```
<font size=5 face=Georgia>

This is One Cool Site

</font>

<p>

<font size=2 face=arial>

You can click below. Do you wanna?

</font>
```

3. Save the file as `fonts-1.htm` and view the file in your browser (see Figure 17.1).

Figure 17.1.
Text control and font faces.

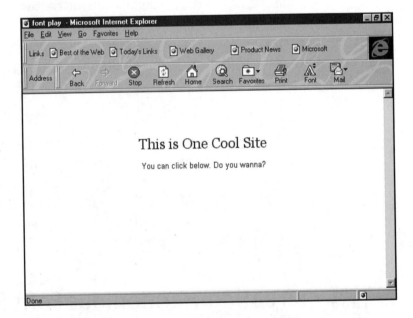

Now you can try the same effect using style sheets. I'll use the inline style for these examples; check with Chapter 3 for other methods of achieving style via style sheets.

4. In another shell instance, add the following:

```
<span style="font: 20pt georgia">This is One Cool Site</span>
```

```
<p style="font: 12pt arial">You can click below. Do you wanna?
</p>
```

5. Save the file as `fonts-2.htm` and view the file in your style sheet-compliant browser (see Figure 17.2).

Figure 17.2.
Text control with style sheets. The type size can be set specifically.

Now let's have some fun and create contrast.

6. Switch the syntax and comments in step 4, so that it looks like this:

```
<p style="font: 12pt arial">You can click below. Do you wanna?
</p>

<span style="font: 20pt georgia">This is One Cool Site</span>
```

7. Save the file as `fonts-3.htm` and view it in your browser (see Figure 17.3). Note how the results are intriguing and inviting? This is contrast!

NOTE: You'll specifically notice the difference between the kind of control available with cascading style sheets over font tags when you employ a specific size control, such as points, over the "size" attribute. This is one reason why style sheets are so exciting: The control they offer has been unavailable to Web designers in the past.

Figure 17.3.
Contrast achieved with style sheets.

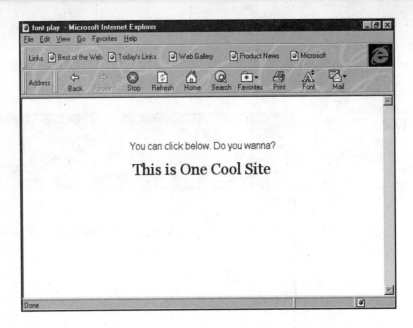

Now you'll move on to other aspects of font control.

Font Color

As with font faces, color can be achieved using the HTML tag attribute, in this case "`color`," or by defining font color via cascading style sheets.

The most important thing to remember is that font colors must be readable. This doesn't mean that they should just be legible, but that reading the text is a pleasant experience. Bright yellow is visually readable against black, but it's not comfortable to read for long sections. Therefore, while you might use a bright yellow against black to achieve a header, avoid it for longer text pieces.

Adding Color to Text with the FONT Tag

This task demonstrates how to create text color within the `<font>` tag.

1. Open `font-1.htm`.

2. Add the following color to the first font call:

   ```
   <font size=5 face=Georgia color="#CC66CC">
   ```

3. Add the second color to the second font string:

```
<font size=2 face=arial color="#FF9933">
```

4. Your resulting syntax looks like this:

```
<font size=5 face=Georgia color="#CC66CC">

This is One Cool Site:

</font>
<p>

<font size=2 face=arial color="#FF9933">

You can click below. Do you wanna?

</font>
```

5. Save the file as `fonts-1a.htm`.

6. View it in your browser. Match the results with the `fonts-1a.htm` file found on the CD-ROM. Note that the color is readable, at least for the short bursts of text used in this instance.

TASK Adding Text Color with Style Sheets

You can also add text color using style sheets. This task will show you how.

1. Open `fonts-3.htm` in your HTML editor.

2. In the first instance, place the following style call:

```
<p style="font: 12pt arial; color: #FF9933">You can click below.
Do you wanna?
</p>
```

3. In the second instance, use this syntax:

```
<span style="font: 20pt georgia; color: #CC66CC">This is One
Cool Site</span>
```

4. Save the work as `fonts-3a.htm` and view it in your browser. Note, again, the color and the contrast produced by the font face and size.

Font Leading

Another form of font control that is now available with cascading style sheets is *leading*. Leading refers to the space between each line of text. By moving text closer or farther apart, you can achieve visual contrast and, therefore, style.

Line height controls are not available in traditional HTML. Because of the less-than-acceptable ways of handling size attributes, as you've seen with the FONT tag, this may be a blessing in disguise. With line height attributes in style sheets, you can use points, pixels, centimeters, inches, and percentages; it's a very flexible, but ultimately strict, method of controlling line height.

DESIGN NOTE: Leading, or line height, is not just a text control issue; it's a spatial control as well. Think about it: You can control space by specifically calling on a certain amount of distance to appear between text components.

Using Line Height

Leading uses the `line-height` attribute, as shown in this task.

1. Open the `fonts-2.htm` file.

2. Add the line height control to the first attribute. Note that this will control the line height above the span.

   ```
   <span style="font: 20pt georgia; line-height: 1in">This is One
   Cool Site</span>
   ```

3. Add the control to the next string. This will add space between the two lines.

   ```
   <p style="font: 12pt arial; line-height: .5in">You can click
   below. Do you wanna?
   </p>
   ```

4. Save your file as `fonts-2a.htm`.

5. View it in your browser and match it to Figure 17.4.

Figure 17.4.

Leading in action.

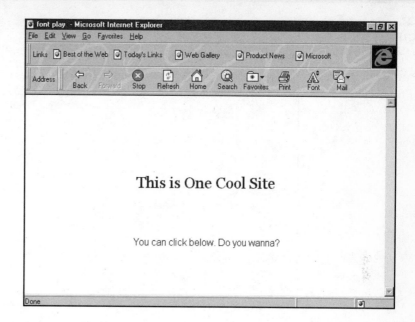

> This is One Cool Site
>
> You can click below. Do you wanna?

Text Technology

Say that ten times fast, I dare you! Tongue-twisting aside, text technology is an important aspect of technical design. This is particularly true on the Web, where the resolution of text is simply not near the quality of print. That reality makes an understanding of the technology helpful in order to create the best, and cleanest, looking text around.

Microsoft has been the leader in browser-based text technologies. They are producing fonts as well as methods to technically manipulate those fonts beyond what can be done with style sheets.

One major issue they've helped address is *anti-aliasing*. This is a technique that is used to smooth fonts. Pixels have edges, so the results of a font set without anti-aliasing is going to look jagged (see Figure 17.5). When creating graphical renditions of fonts, you can set anti-aliasing in any high-end design program.

But when it comes to HTML-based fonts, either through the use of the FONT tag or cascading style sheets, the first challenge is how to address the issue of anti-aliasing. Because there is no graphic control in this instance, the control comes elsewhere.

Figure 17.5.
Text without anti-aliasing.

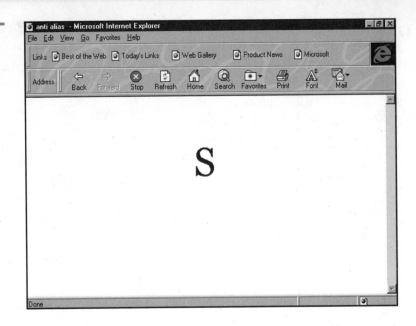

For Windows machines and monitors that can support 16-bit color, a font smoothing utility has been created to address the jagged-edge problem. Figure 17.5 showed you an example of a font without anti-aliasing, or font smoothing, applied. Figure 17.6 shows the same page with the font smoother in action. The difference is subtle, but the results are significantly easier to read, particularly over long stretches of text.

Figure 17.6.
Font smoothing in action. Subtle change, but significant effects.

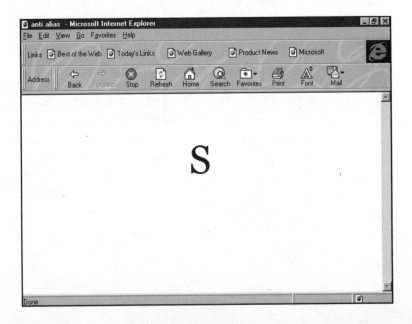

Color and Shape

Color and shape can both be approached through graphics. Color, with style sheets, is becoming more and more browser-based. This makes for quick load times because the need for graphic-based color design is becoming less dependent upon graphics. Shape cannot yet be fully controlled with HTML. However, graphics can combine with HTML attributes to create shapes. This also decreases the load time by reducing the sum total of graphic file sizes.

Web Color Management

Several important concepts can aid you in working effectively with color:

❏ **Select design palettes carefully.** When creating sites, one of the first places to begin in terms of design is to create a palette from which your background colors, text colors, images, image treatments, headers, and links will be determined. Palettes can be found in a variety of graphic design books. You can create your own color combinations as well. Select between three and five colors, making sure you have at least one light color and one dark color within the spectrum selected. Three examples are on the CD-ROM, and you'll use these in an upcoming task. Knowing in advance which colors dominate your site will give your site a cohesive, stylish look.

❏ **Work from a "safe" palette.** Because of the way that colors are managed by different computers, computer graphics cards, and monitors, using the safe palette is a strong assurance that your colors will remain true with any computer that supports 256 colors and above. This is especially important for PC computers using Windows versions prior to the Windows 95 release. In fact, it is precisely the early Windows operating system that caused the need for a safe palette. There are only 216 colors supported by the system (not 256). After you've selected your design palette, select the actual colors from the safe palette. A safe palette is on the CD-ROM.

❏ **If you choose "unsafe" colors, test the results.** There are many instances in which you will want to deviate from the safe palette. This is allowable if you have a good idea that your audience is sophisticated in terms of their end-user technology, and if you test the colors for dithering at lower colors. View your final work at 256 colors and see the results. If the color dithers (moves to the closest color within the system palette), you may find your soft yellow becomes a glowing neon. This is not going to make you or your client too happy.

❏ **Color match link options to the palette.** One of the beauties of BODY tag attributes are that they allow you to set the color for links, visited links, and active links. By using your design palette styles, you'll end up with remarkably clean and, therefore, professional end products.

❏ **Exploit browser-based color.** This means that designers should rely on browser colors as much as possible. This can be done using table cell background color or background color attributes in style sheets. This helps move color away from graphic images that take time to download, freeing you up to use your allotment of downloadable files for truly necessary, higher quality graphics. This is a very effective way of adding a sense of professional style to your work.

TASK   Using Color Effectively

Now you'll get to put these concepts immediately to work.

1. Define your design palette. I've provided one on the CD-ROM, in the images folder that matches this chapter.

2. Pull the colors you selected from a safe palette. Open the safe palette provided and select colors that match the colors in your design palette. I've selected light violet (#996699), rusty orange (#CC6600), and light green (#99CC99) as my primary palette colors. I also use black (#000000) and white (#FFFFFF) as text and accent colors.

3. Create the body attributes, using the palette colors described:

```
<body bgcolor="#99CC99" text="#000000" link="#996699"
vlink="#CC6600" alink="#996699">
```

4. Create a table. In the first cell of the table, use a background color from the palette:

```
<table border=0 width=580 cellpadding=10 cellspacing=10>
<tr>

<td valign=top width=150 bgcolor="#CC6600">

</td>

</tr>
</table>
```

5. Add a second cell that relies on the background color:

```
<td valign=top width=350>

</td>
```

6. Use style sheets to create font and rule styles, filling out the full syntax:

```
<html>
<head>
<title> Color Management </title>
</head>
<body bgcolor="#99CC99" text="#000000" link="#996699"
vlink="#CC6600" alink="#996699">

<table border=0 width=580 cellpadding=10 cellspacing=10>
<tr>

<td valign=top width=150 bgcolor="#CC6600">

<p style="font: 18pt georgia; color: FFFFFF">
Get With It!
</p>

<p style="font: 12pt verdana">

Tips and tricks for a healthy lifestyle include: Duis autem vel
eum iriure dolor in hendrerit in vulputate velit esse molestie
consequat, vel illum dolore eu feugiat nulla facilisis at vero
eros et accumsan et iusto odio dignis.
</p>
</td>

<td valign=top width=350>
<p style="font: 20pt georgia; color: CC6600">
Dr. Day's Attitude Page
</p>

<p style="font: 12pt verdana">
Duis autem vel eum iriure dolor in hendrerit in vulputate velit
esse molestie consequat, vel illum dolore eu feugiat nulla
facilisis at vero eros et accumsan et iusto odio dignissim qui
<a href="nil.htm">blandit praesent luptatum zzril</a> delenit
augue duis dolore te feugait nulla facilisi. Nam liber tempor
cum soluta nobis eleifend option congue nihil imperdiet doming
id quod mazim placerat facer possim assum. Accumsan et iusto
```

```
odio dignissim qui blandit praesent luptatum zzril delenit augue
duis dolore te feugait nulla facilisi.
</p>

<hr width=300 style="color: 99669">
<p align=center style="font: 9pt georgia">

<a href="day.htm">To<b>DAY</b>'s Thought</a> |
<a href="apple.htm">An Apple a <b>DAY</b></a> |
<a href="bread.htm"><b>DAY</b>'s Daily Bread</a>
<p>

</td>
</tr>
</table>

</body>
</html>
```

7. Save the file as `color-1.htm`.

8. View it in your style sheet-compliant browser. Notice specifically how the colors selected are applied. The layout matches Figure 17.7.

Figure 17.7.

The layout of the task. Be sure to view the page in your browser for color application.

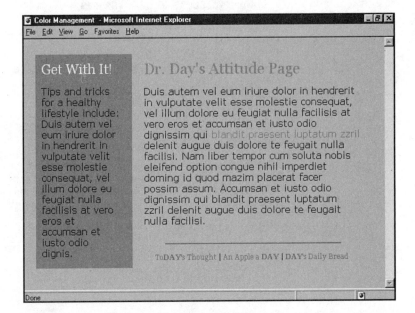

Using Shape

Shapes are powerful. They hold significant, unspoken meanings. It may seem odd to think that shape can convince people that you are a powerful commercial giant, or that your product can be used with confidence, but shapes do this. As a designer, using them with this in mind will subtly, yet effectively, drive your Web site's design and style.

In his book, *A Beginner's Guide to Constructing the Universe*, author Michael S. Schneider studies the meaning of shape by demonstrating how math and nature are intrinsically linked. This intriguing study is of enormous value to Web designers who struggle daily to accommodate the demands of a technical and artistic environment. All shapes can be found in nature, and it is from the natural environment that the artistic and psychological results of shape are rooted.

In general, these shapes express the following ideas:

- ❏ **Circle.** Want to express a sense of community? Suggest that your company or product has endurance? Using circles in your work can do just that. The circle is expressive of safety and wholeness. It also is ascribed to the common descriptions related to women: warmth, comfort, sensuality, and love (see Figure 17.8).

Figure 17.8.
The circular shapes in this page's logo convey community and coherence—a visual representation of the magazine's philosophy.

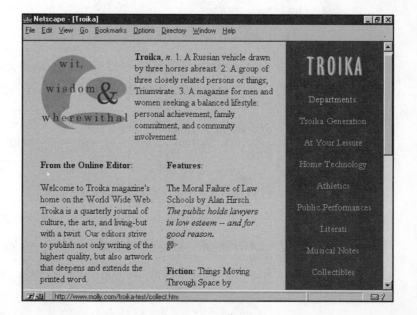

❏ **Rectangle.** If a sense of security is what you're after, rectangles will help you achieve it. Symbolically, they relate to order, logic, and containment. Because a rectangle is the geometric result of adding a fourth point to shape, it is also the foundation for three-dimensional objects. This suggests mass, volume, and anything that is solid.

❏ **Triangle.** Wake up your Web site visitors. Captivate them with the triangle, which represents power, balance, law, science, and religion (the Scales of Justice and Star of David are excellent examples). Triangles are compared to the qualities of men: strength, aggression, and dynamic movement.

But how is shape added? Currently, there are no immediate ways to plot any shape other than a rectangle from within HTML. Images are the primary method of offering alternate shapes. However, you can use HTML combined with images to add shapes, reducing your download times and harnessing the innate power of the browser to handle aspects of a page's design.

Combining a Triangular Image and a Browser-Based Rectangle

This task will show you how to combine color and graphics for maximum color and shape control.

1. Open `color-1.htm`.

2. Add the following table and image above the existing syntax:

```
<table border=0 width=580 cellpadding=0 cellspacing=0>
<tr>

<td valign=top width=175>
<img src="images/tri-1.gif" width=175 height=39>
</td>

</tr>
</table>
```

3. Adjust the cellspacing and padding values in the subsequent table:

```
<table border=0 width=580 cellpadding=10 cellspacing=0>
```

4. Match your syntax to the final code results:

```html
<html>
<head>
<title> Shape One </title>
</head>
<body bgcolor="#99CC99" text="#000000" link="#996699"
vlink="#CC6600" alink="#996699">

<table border=0 width=580 cellpadding=0 cellspacing=0>
<tr>
<td valign=top width=175>
<img src="images/tri-1.gif" width=175 height=39>
</td>

</tr>

</table>
<table border=0 width=580 cellpadding=10 cellspacing=0>
<tr>

<td valign=top width=150 bgcolor="#CC6600">

<p style="font: 18pt georgia; color: FFFFFF">
Get With It!
</p>

<p style="font: 12pt verdana">

Tips and tricks for a healthy lifestyle include: Duis autem vel
eum iriure dolor in hendrerit in vulputate velit esse molestie
consequat, vel illum dolore eu feugiat nulla facilisis at vero
eros et accumsan et iusto odio dignis.
</p>
</td>

<td valign=top width=350>
<p style="font: 20pt georgia; color: CC6600">
Dr. Day's Attitude Page
</p>

<p style="font: 12pt verdana">
Duis autem vel eum iriure dolor in hendrerit in vulputate velit
esse molestie
consequat, vel illum dolore eu feugiat nulla facilisis at vero
eros et accumsan
et iusto odio dignissim qui <a href="nil.htm">blandit praesent
luptatum zzril
</a> delenit augue duis dolore te feugait nulla facilisi. Nam
liber tempor cum
soluta nobis eleifend option congue nihil imperdiet doming id
quod mazim
placerat facer possim assum. Accumsan et iusto odio dignissim
qui blandit praesent luptatum zzril delenit augue duis dolore te
feugait nulla facilisi.
</p>
```

```
<hr width=300 style="color: 99669">
<p align=center style="font: 9pt georgia">

<a href="day.htm">To<b>DAY</b>'s Thought</a> |
<a href="apple.htm">An Apple a <b>DAY</b></a> |
<a href="bread.htm"><b>DAY</b>'s Daily Bread</a>
<p>

</td>
</tr>
</table>

</body>
</html>
```

5. Save the new file as `color-1.htm`.

6. View it in a style sheet-compliant browser.

7. Note the shape (see Figure 17.9). True to form, the triangular top gives a sense of upward movement, which causes you to be alert. The combination of the rectangle and the triangle creates a dynamic and aggressive, yet balanced, sense of mass.

Figure 17.9.

Shape and table-based color combined. The results are a sense of movement and balance.

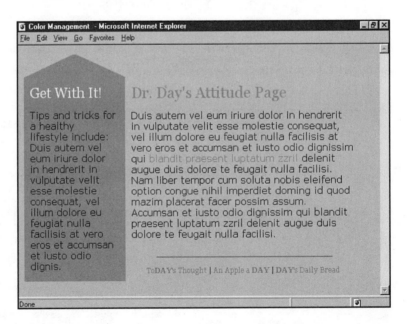

Spatial Relationships: A Closer Look

Spatial relationships have their foundation in the natural environment. Nature uses space in a profound and often magnificent way. Examine your face, for example. Your eyes are a certain distance apart from each other, your forehead and hairline are as well (some more distant than others). No matter what feature you are comparing, it is spaced in a precise manner. If it isn't, your appearance is somehow noted as different than the majority of people.

Interestingly, it isn't only the placement of features that are important, but what lies in between. The expanse of skin from the chin line to the cheekbone is placed upon the bone structure of your skull. In design, the underlying structure of HTML can control the placement as well as the in-between sections, just as nature has created an effective structure for your facial features.

To achieve style and professionalism in design, you must have an understanding of how to orient features on a page. This means knowing that successful visual work relies not just on the where in "where things belong," but the why it should go there.

Two important aspects of spatial placement are alignment and distance. Alignment is where elements are placed on a page: to the right or the left, in the center, at the top, or at the bottom. You've seen this in action with align attributes in image, table cell, paragraph, and division elements in HTML.

Distance is just that. How far apart or how close objects are will immediately affect the way a page is perceived. Grouping objects is sometimes important; other times, it becomes a cramped and difficult situation, leading to what I refer to as the "small-room" phenomenon. This is what I've discussed several times throughout the book—the need to open up a space that appears cramped. The opposite is also true: Too much space between objects lends to a feeling of chaos, which is uncomfortable and unprofessional.

In some senses, the what in "what lies in between" is even more critical than an actual feature. Without the structure and skin between your chin and cheekbone, your face would have little definition. The expanse between features, or elements, on the Web is known as white space. This doesn't mean the space is white, of course, but it is space. There is no object in that field to disturb the space; in fact, the space acts as a cushion to the eye, a momentary place of rest, and a visual guide toward the next object.

 # Spatial Elements at Work

This task will be a bit playful, demonstrating successful and unsuccessful applications of object and element placement, distance, alignment, and white space.

1. Begin with shape-1.htm.

2. Remove all of the width, alignment, cellpadding, and cellspacing values from the syntax:

```
<html>
<head>
<title> Crunch </title>
</head>
<body bgcolor="#99CC99" text="#000000" link="#996699"
vlink="#CC6600" alink="#996699">

<table border=0 cellpadding=0 cellspacing=0>
<tr>
<td>
<img src="images/tri-1.gif" width=175 height=39>
</td>

</tr>

</table>
<table border=0>
<tr>

<td bgcolor="#CC6600">

<p style="font: 18pt georgia; color: FFFFFF">
Get With It!
</p>

<p style="font: 12pt verdana">

Tips and tricks for a healthy lifestyle include: Duis autem vel
eum iriure dolor in hendrerit in vulputate velit esse molestie
consequat, vel illum dolore eu feugiat nulla facilisis at vero
eros et accumsan et iusto odio dignis.
</p>
</td>
```

```
<td>
<p style="font: 20pt georgia; color: CC6600">
Dr. Day's Attitude Page
</p>

<p style="font: 12pt verdana">
Duis autem vel eum iriure dolor in hendrerit in vulputate velit
esse molestie consequat, vel illum dolore eu feugiat nulla
facilisis at vero eros et accumsan et iusto odio dignissim qui
<a href="nil.htm">blandit praesent luptatum zzril</a> delenit
augue duis dolore te feugait nulla facilisi. Nam liber tempor
cum soluta nobis eleifend option congue nihil imperdiet doming
id quod mazim placerat facer possim assum. Accumsan et iusto
odio dignissim qui blandit praesent luptatum zzril delenit augue
duis dolore te feugait nulla facilisi.
</p>

<hr style="color: 99669">
<p style="font: 9pt georgia">

<a href="day.htm">To<b>DAY</b>'s Thought</a> |
<a href="apple.htm">An Apple a <b>DAY</b></a> |
<a href="bread.htm"><b>DAY</b>'s Daily Bread</a>
</p>

</td>
</tr>
</table>


</body>
</html>
```

3. Strip out all of the paragraph markers:

```
<html>
<head>
<title> Crunch</title>
</head>
<body bgcolor="#99CC99" text="#000000" link="#996699"
vlink="#CC6600" alink="#996699">

<table border=0 cellpadding=0 cellspacing=0>
<tr>
<td>
<img src="images/tri-1.gif" width=175 height=39>
</td>

</tr>

</table>
<table border=0>
<tr>
```

```
<td bgcolor="#CC6600">

Get With It!

Tips and tricks for a healthy lifestyle include: Duis autem vel
eum iriure dolor in hendrerit in vulputate velit esse molestie
consequat, vel illum dolore eu feugiat nulla facilisis at vero
eros et accumsan et iusto odio dignis.
</td>

<td>

Dr. Day's Attitude Page

Duis autem vel eum iriure dolor in hendrerit in vulputate velit
esse molestie consequat, vel illum dolore eu feugiat nulla
facilisis at vero eros et accumsan et iusto odio dignissim qui
<a href="nil.htm blandit ."> praesent luptatum zzril</a> delenit
augue duis dolore te feugait nulla facilisi. Nam liber tempor
cum soluta nobis eleifend option congue nihil imperdiet doming
id quod mazim placerat facer possim assum. Accumsan et iusto
odio dignissim qui blandit praesent luptatum zzril delenit augue
duis dolore te feugait nulla facilisi

<hr style="color: 99669">

<a href="day.htm">To<b>DAY</b>'s Thought</a> |
<a href="apple.htm">An Apple a <b>DAY</b></a> |
<a href="bread.htm"><b>DAY</b>'s Daily Bread</a>

</td>
</tr>
</table>

</body>
</html>
```

4. Save the file as crunch.htm and compare your results with Figure
   17.10—not too attractive! It's got color, but it sure doesn't have
   style. And, it looks completely unprofessional.

Think about the attributes you removed:

❑ Width

❑ Align

❑ Valign

❑ Cellpadding

❑ Cellspacing

❑ Paragraph formatting

Each of these control an aspect of spatial relationship. Without the controls, there's no style.

Figure 17.10.

Crunch! All of the style has been removed from this page.

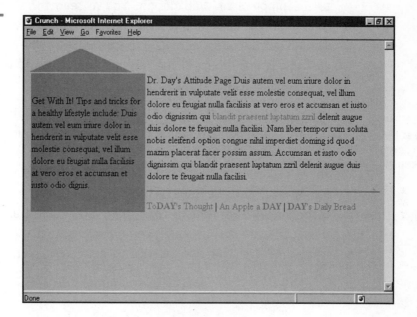

Workshop Wrap-Up

You need your space, as does everyone. Style is the link between well-designed and so-so presentations.

But how do you get them? This chapter showed you how the combined effort of style sheets, tables, and frames can not only create the opportunity for layout tools, but when used well, elevate your sites to a level that says "professional."

Web typography is in its infancy, but it's growing, particularly with the incumbent use of style sheets to successfully control type and type layout. Color control relies heavily on tables, especially when seeking to increase the use of browser-based colors rather than server-sided image data. To get shapes, combine tables and graphics where you can for optimal results.

With HTML, there is no tool more powerful that solves the issues of alignment, distance, and white space as tables. This is precisely why they are so significant to the progress of Web design. You've seen this in action consistently throughout the book, and you learned how to do this with tables, even if you weren't overtly conscious of it. Go back and look at the examples. Look at the way things are grouped, the distance graphics and text have from one another, their alignment, and the spaces in-between.

networkMCI is available at `http://www.mci.com/networkmci/`.

Ways of achieving space include the use of frames to control static and dynamic space, and to confine space where that is desired. This is (at the risk of repeating myself) why frames cause problems when not used carefully. They can place too much control on small spaces. Or, if you have too many frames on a page, the result is chaotic and disturbing. You'll notice that none of my primary teaching in this book gave you a frame example with more than three frame areas. I have rarely come across a site that used more than three frame areas well. The one exception is networkMCI, and even that design is on the fence. The reason it works with its five framed areas is that they are well planned and deployed.

Space can also be achieved through the use of style sheets. Margin control adds a new dynamic, and, when combined with other forms of layout, the results are potent. Read more about margin control and combined style sheet and table layouts in Chapters 3, 18, and 19.

Style—you can get it. And, if you want professional Web sites, you should.

Next Steps

The next chapter will show you how to combine tables and style sheets for practical applications such as menus, order forms, and product lists. For other items of interest, you may want to look at the following:

❏ Chapter 19, "Style Sheets at Work and Play," which covers the use of tables and style sheets to master text-heavy documents

❏ Chapter 20, "Real-time Example: MainStay Communications—Style Sheets in Action," which is a real-time example of the concepts within this chapter in very professional action

Q&A

Q: I've been using graphics to set my fonts. They work well, and I always have specific size, color, face, and anti-aliasing control. Is there anything wrong with this?

A: Nothing. In fact, it's a good option in many cases. However, advancing technology is suggesting other ways to do the same thing, with less wear and tear on the Net, as well as on you. Start playing with style sheets for font control. I think you'll agree that there are a lot of advantages in using client-side power.

Q: I'm a graphic designer, and the concepts you are introducing here are pretty basic. Where can I go to get more advanced graphic-design information for the Web?

A: There are several good graphic resources on the Web itself. If you're a Macintosh user, visit http://www.apple.com/ for platform-specific ideas and resources. PC developers can visit Microsoft's Site Builder's Network at http://www.microsoft.com/workshop/ for a variety of information on typography and Web graphic design. For both platforms, visit http://www.adobe.com/ for top-line news and products, and http://www.wdvl.com/ for the Web Developer's Virtual Library, which offers extensive local and linked resources to graphic designers.

Q: I'm *not* a graphic designer. This information is very new and somewhat detailed for me. Is there anywhere I can go for "basic training" in graphic design theory?

A: Check with your local college or art school for graphic design courses. Many resources exist within your community. Seek out books on the subject, and visit all of the preceding Web sites to follow the concepts being discussed.

eighteen

Combining Tables, Frames, and Style Sheets

In this chapter, you'll have the opportunity to use all of the lessons learned in this book. By combining tables, frames, and style sheets, and applying the elements of style as described in Chapter 17, "Creating Professional Presentations," an attractive site emerges. Both visually agreeable and functionally strong, this site maximizes the combination of table- and frame-based layout, with style sheets employed to add vivacity to the site through the use of font and color control.

The example is colorful, beginning with a strong design palette and then inverting palette elements to achieve visual contrast. The changing layout styles aren't disruptive because the palette provides the repetition and consistency necessary to maintain the separate aspects of the design. Shape enhances the menu, and is also found within the decorative text headers and accents.

Of special interest is how browser-based color and design offer enormous time-saving value. Even with five graphics, the site, which is made up of fifteen HTML files, comes to a total memory value of 64 kilobytes. Bear in mind that 60 kilobytes is what most designers use as a guide for maximum file size of one HTML document and its related graphics. This demonstrates the power of browser-based color and style. Load times are fast and server space is kept to a minimum. There's no wear and tear on the user, and the end product is colorful, interesting, and downright fun.

DESIGN NOTE: The design palette is in the Chapter 18 `images` folder on the CD-ROM. You'll want to check it out, and see how the colors in the palette are used throughout the site to create contrast as well as continuity.

This chapter will focus mostly on task, taking you through each section of the code and commenting on the usage. I've focused on inline style versus other types of style sheets (embedded or linked) in order to show you how to get maximum flexibility with the inline method.

DESIGN NOTE: If you can't see the font styles locally, it's because you don't have the fonts on your machine. Remember that font styles are dependent upon what someone has. When you design for style and you don't know what the majority of your end-users have, stick to common styles. In this situation, I felt the results of decorative font styles and design concepts were more important to demonstrate than sticking to the standard styles of font, which have been used up until now. If you have a decorative and Sanserif font similar to the ones I'm using, go ahead and replace my font calls with the ones you have. The design will change a bit, but you'll get the picture—literally.

Creating the Splash Page

The entrance to the site uses a combination of tables and style sheets to achieve its design.

1. In your HTML editor, begin with the following shell syntax:

```
<html>
<head>
<title>New Asia General Store</title>
</head>

<body bgcolor="#663333" text="#000000" link="#FF6666"
vlink="#FFCC99" alink="#FFCC00">

</body>
</html>
```

2. Add the main table container:

```
<table border=0 width=600 cellpadding=10 cellspacing=10>
<tr>

</tr>
</table>
```

3. Build the first cell's container, noting the vertical alignment, width, and color selections:

```
<td valign=top width=400 bgcolor="#FF6666">

</td>
```

4. Add the contents to the cell, including header, text, and graphics. Pay attention to the inline style calls:

```
<h1 style="font: 26pt mandarind; color: 663333">New Asia
<br>General Store</h1>

<p style="font: 12pt arial">
Occumsan Aliquam <i>dignissim qui</i> blandit praesent luptatum
zzril delenit augue duis

<img src="images/na-rice.jpg" width=200 height=150 hspace=10
vspace=10 align=left>
```

```
dolore te feugait nulla facilisi. Nam liber tempor cum soluta
nobis eleifend option congue <b>nihil imperdiet doming id quod
</b> mazim placerat facer possim assum. Eros Et Accumsan
dignissim qui blandit praesent luptatum zzril delenit augue duis
dolore te feugait nulla
 facilisi.
</p>
```

5. Create the second cell container. In this section, you'll see how there's no color argued, and the vertical alignment is placed in the middle of the table rather than the top:

```
<td valign=middle width=180>

</td>
```

6. Add the second cell's contents, which creates the main page navigation:

```
<a href="about.htm" style="font: 14pt mandarind">About New
Asia</a>
<p>

<a href="store.htm" style="font: 14pt mandarind">The Store</a>
<p>

<a href="rest.htm" style="font: 14pt mandarind">The Restaurant
</a>
<p>

<a href="menu.htm" style="font: 14pt mandarind">Products</a>
<p>

<a href="order.htm" style="font: 14pt mandarind">Orders</a>
<p>


<hr width=200 style="color: FFCC99">

<p style="font: 9pt arial; color: FFCC99">
Eros Et Accumsan dignissim qui <a href="menu.htm" style="color:
FF6666">
blandit praesent luptatum zzril</a> delenit augue duis dolore te
feugait nulla facilisi.
</p>
```

7. Save the file as index.htm.

8. View it in a style sheet–compliant browser, paying attention to the use of color.

9. Compare the layout with Figure 18.1.

Figure 18.1.

Table and style sheet splash.

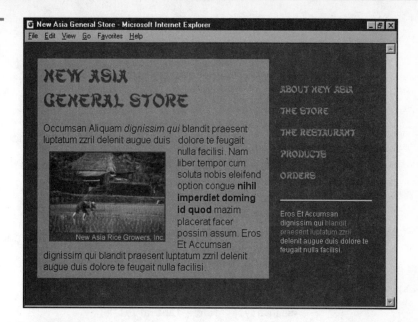

CAUTION: Be sure the browser you are using to test your pages is fully cascading style sheet–compliant. This means you should use Internet Explorer 3.0 or above. At the time of this writing, Netscape 4.0 betas are not fully compliant.

Creating a Content Page with a Specific Style

This content page uses a table with multiple cells and staggered cell background color, as well as cascading style sheets, to achieve its design.

1. In your HTML editor, begin with the following:

```
<html>
<head>
<title>About New Asia</title>
</head>
<body bgcolor="#663333" text="#000000" link="#FF6666"
vlink="#FFCC99" alink="#FFCC00">

</body>
</html>
```

2. Add the decorative text header:

```
<center>

<h1 style="font: 26pt mandarind; color: FF6666">About New Asia</h1>

</center>
```

3. Define the table container, noting width, padding, and spacing:

```
<table border=0 width=600 cellpadding=10 cellspacing=10>
<tr>

</tr>
</table>
```

4. The first table cell has the following parameters and contents:

```
<td valign=top width=150 bgcolor="#FFCC99">

<h1 style="font: 16pt mandarind">food</h1>

<span style="font: 12pt arial">
Nam liber tempor cum soluta nobis eleifend option congue
<b>nihil imperdiet doming id quod</b>
mazim placerat facer possim assum.
</span>

</td>
```

5. Add the second table cell. Note the color and width. This is a "spacer," but it also exploits color, creating a striped effect:

```
<td valign=top width=10 bgcolor="#FF6666">

</td>
```

6. Now place the subsequent cell, attributes, and elements:

```
<td valign=top width=150 bgcolor="FFCC99">

<h1 style="font: 16pt mandarind">beverages</h1>

<span style="font: 12pt arial">
Nam liber tempor cum soluta nobis eleifend <a
href="menu.htm">option congue</a>
nihil imperdiet doming id quod mazim placerat facer possim
assum.
</span>

</td>
```

7. Place another colored spacer:

```
<td valign=top width=10 bgcolor="#FF6666">

</td>
```

8. Add the final table cell before the closing table tag.

```
<td valign=top width=150 bgcolor="#FFCC99">
<h1 style="font: 16pt mandarind">sundries</h1>
<span style="font: 12pt arial">

Nam liber tempor cum soluta nobis eleifend option congue nihil
imperdiet doming id quod mazim <a
href="menu.htm">placerat facer possim</a> assum.

</span>
</td>
```

9. Include bottom-based navigation options:

```
<p>

<center>

<a href="about.htm" style="font: 12pt mandarind">About New
Asia</a>
. | .

<a href="store.htm" style="font: 12pt mandarind">The Store</a>
. | .

<a href="rest.htm" style="font: 12pt mandarind">The Restaurant</
a>
. | .

<a href="menu.htm" style="font: 12pt mandarind">Products</a>
. | .

<a href="order.htm" style="font: 12pt mandarind">Orders</a>

</center>
```

10. Save the file as about.htm and view it in your browser.

11. Match the design layout to Figure 18.2.

The . | . used between text navigation options is simply a variation on the earlier | .

Figure 18.2.
Content page using table cell backgrounds reflects the concept of contrast.

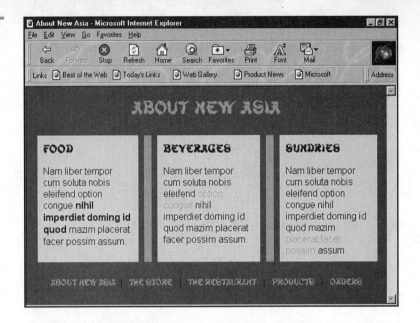

DESIGN NOTE: The columns and colors, along with the centered heading and related decorative font, create a sense of a pagoda-style building. This type of subtlety is what can make or break a design. You might not have noticed it at first, but when you look at it now that I've told you, you can see what I mean. Even if a Web visitor doesn't actually see the effects you're after, they sense it. This is the impact of style.

Creating a Content Page in Another Style

This task uses a table with rows, style sheets, and images to create the layout.

1. In your HTML editor place the shell:

```
<html>
<head>
<title>New Asia Store</title>
</head>
```

```
<body bgcolor="#663333" text="#000000" link="#000000"
vlink="#FFCC99" alink="#FFCC00">

</body>
</html>
```

2. Prepare a table shell, anticipating two rows:

```
<table border=0 width=600 cellpadding=10 cellspacing=10>
<tr>

</tr>

<tr>

</tr>
</table>
```

3. Add the table cell data for the first row:

```
<td valign=middle bgcolor="#FFCC99">

<h1 style="font: 26pt mandarind; color: 663333">New Asia Store</
h1>

<p style="font: 12pt arial; color: FF6666">

Occumsan Aliquam <i>dignissim qui</i> blandit praesent luptatum
zzril delenit augue duis dolore te feugait nulla facilisi. Nam
liber tempor cum soluta nobis eleifend option congue <b>nihil
imperdiet doming id quod</b>
mazim placerat facer possim assum. Eros Et Accumsan dignissim
qui blandit praesent luptatum zzril delenit augue duis dolore te
feugait nulla facilisi.
</p>
</td>
```

4. Add the table cell data in the second row, including an image and the bottom-based navigation:

```
<td valign=middle bgcolor="FF6666">
<p style="font: 12pt arial; color: FFCC99">

<img src="images/dragon.gif" width=150 height=161 hspace=10
vspace=10 align=left>
Occumsan Aliquam <i>dignissim qui</i> blandit praesent luptatum
zzril delenit augue duis dolore te feugait nulla facilisi. Nam
liber tempor cum soluta nobis eleifend option congue <b>nihil
imperdiet doming id quod</b> mazim placerat facer possim assum.

</p>
```

```
<div align=center>
<a href="about.htm" style="font: 12pt mandarind">About New
Asia</a>
. | .

<a href="store.htm" style="font: 12pt mandarind">The Store</a>
. | .

<a href="rest.htm" style="font: 12pt mandarind">The Restaurant</
a>

<a href="menu.htm" style="font: 12pt mandarind">Products</a>
. | .

<a href="order.htm" style="font: 12pt mandarind">Orders</a>

</div>
```

5. Save the file as store.htm.

6. View it in your browser.

7. Compare the layout to Figure 18.3.

Figure 18.3.

Content page with horizontal rather than vertical structure.

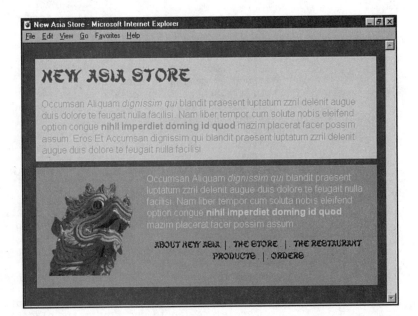

NOTE: Even though the previous page uses rows, creating horizontal rather than the earlier vertical design, continuity is not lost. This is because you've maintained consistent color and text choices.

DESIGN NOTE: You'll notice that I often bold or italicize sections of sentences within paragraphs. This adds to visual interest, as well as drawing the idea to the important, highlighted information stylized text should hold. It's a fun way to add contrast to a page, but choose your selections in moderation.

TASK   Creating a Content Page, Style III

This page is reminiscent of the splash page. I've merely altered the order in which the cells are placed within the basic table structure. Furthermore, I've realigned some of the text and added a different image. You will see that the main feel of the first page has been recreated. This allows for continuity, or a grounding, that Web visitors will only subtly notice, if they notice at all.

1. Begin with the following:

```
<html>
<head>
<title>New Asia Restaurant, Inc.</title>
</head>

<body bgcolor="#663333" text="#000000" link="#FF6666"
vlink="#FFCC99" alink="#FFCC00">

</body>
</html>
```

2. Now design the table:

```
<table border=0 width=600 cellpadding=10 cellspacing=10>
<tr>

</tr>
</table>
```

3. Add the first cell and its contents, which contain the navigation and a small paragraph:

```
<td valign=middle align=right width=180>

<a href="about.htm" style="font: 14pt mandarind">About New
Asia</a>
<p>

<a href="store.htm" style="font: 14pt mandarind">The Store</a>
<p>

<a href="rest.htm" style="font: 14pt mandarind">The Restaurant
</a>
<p>

<a href="menu.htm" style="font: 14pt mandarind">Products</a>
<p>

<a href="order.htm" style="font: 14pt mandarind">Orders</a>
<p>


<hr width=200 style="color: FFCC99">

<span style="font: 9pt arial; color: FFCC99">

Eros Et Accumsan dignissim qui <a href="menu.htm" style="color:
FF6666"> blandit praesent luptatum zzril</a> delenit augue duis
dolore te feugait nulla facilisi.

</span>

</td>
```

4. Follow that with the next cell, header and paragraph text, and image. Note the use of background color in the table cell:

```
<td valign=top width=400 bgcolor="#FF6666">

<h1 align=right style="font: 26pt mandarind; color: 663333">New
Asia <br>Restaurant, Inc.</h1>

<p style="font: 12pt arial">
Occumsan Aliquam <i>dignissim qui</i> blandit praesent luptatum
zzril delenit augue duis

<img src="images/na-rest.jpg" width=175 height=130 hspace=10
vspace=10 align=right>
```

```
dolore te feugait nulla facilisi. Nam liber tempor cum soluta
nobis eleifend option congue <b>nihil imperdiet doming id quod</
b> mazim placerat facer possim assum. Eros Et Accumsan dignissim
qui blandit praesent luptatum zzril delenit augue duis dolore te
feugait nulla facilisi.
</p>

</td>
```

5. Save the file as rest.htm.

6. View it in your browser.

7. Match the design to Figure 18.4.

Figure 18.4.
This page is inspired thematically by the splash, but uses different attributes to create an entirely different layout.

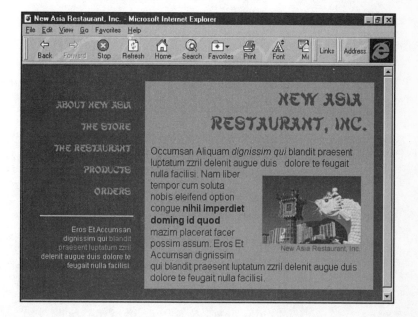

DESIGN NOTE: You might have noticed that another element that is shifting positions is the navigation. I've set it to the right, the left, and the bottom. Again, it's consistency that's making the difference here.

Adding Frames—The Frameset

I'd like to add frames into the mix to provide a little diversity. More importantly, there are potentially long lists of products in a variety of sections. Therefore, I've created a left borderless frame menu with a right target for the product lists within the section.

1. Begin with the shell syntax:

```
<html>
<head>
<title>Product Frameset</title>
</head>

</html>
```

2. Add the frameset parameters:

```
<frameset cols="175,*" frameborder=0 framespacing=0 border=0>

</frameset>
```

3. Now place the two frames and their respective attributes:

```
<frame src="prod-m.htm" name=menu noresize scrolling="auto">
<frame src="prod-r.htm" name=right noresize scrolling="auto">
```

4. Save the file as menu.htm.

Making the Menu

Using two graphics in combination with a table-cell background, you'll create a shaped menu with style sheets controlling font and line-height (leading).

1. In your HTML editor create the shell:

```
<html>
<head>
<title>Product Menu</title>
</head>
<body bgcolor="#663333" text="#000000" link="#663333"
vlink="#FFCC99" alink="#FFCC00">

</body>
</html>
```

2. The first image is put into place with its own table as follows:

```
<table border=0 cellpadding=0 cellspacing=0>
<tr>
```

```
<td>
<img src="images/pagoda.gif" width=150 height=33>
</td>

</tr>
</table>
```

3. The main table appears right underneath. Note the table cell color, the style calls for the link navigation, and especially the difference in cellpadding. This controls white space, as covered in Chapter 17.

```
<table width=150 border=0 cellpadding=10 cellspacing=0>
<tr>

<td bgcolor="#FF6666" align=middle>

<a href="teas.htm" style="font: 18pt mandarind"
target="right">teas</a>
<p>

<a href="spice.htm" style="font: 18pt mandarind"
target="right">spices</a>
<p>

<a href="oils.htm" style="font: 18pt mandarind"
target="right">perfumes</a>
<p>

<a href="music.htm" style="font: 18pt mandarind"
target="right">asian music</a>
<p>

<a href="art.htm" style="font: 18pt mandarind"
target="right">asian art</a>
<p>

<a href="books.htm" style="font: 18pt mandarind"
target="right">asian books</a>
<p>

<a href="heal.htm" style="font: 18pt mandarind"
target="right">healing</a>
<p>

</td>
</tr>
</table>
```

4. The bottom graphic also uses a table to help fit it snugly up against the table above it:

```
<table border=0 cellpadding=0 cellspacing=0>
<tr>
```

```
<td>
<img src="images/pagoda-d.gif" width=150 height=33>
</td>

</tr>
</table>
```

5. Save the file as prod-m.htm.

CAUTION: Be sure tables that combine to create a single image are kept close together in the code. Also, if you are having trouble, look at cellpadding and, especially, cellspacing. If one table has it and another doesn't, that might throw the visual appearance off. Other attributes to be cautious of are alignment and vertical alignment. By playing with these various attributes, you'll come up with the final results you are after.

TASK

Creating a Template for Product Lists

In this task, you'll create the first product list. You can use this as a template for ensuing lists. You'll see as you move through the product list that keeping consistent in this area helps a visitor quickly access the information that he or she is after.

1. Create the HTML shell:

```
<html>
<head>
<title>New Asia: Teas </title>
</head>

<body bgcolor="#FF6666" text="#FFCC99" link="#663333"
vlink="#FF6666" alink="#FF6666">

</body>
</html>
```

2. Add the header information. I've set it to the right to balance out the left menu.

```
<div align=right style="font: 22pt mandarind"> Teas </div>
```

Build the table shell. Notice the short table that accommodates the frame environment but still maintains plenty of white space and margins:

```
<table border=0 width=430 cellpadding=10 cellspacing=0>
<tr>

</tr>
</table>
```

4. Begin with the table cell top data and the ensuing ordered list. Note the style call inside the `<td>` tag:

```
<td style="font: 12pt arial">

<ol>

<li>Nam liber tempor cum soluta nobis eleifend <a href=
"menu.htm">option congue </a> nihil imperdiet doming id quod
mazim placerat facer possim assum.
<p>

<li>Nam liber tempor cum soluta nobis eleifend option
conguenihil imperdiet doming <b>id quod mazim</b> placerat facer
possim assum.
<p>

<li>Nam liber tempor cum soluta nobis eleifend option congue
nihil imperdiet doming id <i>quod mazim placerat </i>facer
possim assum.
<p>

</ol>
```

5. Underneath the end tag for the ordered list, add a division tag to center the text-based navigation:

```
<div align=center>
<a href="about.htm" style="font: 12pt mandarind" target="_top">
About New Asia</a>
. | .

<a href="store.htm" style="font: 12pt mandarind"
target="_top">The Store</a>
. | .

<a href="menu.htm" style="font: 12pt mandarind" target="_top">
The Restaurant</a>

<a href="menu.htm" style="font: 12pt mandarind"
target="_top">Products</a>
. | .
```

```
<a href="order.htm" style="font: 12pt mandarind"
target="_top">Orders</a>

</div>
```

6. Save the file as prod-r.htm.

7. Open the menu.htm file in your browser.

8. Match the layout results to Figure 18.5.

Figure 18.5.
The frame-based section.

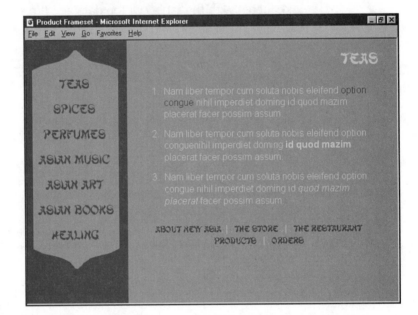

CAUTION: You'll want to pay attention to the way you link back to the rest of the site, which isn't framed. The links to the site's main level from within the product list all have the pages load in the entire main window. This is done by using the magic target name _top.

 ## Using the Template

Because you've created the previous page as both a part of the site and for creation of all the product pages, I'll walk you through the quick method for using the template.

1. Open the prod-r.htm file in your HTML editor.

2. Change the title to the correct page title:

```
<title>New Asia: Healing</title>
```

3. Change the header text to the appropriate name:

```
<div align=right style="font: 22pt mandarind">
Ancient Healing Arts
</div>
```

4. Of course, change any of the actual data lists to match the appropriate product sections.

5. Save the file with the new name—in this case, `heal.htm`.

6. View the `menu.htm` in your browser and click through to the Healing page. Your results should match Figure 18.6.

7. Repeat the process for each of the pages, until you've created all of the required links for this section.

Figure 18.6.
Another view of the frame layout.

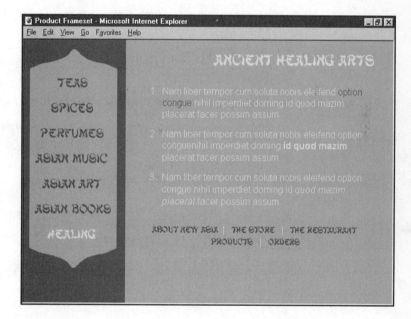

Templates, wherever you can create them, are a great idea. They'll help speed up your work and lower the wear and tear on you.

 The Order Page

If you require an order form, here's a sample. Of course, you'll have to find out what kind of process your Web server allows for the literal syntax. This gives you a look at layout with tables, style sheets, and at specific form elements, including checkboxes and drop-down selections.

1. Begin with the shell:

```
<html>
<head>
<title>New Asia: Orders</title>
</head>
<body bgcolor="#663333" text="#FFCC99" link="#FF6666"
vlink="#FFCC99"alink="#FFCC00">

</body>
</html>
```

2. Add the title header. I've used a right alignment. Also try a left or center for variety.

```
<div align=right style="font: 22pt mandarind; color: FF6666">
New Asia Orders </div>
```

3. Place the table head and first part of the table cell:

```
<table border=0 width=500 cellpadding=10 cellspacing=0>
<tr>

<td valign=top>
```

4. Begin the form:

```
<form action="http://molly.com/htbin/buildlist.pl" method=post>

Please use the following order form to order New Asia Products:
</p>

<b>Choose Items:</b><br>
Check the items that interest you.
<p>
```

5. Begin the table head for the nested and centered inner table:

```
<table border=0 valign=top>
<tr>
```

6. Add the first table cell and data. Note the checkbox options:

```
<td width=200 valign=top>

<input type="checkbox" name="sections" value="Teas">
Teas<br>

<input type="checkbox" name="sections" value="spices">
Spices<br>
```

```
<input type="checkbox" name="sections" value="Food">
Food<br>

</td>
```

7. Add the second table cell and data:

```
<td width=200 valign=top>

<input type="checkbox" name="sections" value="Books">
Books<br>

<input type="checkbox" name="sections" value="Music">
Music<br>

<input type="checkbox" name="sections" value="art">
Asian Art<br>

</td>
```

8. Close the nested table, the division, and add a paragraph for some spacing:

```
</td>
</tr>
</table>
</div>
<p>
```

9. Continue the main table content, including the drop-down menus:

```
Preferred Ship Dates on International Orders:
<br>

<select name="date">
<option value="03-20-97">03-20-97
<option value="03-27-97">03-27-97
<option value="04-03-97">04-03-97
<option selected value="04-10-97">04-10-97

</select>
<input type="hidden" name="uniqueid" value="51860832778">
<p>

Payment Method:
<br>

<select name="Pay">
<option value="Visa">Visa
<option value="mcard">Mastercard
<option value="Amex">American Express
<option selected value="nac">New Asia Credit
</select>
<p>

<input type="submit" name="order" value="order">
<p>
```

10. Add a horizontal bar for style, and follow up with the bottom-based navigation:

```
<hr style="color: FFCC99">

<div align=center>

<a href="about.htm" style="font: 12pt mandarind">About New
Asia</a>
. | .

<a href="store.htm" style="font: 12pt mandarind">The Store</a>
. | .

<a href="rest.htm" style="font: 12pt mandarind">The Restaurant</
a>
. | .

<a href="menu.htm" style="font: 12pt mandarind">Products</a>

</div>

</td>

</tr>
</table>
</div>
```

11. Save the file as order.htm.

12. View the file in your browser. Your results should match Figure 18.7.

Figure 18.7.
The order form.

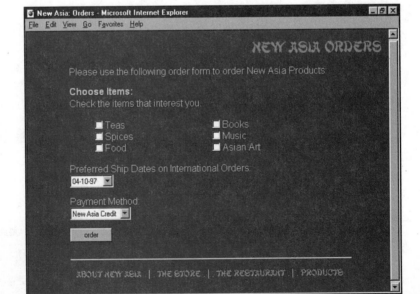

If you plug in the correct syntax for your Web server and place this online, the form will be active. Checkboxes allow individuals to make or remove selections with a click of the mouse (see Figure 18.8). Drop-down menus are a powerful way of putting a lot of information into a selection, yet keeping visible data tight (see Figure 18.9).

Figure 18.8.
The order form's checkboxes. Click to select; click again to deselect.

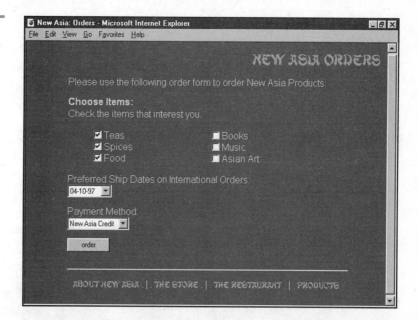

Figure 18.9.
A drop-down menu: small space, but lots of power.

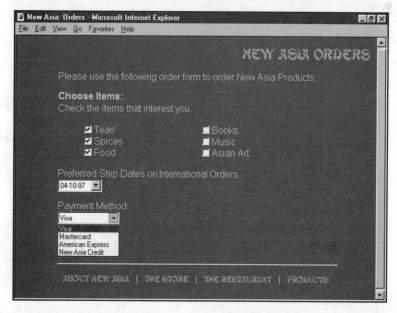

Workshop Wrap-Up

The power of this chapter is that it employs the best of the techniques you've learned in much of this book, yet does so in a straightforward fashion. You should, by now, feel pretty comfortable with your skills. If something is still elusive to you, look back over your work and find out if you can solve the weak area by repeating tasks that were more challenging for you.

Style sheets are wonderful because they add so many possibilities to design, particularly the introduction of some semblance of font control. Combine this with the browser color you can exploit in table cells, the static and spatial power of frames, and interesting navigation options, and you have a designer's toolbox that is very strong.

The pervasive caution is the cross-browser support issue. Internet Explorer is the only popular browser at this time that has style sheets completely integrated with its technology. Netscape is currently struggling to match that compliance, but right now it doesn't meet it. Figure 18.10 shows a page from this chapter's tasks in the 4.0 professional release, and the style sheets are not working as easily as they do with their native Microsoft product.

Figure 18.10.

A style sheet as viewed through Netscape 4.0 professional release 3. The results are not consistent.

Therefore, patience and perseverance must also be part of your design bag of tricks. Learn the technologies, refine them, and flex them to the main browser releases as they come out. None of this is static; it's going to keep changing, evolving, and it's your job to grow with it.

Next Steps

Chapter 19, "Style Sheets at Work and Play," moves into an area untouched so far: how to deal with large data management, particularly as it pertains to text and intranets.

Be sure to revisit the very first chapters of this book, 1–3, for a complete overview of the way tables, frames, and style sheets work. Then think of them in the context of this chapter.

Enjoy the following as well:

- ❏ Chapter 20, "Real-Time Example: MainStay Communications—Style Sheets in Action," which has a real-life look at a corporate Web site

- ❏ Appendix A, "Directory of Resources," which is a fantastic list of resources to help you move ahead in your Web studies

- ❏ Appendix C, "Current HTML Standards," which is a specialty list of tags and browser compatibility for tables, frames, and style sheets

Q&A

Q: Why do you sometimes put the style sheet syntax in paragraphs and other times in headers? This is confusing. I see you use span and division a lot, as well.

A: My objective with this is to show you that you can use inline styles with almost any tag successfully. The one questionable issue is, again, browser-based. It appears as though certain inline styles are inconsistent in current versions of Netscape 4.0.

Q: I'm jazzed by style sheets. Where can I learn about them in real depth?

A: The World Wide Web Consortium, which is the standards committee for HTML and related technology approval, keeps extensive documentation on anything and everything to do with style sheets. Visit `http://www.w3.org/` for more information.

nineteen
Style Sheets at Work and Play

Because style sheets are so flexible, you're going to spend a little time designing a variety of templates to get a hands-on sense of that flexibility. More importantly, these designs are immediately applicable to a range of common Web design jobs. By simply changing some of the styles, such as fonts, colors, alignment, headers, or paragraph styles, you can stock up on a very diverse collection of style-sheet–based offerings.

All of these examples use the embedded style, and in some cases I've extrapolated the style and shown how to make a linked style sheet to control numerous pages with the same style elements. There's a lot of variation within the style sheets themselves. Sometimes I've used tables to lay out a page, and other times, merely a straightforward HTML document. I also

It cannot be said enough: Know your audience. This will help determine how much you are realistically able to currently employ style sheets.

demonstrate the use of grouping and class, as well as showing how you can override style sheet calls by reverting to plain-speaking HTML tags within your document.

This chapter should serve not only as a practical taste of what style sheets can do, but as inspiration to spend time on your own, using style sheets in very creative design applications. You will see how you can, by using classes, create an untold variety of styles within the same page.

Business Page

Your first template is a business page. This can be used for commercial business purposes, or for an intranet application.

1. Begin with the standard HTML shell:

```
<html>

<head>
<title>The Multi Group: Professional Page</title>
</head>

<body bgcolor="#CCCCCC">


</body>
</html>
```

2. Between the closing HEAD tag and BODY tag, enter the style container:

```
<style>


</style>
```

3. Now add the BODY attributes:

```
BODY {background: #CCCCCC; color: #000000; margin-top:0.00in;
➥margin-left:0.20in; margin-right:0.20in}
```

You'll see how the background and text colors are argued here, and the margins are individually distinguished.

CAUTION: If you remember back to Chapter 3, "In Vogue: Cascading Style Sheets," I discussed the "body" browser bug in Internet

Explorer 3.0, and early beta versions of Netscape 4.0. Body colors in the style sheet are ignored. Therefore, you must put the color in the body tag just to be safe. It's a good idea to get used to putting the background color in the style sheet as well, because the problem is in fact a bug and not a style sheet idiosyncrasy. It's always a good idea to do both, anyway. Many people don't upgrade browsers in a timely fashion, and backwards compatibility, at least as far as you can reasonably take it and include new technologies, is always a good idea.

4. Now select and argue the header style:

```
H1 {font: 24pt Garamond; color: #669966; text-align: right}
```

This makes any first-level header 24-point, Garamond font, with defined color and a right alignment.

5. Add styles paragraph:

```
P {font: 12pt Verdana; color: #FFFFFF; text-align: right;
➥text-indent: 0.5in}
P.1 {font: 11pt verdana; color: #000000; text-align: right;
➥text-indent: 0.5in}
```

The second style is an example of class definition, enabling you to use, in this case, two styles of paragraphs. You can literally add as many classes to a style sheet as you like. In the case of large data management, you can use this to your advantage.

6. Add the link color:

```
A {color: #FFFFFF}
```

7. Continue with the body color:

```
<body bgcolor="#CCCCCC">
```

8. Set up your table, table cells, and content. Place all three within the body container tags. Pay careful attention to the use of table cell color definitions, which override the style background just as if this were a standard HTML page.

```
<table border=0 width=575 cellpadding=10 cellspacing=0>
<tr>
```

```
<td valign=top width=150 bgcolor="#99CC99">

<p style="line-height: 0.5in">

Duis autem

in hendrerit in vulputate

molestie consequat vel

feugiat nulla facilisis

</td>

<td valign=middle width=425>

<h1>The Multi Group</h1>

<p>

s e n s e . a n d . s e n s i t i v i t y
<br>

<i>in</i> the market place
</p>

<p class=1>

Eros Et Accumsan <b>dignissim qui</b> blandit praesent luptatum
zzril delenit augue duis dolore te feugait nulla facilisi. Nam
liber tempor cum soluta nobis eleifend option congue nihil
imperdiet<b> doming id quod mazim</b> placerat
facer possim assum. Iusto odio dignissim qui blandit praesent
luptatum zzril delenit augue duis dolore te feugait nulla
facilisi. Nam <i>liber tempor </i> cum soluta nobis eleifend
option congue nihil imperdiet doming id quod mazim placerat
facer possim assum. Accumsan et iusto odio dignissim qui
blandit. Eros Et Accumsan dignissim qui blandit praesent
luptatum zzril delenit augue duis dolore <b>te feugait nulla</b>
facilisi. Nam <i>liber tempor </i> cum soluta nobis.
</p>

</td>

</tr>
</table>
```

9. Save the file as `mg.htm`.

10. View it in your style sheet–compliant browser. Figure 19.1 shows the results.

Figure 19.1.

Business-oriented splash page.

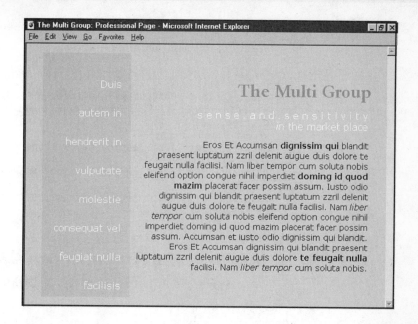

I must continue to remind you of the limitation of font styles. What I have on my computer, you may not have on yours. Although I've focused on using fonts in these instances that I have on my machine, you will do well to study Chapter 3 again. This time, look specifically at the ways you can achieve some semblance of font control.

DESIGN NOTE: The Multi Group example is very consistent with a splash or front page. Let's say you were designing different levels of a company's Web site. You can use this style at each level, embedding the same style in those specific pages, or linking those pages to a master style sheet.

 # Employee Newsletter

This task uses simple HTML layout with style to create a very attractive look.

1. Create the shell:

```
<html>
<head>
<title>P.J. Dailey: News</title>
</head>

<body bgcolor="#000000">

</body>
</html>
```

2. Between the HEAD and BODY, place your embedded style sheet, paying attention to color, alignment, and class:

```
<style>

BODY: {color: #000000; margin-left: 0.75in;
➥margin-right: 0.75in; margin-top: 0.00in}
H1.right {font: 18pt "lucida handwriting"; color: #999966;
➥text-align: right}
H1.left {font: 18pt "lucida handwriting"; color: #999966;
➥text-align: left}
P {font: 12pt "arial narrow"; color: #CCCC99; margin-indent:
➥0.5in}
P.1 {font: 11pt/11pt "arial narrow"; color: #FFFFFF}
HR {color: #CCCC99}

</style>
```

3. Within the body, lay out the headers and dummy text:

```
<h1 class=right>P.J. Dailey News . . .</h1>

<p>

Eros Et Accumsan <b>dignissim qui</b> blandit praesent luptatum
zzril delenit augue duis dolore te feugait nulla facilisi. Nam
liber tempor cum soluta nobis eleifend option congue nihil
imperdiet<b> doming id quod mazim</b> placerat facer possim
assum.
</p>

<hr>


<h1 class=left>te feugait</h1>

<p class=1>

Eros Et Accumsan <b>dignissim qui</b> blandit praesent luptatum
zzril delenit augue duis dolore te feugait nulla facilisi. Nam
liber tempor cum soluta nobis eleifend option congue nihil
imperdiet!

</p>

<hr>

<h1 class=right>liber tempor</h1>

<p>
```

```
Eros Et Accumsan <b>dignissim qui</b> blandit praesent luptatum
zzril delenit augue duis dolore te feugait nulla facilisi. Nam
liber tempor cum soluta nobis eleifend option congue nihil
imperdiet<b> doming id quod mazim</b> placerat facer possim
assum.

</p>
```

4. Save the file as `pj.htm`.

5. View the file in your browser.

6. Match the layout results to Figure 19.2.

Figure 19.2.

Interoffice newsletter example.

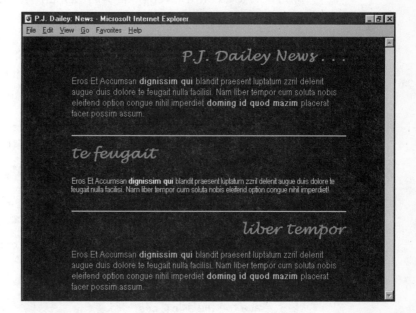

DESIGN NOTE: The P. J. Dailey page provides a great example of how to combine headers and body text. With very few exceptions, you don't want to break up a header from the related text with a horizontal rule. This is a mistake that many people make. Furthermore, this example shows how horizontal rules can successfully be used without appearing cliché. The addition of style breaks the typical and ugly use of horizontal rules on the Web. By defining color and having plenty of white space, the problems seen with most rules disappears. At all costs, avoid using horizontal rules that stretch from margin to margin.

Also, the use of headers and text together creates a rationale for using the rules at all, not just for paragraph breaks. If a paragraph break is what you're after, use a paragraph break, not a rule.

TASK Creating a Linked Style Sheet

Beacause the P. J. Dailey example could be applied to many pages, I'll show you how to create a linked page. All you then need to do is link the individual pages to this page, and they will all pick up the styles defined within the sheet.

1. Open up a fresh page in your HTML editor.

2. Take the embedded style out of the originating page, and place the following into the fresh editing environment:

```
<style>

BODY: {color: #000000; margin-left: 0.75in; margin-right:
➥0.75in; margin-top: 0.00in}
H1.right {font: 18pt "lucida handwriting"; color: #999966;
➥text-align: right}
H1.left {font: 18pt "lucida handwriting"; color: #999966;
➥text-align: left}
P {font: 12pt "arial narrow"; color: #CCCC99;
➥margin-indent: 0.5in}
P.1 {font: 11pt/11pt "arial narrow"; color: #FFFFFF}
HR {color: #CCCC99}

</style>
```

3. Save the file as `pj.css`.

4. Place the following link below the TITLE and before the `</head>` tag on every page you want to have influenced by this style:

```
<link rel=stylesheet href="pj.css" type="text/css">
```

NOTE: Because you're linking styles, it's not necessary to embed this information in any of the individual pages to be influenced by the link. However, if you want to alter individual pages that will take on most of the attributes of the linked style sheet, yet contain a few individual changes, you can embed a style sheet into that page with minor changes. Furthermore, if you want to alter only one or two smaller sections in a handful of pages, drawing from the linked page and embedded style, you can use inline style to cover that smaller section. The CSS-compliant browser will read inline over embedded and embedded over linked. Riddle: What does this cause? Answer: A cascade.

5. Save and test your files.

Price List

This example uses a bordered table within the page as a grid. Pay specific attention to the classes defined for the table cells. This further demonstrates the power and flexibility of style sheets.

1. Create the shell:

```
<html>

<head>
<title>Beautiful Dreamer Music: Price List V2</title>

</head>

<body bg color="#CCCC99">

</body>
</html>
```

2. Add the style:

```
<style>

BODY {background: #CCCC99; color: #000000; margin-left: 0.5in;
➥margin-right: 0.5in}
H1 {font: 20pt "book antiqua"; color: #666633; text-align: left}
H2 {font: 18pt "book antiqua"; color: #666633; text-align: left}
P {font: 12pt arial; color: #000000}
B {font: 12pt "book antiqua"; color: #666633; font-weight: bold}
HR {color: #CC9999}
TD {font: 11pt "book antiqua"}
TD.grey {background: #999999; font: 11pt arial}
TD.mauve {background: #CC9999; font: 11pt arial}
A {text-decoration: none; color: #CC9999; font-weight: bold}

</style>
```

3. The following are the main header and body text:

```
<h1>Beautiful Dreamer Music</h1>

<p>

Eros Et Accumsan dignissim qui blandit praesent luptatum zzril
delenit augue duis dolore te feugait nulla facilisi. Nam liber
tempor cum soluta nobis eleifend option congue nihil imperdiet
doming id quod <a href="nil.htm">mazim placerat facer</a> possim
assum.

</p>
```

4. The following are the secondary header and table:

```
<hr width=45%>

<h2>Prices:</h2>

<table border=1 width=500 cellpadding=10 cellspacing=0>
<tr>

<td class=mauve width=50>

<b>Eros</b>

</td>

<td class=grey width=50>

<b>Qui </b>

</td>


<td class=mauve width=50>

<b>Zzril </b>

</td>

</tr>

<tr>

<td class=mauve width=50>
```

```
Eros<br>
dignissim <br>
blandit <br>
luptatum

</td>

<td class=grey width=50>

Eros<br>
qui <br>
blandit <br>
luptatum

</td>


<td class=mauve width=50>

Accumsan<br>
dignissim <br>
praesent <br>
zzril

</td>

</tr>

<tr>

<td colspan=3 align=right>

<i>eros et accumsan dignissim, st.</i>   
Total: $18,000.00

</td>

</tr>
</table>
</div>
```

5. Save your work as bd.htm.

6. View your work and compare it with Figure 19.3.

Figure 19.3.
*Price sheet page
version 1.*

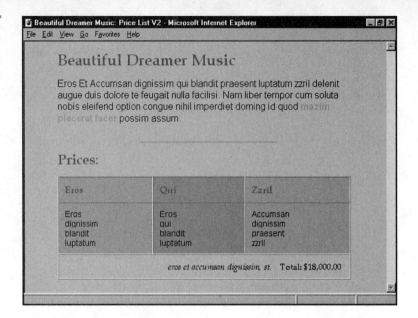

TASK   Price List: Reverse Style

Now let's have some fun and reverse the headers and body text of this example. This shows how dramatic variation can be achieved quite simply with style sheets.

1. To reverse the style, simply change the attributes of the style section:

```
<style>

BODY {background: #CCCC99; color: #000000; margin-left: 0.5in;
➥margin-right: 0.5in}
H1 {font: 20pt "arial"; color: #666633; text-align: left}
H2 {font: 18pt "arial"; color: #666633; text-align: left}
P {font: 12pt "book antiqua"; color: #000000}
B {font: 12pt "arial"; color: #666633; font-weight: bold}
HR {color: #CC9999}
TD {font: 11pt "arial"}
TD.grey {background: #999999; font: 11pt "book antiqua"}
TD.mauve {background: #CC9999; font: 11pt "book antiqua"}
A {text-decoration: none; color: #CC9999; font-weight: bold}

</style>
```

2. Continue with the body text and attributes:

```
<body bgcolor="#CCCC99">

<h1>Beautiful Dreamer Music</h1>

<p>

Eros Et Accumsan dignissim qui blandit praesent luptatum zzril
delenit augue duis dolore te feugait nulla facilisi. Nam liber
tempor cum soluta nobis eleifend option congue nihil imperdiet
doming id quod <a href="nil.htm">mazim placerat facer</a> possim
assum.

</p>

<hr width=45%>

<h2>Prices:</h2>

<table border=1 width=500 cellpadding=10 cellspacing=0>
<tr>

<td class=mauve width=50>

<b>Eros</b>

</td>

<td class=grey width=50>

<b>Qui </b>

</td>


<td class=mauve width=50>

<b>Zzril </b>

</td>

</tr>

<tr>

<td class=mauve width=50>
```

```
Eros<br>
dignissim <br>
blandit <br>
luptatum

</td>

<td class=grey width=50>

Eros<br>
qui <br>
blandit <br>
luptatum

</td>


<td class=mauve width=50>

Accumsan<br>
dignissim <br>
praesent <br>
zzril

</td>

</tr>

<tr>

<td colspan=3 align=right>

<i>eros et accumsan dignissim, st.</i>    Total:
$18,000.00

</td>

</tr>
</table>
</div>
```

3. Add the style and body syntax into the HTML shell.

4. Save the file as bd-r.

5. View it in your browser, and compare it to Figure 19.4.

Figure 19.4.

*Price sheet page
version II.*

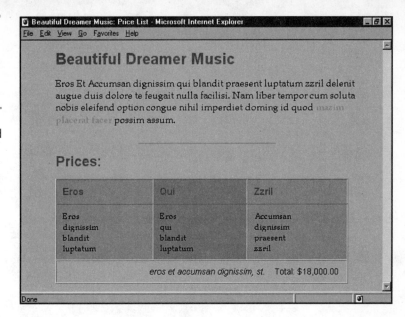

Some people use
comment tags around
their style sheet calls.
This hides them from
non-style sheet
browsers. You can
then design the page
to be viewable in a
non-compliant
browser, but still
allow for readability
and some semblance
of style.

Creating a Party Invitation Using Style Sheets

Want to get colorful? This task uses style sheets to achieve a fun design.

1. Begin with the HTML shell syntax:

```
<html>

<head>
<title>business party announcement</title>
</head>

<body bgcolor="#FFFFFF">

</body>
</html>
```

2. Add the style. In this example, you'll see grouping in action with the margin attribute in the BODY syntax:

```
<style>

BODY {color: #FFFFFF; margin: 0.0 0.05 0.05}
H1 {font: 25pt "LasVegasD"; color:#FF3333; text-align: right}
H2 {font: 20pt "LasVegasD"; color: #FF3333; text-align: left}
```

```
P {font: 13pt "verdana"; color: #333399}
HR {color: #FF3333}
A {color: #FFCC33; text-decoration: none}

</style>
```

3. Add your table and contents:

```
<table border=0 width=580 cellpadding=10 cellspacing=0>
<tr>

<td width=400 bgcolor="#FFFF00">

<h1>Viva Las Vegas Party!!!</h1>

<p>

<b>Las Vegas-style</b> party for all employees of AJbest Books.
Eros Et Accumsan dignissim qui blandit praesent luptatum zzril
delenit augue duis dolore te feugait nulla facilisi.

</p>

<p>

<b>Nam: </b>liber tempor cum soluta nobis

</p>

<p>

<b>Nam: </b>liber tempor cum soluta nobis

</p>

<p>

<b>Nam: </b>liber tempor cum soluta nobis

</p>
</td>

<td width=170>

<h2>win big . . .</h2>

<p align=right>

Eros Et Accumsan dignissim qui <a href="http://win.htm/">blandit
praesent</a> luptatum zzril delenit augue duis dolore te feugait
nulla facilisi. Nam liber tempor!
```

```
</p>

<hr>

<p align=right>

<i>email: <ahref="mailto:helene@ajbooks.biz">helene@ajbooks.
biz</a></i>

</td>

</tr>
</table>
```

4. Save the file as `vlv.htm` and view it in your browser.

5. Figure 19.5 shows the layout of this bright online invitation.

Figure 19.5.
Business party invitation.

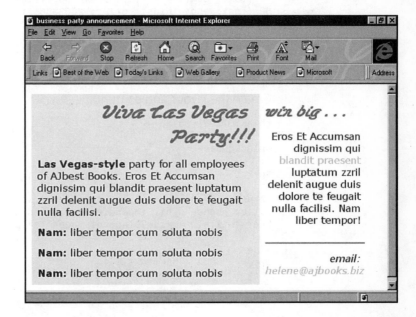

Looking for more style sheet references? Visit `http://www.htmlhelp.com/reference/css/references.html`.

Kids' News

Here again is an example of a standard HTML design using rules that creates an attractive, vivacious, and very fun page.

1. Start with the shell:

```
<html>
<head>
<title>KidTIME!</title>
</head>

<body bgcolor="FFFFFF">

</body>
</html>
```

2. Add the style:

```
<style>

BODY {color: #FFFFFF; margin: 0.05in 0.75in}
H1 {font: 20pt "Kids"; color:#663366; text-align: right}
H2 {font: 18pt "Kids"; color: #663366; text-align: left}
P {font: 13pt "arial narrow"; color: #009933}
HR {color: #FF9900}
A {color: #FF9900; text-decoration: none}

</style>
```

3. Create the layout and content:

```
<h1>KidTIME!</h1>

<blockquote>

<p>

<b>Hey Kids!</b> Nam liber tempor cum soluta nobis eleifend
option congue nihil imperdiet doming id quod <a
href="nil.htm">mazim placerat facer</a> possim assum.

</p>

<hr>

<h2>You Know It!</h2>

<p>

Nam liber tempor cum soluta nobis eleifend option congue nihil
imperdiet doming id quod <a href="nil.htm">mazim placerat
facer</a> possim assum.
</p>

<hr>

<h2>Cool KATsss</h2>

<p>
```

```
Nam liber tempor cum soluta nobis eleifend option congue nihil
imperdiet doming id quod <a href="nil.htm">mazim placerat
facer</a> possim assum.

</p>

</blockquote>
```

4. Save the file as `kids.htm`.

5. View it in your browser and compare it to Figure 19.6.

Figure 19.6.

Light and bright kids' page.

TASK # Another Linked Style Sheet

Now you'll create the preceding fun kids' magazine in the linked style.

1. Open up a fresh page in your HTML editor.

2. Take the embedded style out of the originating page and place it into the fresh editing environment:

```
<style>

BODY {color: #FFFFFF; margin: 0.05in 0.75in}
H1 {font: 20pt "Kids"; color:#663366; text-align: right}
H2 {font: 18pt "Kids"; color: #663366; text-align: left}
P {font: 13pt "arial narrow"; color: #009933}
```

```
HR {color: #FF9900}
A {color: #FF9900; text-decoration: none}

</style>
```

3. Save the file as `kids.css`.

4. Place the following link below the `TITLE` and before the `</head>` tag on every page you want to have influenced by this style:

   ```
   <link rel=stylesheet href="pj.css" type="text/css">
   ```

5. Save and test your files.

TASK   Online Book Cover

This task shows you a very sophisticated look and feel gained through style. Pay special attention to another way of using class. In this case, I've defined attributes, not tags, and given them a name in the `.namegoeshere` style. What this allows me to do is call that class within any HTML section I'd like; therefore, the style that string contains will be used. Also note the use of graphics. Even with three graphics on the page, the total HTML and graphic combination results in only 11 kilobytes.

1. Create the shell:

   ```
   <html>
   </head>
   <title>Dare to Dream: Poems by Women of War</title>
   </head>

   <body bgcolor=#000000>

   </body>
   </html>
   ```

2. Add the style, paying attention to the defined classes `.HEAD` and `.SUB`:

   ```
   <style>

   BODY {font: 16pt "garamond"; font-style: "italic";color:
   ➥#66CCCC;text-align: center;background: #000000}
   .HEAD {font: 15pt "arial narrow"; font-weight: bold; text-align:
   ➥center; font-style: none}
   .SUB  {line-height: 20pt}

   </style>
   ```

3. Add the table and contents, noting each step of the way the use of class:

```
<table border=0 width=500 cellpadding=5 cellspacing=0>
<tr>

<td width=200 class=head>

d a r e   t o   d r e a m

 </td>

<td width=200>

<img src="images/wow1.gif" width=100 height=147>

</td>

</tr>
<tr>

<td width=200>

<img src="images/wow2.gif" width=75 height=116>

</td>

<td class=sub width=200>

. . . a journey into<br> lives <br> and lifetimes

</td>

</tr>
<tr>

<td width=200>

a series of poems<br>
~ by ~ <br>
women of war

</td>

<td width=200>

<img src="images/wow3.gif" width=175 height=110>

</td>

</tr>
</table>
```

4. Save the file as `dtd.htm`.

5. View it in your browser and compare it to Figure 19.7.

Figure 19.7.

An elegant, artistic book cover.

For a detailed description of Internet Explorer 3.0 for Windows 95 and NT, visit `http://www.shadow.net/%7Ebraden/nostyle/ie3.html`. Use a Macintosh and want more information? Point your browser to `http://www.cwru.edu/lit/homes/eam3/css1/css1.html`.

Workshop Wrap-Up

I hope you enjoyed the tasks in this book. My main concern is that you have gotten a taste of what style sheets can do, how they work, and the many flexible ways of using them.

As always, you have to determine how to apply style sheets in your own work. For the purposes of this book, I've covered enough territory to get you started. If you feel you don't quite grasp the basic ideas, go back to the quick start section of this book. Chapter 3, "In Vogue: Cascading Style Sheets," covers the primary concepts of style sheets, and you can read this again before moving out on your own.

If style sheets are something that you are definitely considering working with more regularly, I encourage you to visit the World Wide Web Consortium (`http://www.w3.org/`) for very explicit discussions regarding style sheet development, implementation into browsers, and use in design. There's a lot of very technical information that I could not cover in this book, and if this book has served you well, you will be interested in learning more about the technology underlying the style.

Next Steps

It's time to breathe a sigh of relief. All of the task-oriented chapters are done with, and Chapter 20, "Real-Time Example: MainStay Communications—Style Sheets in Action," provides a real-life example of a Web site using style sheets to drive the design.

Be sure to revisit Chapter 3 and, if you haven't already, the appendixes at the end of the book. Appendix C, "Current HTML Standards," in particular is very effective in terms of layout and style in its entirety.

Q&A

Q: Sometimes I notice you use quotations around font names, other times you don't. What's the deal?

A: If a font name is more than one word, you'll need to put quotations around it; otherwise, it isn't mandatory to do so.

Q: I made a style sheet and when I pull up the page in my browser, I just get a blank page. What am I doing wrong?

A: Look at your style sheet very carefully. Style sheet syntax is moody: You have to have everything in just the right place in order for it to function well. If you find no problems there, and you are using a table to lay out the information, go through the table and make sure all of your cells, rows, and final table tags are in place.

Q: I don't have any of your fonts. Where can I get some?

A: All computers come with standard fonts. You can get tons of common fonts on inexpensive CD-ROMs. You can search the Web for a variety of free, low-cost, and top-of-the-line fonts, also.

twenty

Real-Time Example: MainStay Communications —Style Sheets in Action

This example shows progress at work. MainStay Communications is a high-end Web design and New Media Analysis company. Okay, to be honest, it's my company. I'm taking the opportunity to use the lessons learned in this past section and apply them to a real-life experience. This will help you feel as though the techniques in this book are within your reach.

Because my desire is to reach an audience only interested in design techniques such as the ones I've taught in this book, my use of style sheets is defended. More than that, the site is viewable in Netscape Navigator. It's not beautiful, but it's completely accessible.

Visit MainStay at
`http://ybi.com/`
`mainstay/`.

The beauty of the site is a simple one. There aren't a lot of hoops and whistles and bells. In fact, there are only two graphics in the entire site: the GIF animation when you enter and the MainStay Communications logo that is placed throughout the site.

As you move through the site, you'll see many of the concepts you've worked through used within the pages. This can help you to synthesize the learning into a tangible experience. The focus points in this chapter include

❏ The creation of a professional presentation

❏ Text control

❏ Use of a standardized design palette

❏ Use of fonts and point sizes

❏ Use of margins

❏ Contrast

❏ Text color

❏ Background color

❏ Use of shape

❏ Creation of white space

❏ Awareness of alignment and distance

The Main Point

Pulling off style isn't necessarily an easy thing to do. However, as I mentioned earlier, it's not so much what you do, but how you do it. Your tastes and mine are likely to be different. If I've made my choices well, at least what I've created is not going to offend my Web visitors, or certainly not the audience members for whom I'm creating the site. Sure, if this design were for a punk rock band, I'd be out of business in a second.

To achieve this style, I've employed the previously mentioned elements using cascading style sheets and tables as the main ingredients. And, I've done it in an interesting way: I've used one style sheet to create the entire site. By linking each individual page to this style sheet, I've created a very stable solution to the consistency problem in design.

Selecting each style ahead of time, I determined what I was going to need in order to carry the site off. After I had all of the content in place and an outline of the site, the first thing I did was determine my design palette, so I'd have the colors I was going to work with. Then, I selected my fonts, headers, and confirmed my overall concept.

I'm going to start off by showing you the main style sheet, and then step you through each individual page of the site and discuss how it was created, pointing out how the style was achieved in each specific case.

 # Creating the Linked Style Page

As you recall from your lessons, a linked page must have the extension `.css` and reside on the server with your data.

1. Begin with a fresh editing page, and place the `<style>` tags in container fashion on the page:

```
<style>


</style>
```

2. Now add the BODY and HEADER attributes, as follows:

```
BODY {background: #FFFFFF; color: #000000; font: 12pt "arial";
➥margin: 0.00 0.50in 0.50in}
H1 {font: 14pt "georgia"; color: #000099; text-align: left}
H1.green {font: 14pt "georgia"; color: #009900; text-align:
➥left}
```

3. Now create classes for text styles. I've used .text1, .text2, and so forth to indicate differences between the styles:

```
.text1 {font: 12pt "arial"; color: #FFFFFF; text-align: right}
.text2 {font: 12pt "arial"; color: #FFFFFF; text-align: left}
.text3 {font: 11pt "arial"; color: #FFFFFF; text-align: center}
.text4 {font: 11pt "arial"; color: #000099}
.text5 {font: 11pt "arial"; color: #009900}
```

4. Add classes for background colors:

```
.back1 {background: #000099}
.back2 {background: #009900; color: #FFFFFF}
```

5. Finally, add two styles that are just color, so you can add the specific color to any tag you choose:

```
.1 {color: #009900}
.2 {color: #000099}

</style>
```

6. Save the style sheet, remembering to use a `.css` extension.

As you can see, I've created a precise series of options for myself, giving maximum flexibility from page to page without getting too complicated about it. In simple terms, I've made the default background color white and the default text color black. My header fonts are a serif, called Georgia. My main text is all comprised of the sanserif font, Arial. I've also used a variety of color options from my palette, as well as alignments and color calls.

TIP: Keep your eyes on the way I've named classes. This is a completely arbitrary act. You can name your class styles anything you want as long as they are preceded with a ".". However, it's a good idea to use names that make sense, even if it's only to you.

The Splash Page

I wanted to have some fun with this one, so what I did was create an animated GIF. Because it's the only thing on the page, save for a small comment regarding the use of style sheets within the site, I figured I could get away with a large file. It comes in at 43 kilobytes, not really too shabby at all. And, the results are worth it. Although the site is professional through and through, it begins on a light note.

The syntax for the first page appears as follows. You'll note that this page is linked to the style sheet right off the bat:

```
<html>
<head>
<title>Welcome to MainStay Communications</title>
```

```
<link rel=stylesheet href="ms.css" type="text/css">

</head>

<body bgcolor="FFFFFF">

<center>

<a href="ms.htm"><img src="images/main-ani.gif" width=400 height=375
border=0>
</a>


<p style="font-family: arial; font-size: 9pt">This site uses
cascading style sheets. It is best viewed with a compliant browser.
</p>

</center>

</body>
</html>
```

Figures 20.1, 20.2, and 20.3 show three different views of the animation.

Figure 20.1.
*The first view of the
MainStay home page.*

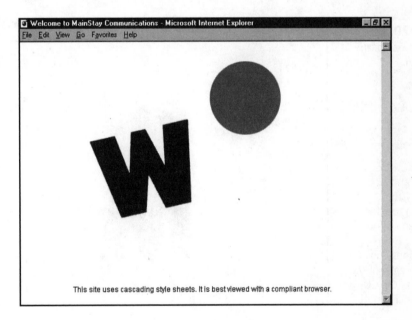

Figure 20.2.
A mid-section view of the animation.

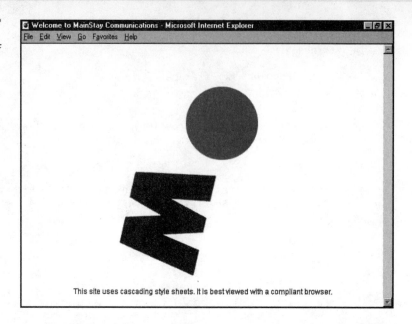

Figure 20.3.
The final view of the animation.

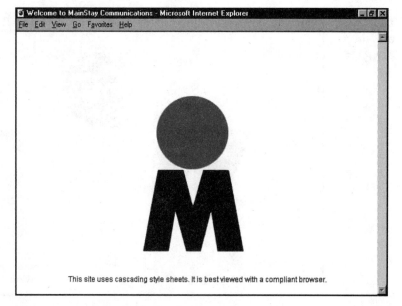

A terrific and compact GIF animation tool for the PC can be found at `http://www.gamani.com/tools`. A copy of the demo is on the CD-ROM. Check it out!

Studying the Main Page

The first page after entering the site is a brief overview of the company. You'll notice I used tables and style sheets to gain a combined effect of shape and weight. MainStay, as the name and logo implies, is a stable new media company. No matter what technologies come and go, the implication is here to weather the storm.

1. Here is the main page's syntax. Observe the `<link>` tag and its attributes, which point to the MainStay linked style sheet.

```
<html>
<head>
<title>MainStay Communications: Company </title>

<link rel=stylesheet href="ms.css" type="text/css">

</head>
```

2. Next, I've placed a body color attribute to avoid the background bug mentioned in Chapter 3, "In Vogue: Cascading Style Sheets," and to provide a background for non–style sheet-compliant browsers. This ensures that any browser will see the white background, rather than a gray one.

```
<body bgcolor="#FFFFFF">
```

3. Now I've created a table, with two table cells in the first row. Pay close attention to the use of `class` and `style` attributes:

```
<div align=center>

<table class=back1 border=0 width=500 cellpadding=10
cellspacing=0>
<tr>

<td style="background: #FFFFFF" valign=middle align=middle
width=200>

<img src="images/mainstay.gif" width=73 height=86>

</td>

<td class=text1 valign=top width=200>

MainStay Communications has been working in the area of media
communications for over a decade. MainStay creates powerful
interactive media, online presence, and marketing provision
through Commercial Online Services, the Internet and the
World Wide Web.

</td>

</tr>
```

4. The second row in the table contains only one table cell. You'll see I've used the `colspan` attribute to stretch it across the two columns created by the first row.

```
<tr>

<td class=text2 valign=top width=200 colspan=2>

Located in Tucson, Arizona, MainStay utilizes the talents of
graphic, audio and video designers, animators, Internet and
commercial online service providers, technical writers and
computer programmers to create complete, award-winning
communications strategies for your company's needs.

</td>

</tr>

</table>
</div>
<p>
```

5. After the table, I've placed text-based navigation options, and then closed the division, body of code, and HTML page with the appropriate tags:

```
<div class=text5 align=center>

<a href="ms.htm">Company</a> |
<a href="clients.htm">Clients</a> |
<a href="web.htm">Web Design</a> |
<a href="media.htm">Media Analysis</a> |
<a href="papers.htm">White Papers</a> |
<a href="fees.htm">Fees</a> |
<a href="contact.htm">Contact</a>

</div>

</body>
</html>
```

You'll see that the primary way of using the style sheet has been to define class within tags. The advantage to this is that you don't have to name every tag you're going to use. Using class calls means that you can add that style, whatever it is, to any HTML tag.

Figure 20.4 shows the results of MainStay's Company page.

Figure 20.4.

MainStay Company page. Note the sense of firmness communicated through the use of shape (rectangles) and weight.

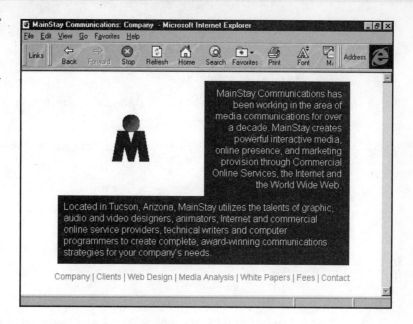

MainStay Communications: Company - Microsoft Internet Explorer

MainStay Communications has been working in the area of media communications for over a decade. MainStay creates powerful interactive media, online presence, and marketing provision through Commercial Online Services, the Internet and the World Wide Web.

Located in Tucson, Arizona, MainStay utilizes the talents of graphic, audio and video designers, animators, Internet and commercial online service providers, technical writers and computer programmers to create complete, award-winning communications strategies for your company's needs.

Company | Clients | Web Design | Media Analysis | White Papers | Fees | Contact

Examining the Client Page

Who a company has worked for often reflects the quality of its experience. You'll want to decide if incorporating this type of information in your commercial site design is right for a given client. In this case, I included an annotated list of national, international, and regional clients. I've drawn the eye to regional clients because it creates nice visual contrasts as well as making the suggestion that the company is not just corporate, but maintains home-town ties. This communicates a sense of broad experience as well as personal attention to clients.

1. You will notice the linked style sheet right at the top, between the `</title>` and the `</head>` tags:

```
<html>
<head>
<title>MainStay: Clients</title>

<link rel=stylesheet href="ms.css" type="text/css">

</head>
```

2. Note how the body background color is defined:

```
<body bgcolor="FFFFFF">

<div align=center>
```

3. The first table begins with standard attributes, images, and no background coloration:

```
<table border=0 width=550 cellpadding=0 cellspacing=0>
<tr>
<td width=9>

</td>

<td valign=top align=left>

<img src="images/mainstay.gif" width=73 height=86>

</td>
</tr>
</table>
```

4. Another table is placed below the first, forming a stack. The table's attributes are standard, but the first table cell uses an inline class call to pull attributes from the style sheet:

```
<table border=0 width=550 cellpadding=10 cellspacing=0>
<tr>

<td class=text4 valign=top width=300>

<h1>Selected Clients: National</h1>

General Electric Information Services<br>
Microsoft Corporation<br>
The Microsoft Network<br>
National Academy of Elder Law Attorneys<br>
National Association of Senior Living Industries<br>
TCI<br>

<h1>International</h1>

Interactive Press, Mexico<br>
Scouting of Germany<br>
Sedgwick China

</td>
```

5. The following cell also demonstrates a class call from the style sheet, as well as standard attributes:

```
<td class=text3 bgcolor="#009900"valign=middle width=200>

<h1 style="text-align: center">Regional</h1>

Alternative Concepts of Nevada<br>
Arizona Bookstore<br>
CoreWave<br>
Gadabout Salons<br>
MainStream Media<br>
Ramada Inn <br>
Saguaro Credit Union <br>
Sulphur Springs Valley Electric<br>
Wilde Rose Coffee Company
</td>

</tr>
</table>
</div>
<p>
```

6. The table is closed, as is the division. A new division using class calls assigns the style to the text-based navigation before the code is completed:

```
<div class=text5 align=center>

<a href="ms.htm">Company</a> |
<a href="clients.htm">Clients</a> |
<a href="web.htm">Web Design</a> |
<a href="media.htm">Media Analysis</a> |
<a href="papers.htm">White Papers</a> |
<a href="fees.htm">Fees</a> |
<a href="contact.htm">Contact</a>

</div>

</body>
</html>
```

Figure 20.5 shows the page's layout.

Figure 20.5.
MainStay client page. Professionalism and warmth are suggested by this design.

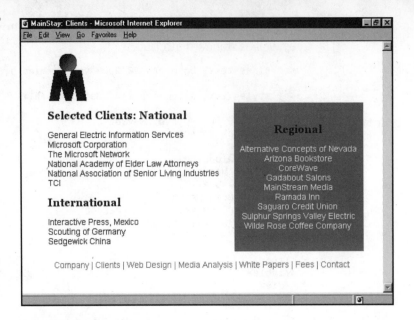

DESIGN NOTE: You'll notice I've used centered text within the table cell to the right. I typically avoid centering text because it isn't as attractive as you might think. Where it does work is in limited sections that visually call for the balance and shape that centered alignment creates. In this case, there is the additional value of contrast because of the reversed text color.

TASK

Working with the Services Page

For the Web design section, I decided to go simple and straight to the point. My feeling is that if a client needs more information, he or she will get in touch. Otherwise, why give away the store? You'll notice that almost all of these pages are written right to the point. The reason is because of attention span. I don't want to bore a visitor with all the amazing things the company can do. Instead, I show it through my design and through my client list. The rest is up to them.

1. The syntax begins with the title and the all-important style sheet link:

```
<html>
<head>
<title>MainStay: Web Design Services</title>

<link rel=stylesheet href="ms.css" type="text/css">

</head>
```

2. I continue with the background color:

```
<body bgcolor="FFFFFF">
```

3. Block-quoting ensures that the main body of text, which isn't placed within a table, will have sufficient margins. Note that I've placed the table *within* the blockquote. This keeps the table within the defined margins so that it lines up nicely with the following text:

```
<blockquote>
```

4. The table uses straightforward attributes. The job of this table is to contain and align the graphic:

```
<table border=0 width=550 cellpadding=0 cellspacing=0>
<tr>

<td valign=top align=left>

<img src="images/mainstay.gif" width=73 height=86>

</td>
</tr>
</table>
```

5. The following header incorporates a class call:

```
<h1 class=green>Web Site Design</h1>
```

6. The <span> tag is used to call style from the linked sheet to the body of text. Note how this rhythm repeats throughout the page:

```
<span class=text4>

Graphic Design, Custom Layout and HTML Scripting, Programming
(CGI, Perl, ActiveX, Java, JavaScript, Visual Basic,
VBScript, etc).
</span>


<h1 class=green>Presence</h1>
```

```
<span class=text4>

Presence packages can include dedicated server space, POP Mail
Accounts, PPP or SLIP Accounts, Registered Domains,
Maintenance, Technical Training, Support and Assistance.

</span>

<h1 class=green>The Complete Networking Package</h1>

<span class=text4>

Interested in becoming an Internet Service Provider or maintain-
ing your own Web Server? MainStay Communications provides
consultation, development of networking systems, and implementa-
tion of hardware and software for Internet-based Server and
Service Provision.

</span>
</blockquote>
<p>
```

Even when I have a defined margin, I often use block-quotes. This can really help pull in the margin when you're not using tables. I like a lot of white space. It's easier on my eyes, which spend a lot time in front of a computer. Other visitors will appreciate it, too. It makes reading much easier.

7. The `</blockquote>` tag closes off the body of text. Then, a division with the text-based navigation is added before the page is completed:

```
<div class=text5 align=center>

<a href="ms.htm">Company</a> |
<a href="clients.htm">Clients</a> |
<a href="web.htm">Web Design</a> |
<a href="media.htm">Media Analysis</a> |
<a href="papers.htm">White Papers</a> |
<a href="fees.htm">Fees</a> |
<a href="contact.htm">Contact</a>

</div>

</body>
</html>
```

The Web design page can be seen in Figure 20.6.

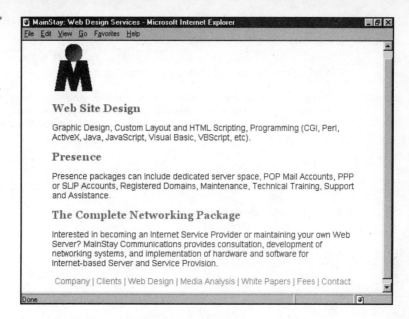

Figure 20.6.

MainStay's Web design page. Simple design is sometimes the most effective for the task at hand.

Reversing Direction

To be a bit playful, I've reversed the earlier shape created with table cell background colors. You'll also note that the class calls in this case cause the text to reverse as well. The end design maintains consistency with the rest of the site, but also adds a little visual pick-me-up for the visitor.

Match this code to that used for the Company page earlier in the chapter:

```
<html>
<head>
<title>MainStay Communications: Media Analysis</title>

<link rel=stylesheet href="ms.css" type="text/css">

</head>

<body bgcolor="#FFFFFF">

<div align=center>
```

```
<table class=back1 border=0 width=500 cellpadding=10 cellspacing=0>
<tr>

<td class=text2 valign=top width=200 height=200>

Interactive media, new media, Internet and Intranet, promotions and
marketinganalysis are available by project proposal, with
consultations billed as per the enclosed Terms and Conditions.
Initial consultation is free.

</td>

<td style="background: #FFFFFF" valign=middle align=middle width=200>

<img src="images/mainstay.gif" width=73 height=86>

</td>

</tr>

<tr>

<td class=text1 valign=top width=200 colspan=2>

MainStay Communications offers public presentations and corporate
training in new media, interactive media, Internet and Intranet, and
fundamentals of Web design. Fees are by proposal or at the hourly
rate stated in Terms and Conditions.

</td>

</tr>

</table>
</div>
<p>

<div class=text5 align=center>

<a href="ms.htm">Company</a> |
<a href="clients.htm">Clients</a> |
<a href="web.htm">Web Design</a> |
<a href="media.htm">Media Analysis</a> |
<a href="papers.htm">White Papers</a> |
<a href="fees.htm">Fees</a> |
<a href="contact.htm">Contact</a>

</div>

</body>
</html>
```

DESIGN NOTE: As you see, multiple table rows come in handy when you're after visual effects like the ones shown here. Using the `colspan` argument, I've been able to create the right-angle design.

Figure 20.7 demonstrates this reverse style in action.

Figure 20.7.
Reversing an earlier theme helps maintain consistency, but offers some fresh information to the visitor's eye.

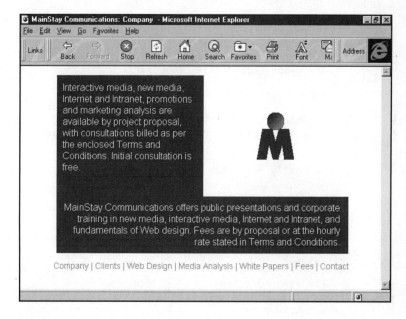

Your Papers, Please

One way of helping clients is to provide them with information on your products. In this case, I have currently linked to one article: "Client Strategies and Concepts." This is basically a worksheet that allows clients to do some preliminary planning on their own before calling the company with questions. Note how I've added a style call to the `<li>` tag, and to the horizontal rule. This call applies one kind of style: color.

```
<html>
<head>
<title>MainStay: Web Design Services</title>

<link rel=stylesheet href="ms.css" type="text/css">

</head>
```

One way of naming classes is by referring to what they do, as in the case of **green** and **blue**. You'll always know that calling on a class named that succinctly will do exactly what it says it will.

```
<body bgcolor="FFFFFF">

<blockquote>

<table border=0 width=550 cellpadding=0 cellspacing=0>
<tr>

<td valign=top align=left>

<img src="images/mainstay.gif" width=73 height=86>

</td>
</tr>
</table>

<h1 class=green>White Papers</h1>

<span class=text4>

MainStay Communications offers the following papers and information
to aid clients and potential clients in preparing for a Web site.
<p>

Currently available papers include:
<p>

<li class=2><a href="sandc.htm" class=text5>Client Strategies and
Concepts</a>
<p>

</span>

<hr class=2 width=75% align=center>

</blockquote>
<p>

<div class=text5 align=center>

<a href="ms.htm">Company</a> |
<a href="clients.htm">Clients</a> |
<a href="web.htm">Web Design</a> |
<a href="media.htm">Media Analysis</a> |
<a href="papers.htm">White Papers</a> |
<a href="fees.htm">Fees</a> |
<a href="contact.htm">Contact</a>

</div>

</body>
</html>
```

In Figure 20.8, you can see the results of the preceding syntax.

Figure 20.8.
The White Papers page.

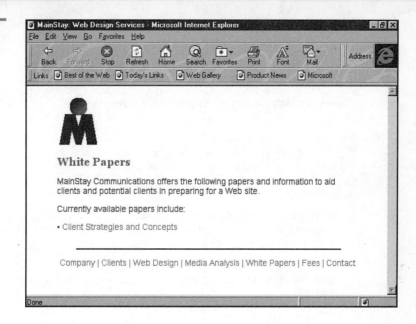

Quick, Link!

To read the paper, just click the link. In this instance, I've again used a very standard, simple HTML layout. Note the use of <ol>, the ordered list tag.

```
<html>
<head>
<title>MainStay: Web Design Services</title>

<link rel=stylesheet href="ms.css" type="text/css">

</head>

<body bgcolor="FFFFFF">

<blockquote>

<table border=0 width=550 cellpadding=0 cellspacing=0>
<tr>

<td valign=top align=left>

<img src="images/mainstay.gif" width=73 height=86>

</td>
</tr>
</table>

<h1 class=green>Client Strategies and Concepts:</h1>
```

```
<span class=text4>

In order to provide the best services possible, MainStay asks that
you think about the following aspects of your company, services, and
ideas before inquiring aftera consultation. This will save you time
<i>and money!</i>. Please note: "product" can refer to organization
or project; company to organization, etc.

<ol>

<li> What is the specific intent of this project? (an example might
be "to sell 4,000,000 units of product X in the
fourth quarter of 1996)
<p>

<li> Who is the current audience (client, buyer) of your product?
(again, be very specific: "U.S. males age 20-25, middle
class or higher, college educated)
<p>

<li> What audience(s) would you like to expand your services to
reach?
<p>

<li>Describe the details of your product:
<p>

<li>What current forms of marketing and distribution do you use?
(newspaper ads, television ads, radio, word-of-mouth,
Internet, etc.)
<p>

<li>Do you consider your product visual? If so, how so? (color and
style of packaging, advertising, specific colors and fonts used,
etc.)
<p>

<li>Describe a television, newspaper, or other advertisement
that appeals to you:
<p>

<li>Describe an ad that you strongly dislike:
<p>
```

```
<li>Do you or your company have any specific philosophical ideas,
philanthropical activities, or religious/political
sensitivies?
<p>

<li>Please tell us anything about your company and product that you
feel is unusual, important, and outstanding.

</ol>

</span>

</blockquote>
<p>
<p>

<div class=text5 align=center>

<a href="ms.htm">Company</a> |
<a href="clients.htm">Clients</a> |
<a href="web.htm">Web Design</a> |
<a href="media.htm">Media Analysis</a> |
<a href="papers.htm">White Papers</a> |
<a href="fees.htm">Fees</a> |
<a href="contact.htm">Contact</a>

</div>

</body>
</html>
```

CAUTION: Although this page prints out nicely, there is a problem with reversed text, as on earlier pages in this example. If you really think a client is going to want to print something out, make sure that the information that is absolutely necessary will print, or provide a downloadable file for them to print out on their own.

For a glimpse of the example code in real-life color, check Chapter 20's folder on the CD-ROM for the file, which you can load in your browser. For a quick glance, Figure 20.9 will do the trick.

Figure 20.9.

The actual question-naire. You can print this page out and use it as a reference or worksheet for your own clients.

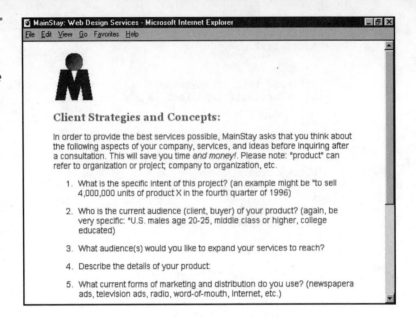

MainStay: Web Design Services - Microsoft Internet Explorer

File Edit View Go Favorites Help

Client Strategies and Concepts:

In order to provide the best services possible, MainStay asks that you think about the following aspects of your company, services, and ideas before inquiring after a consultation. This will save you time *and money!*. Please note: "product" can refer to organization or project; company to organization, etc.

1. What is the specific intent of this project? (an example might be "to sell 4,000,000 units of product X in the fourth quarter of 1996)

2. Who is the current audience (client, buyer) of your product? (again, be very specific: "U.S. males age 20-25, middle class or higher, college educated)

3. What audience(s) would you like to expand your services to reach?

4. Describe the details of your product:

5. What current forms of marketing and distribution do you use? (newspapera ads, television ads, radio, word-of-mouth, Internet, etc.)

Cha-Ching!

It's not usually a good idea to put your prices on the Web. However, if you're very particular about who is going to get in touch with you, it can be a good idea. I like to show my prices so people can figure out whether they want to use the services provided by MainStay Communications. The advantage is that they have a starting point for their questions, and the company doesn't have to be overwhelmed with questions from people who know that these services are not within their budget.

The terms and conditions are very simply stated, in the same style as the white paper—simple, clean, and printable. You might take a close look at the information within and adapt it to your own needs. You're welcome to do so, but be careful to check with an attorney about any language or specifics that might apply to your unique needs.

```
<html>
<head>
<title>MainStay: Fees, Terms, and Conditions</title>

<link rel=stylesheet href="ms.css" type="text/css">

</head>
```

```
<body bgcolor="FFFFFF">

<blockquote>

<table border=0 width=550 cellpadding=0 cellspacing=0>
<tr>

<td valign=top align=left>

<img src="images/mainstay.gif" width=73 height=86>

</td>
</tr>
</table>

<h1 class=green>MainStay Communications Consulting:<br>
Terms and Conditions</h1>

<span class=text4>
<ol>

<li>For fixed price work, MainStay Communications's fee is by
proposal only.
<p>

<li>If you prefer to be billed hourly for services, the rate is
$200 per hour per service. Minimum is one hour.
<p>

<li> Because of the demands for services provided, a two-to-four week
notice is preferred. If you require services within 48 hours of your
initial contact, be aware that the fee will be charged at 150%
"panic" rate.
<p>

<li>Unless otherwise noted, any specific information exchanged is
considered to be in strict confidentiality, and will not be disclosed
it to any third party.Unless you ask specifically, our business
relationship is not considered secret nor is the general nature of
our work together.
<p>

<li>Accounting can be handled any way you prefer. Normally, invoices
for accumulated time are sent out once a month. If you prefer other
arrangements, this is fine, but should be stated ahead of time.
Please note that a 15% late fee on invoices which are more than one
month overdue will be enforced. Your accounting department should be
told that our billing is based on a "Net 30" invoice.
<p>

<li>Our relationship is based on mutual respect and common business
practice.All work provided is exclusive to you and your company.
Products and services are only recommended when they have been used
and tested to standards.
<p>
```

A common question from Web designers is "How much should I charge?" I recommend starting at $100 an hour for your services. Then, go up or down depending on the level of your experience, education, and what your market will bear.

```
</ol>

</span>

<hr class=2 width=75% align=center>

</blockquote>
<p>

<div class=text5 align=center>

<a href="ms.htm">Company</a> |
<a href="clients.htm">Clients</a> |
<a href="web.htm">Web Design</a> |
<a href="media.htm">Media Analysis</a> |
<a href="papers.htm">White Papers</a> |
<a href="fees.htm">Fees</a> |
<a href="contact.htm">Contact</a>

</div>

</body>
</html>
```

Figure 20.10 shows the terms and conditions page, also an easy-to-print page that clients can take away from their computers to muse over.

Figure 20.10.
The Terms and Conditions page.

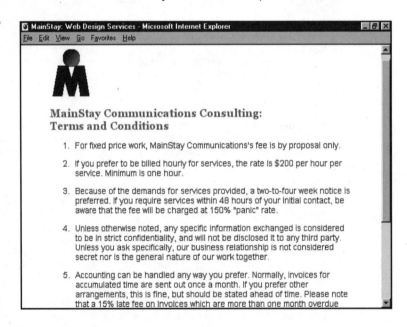

Get in Touch

Finally, it's always a good idea to make sure people can get in touch. Going back to an earlier theme, choice, it's also nice to give them a variety of options. I use voice, fax, postal, and electronic mail.

This page uses a table layout, going back to another, earlier theme, for its design. Again, the idea is consistency with a bit of diversity. It makes for a visually interesting experience.

```html
<html>
<head>
<title>MainStay: Contact</title>

<link rel=stylesheet href="ms.css" type="text/css">

</head>

<body bgcolor="FFFFFF">

<div align=center>

<table border=0 width=550 cellpadding=10 cellspacing=0>
<tr>

<td class=text4 valign=top width=300>

<h1>Making Contact</h1>

You can get in touch with MainStay communications in the following
ways:
<p>

<h2>Toll-Free (U.S. Only) Voice:</h2>

1-800-300-9097
<p>

<h2>FAX:</h2>

520-323-2751
<p>

<h2>Postal Mail</h2>

MainStay Communications<br>
3400 East Speedway Boulevard Suite 118-111<br>
Tucson, Arizona 85716<br>
U.S.A.
<p>

</td>
```

```
<td class=text3 bgcolor="009900" valign=top width=200>

<h1 style="text-align: center">email is easiest!</h1>

MainStay Communications appreciates that if you can, you contact us
via electronic mail. Simply click the link below, and
let us know what services you are interested in.
<p>

<a href="mailto:ybi@ybi.com">email MainStay
<p>

<img src="images/mainstay.gif" width=73 height=86 border=0>
</a>
</td>

</tr>
</table>
</div>
<p>

<div class=text5 align=center>

<a href="ms.htm">Company</a> |
<a href="clients.htm">Clients</a> |
<a href="web.htm">Web Design</a> |
<a href="media.htm">Media Analysis</a> |
<a href="papers.htm">White Papers</a> |
<a href="fees.htm">Fees</a> |
<a href="contact.htm">Contact</a>

</div>

</body>
</html>
```

Figure 20.11 wraps up this real-time tour with a look at the contact page.

Figure 20.11.
The Contact page makes it easy to get in touch, offering a variety of options.

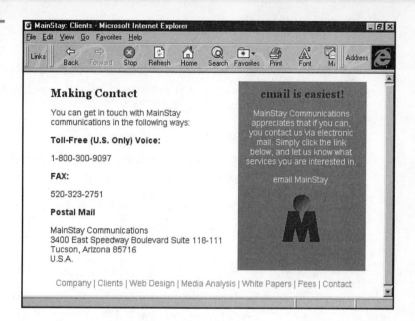

Workshop Wrap-Up

This tour of MainStay Communications not only provides a tangible experience for you as a designer interested in using style sheets, but also gives you some hard-copy material to use for your own design business.

My hopes are that you'll take the lessons in this book to great places, for your own individual success and for the greater good of the Web.

Each person who comes to the Web as a potential designer has something to offer. As those skills get stronger, the Web becomes more interesting. Instead of cliché and overused techniques and technologies, there's a new and fresh look behind every link.

It's true that not everyone can be good at everything. I personally don't consider myself a great designer. I think I'm a fairly competent coder, particularly because I can do it by hand instead of relying on a software package that does it all for me. There's a certain sense of pride in knowing that if I need to get under the hood and fix something, my skills are good enough to do that troubleshooting.

Each person who works hard at Web design concepts and technologies will eventually find his or her niche. I think my best quality is synthesis. I may not be the best designer, and I'm absolutely no use at all when it comes to actual programming, but I understand how to take Web technologies and pull them together. This is my strength.

What's yours? Think about it! This is an important process in the education of a Web designer. You must come to a point where confidence is built from the knowledge that your individual talents are worthwhile and necessary.

Ultimately, the Web will be a better place for the contributions you will offer.

Next Steps

There are four appendixes, each with a wealth of information including resources and HTML references. The CD-ROM, which you should be very familiar with by now, offers some terrific shareware and demo programs for you to enjoy.

Q&A

Q: I learned a lot working through these steps. But I still feel I have so much more to learn. Where can I go for more task-oriented books, and books on Web design in general?

A: If you enjoyed the way this book works, be sure to check out the other books in the Laura Lemay Web Workshop series. They are written by a number of very knowledgeable authors who bring experience and wit to their writing. More information is in the back section. Also, you can visit the Information SuperLibrary from Macmillan Computer Publishing. This site is a very comprehensive database of all the computer and Internet-oriented books in the Macmillan family. Point your browser to `http://www.mcp.com/mcp/`.

P A R T

Appendixes

Directory of
Resources

The following list includes a variety of resources online and offline that would be of interest to Web designers.

HTML Resources

- ❏ The HTML Reference Manual (from Sandia National Laboratories)

    `http://www.sandia.gov/sci_compute/html_ref.html`

- ❏ HTML Writers Guild

    `http://www.hwg.org/`

- ❏ NCSA—A Beginner's Guide to HTML

    `http://www.ncsa.uiuc.edu/General/Internet/WWW/HTMLPrimer.html`

- ❏ The Web Developer's Virtual Library

    `http://WWW.Stars.com/`

- ❏ World Wide Web Consortium's HyperText Markup Language (HTML) Working and Background Materials

    `http://www.w3.org/pub/WWW/MarkUp/MarkUp.html`

- ❏ World Wide Web FAQ

    `http://www.boutell.com/faq/`

- ❏ Yale/CAIM WWW Style Manual

    `http://info.med.yale.edu/caim/StyleManual_Top.HTML`

Mail Lists (Listservs) and Usenet Newsgroups

- ❏ ADV-HTML

    To subscribe to ADV-HTML, send the following command in the body of an e-mail message to `listserv@ua1vm.ua.edu`:

    `subscribe ADV-HTML Your Name`

- ❏ alt.html

❏ `comp.infosystems.www.authoring.html`

❏ HTML-L

To subscribe to HTML-L, send the following command in the body of an e-mail message to `listserv@vm.ege.edu.tr`:

`subscribe HTML-L` *Your Name*

❏ HTML Writers Guild: Mailing Lists

`http://www.hwg.org/lists/index.html`

hwg-news (Mandatory for all hwg members)

hwg-main; "Discussion of all aspects of creating Web services"

hwg-main-digest; "As above, but in digest version"

hwg-basics; "Basic HTML, including inline images"

hwg-business; "Marketing, contracts, ethics, sales, etc."

hwg-ops; "Guild-related business"

❏ Netscape

To subscribe to Netscape, send the following command in the body of an e-mail message to `listserv@irlearn.ucd.ie`:

`subscribe NETSCAPE` *Your Name*

❏ Web-Consultants

You can find out how to subscribe to the Web-Consultants list and the Web-Consultants Jobline list at `http://just4u.com/webconsultants/mlists.htm`.

❏ www-html

To subscribe to www-html, send the request, subscribe, in the body of an e-mail message to `www-html-request@w3.org`.

Books

❏ *The HTML Sourcebook: a Complete Guide to HTML 3.0*

Ian S. Graham
2nd Edition
John Wiley & Sons, 1996
ISBN: 0471142425

`http://www.utirc.utoronto.ca/HTMLdocs/NewHTML/htmlindex.html`

❏ *Teach Yourself Web Publishing with HTML 3.2 in 14 Days, Professional Reference Edition*

Laura Lemay
Professional Reference Edition
Sams.net, 1996
ISBN: 1575210967

❏ *HTML and CGI Unleashed, Professional Reference Edition*

John December, Mark Ginsburg
Book & CD-ROM Edition
Sams, 1996
ISBN: 0672301777

❏ *Web Publishing Unleashed, Professional Reference Edition*

William Robert Stanek
Book & CD-ROM Edition
Sams, 1997
ISBN: 30987198x

❏ *The Webmaster's Guide to HTML: for Advanced Web Developers*
(J. Ranade Workstation Series)

Nathan J. Muller, Linda L. Tyke (Illustrator)
Book & Disk Edition
McGraw Hill, 1995
ISBN: 0079122736

❑ *Web Programming Secrets with HTML, CGI, and PERL*

Ed Tittel, Mark Gaither, Sebastian Hassinger, Mike Erwin
Book & Disk Edition
IDG Books Worldwide, 1996
ISBN: 156884848X

Conferences and Events

❑ An in-depth view of forms, tables, and CGI

http://WWW.Stars.com/Seminars/

❑ General Events Information

http://conferences.calendar.com

❑ Mecklermedia/Internet World Events

A complete list of the events sponsored by Mecklermedia (*Internet World*) is available at http://events.iworld.com.

Contact: Ann Zmitrovich (annz@mecklermedia.com)

Phone: 203-341-2967

❑ Softbank Expo's Upcoming Event Calendar and Product Fact Sheet

http://www.sbexpos.com/sbexpos/public_relations/
product_fact_sheet.html

Also, check http://www.interop.com.

Other Resources

❑ WebTechs Validation Service

http://www.webtechs.com/html-val-svc/

❑ Yahoo!

http://www.yahoo.com/Computers_and_Internet/Software/
Data_Formats/HTML

Web Graphic Design Resources

The following resources can help provide more information on how to approach graphics for the Web.

Web Sites

❏ The 3-D Café

   http://www.3dcafe.com/

❏ Creating Graphics for the Web

   http://www.widearea.co.uk/designer/

❏ Graphics Formats for the WWW

   http://www.w3.org/pub/WWW/Graphics/

❏ Adobe

   http://www.adobe.com

❏ Corel/WordPerfect

   http://www.corel.ca

❏ David Siegel's Net Tips for Writers and Designers

   http://www.dsiegel.com/tips/tips_home.html

❏ Kai's Power Tips and Tricks for Adobe Photoshop

   http://the-tech.mit.edu/KPT/

❏ Paint Shop Pro

   http://www.jasc.com/index.html

❏ Royal Frazier

   http://members.aol.com/royalef/index.html

❏ Web Developer's Virtual Library

   http://www.stars.com/Graphics/

Listservs and Newsgroups

❑ `alt.corel.graphics`

❑ `comp.graphics.misc`

❑ `comp.graphics.apps.photoshop`

❑ `comp.infosystems.www.authoring.images`

❑ Corel

`http://www.corelnet.com/corelnet/newtalk/newtalk.htm`

❑ DIRECT-L

Macromedia Director support list to provide a forum for discussions of the software program.

To subscribe to DIRECT-L, send the following command in the body of an e-mail message to `LISTSERV@uafsysb.uark.edu`:

`subscribe DIRECT-L` *Your Name*

❑ Graphics

The Graphics mailing list discusses the history, theory, practice, and techniques of graphic design. To subscribe to the Graphics mailing list, send the following command in the body of an e-mail message to `listserv@ulkyvm.louisville.edu`:

`subscribe graphics` *Your Name*

❑ Lynda's Homegurrl Web Design List

To subscribe to Lynda's Homegurrl Web Design List, follow the instructions available at `http://www.lynda.com/webdesign.html`.

❑ Photoshop

To subscribe, send the following command in the body of an e-mail message to `listproc2@bgu.edu`:

`subscribe PHOTSHOP` *Your Name*

Books

❏ *Creating Great Web Graphics*

Laurie McCanna
Holt Publishing
ISBN: 1558284796

http://www.mccannas.com/book/overview.htm

and

http://www.dru.nl/bedrijven/broese/specials/eoug96/int7.htm.

❏ *Designing Web Graphics, 2nd Edition*

Lynda Weinman
New Riders Publishing, 1997
ISBN:1562057154

❏ *Photoshop for Windows 95 Bible*

Deke McClelland
IDG Books Worldwide, 1996
ISBN: 156884882X

Conferences, Courses, and Events

❏ Adobe Internet Conference Overview

http://www.adobe.com/events/aic/main.html

❏ Designing Effective User Interfaces

http://cs.wpi.edu/~matt/courses/cs563/talks/smartin/
int_design.html

❏ The MasterClass Series: Training in HCI (Human-Computer Interface)

http://www.system-concepts.com/masterclass/

Visit the following Web site for up-to-date information on these courses:

❏ SIGGRAPH Online

http://www.siggraph.org/

SIGGRAPH Online is the Association for Computing Machinery's Special Interest Group on Computer Graphics. The calendar of SIGGRAPH events is at `http://www.siggraph.org/calendar/calendar.html`.

Other Resources

❏ Computer User Groups on the World Wide Web

`http://annarbor.apcug.org/others/index.htm`

Web Multimedia Resources

The following Internet resources are helpful to those wanting more information on how to produce multimedia:

Web Sites

❏ The Apple QuickTime VR Download Site

`http://qtvr.quicktime.apple.com/`

❏ Jack Decker's Personal Audio-Video Home Page

`http://www.novagate.com/~jack/audiovid.html`

❏ Macromedia Products

`http://www.macromedia.com/`

❏ The MICE Multimedia Index

`http://boom.cs.ucl.ac.uk/mice/`

❏ Microsoft Internet Explorer

`http://www.microsoft.com/ie/default.htm`

❏ Netscape Navigator Plug-Ins

`http://home.netscape.com/comprod/products/navigator/version_2.0/plugins/index.html`

❏ QTVR: a Practical Guide

`http://www.sils.umich.edu/~mbonn/guide.html`

❏ University of Geneva Multimedia Sources

`http://viswiz.gmd.de/MultimediaInfo/`

`http://fourier.dur.ac.uk:8000/mm.html`

Listservs and Newsgroups

❏ Image-L

Send e-mail to `listserv@vm3090.ege.edu.tr` with

`SUB IMAGE-L Your Name`

in the body of the message and a blank subject line.

❏ Multimedia Discussion List

Send e-mail to `majordomo@cleo.murdoch.edu.au` with

`subscribe multimedia`

in the body of the message and a blank header.

❏ `news:clari.tw.new_media`

This is a newsfeed dealing with multimedia and other new technologies.

❏ `news:comp.multimedia`

This is a general multimedia newsgroup.

❏ `news:comp.os.ms-windows.programmer.graphics`

This is a technical MS-Windows graphics programming list.

❏ Voice on the Net (VON) Mailing List

This is a mailing list dedicated to broader discussion of all of the various audio/video products and technologies. To subscribe, send e-mail to `majordomo@pulver.com`. Leave the subject blank, and in the body write the following:

`subscribe von-digest`

❏ Web Multimedia Fusion

`http://www.emf.net/~mal/vcd-dev.html`

Conferences and Events

❏ Antares Virtual Reality

`http://www.avrs.com/antares/edu.html`

Educational software and classes are offered through Antares Virtual Reality Systems.

❏ Asymetrix Seminars

`http://www.asymetrix.com/events.html`

Seminars are available from Asymetrix, a proprietary multimedia tool vendor.

❏ CSU Master of Arts in Multimedia

`http://monet.mcs.csuhayward.edu/mmm/`

Pick up an outline for the Master of Arts in Multimedia Program at California State University at Hayward.

3-D imaging techniques are the focus of this tutorial. This company also has seminars on creating a Web site. The base address provides information on these services.

❏ Texas A&M

`http://mccnet.tamu.edu/Internet_Seminars.html`

Descriptions appear for free seminars at Texas A&M on the second Tuesday of every month.

❏ University of California at Berkeley

`http://www-plateau.cs.berkeley.edu/courseware/`

Descriptions are offered for courseware at UC Berkeley. Many lectures are broadcast on the Internet backbone.

❏ Virginia Commonwealth University: Multimedia Seminars

`http://www.vcu.edu/mdcweb/new/seminars/seminars.html`

Find multimedia seminars at Virginia Commonwealth University.

Books

❏ *Designing Multimedia: a Visual Guide to Multimedia and Online Graphic Design*

Lisa Lopuck
Peachpit Press, 1996
ISBN: 0201883988

❏ *Multimedia: Making It Work, Second Edition*

Tay Vaughan
Osborne, 1994
with CD-ROM
ISBN: 0078820359

❏ *Multimedia Power Tools, Second Edition*

Peter Jerram and Michael Gosney
Random House, 1996
with CD-ROM
ISBN: 0679763465

❏ *Multimedia Systems Design*

Prabhat K. Andleigh and Kiran Thakrar
Prentice Hall, 1996
ISBN: 0130890952

❏ *Shockwave for Director User's Guide*

Sasha Magee and Noel Rabinowitz
New Riders Publishing, 1996
with CD-ROM
ISBN: 1566205595X

Other Resources

The following is an e-mail–based multimedia course:

`MULTIMED-Request@URIACC.URI.EDU`

Web Programming

Web Designers can help increase Web-related programming skills by researching the following references.

Web Sites

❏ Aereal Serch

`http://www.virtpark.com/theme/cgi-bin/serch.html`

❏ Earthweb's Gamelan Java Directory

`http://www.gamelan.com`

❏ The Java Message Exchange

`http://porthos.phoenixat.com/~warreng/WWWBoard/wwwboard.html`

❏ The JavaScript Index

`http://www.c2.org/~andreww/javascript/`

❏ The Microsoft Internet Developer's site

`http://www.microsoft.com/intdev/welcome.htm`

❏ Netscape's JavaScript Authoring Guide

`http://www.netscape.com/eng/mozilla/Gold/handbook/javascript/index.html`

❏ Netscape JavaScript Link List

`http://www.netscape.com/comprod/products/navigator/version_2.0/script/index.html`

❏ Netscape's JavaScript Tutorial

`http://www.netscape.com/comprod/products/navigator/version_2.0/script/script_info/tutorial/main.htm`

❏ PERL Manual and Searchable Index

`http://www.cs.cmu.edu/htbin/perl-man`

❏ Virtual Cities Repository

http://www.vir.com/~farid/ctrepos.htm

❏ VR for the People

http://gnn.com/gnn/wr/sept29/features/vrml/index.html

❏ VRML Futures Forum

http://vag.vrml.org/

❏ The VRML Repository

http://www.sdsc.edu/vrml/

❏ VRML Resources

http://vrml.wired.com/

❏ VRML Resources from Silicon Graphics

http://webspace.sgi.com/

❏ The World Wide Web Consortium

http://www.w3.org/pub/WWW/

Listservs and Usenet Newsgroups

❏ CGI List

This is a common gateway interface discussion.

Send e-mail to listserv@vm.ege.edu.tr with

SUB CGI-L *Your Name*

in the body of the message and a blank subject line.

❏ JavaScript Talk

http://www.farhorizons.com/jstalk/jstalk.html

❏ JavaScript Mailing List

Send e-mail to javascript-request@netural.com with SUBSCRIBE in the body of the message and a blank subject line.

❏ `news:comp.lang.java`

This is a Java newsgroup.

❏ `news:comp.lang.javascript`

This is a JavaScript newsgroup.

❏ `news:comp.lang.perl`

Check this for Perl information and discussion.

❏ `news:comp.lang.basic.visual`

This offers MS Visual Basic general news.

❏ OpenDoc Standards and Java Discussion

`http://www.cuesys.com/lists/jod/`

❏ STRONG-JAVA Mailing List

`http://www.entmp.org/cgi-bin/lwgate/STRONG-JAVA/`

This offers subscription information about the STRONG-JAVA mailing list. Beginners are strongly discouraged.

❏ VRML Standards

To join the VRML standards discussion, please subscribe to the www-vrml mailing list. Send e-mail to `majordomo@wired.com` with the subject line blank and the following in the message body:

`subscribe www-vrml` *your e-mail address*

Conferences, Learning Resources, Organizations

❏ Algorithm Incorporated

`http://www.algorithm.com/virtual/virtual.html`

❏ Association for Women in Computing

`http://www.halcyon.com/monih/awc.html`

❏ Interface Online Training Center

`http://www.iftech.com/iti/itioltc.htm`

❏ SIGGRAPH 96

`http://www.siggraph.org/conferences/siggraph96/siggraph96.html`

❏ Team WebGrrls

`http://www.women.org/`

❏ Women Online

`http://women-online.com/`

Books

❏ *Beyond HTML*

Richard Karpinki
Osborne, 1996
ISBN: 0078821983

❏ *CGI Programming on the World Wide Web*

Shishir Gundavaram
O'Reilly & Associates, 1996
ISBN: 1565921682

❏ *Danny Goodman's JavaScript Handbook*

Danny Goodman
IDG Books, 1996
with CD-ROM
ISBN: 0764530038

❏ *Learning Perl (the Llama Book)*

Randal L. Schwartz
O'Reilly & Associates, 1993
ISBN: 1565920422

❏ *Programming Perl (the Camel Book)*

Larry Wall & Randal L. Schwartz
O'Reilly & Associates, 1991
ISBN: 0937175641

❏ *Teach Yourself Java 1.1 in 21 Days, 2nd Edition*

Laura Lemay and Charles L. Perkins
Sams.net, 1997
with CD-ROM
ISBN: 1575211424

❏ *Special Edition Using CGI, 2nd Edition*

Jeffry Dwight, Michael Erwin, and Robert Niles
Que, 1997
with CD-ROM
ISBN: 0789711397

❏ *Teach Yourself VRML 2 in 21 Days*

Chris Marrin and Bruce Campbell
Sams.net, 1997
with CD-ROM
ISBN: 1575211939

HTML Quick Reference

This appendix is a reference to the HTML tags you can use in your documents. Unless otherwise noted, all the tags listed here are supported by both Microsoft Internet Explorer 3.0 and Netscape Navigator 3.0. Note that some other browsers do not support all the tags listed.

Appendix C, "Current HTML Standards," examines tags and attributes specific to style sheets, tables, and frames. It provides a look at browser compatibility and references the proposed HTML style sheet specification. Refer to the Netscape (http://home.netscape.com/) or Microsoft (http://www.microsoft.com/) Web sites for details on this and other late-breaking changes to the HTML standard.

Special thanks to Dick Oliver for providing the material for this appendix.

HTML Tags

These tags are used to create a basic HTML page with text, headings, and lists. An (MS) beside the attribute indicates that it is supported only by Microsoft Internet Explorer.

Comments

`<!-- ... -->`	Creates a comment. Can also be used to hide JavaScript from browsers that do not support it.
`<COMMENT>...</COMMENT>`	The new official way of specifying comments.

Structure Tags

`<HTML>...</HTML>`	Encloses the entire HTML document.
`<HEAD>...</HEAD>`	Encloses the head of the HTML document.
`<BODY>...</BODY>`	Encloses the body (text and tags) of the HTML document.

Attributes:

`BACKGROUND="..."`	The name or URL of the image to tile on the page background.
`BGCOLOR="..."`	The color of the page background.
`TEXT="..."`	The color of the page's text.
`LINK="..."`	The color of unfollowed links.
`ALINK="..."`	The color of activated links.
`VLINK="..."`	The color of followed links.
`BGPROPERTIES="..."`(MS)	Properties of background image. Currently allows only the value `FIXED`, which prevents the background image from scrolling.

	`TOPMARGIN="..."`(MS)	Top margin of the page, in pixels.
	`BOTTOMMARGIN="..."`(MS)	Bottom margin of the page, in pixels.
`<BASE>`		Indicates the full URL of the current document. This optional tag is used within `<HEAD>`.

Attributes:

	`HREF="..."`	The full URL of this document.
`<ISINDEX>`		Indicates that this document is a gateway script that allows searches.

Attributes:

	`PROMPT="..."`	The prompt for the search field.
	`ACTION="..."`	Gateway program to which the search string should be passed.
`<LINK>`		Indicates a link between this document and some other document. Generally used only by HTML-generating tools. `<LINK>` represents a link from this entire document to another, as opposed to `<A>`, which can create multiple links in the document. Not commonly used.

Attributes:

	`HREF="..."`	The URL of the document to call when the link is activated.
	`NAME="..."`	If the document is to be considered an anchor, the name of that anchor.

continues

REL="..."	The relationship between the linked-to document and the current document; for example, "TOC" or "Glossary".
REV="..."	A reverse relationship between the current document and the linked-to document.
URN="..."	A Uniform Resource Number (URN), a unique identifier different from the URL in HREF.
TITLE="..."	The title of the linked-to document.
METHODS="..."	The method by which the document is to be retrieved; for example, FTP, Gopher, and so on.
<META>	Indicates meta-information about this document (information about the document itself); for example, keywords for search engines, special HTTP headers to be used for retrieving this document, expiration date, and so on. Meta-information is usually in the form of a key/value pair. Used in the document <HEAD>.

Attributes:

HTTP-EQUIV="..."	Creates a new HTTP header field with the same name as the attribute's value; for example, HTTP-EQUIV="Expires". The value of that header is

	specified by the CONTENT attribute.
NAME="..."	If meta data is usually in the form of key/value pairs, NAME indicates the key; for example, Author or ID.
CONTENT="..."	The content of the key/value pair (or of the HTTP header indicated by HTTP-EQUIV).
<NEXTID>	Indicates the document "next" to this one (as might be defined by a tool to manage HTML documents in series). <NEXTID> is considered obsolete.

Headings and Title

<H1>...</H1>	A first-level heading.
<H2>...</H2>	A second-level heading.
<H3>...</H3>	A third-level heading.
<H4>...</H4>	A fourth-level heading.
<H5>...</H5>	A fifth-level heading.
<H6>...</H6>	A sixth-level heading.
<TITLE>...</TITLE>	Indicates the title of the document. Used within <HEAD>.

All heading tags accept the following attribute:

Attributes:

ALIGN="..."	Possible values are CENTER, LEFT, and RIGHT.

Paragraphs and Regions

<P>...</P>	A plain paragraph. The closing tag (</P>) is optional.

Attributes:

ALIGN="..."	Align text to CENTER, LEFT, or RIGHT.
<DIV>...</DIV>	A region of text to be formatted.

Attributes:

ALIGN="..."	Align text to CENTER, LEFT, or RIGHT.

Links

<A>...</A>	With the HREF attribute, creates a link to another document or anchor; with the NAME attribute, creates an anchor that can be linked to.

Attributes:

HREF="..."	The URL of the document to be called when the link is activated.
NAME="..."	The name of the anchor.
REL="..."	The relationship between the linked-to document and the current document; for example, "TOC" or "Glossary" (not commonly used).
REV="..."	A reverse relationship between the current document and the linked-to document (not commonly used).
URN="..."	A Uniform Resource Number (URN), a unique identifier different from the URL in HREF (not commonly used).

	TITLE="..."	The title of the linked-to document (not commonly used).
	METHODS="..."	The method by which the document is to be retrieved; for example, FTP, Gopher, and so on (not commonly used).
	TARGET="..."	The name of a frame that the linked document should appear in.

Lists

<OL>...</OL>		An ordered (numbered) list.

Attributes:

	TYPE="..."	The type of numerals to label the list. Possible values are A, a, I, i, 1.
	START="..."	The value with which to start this list.

<UL>...</UL>		An unordered (bulleted) list.

Attributes:

	TYPE="..."	The bullet dingbat to use to mark list items. Possible values are DISC, CIRCLE (or ROUND), and SQUARE.

<MENU>...</MENU>	A menu list of items.
<DIR>...</DIR>	A directory listing; items are generally smaller than 20 characters.
<LI>	A list item for use with <OL>, <UL>, <MENU>, or <DIR>.

Attributes:

TYPE="..."	The type of bullet or number to label this item with. Possible values are DISC, CIRCLE (or ROUND), SQUARE, A, a, I, i, 1.
VALUE="..."	The numeric value this list item should have (affects this item and all below it in <OL> lists).

<DL>...</DL>	A definition or glossary list.

Attributes:

COMPACT	The COMPACT attribute specifies a formatting that takes less whitespace to present.

<DT>	A definition term, as part of a definition list.
<DD>	The corresponding definition to a definition term, as part of a definition list.

Character Formatting

<EM>...</EM>	Emphasis (usually italic).
<STRONG>...</STRONG>	Stronger emphasis (usually bold).
<CODE>...</CODE>	Code sample (usually Courier).
<KBD>...</KBD>	Text to be typed (usually Courier).
<VAR>...</VAR>	A variable or placeholder for some other value.
<SAMP>...</SAMP>	Sample text (seldom used).
<DFN>...<DFN>	A definition of a term.
<CITE>...</CITE>	A citation.
<B>...</B>	Boldface text.
<I>...</I>	Italic text.

`<TT>...</TT>`	Typewriter (monospaced) font.
`<PRE>...</PRE>`	Preformatted text (exact line endings and spacing will be preserved—usually rendered in a monospaced font).
`<BIG>...</BIG>`	Text is slightly larger than normal.
`<SMALL>...</SMALL>`	Text is slightly smaller than normal.
`<SUB>...</SUB>`	Subscript.
`<SUP>...</SUP>`	Superscript.
`<STRIKE>...</STRIKE>`	Puts a strikethrough line in text.

Other Elements

`<HR>`	A horizontal rule line.

Attributes:

`SIZE="..."`	The thickness of the rule, in pixels.
`WIDTH="..."`	The width of the rule, in pixels or as a percentage of the document width.
`ALIGN="..."`	How the rule line will be aligned on the page. Possible values are LEFT, RIGHT, and CENTER.
`NOSHADE`	Causes the rule line to be drawn as a solid line instead of a transparent bevel.
`COLOR="..."` (MS)	Color of the horizontal rule.

` `	A line break.

Attributes:

`CLEAR="..."`	Causes the text to stop flowing around any images. Possible values are RIGHT, LEFT, ALL.

`<NOBR>...</NOBR>`	Causes the enclosed text not to wrap at the edge of the page.
`<WBR>`	Wraps the text at this point only if necessary.
`<BLOCKQUOTE>... </BLOCKQUOTE>`	Used for long quotes or citations.
`<ADDRESS>...</ADDRESS>`	Used for signatures or general information about a document's author.
`<CENTER>...</CENTER>`	Centers text or images.
`<BLINK>...</BLINK>`	Causes the enclosed text to blink in an irritating manner.
`<FONT>...</FONT>`	Changes the size of the font for the enclosed text.

Attributes:

`SIZE="..."`	The size of the font, from 1 to 7. Default is 3. Can also be specified as a value relative to the current size—for example, +2.
`COLOR="..."`	Changes the color of the text.
`FACE="..."`	Name of font to use if it can be found on the user's system. Multiple font names can be separated by commas, and the first font on the list that can be found will be used.

`<BASEFONT>`	Sets the default size of the font for the current page.

Attributes:

`SIZE="..."`	The default size of the font, from 1 to 7. Default is 3.

Images, Sounds, and Embedded Media

`<IMG>`	Inserts an inline image into the document.

Attributes:

ISMAP	This image is a clickable image map.
`SRC="..."`	The URL of the image.
`ALT="..."`	A text string that will be displayed in browsers that cannot support images.
`ALIGN="..."`	Determines the alignment of the given image. If LEFT or RIGHT, the image is aligned to the left or right column, and all following text flows beside that image. All other values such as TOP, MIDDLE, BOTTOM, or the Netscape-only TEXTTOP, ABSMIDDLE, BASELINE, ABSBOTTOM determine the vertical alignment of this image with other items in the same line.
`VSPACE="..."`	The space between the image and the text above or below it.
`HSPACE="..."`	The space between the image and the text to its left or right.
`WIDTH="..."`	The width, in pixels, of the image. If WIDTH is not the actual width, the image is scaled to fit.

continues

HEIGHT="..."	The width, in pixels, of the image. If HEIGHT is not the actual height, the image is scaled to fit.
BORDER=":.."	Draws a border of the specified value in pixels to be drawn around the image. In the case of images that also are links, BORDER changes the size of the default link border.
LOWSRC="..."	The path or URL of an image that will be loaded first, before the image specified in SRC. The value of LOWSRC is usually a smaller or lower resolution version of the actual image.
USEMAP="..."	The name of an image map specification for client-side image mapping. Used with <MAP> and <AREA>.
DYNSRC="..." (MS)	The address of a video clip or VRML world (dynamic source).
CONTROLS (MS)	Used with DYNSRC to display a set of playback controls for inline video.
LOOP="..." (MS)	The number of times a video clip will loop. (-1 or INFINITE means to loop indefinitely.)

	START="..." (MS)	When a DYNSRC video clip should start playing. Valid options are FILEOPEN (play when page is displayed) or MOUSEOVER (play when mouse cursor passes over the video clip).
<BGSOUND> (MS)		Plays a sound file as soon as the page is displayed.

Attributes:

	SRC="..."	The URL of the WAV, AU, or MIDI sound file to embed.
	LOOP="..." (MS)	The number of times a video clip will loop. (-1 or INFINITE means to loop indefinitely.)
<SCRIPT>		An interpreted script program.

Attributes:

	LANGUAGE="..."	Currently, only JAVASCRIPT is supported by Netscape. Both JAVASCRIPT and VBSCRIPT are supported by Microsoft.
	SRC="..."	Specifies the URL of a file that includes the script program.
<OBJECT>		Inserts an image, video, Java applet, or ActiveX control into a document.

NOTE: Usage of the <OBJECT> tag is not yet finalized. Check http://www.w3.org/ for the latest attributes supported by the HTML 3.2 standard.

`<APPLET>`		Inserts a self-running Java applet.
Attributes:		
	`CLASS="..."`	The name of the applet.
	`SRC="..."`	The URL of the directory where the compiled applet can be found (should end in a slash / as in `http://mysite/ myapplets/`). Do not include the actual applet name, which is specified with the `CLASS` attribute.
	`ALIGN="..."`	Indicates how the applet should be aligned with any text that follows it. Current values are `TOP`, `MIDDLE`, and `BOTTOM`.
	`WIDTH="..."`	The width of the applet output area in pixels.
	`HEIGHT="..."`	The height of the applet output area in pixels.
`<PARAM>`		Program-specific parameters (always occurs within `<APPLET>` or `<OBJECT>` tags).
Attributes:		
	`NAME="..."`	The type of information being given to the applet or ActiveX control.
	`VALUE="..."`	The actual information to be given to the applet or ActiveX control.
	`REF`	Indicates that this `<PARAM>` tag includes the address or location of the object.

`<EMBED>`		Embeds a file to be read or displayed by a Plug-in application.

NOTE: In addition to the following standard attributes, you can specify applet-specific attributes to be interpreted by the plug-in which displays the embedded object.

Attributes:

`SRC="..."`	The URL of the file to embed.
`WIDTH="..."`	The width of the embedded object in pixels.
`HEIGHT="..."`	The height of the embedded object in pixels.
`ALIGN="..."`	Determines the alignment of the media window. Values are the same as for the `<IMG>` tag.
`VSPACE="..."`	The space between the media and the text above or below it.
`HSPACE="..."`	The space between the media and the text to its left or right.
`BORDER="..."`	Draws a border of the specified size in pixels to be drawn around the media.
`<NOEMBED>...</NOEMBED>`	Alternate text or images to be shown to users who do not have a plug-in installed.
`<MAP>...</MAP>`	A client-side image map, referenced by `<IMG USEMAP="...">`. Includes one or more `<AREA>` tags.

`<AREA>`	Defines a clickable link within a client-side image map.

Attributes:

`SHAPE="..."`	The shape of the clickable area. Currently, only `RECT` is supported.
`COORDS="..."`	The left, top, right, and bottom coordinates of the clickable region within an image.
`HREF="..."`	The URL that should be loaded when the area is clicked.
`NOHREF`	Indicates that no action should be taken when this area of the image is clicked.

Forms

`<FORM>...</FORM>`	Indicates an input form.

Attributes:

`ACTION="..."`	The URL of the script to process this form input.
`METHOD="..."`	How the form input will be sent to the gateway on the server side. Possible values are `GET` and `POST`.
`ENCTYPE="..."`	Normally has the value `application/x-www-form-urlencoded`. For file uploads, use `multipart/form-data`.
`NAME="..."`	A name by which JavaScript scripts can refer to the form.

`<INPUT>`		An input element for a form.
Attributes:		
	`TYPE="..."`	The type for this input widget. Possible values are CHECK BOX, HIDDEN, RADIO, RESET, SUBMIT, TEXT, SEND FILE, or IMAGE.
	`NAME="..."`	The name of this item, as passed to the gateway script as part of a name/value pair.
	`VALUE="..."`	For a text or hidden widget, the default value; for a check box or radio button, the value to be submitted with the form; for Reset or Submit buttons, the label for the button itself.
	`SRC="..."`	The source file for an image.
	`CHECKED`	For check boxes and radio buttons, indicates that the widget is checked.
	`SIZE="..."`	The size, in characters, of a text widget.
	`MAXLENGTH="..."`	The maximum number of characters that can be entered into a text widget.
	`ALIGN="..."`	For images in forms, determines how the text and image will align (same as with the `<IMG>` tag).
`<TEXTAREA>...</TEXTAREA>`		Indicates a multiline text entry form element. Default text can be included.

Attributes:

`NAME="..."`		The name to be passed to the gateway script as part of the name/value pair.
`ROWS="..."`		The number of rows this text area displays.
`COLS="..."`		The number of columns (characters) this text area displays.
`WRAP="..."`		Controls text wrapping. Possible values are `OFF`, `VIRTUAL`, and `PHYSICAL`.

`<SELECT>...</SELECT>`   Creates a menu or scrolling list of possible items.

Attributes:

`NAME="..."`		The name that is passed to the gateway script as part of the name/value pair.
`SIZE="..."`		The number of elements to display. If `SIZE` is indicated, the selection becomes a scrolling list. If no `SIZE` is given, the selection is a pop-up menu.
`MULTIPLE`		Allows multiple selections from the list.

`<OPTION>`   Indicates a possible item within a `<SELECT>` element.

Attributes:

`SELECTED`		With this attribute included, the `<OPTION>` will be selected by default in the list.

VALUE="..."	The value to submit if this <OPTION> is selected when the form is submitted.

Tables

<TABLE>...</TABLE>	Creates a table that can contain a caption (<CAPTION>) and any number of rows (<TR>).

Attributes:

BORDER="..."	Indicates whether the table should be drawn with or without a border. In Netscape, BORDER can also have a value indicating the width of the border.
CELLSPACING="..."	The amount of space between the cells in the table.
CELLPADDING="..."	The amount of space between the edges of the cell and its contents.
WIDTH="..."	The width of the table on the page, in either exact pixel values or as a percentage of page width.
ALIGN="..." (MS)	Alignment (works like IMG ALIGN). Values are LEFT or RIGHT.
BGCOLOR="..."	Background color of all cells in the table that do not contain their own BACKGROUND or BGCOLOR attribute.

continues

`BACKGROUND="..."` (MS)	Background image to tile within all cells in the table that do not contain their own `BACKGROUND` or `BGCOLOR` attribute.
`BORDERCOLOR="..."` (MS)	Border color (used with `BORDER="..."`).
`BORDERCOLORLIGHT="..."` (MS)	Color for light part of 3D-look borders (used with `BORDER="..."`).
`BORDERCOLORDARK="..."` (MS)	Color for dark part of 3D-look borders (used with `BORDER="..."`).
`VALIGN="..."` (MS)	Alignment of text within the table. Values are `TOP` and `BOTTOM`.
`FRAME="..."` (MS)	Controls which external borders will appear around a table. Values are `void` (no frames), `above` (top border only), `below` (bottom border only), `hsides` (top and bottom), `lhs` (left-hand side), `rhs` (right-hand side), `vsides` (left and right sides), and `box` (all sides).
`RULES="..."` (MS)	Controls which internal borders appear in the table. Values are `none`, `basic` (rules between `THEAD`, `TBODY`, and `TFOOT` only), `rows` (horizontal borders only), `cols` (vertical borders only), and `all`.
`<CAPTION>...</CAPTION>`	The caption for the table.

continues

Attributes:

`ALIGN="..."`	The position of the caption. Possible values are TOP and BOTTOM.
`<TR>...</TR>`	Defines a table row, containing headings and data (`<TR>` and `<TH>` tags).

Attributes:

`ALIGN="..."`	The horizontal alignment of the contents of the cells within this row. Possible values are LEFT, RIGHT, and CENTER.
`VALIGN="..."`	The vertical alignment of the contents of the cells within this row. Possible values are TOP, MIDDLE, BOTTOM, and BASELINE.
`BGCOLOR="..."`	Background color of all cells in the row that do not contain their own BACKGROUND or BGCOLOR attributes.
`BACKGROUND="..."(MS)`	Background image to tile within all cells in the row that do not contain their own BACKGROUND or BGCOLOR attributes.
`BORDERCOLOR="..."(MS)`	Border color (used with BORDER="...").
`BORDERCOLORLIGHT="..."(MS)`	Color for light part of 3D-look borders (used with BORDER="...").

continues

BORDERCOLORDARK="..."(MS)	Color for dark part of 3D-look borders (used with BORDER="...").

`<TH>...</TH>`   Defines a table heading cell.

Attributes:

ALIGN="..."	The horizontal alignment of the contents of the cell. Possible values are LEFT, RIGHT, and CENTER.
VALIGN="..."	The vertical alignment of the contents of the cell. Possible values are TOP, MIDDLE, BOTTOM, and BASELINE.
ROWSPAN="..."	The number of rows this cell will span.
COLSPAN="..."	The number of columns this cell will span.
NOWRAP	Does not automatically wrap the contents of this cell.
WIDTH="..."	The width of this column of cells, in exact pixel values or as a percentage of the table width.
BGCOLOR="..."	Background color of the cell.
BACKGROUND="..." (MS)	Background image to tile within the cell.
BORDERCOLOR="..." (MS)	Border color (used with BORDER="...").

`BORDERCOLORLIGHT="..."` (MS)	Color for light part of 3D-look borders (used with `BORDER="..."`).
`BORDERCOLORDARK="..."` (MS)	Color for dark part of 3D-look borders (used with `BORDER="..."`).

`<TD>...</TD>`   Defines a table data cell.

Attributes:

`ALIGN="..."`	The horizontal alignment of the contents of the cell. Possible values are `LEFT`, `RIGHT`, and `CENTER`.
`VALIGN="..."`	The vertical alignment of the contents of the cell. Possible values are `TOP`, `MIDDLE`, `BOTTOM`, and `BASELINE`.
`ROWSPAN="..."`	The number of rows this cell will span.
`COLSPAN="..."`	The number of columns this cell will span.
`NOWRAP`	Does not automatically wrap the contents of this cell.
`WIDTH="..."`	The width of this column of cells, in exact pixel values or as a percentage of the table width.
`BGCOLOR="..."`	Background color of the cell.
`BACKGROUND="..."` (MS)	Background image to tile within the cell.

continues

BORDERCOLOR="..." (MS)	Border color (used with BORDER="...").
BORDERCOLORLIGHT="..." (MS)	Color for light part of 3D-look borders (used with BORDER="...").
BORDERCOLORDARK="..." (MS)	Color for dark part of 3D-look borders (used with BORDER="...").

Frames

<FRAMESET>...</FRAMESET>	Divides the main window into a set of frames that can each display a separate document.

Attributes:

ROWS="..."	Splits the window or frameset vertically into a number of rows specified by a number (such as 7), a percentage of the total window width (such as 25%), or as an asterisk (*) indicating that a frame should take up all the remaining space or divide the space evenly between frames (if multiple * frames are specified).
COLS="..."	Works similar to ROWS, except that the window or frameset is split horizontally into columns.

	`BORDER="..."`	Size of frame border in pixels (0 turns off borders). This tag is Netscape-specific— Microsoft IE uses `FRAMEBORDER` and `FRAMESPACING` instead.
	`FRAMEBORDER="..."` (MS)	Specifies whether to display a border for a frame. Options are `YES` and `NO`.
	`FRAMESPACING="..."` (MS)	Space between frames, in pixels.
`<FRAME>`		Defines a single frame within a `<FRAMESET>`.

Attributes:

	`SRC="..."`	The URL of the document to be displayed in this frame.
	`NAME="..."`	A name to be used for targeting this frame with the `TARGET` attribute in `<A HREF>` links.
	`<MARGINWIDTH>`	The amount of space to leave to the left and right side of a document within a frame, in pixels.
	`<MARGINHEIGHT>`	The amount of space to leave above and below a document within a frame, in pixels.
	`SCROLLING="..."`	Determines whether a frame has scrollbars. Possible values are `YES`, `NO`, and `AUTO`.

continues

NORESIZE		Prevents the user from resizing this frame (and possibly adjacent frames) with the mouse.
</NOFRAME>...</NOFRAMES>		Provides an alternative document body in <FRAMESET> documents for browsers that do not support frames (usually encloses <BODY>...</BODY>).

Character Entities

Table B.1 contains the possible numeric and character entities for the ISO-Latin-1 (ISO8859-1) character set. Where possible, the character is shown.

NOTE: Not all browsers can display all characters, and some browsers might even display characters different from those that appear in the table. Newer browsers seem to have a better track record for handling character entities, but be sure to test your HTML files extensively with multiple browsers if you intend to use these entities.

Table B.1. ISO-Latin-1 character set.

Character	Numeric Entity	Character Entity (if any)	Description
	&#00;-&#08;		Unused
	&#09;		Horizontal tab
	&#10;		Line feed
	&#11;-&#31;		Unused
	&#32;		Space
!	&#33;		Exclamation mark
"	&#34;	&quot;	Quotation mark
#	&#35;		Number sign

Character	Numeric Entity	Character Entity (if any)	Description
$	&#36;		Dollar sign
%	&#37;		Percent sign
&	&#38;	&amp;	Ampersand
'	&#39;		Apostrophe
(	&#40;		Left parenthesis
)	&#41;		Right parenthesis
*	&#42;		Asterisk
+	&#43;		Plus sign
,	&#44;		Comma
-	&#45;		Hyphen
.	&#46;		Period (full stop)
/	&#47;		Solidus (slash)
0–9	0 - 9		Digits 0–9
:	&#58;		Colon
;	&#59;		Semicolon
<	&#60;	&lt;	Less than
=	&#61;		Equal sign
>	&#62;	&gt;	Greater than
?	&#63;		Question mark
@	&#64;		Commercial "at"
A–Z	A-Z		Letters A–Z
[	&#91;		Left square bracket
\	&#92;		Reverse solidus (backslash)
]	&#93;		Right square bracket

continues

Table B.1. continued

Character	Numeric Entity	Character Entity (if any)	Description
^	&#94;		Caret
—	&#95;		Horizontal bar
`	&#96;		Grave accent
a–z	a-z		Letters a–z
{	&#123;		Left curly brace
|	&#124		Vertical bar
}	&#125;		Right curly brace
~	&#126;		Tilde
	&#127;-		Unused
¡	&#161;	&iexcl;	Inverted exclamation mark
¢	&#162;	&cent;	Cent sign
£	&#163;	&pound;	Pound sterling
¤	&#164;	&curren;	General currency sign
¥	&#165;	&yen;	Yen sign
¦	&#166;	¦ or brkbar;	Broken vertical bar
§	&#167;	&sect;	Section sign
¨	&#168;	&uml;	Umlaut (dieresis)
©	&#169;	© (Netscape only)	Copyright
ª	&#170;	&ordf;	Feminine ordinal
‹	&#171;	&laquo;	Left angle quote, guillemot left
¬	&#172;	&not;	Not sign
-	&#173;	&shy;	Soft hyphen
®	&#174;	® (Netscape only)	Registered trademark

Character	Numeric Entity	Character Entity (if any)	Description
-	&#175;	&hibar;	Macron accent
°	&#176;	&deg;	Degree sign
±	&#177;	&plusmn;	Plus or minus
²	&#178;	&sup2;	Superscript two
³	&#179;	&sup3;	Superscript three
´	&#180;	&acute;	Acute accent
µ	&#181;	&micro;	Micro sign
¶	&#182;	&para;	Paragraph sign
·	&#183;	&middot;	Middle dot
¸	&#184;	&cedil;	Cedilla
¹	&#185;	&sup1;	Superscript one
º	&#186;	&ordm;	Masculine ordinal
›	&#187;	&raquo;	Right angle quote, guillemot right
¼	&#188;	&frac14;	Fraction one-fourth
½	&#189;	&frac12;	Fraction one-half
¾	&#190;	&frac34;	Fraction three-fourths
¿	&#191;	&iquest	Inverted question mark
À	&#192;	&Agrave;	Capital A, grave accent
Á	&#193;	&Aacute;	Capital A, acute accent

continues

Table B.1. continued

Character	Numeric Entity	Character Entity (if any)	Description
Â	&#194;	&Acirc;	Capital A, circumflex accent
Ã	&#195;	&Atilde;	Capital A, tilde
Ä	&#196;	&Auml;	Capital A, dieresis or umlaut mark
Å	&#197;	&Aring;	Capital A, ring
Æ	&#198;	&AElig;	Capital AE diphthong (ligature)
Ç	&#199;	&Ccedil;	Capital C, cedilla
È	&#200;	&Egrave;	Capital E, grave accent
É	&#201;	&Eacute;	Capital E, acute accent
Ê	&#202;	&Ecirc;	Capital E, circumflex accent
Ë	&#203;	&Euml;	Capital E, dieresis or umlaut mark
Ì	&#204;	&Igrave;	Capital I, grave accent
Í	&#205;	&Iacute;	Capital I, acute accent
Î	&#206;	&Icirc;	Capital I, circumflex accent

Character	Numeric Entity	Character Entity (if any)	Description
Ï	&#207;	&Iuml;	Capital I, dieresis or umlaut mark
Ð	&#208;	&ETH;	Capital Eth, Icelandic
Ñ	&#209;	&Ntilde;	Capital N, tilde
Ò	&#210;	&Ograve;	Capital O, grave accent
Ó	&#211;	&Oacute;	Capital O, acute accent
Ô	&#212;	&Ocirc;	Capital O, circumflex accent
Õ	&#213;	&Otilde;	Capital O, tilde
Ö	&#214;	&Ouml;	Capital O, dieresis or umlaut mark
×	&#215;	Multiply sign	
Ø	&#216;	&Oslash;	Capital O, slash
Ù	&#217;	&Ugrave;	Capital U, grave accent
Ú	&#218;	&Uacute;	Capital U, acute accent
Û	&#219;	&Ucirc;	Capital U, circumflex accent
Ü	&#220;	&Uuml;	Capital U, dieresis or umlaut mark
Ý	&#221;	&Yacute;	Capital Y, acute accent

continues

Table B.1. continued

Character	Numeric Entity	Character Entity (if any)	Description
Þ	&#222;	&THORN;	Capital THORN, Icelandic
ß	&#223;	&szlig;	Small sharp s, German (sz ligature)
à	&#224;	&agrave;	Small a, grave accent
á	&#225;	&aacute;	Small a, acute accent
â	&#226;	&acirc;	Small a, circumflex accent
ã	&#227;	&atilde;	Small a, tilde
ä	&#228;	&aauml;	Small a, dieresis or umlaut mark
å	&#229;	&aring;	Small a, ring
æ	&#230;	&aelig;	Small ae diphthong (ligature)
ç	&#231;	&ccedil;	Small c, cedilla
è	&#232;	&egrave;	Small e, grave accent
é	&#233;	&eacute;	Small e, acute accent
ê	&#234;	&ecirc;	Small e, circumflex accent
ë	&#235;	&euml;	Small e, dieresis or umlaut mark
ì	&#236;	&igrave;	Small i, grave accent

Character	Numeric Entity	Character Entity (if any)	Description
í	&#237;	&iacute;	Small i, acute accent
î	&#238;	&icirc;	Small i, circumflex accent
ï	&#239;	&iuml;	Small i, dieresis or umlaut mark
ð	&#240;	&eth;	Small eth, Icelandic
ñ	&#241;	&ntilde;	Small n, tilde
ò	&#242;	&ograve;	Small o, grave accent
ó	&#243;	&oacute;	Small o, acute accent
ô	&#244;	&ocirc;	Small o, circumflex accent
õ	&#245;	&otilde;	Small o, tilde
ö	&#246;	&ouml;	Small o, dieresis or umlaut mark
÷	&#247;		Division sign
ø	&#248;	&oslash;	Small o, slash
ù	&#249;	&ugrave;	Small u, grave accent
ú	&#250;	&uacute;	Small u, acute accent
û	&#251;	&ucirc;	Small u, circumflex accent
ü	&#252;	&uuml;	Small u, dieresis or umlaut mark

continues

Table B.1. continued

Character	Numeric Entity	Character Entity (if any)	Description
ý	&#253;	&yacute;	Small y, acute accent
þ	&#254;	&thorn;	Small thorn, Icelandic
ÿ	&#255;	&yuml;	Small y, dieresis or umlaut mark

C Current HTML Standards

Tables

Tags and Attributes	NNav	IE	Mosaic	HTML	CSS	Lynx
<TABLE>...</TABLE>	1.1	2	3	3	–	X
ALIGN	1.1	2	–	3	–	–
BACKGROUND	–	2	–	–	–	–
BGCOLOR	3.0b	2	3	–	–	–
BORDER	–	2	3	3	–	–
BORDERCOLOR	–	2	–	–	–	–
BORDERCOLORDARK	–	2	–	–	–	–
BORDERCOLORLIGHT	–	2	–	–	–	–
BORDERSTYLE	–	–	–	–	–	–
CELLPADDING	1.1	2	3	3.2	–	–
CELLSPACING	1.1	2	3	3.2	–	–
CLASS	–	3	–	3.2+	X	–
CLEAR	–	3	–	3*	–	–
COLSPEC	–	–	–	3*	–	–
DIR	–	–	–	3.2+	–	–
DP	–	–	–	3*	–	–
FLOAT	–	–	–	3.2+?	–	–
FRAME	–	2	–	–	–	–
HEIGHT	1.1	2	3	–	–	–
ID	–	3	–	3.2+	X	–
LANG	–	–	–	3.2+	–	–
NOFLOW	–	–	–	3*	–	–
NOWRAP	–	3	–	3*	–	–
RULES	–	2	–	3.2+	–	–
STYLE	–	3	–	–	–	–
UNITS	–	–	–	3*	–	–
VALIGN	–	2	–	–	–	–
WIDTH	1.1	2	3	3	–	–

	NNav	IE	Mosaic	HTML	CSS	Lynx
<CAPTION>…</CAPTION>	1.1	X	2	3	-	X
ALIGN	1.1	X	3	-	-	-
VALIGN	-	X	-	-	-	-

	NNav	IE	Mosaic	HTML	CSS	Lynx
<TBODY>…</TBODY>	-	X	-	3	-	-
CLASS	-	3	-	-	-	-
ID	-	3	-	-	-	-
STYLE	-	3	-	-	-	-

	NNav	IE	Mosaic	HTML	CSS	Lynx
<TD>…</TD>	1.1	X	2	3	-	X
ALIGN	1.1	X	2	3.2	-	-
BACKGROUND	-	X	-	-	-	-
BGCOLOR	3.0b	X	3	-	-	-
BORDERCOLOR	-	X	-	-	-	-
BORDERCOLORDARK	-	X	-	-	-	-
BORDERCOLORLIGHT	-	X	-	-	-	-
CLASS	-	3	-	-	-	-
COLSPAN	-	X	2	3.2	-	-
HEIGHT	1.1	X	-	3.2	-	-
ID	-	3	-	-	-	-
NOWRAP	X	X	-	3.2	-	-
ROWSPAN	1.1	X	2	3.2	-	-
STYLE	-	3	-	-	-	-
VALIGN	1.1	X	2	3.2	-	-
WIDTH	1.1	X	3	-	-	-
WIDTH%	1.1	X	-	3.2	-	-

	NNav	IE	Mosaic	HTML	CSS	Lynx
<TEXTAREA>...</TEXTAREA>	1	X	X	3	-	-
COLS	1	X	X	-	-	-
NAME	1	X	X	-	-	-
ROWS	1	X	X	-	-	-
WRAP	2	-	-	-	-	-

	NNav	IE	Mosaic	HTML	CSS	Lynx
<TFOOT>...</TFOOT>	-	X	-	3	-	-
CLASS	-	3	-	-	-	-
ID	-	3	-	-	-	-
STYLE	-	3	-	-	-	-

	NNav	IE	Mosaic	HTML	CSS	Lynx
<TH>...</TH>	1.1	X	2	3	-	X
ALIGN	1.1	X	2	3	-	-
AXES	-	-	-	3	-	-
AXIS	-	-	-	3	-	-
BACKGROUND	-	X	-	-	-	-
BGCOLOR	3.0b	X	-	-	-	-
BORDERCOLOR	-	X	-	-	-	-
BORDERCOLORDARK	-	X	-	-	-	-
BORDERCOLORLIGHT	-	X	-	-	-	-
CLASS	-	-	-	3.2+	X	-
COLSPAN	X	X	2	3*	-	-
DIR	-	-	-	3.2+	-	-
DP	-	-	-	3*	-	-
ID	-	-	-	3.2+	X	-
HEIGHT	-	X	-	-	-	-
LANG	-	-	-	3.2+	-	-

	NNav	IE	Mosaic	HTML	CSS	Lynx
NOWRAP	X	X	-	3	-	-
ROWSPAN	X	X	2	3	-	-
VALIGN	X	X	2	3	-	-
WIDTH	1.1	X	-	-	-	-
WIDTH%	1.1	-	-	3.2	-	-

	NNav	IE	Mosaic	HTML	CSS	Lynx
<THEAD>…</THEAD>	-	X	-	3	-	-
ALIGN	-	3	-	-	-	-
CLASS	-	3	-	-	-	-
ID	-	3	-	-	-	-
STYLE	-	3	-	-	-	-
VALIGN	-	3	-	-	-	-

	NNav	IE	Mosaic	HTML	CSS	Lynx
<TR>…</TR>	1.1	X	2	3	-	X
ALIGN	-	X	2	3	-	-
BGCOLOR	3.0b	X	-	-	-	-
BORDERCOLOR	-	X	-	-	-	-
BORDERCOLORDARK	-	X	-	-	-	-
BORDERCOLORLIGHT	-	X	-	-	-	-
CLASS	-	3	-	3.2+	X	-
DIR	-	-	-	3.2+	-	-
DP	-	-	-	3*	-	-
ID	-	3	-	3.2+	X	-
LANG	-	-	-	3.2+	-	-
NOWRAP	-	3	-	3*	-	-
ROWSPAN	-	-	-	-	-	-

continues

	NNav	IE	Mosaic	HTML	CSS	Lynx
STYLE	-	3	-	-	-	-
VALIGN	X	X	2	3	-	-
WIDTH	-	-	-	-	-	-
WIDTH%	-	-	-	-	-	-

Frames

The following tags and attributes are the currently available HTML syntax for frames.

Tags and Attributes	NNav	IE	Mosaic	HTML	CSS	Lynx
<FRAME>…</FRAME>	2	3	-	3.2+?	-	X
ALIGN	-	3	-	-	-	-
BORDER	2	-	-	-	-	-
BORDERCOLOR	3	-	-	-	-	-
FRAMEBORDER	3	3	-	-	-	-
FRAMESPACING	-	3	-	-	-	-
HSPACE	-	3	-	-	-	-
MARGINHEIGHT	2	3	-	-	-	-
MARGINWIDTH	2	3	-	-	-	-
NAME	1	3	-	-	-	X
NORESIZE	2	3	-	-	-	-
SCROLLING	2	3	-	-	-	-
SRC	2	3	-	-	-	-
VSPACE	-	3	-	-	-	-

	NNav	IE	Mosaic	HTML	CSS	Lynx
<FRAMESET>…</FRAMESET>	2	3	-	3	-	
COLS	2	3	-	-	-	-
BORDER	2	-	-	-	-	-
LAYOUT	-	3	-	-	-	-

	NNav	IE	Mosaic	HTML	CSS	Lynx
FRAMEBORDER	-	3	-	-	-	-
ROWS	2	3	-	-	-	-

	NNav	IE	Mosaic	HTML	CSS	Lynx
<IFRAME>…</IFRAME>	-	3	-	-	-	-
ALIGN	-	3	-	-	-	-
FRAMEBORDER	-	3	-	-	-	-
HEIGHT	-	3	-	-	-	-
MARGINHEIGHT	-	3	-	-	-	-
MARGINWIDTH	-	3	-	-	-	-
NAME	-	3	-	-	-	-
SCROLLING	-	3	-	-	-	-
SRC	-	3	-	-	-	-
WIDTH	-	3	-	-	-	-

	NNav	IE	Mosaic	HTML	CSS	Lynx
<NOFRAMES>…</NOFRAMES>	-	2	3	-	3.2	-

	NNav	IE	Mosaic	HTML	CSS	Lynx
<A>,<BASE>,<AREA>,<FORM>	2	-	-	-	-	-
BASE	2	-	-	-	-	-
AREA	2	-	-	-	-	-
FORM	2	-	-	-	-	-
TARGET	2	-	-	-	-	-

	NNav	IE	Mosaic	HTML	CSS	Lynx
<LAYER>…</LAYER>	4	-	-	-	-	-
ABOVE	4	-	-	-	-	-
BACKGROUND	4	-	-	-	-	-

continues

	NNav	IE	Mosaic	HTML	CSS	Lynx
BELOW	4	-	-	-	-	-
BGCOLOR	4	-	-	-	-	-
CLIP	4	-	-	-	-	-
LEFT	4	-	-	-	-	-
NAME	4	-	-	-	-	-
TOP	4	-	-	-	-	-
VISIBILITY	4	-	-	-	-	-
WIDTH	4	-	-	-	-	-
Z-INDEX	4	-	-	-	-	-

	NNav	IE	Mosaic	HTML	CSS	Lynx
<ILAYER>…</ILAYER>	4	-	-	-	-	-
ABOVE	4	-	-	-	-	-
BACKGROUND	4	-	-	-	-	-
BELOW	4	-	-	-	-	-
BGCOLOR	4	-	-	-	-	-
CLIP	4	-	-	-	-	-
LEFT	4	-	-	-	-	-
NAME	4	-	-	-	-	-
TOP	4	-	-	-	-	-
VISIBILITY	4	-	-	-	-	-
WIDTH	4	-	-	-	-	-
Z-INDEX	4	-	-	-	-	-

Style Sheets

These tags and attributes are the currently available HTML for style sheets. A - indicates that the browser does not support the tag or attribute.

Tags and Attributes	NNav	IE	Mosaic	HTML	CSS	Lynx
<STYLE>...</STYLE>	4	3	-	3	X	-
NOTATION	-	-	-	3	-	-
TYPE	4	3	-	3	-	-
TITLE	-	3	-	3	-	-

	NNav	IE	Mosaic	HTML	CSS	Lynx
<LINK>	2	3	X	X	-	-
HREF	-	3	-	3	-	-
LINK	-	3	-	-	-	-
METHODS	-	-	-	3	-	-
REL="stylesheet"	-	3	-	3	-	-
REV	-	-	-	3	-	-
TITLE	-	3	-	3	-	-
TYPE	-	3	-	-	-	-

	NNav	IE	Mosaic	HTML	CSS	Lynx
<SPAN>...</SPAN>	-	-	-	3.2+	X	-
CLASS	-	-	-	3.2+	X	-
ID	-	-	-	3.2+	X	-
STYLE	-	-	-	3.2+	X	-

	NNav	IE	Mosaic	HTML	CSS	Lynx
<DIV>...</DIV>	3	-	-	3.2+	X	-
CLASS	-	-	-	3.2+	X	-
ID	-	-	-	3.2+	X	-
STYLE	-	-	-	3.2+	X	-

Browser Timeline

The following chart shows the browser type, version, and release dates of the beta and final product.

		Beta	Product
Release Dates:	Netscape 1.0	Oct-94	Dec-94
	Netscape 1.1	Mar-95	Apr-95
	Netscape 1.2	Jun-95	Jul-95
	Netscape 2.0	Sep-95	Mar-96
	Netscape 3.0	Apr-96	Aug-96
	Netscape 4.0	Dec-96	
	MSIE 1.0		Aug-95
	MSIE 2.0	Oct-95	Nov-95
	MSIE 3.0	May-96	Aug-96
	MSIE 3.01 update	n/a	Oct-96
	MSIE 4.0	Mar-97	
	NSCA Mosaic 1.0	Jun-93	Nov-93
	NCSA Mosaic 2.0	Mar-95	Oct-95
	NCSA Mosaic 2.1	n/a	Jan-96
	NCSA Mosaic 3.0	Apr-96	Jan-97 Final release
	HTML 1.0	Jun-93	
	HTML 2.0	Jul-94	Sep-95
	HTML+	Nov-93	
	HTML 3.0	Mar-95	n/a
	HTML 3.2	1996	Jan-97
	HTML 3.2+	Ongoing	
	CSS1	Jan-96	Dec-96

d

What's on the
CD-ROM

On the *Laura Lemay's Web Workshop: Designing with Style Sheets, Tables, and Frames* CD-ROM, you will find sample files that have been presented in this book, along with a wealth of other applications and utilities.

> NOTE: Please refer to the `readme.wri` file on the CD-ROM (Windows) or the Guide to the CD-ROM (Macintosh) for the latest listing of software.

Windows Software

ActiveX

❑ Microsoft ActiveX Control Pad and HTML Layout Control

Explorer

❑ Microsoft Internet Explorer 3

Graphics, Video, and Sound Applications

❑ Cell Assembler

❑ Goldwave sound editor, player, and recorder

❑ MapThis imagemap utility

❑ MPEG2PLY MPEG viewer

❑ MPEGPLAY MPEG viewer

❑ Paint Shop Pro 3.12

❑ SnagIt

❑ ThumbsPlus

HTML Tools

❑ W3e HTML Editor

❑ Hot Dog 32-bit HTML editor

❑ HoTMeTaL HTML editor

❑ HTMLed HTML editor

❑ WebEdit Pro HTML editor

❑ Web Weaver HTML editor

Java

- ❏ Trial version of Jamba for Windows 95/NT
- ❏ Jpad IDE
- ❏ JPad Pro Java IDE demo
- ❏ Kawa IDE
- ❏ Studio J++ demo
- ❏ Javelin IDE demo
- ❏ JDesigner Pro database wizard for Java

Utilities

- ❏ Adobe Acrobat viewer
- ❏ WinZip for Windows NT/95
- ❏ WinZip Self-Extractor

Macintosh Software

Graphics, Video, and Sound Applications

- ❏ Graphic Converter v2.1.4
- ❏ GIFConverter v2.3.7
- ❏ Fast Player v1.1
- ❏ Sparkle 2.4.5
- ❏ SoundApp v1.5.1

HTML Tools

- ❏ BBEdit 3.5.1
- ❏ BBEdit 4 demo
- ❏ HTML Web Weaver v2.5.2
- ❏ WebMap v1.01 imagemap creator

- ❏ HTML.edit v1.7
- ❏ HTML Editor for the Macintosh v1.0

Utilities

- ❏ ZipIt for Macintosh
- ❏ ScrapIt Pro
- ❏ Adobe Acrobat

About Shareware

Please read all documentation associated with third-party products (usually contained with files named `readme.txt` or `license.txt`) and follow all guidelines.

ActiveX A relatively new technology that makes it easy to embed animated objects, data, and computer code on Web pages. With ActiveX2ntrols, a Web browser that supports ActiveX can play just about any item you might encounter on a Web page.

anchor A named point on a Web page. (The same HTML tag is used to create Hypertext links and anchors, which explains why the tag is named <A>.)

animated GIF An animated graphic exploiting looping and timing features in the GIF89a format.

ASCII file A text file that conforms to the American Standard Code for Information Interchange.

attributes Special code words used inside an HTML tag to control exactly what the tag does.

bandwidth The maximum information-carrying capacity of an electronic connection or network.

binary file An executable file or a file that is in not in ASCII text format.

browse To wander around a portion of the Internet looking for items of interest. Also known as *surfing* or *cruising.*

browser A software program for viewing HTML pages.

cache A temporary storage area that a Web browser uses to store pages that it has recently opened. The cache enables the browser to quickly load these pages if you decide to return to them.

cascading style sheets Invented by Haåkon Lie, CSSs are a new addition to HTML 3.0 that allow page designers to have greater control over the rendering of a document. Browsers that support style sheets will allow font and color attributes to be specified. CSS1 is the first phase of cascading style sheets.

client-side image maps A new HTML method for linking an image to more than one address. The advantage of this approach is that the browser can display the destination URL of a region when the mouse passes over it, and some network traffic is saved because the browser can directly request the new document when a click is made.

comment Text in an HTML document (or computer program) that will only be seen by the people who edit the source for that page. Comments are normally invisible when a page is viewed with a Web browser.

common gateway interface (CGI) An interface for external programs to talk to a Web server. Programs that are written to use CGI are called CGI programs or CGI scripts, and are commonly used for processing HTML forms.

compression   The process of making a computer file smaller so that it can be copied more quickly between computers.

cyberspace   A broad expression used to describe the activity, communication, and culture happening on the Internet and other computer networks.

definition list   An indented list without a number or symbol in front of each item. (See also *ordered list* and *unordered list*.)

digital   Electronic circuits generally considered to use an on or off sequence of values to convey information.

digitized   Converted to a digital format suitable for storage.

direct connection   A permanent, 24-hour link between a computer and the Internet. A computer with a direct connection can use the Internet at any time.

directory service   An Internet service that maintains a database on individuals, including e-mail, fax, and telephone numbers, that is searchable by the public.

domain   The address of a computer on the Internet. A user's Internet address is made up of a username and a domain name.

domain name system (DNS)   An Internet addressing system that uses a group of names that are listed with dots (.) between them, working from the most specific to the most general group. In the United States, the top (most general) domains are network categories such as edu

(education), com (commercial), and gov (government). In other countries, a two-letter abbreviation for the country is used, such as ca (Canada) or au (Australia).

download   To retrieve a file or files from a remote machine to your local machine.

e-mail (electronic mail)   A system that enables a person to compose a message on a computer and transmit that message through a computer network, such as the Internet, to another computer user.

e-mail address   The word-based Internet address of a user, typically made up of a username, an at (@) sign, and a domain name (that is, *user@domain*). E-mail addresses are translated from the numeric IP addresses by the domain name system (DNS).

encryption   The process of encoding information so that it is secure to other Internet users.

FAQ   Short for *frequently asked questions*, a computer file containing the answers to frequently asked questions about a particular Internet resource.

Favorites menu   In Internet Explorer, a menu that contains a list of your favorite Web pages and Internet resources. You can add items to this menu at any time. Favorites are equivalent to bookmarks in Netscape Navigator.

firewall   A security device placed on a LAN to protect it from Internet intruders. This can be a special kind of hardware router, a piece of software, or both.

form A page that includes areas to be filled out by the reader. HTML forms allow information to be sent back to the company or individual who made (or maintains) the page.

frame A rectangular region within the browser window that displays a Web page, alongside other pages in other frames.

freeware Software available to anyone, free of charge; unlike shareware, which requires payment.

FTP (File Transfer Protocol) The basic method for copying a file from one computer to another through the Internet.

graphical editor A program that allows you to edit an approximation of what a Web page would look like when viewed with a Web browser. Graphical editors usually hide the actual HTML tags they are creating from view.

graphics Digitized pictures and computer-generated images.

Helper application An application that is configured to launch and view files that are unreadable to a Web browser.

HTML (HyperText Markup Language) The document formatting language used to create pages on the World Wide Web.

HTTP (HyperText Transfer Protocol) The standard method for exchanging information between HTTP servers and clients on the Web. The HTTP specification lays out the rules of how Web servers and browsers must work together.

hypertext Text that allows readers to jump spontaneously among onscreen documents and other resources by selecting highlighted keywords that appear on each screen. Hypertext appears most often on the World Wide Web.

image compression The mathematical manipulation that images are put through to squeeze out repetitive patterns. It makes them load and display much faster.

image map An image on a Web page that leads to two or more different links, depending on which part of the image someone clicks. Modern Web browsers use client-side image maps, but you can also create server-side image maps for compatibility with old browsers.

interlaced GIF An image file that will appear blocky at first, and then more and more detailed as it continues downloading. (Similar to a *progressive JPEG* file.)

Internet A large, loosely organized integrated network connecting universities, research institutions, government, businesses, and other organizations so that they can exchange messages and share information.

Internet Explorer An advanced Web browser created by Microsoft Corporation. Internet Explorer is powerful and easy to use.

Internet service provider (ISP) The company that provides you or your company with access to the Internet. ISPs usually have several servers and a high-speed link to the Internet backbone.

intranet A private network with access restricted to one organization, but which uses the same standards and protocols as the global public Internet.

ISDN (Integrated Digital Services Network) Essentially operates as a digital phone line. ISDN delivers many benefits over standard analog phone lines, including multiple simultaneous calls and higher-quality data transmissions. ISDN data rates are 56Kbps to 128Kbps.

Java The Web-oriented language developed by Sun Microsystems.

Kbps (kilobits per second) A rate of transfer of information across a connection such as the Internet.

LAN (local area network) A computer network limited to a small area.

link An icon, a picture, or a highlighted string of text that connects the current Web page to other Web pages, Internet sites, graphics, movies, or sounds. On the Web, you skip from page to page by clicking on links.

Mbps (megabits per second) A rate of transfer of information across a connection such as the Internet (equal to 1,000Kbps).

modem (modulator/demodulator) A device to convert the digital signals of a computer to an analog format for transmission across telephone lines.

multimedia A description for systems capable of displaying or playing text, pictures, sound, video, and animation.

navigation Movement within a computer environment (for example, navigation of a Web site).

Netscape Short for Netscape Communications Corporation, a software company that developed and markets a popular World Wide Web browser called Navigator. Some people casually refer to Navigator as Netscape.

network A set of computers interconnected so that they can communicate and share information. Most major networks are connected to the global network-of-networks, called the Internet.

ordered list An indented list that has numbers or letters in front of each item. (See also *unordered list* and *definition list*.)

password A secret code, known only to the user, that allows that user to access a computer that is protected by a security system.

pixel An individual dot of color in a computer graphics image.

POTS Plain old telephone service.

PPP (Point-to-Point Protocol) A communications protocol that enables a dial-up Internet connection.

progressive JPEG An image file that appears blurry at first, and then gradually comes into focus. (Similar to an *interlaced GIF* file.)

protocol Specific rules and conventions defining how data may be exchanged between any two devices.

provider   A general reference to an Internet access provider, a company that has its own dedicated access to the Internet and can therefore sell dial-up IP accounts to Internet users.

public domain   Material that is freely usable by anyone, but still could be copyrighted.

relative address   An address describing the path from one Web page to another, instead of a full (or *absolute*) URL address.

resolution   The number of individual dots, or *pixels*, that make up an image.

resource   A generic term to describe the varied information and activities available to Internet users.

search engine   A program that provides a way to search for specific information.

server   A networked computer that "serves" a particular type of information to users. See also *Web server*.

server-side image maps   A technique for implementing Web page images that lead to more than one link so that the server computer determines which link to go to. This method is now less commonly used than client-side image maps.

shareware   Software programs that users are permitted to acquire and evaluate for free. Shareware is different from freeware in that, if a person likes the shareware program and plans to use it on a regular basis, he or she is expected to send a fee to the programmer.

Shockwave   An interactive multimedia system for the Web that views applications developed by Macromedia Director.

source   The actual text and commands stored in an HTML file, including tags, comments, and scripts that may not be visible when the page is viewed with a Web browser.

surfing   Another term for browsing.

table   Text and/or images arranged into orderly rows and columns. HTML provides several tags specifically for creating tables.

tag   A coded HTML command used to indicate how part of a Web page should be displayed.

T-1 line   A digital circuit capable of transferring data at 1.544Mbps.

T-3 line   A digital circuit equivalent to 28 T-1 lines.

TCP/IP (Transmission Control Protocol/ Internet Protocol)   The agreed-on set of computer communications rules and standards that allows communications between different types of computers and networks that are connected to the Internet.

text editor   Any program that allows you to edit text with your computer.

unordered list   An indented list with a special bullet symbol in front of each item. (See also *ordered list* and *definition list*.)

URL (uniform resource locator)   Also commonly called a location or address. This is an addressing system that locates documents on the Internet.

username   Used with a password to gain access to a computer. A dial-up IP user typically has a username and password for dialing the access provider's Internet server.

VBScript   A script language developed by Microsoft. A technical competitor to Java and JavaScript applications.

VRML (Virtual Reality Modeling Language)
A three-dimensional navigation specification used to create 3-D worlds.

Web server   A computer on the Internet that hosts data that can be accessed by Web browsers using the HTTP protocol.

World Wide Web (WWW or the Web)   A set of Internet computers and services that provide an easy-to-use system for finding information and moving among resources. WWW services feature hypertext, hypermedia, and multimedia information, which can be explored through browsers such as Netscape or Internet Explorer.

INDEX

A VIACOM SERVICE

The Information SuperLibrary™

Bookstore

Search

What's New

Reference

Software

Newsletter

Company Overviews

Yellow Pages

Internet Starter Kit

HTML Workshop

Win a Free T-Shirt!

Macmillan Computer Publishing

Site Map

Talk to Us

CHECK OUT THE BOOKS IN THIS LIBRARY.

You'll find thousands of shareware files and over 1600 computer books designed for both technowizards and technophobes. You can browse through 700 sample chapters, get the latest news on the Net, and find just about anything using our massive search directories.

All Macmillan Computer Publishing books are available at your local bookstore.

We're open 24-hours a day, 365 days a year.

You don't need a card.

We don't charge fines.

And you can be as **LOUD** as you want.

The Information SuperLibrary
http://www.mcp.com/mcp/   ftp.mcp.com

Copyright © 1997, Macmillan Computer Publishing-USA, A Simon & Schuster Company

Laura Lemay's Guide to Sizzling Web Site Design

Molly E. Holzschlag

This book is more than just a guide to the hottest Web sites, it's a behind-the-scenes look at how those sites are created. The latest Web technologies are discussed in detail, showing readers how these technologies have been applied, and how they can implement those features on their own Web pages.

$45.00 USA/$63.95 CDN   *User Level: Casual—Accomplished*
ISBN: 1-57521-221-8   *Internet—Web Publishing*   *400 pages*

Laura Lemay's Web Workshop: Graphics and Web Page Design

Laura Lemay, Jon M. Duff, and James L. Mohler

With the number of Web pages increasing daily, only well-designed pages will stand out and grab the attention of those browsing the Web. This book illustrates how to design attractive Web pages that will be visited over and over again.

$55.00 USA/$77.95 CDN   *User Level: Accomplished*
ISBN: 1-57521-125-4   *Internet—Online/Communications*   *500 pages*

Laura Lemay's Web Workshop: 3D Graphics and VRML 2

Laura Lemay, Kelly Murdock, and Justin Couch

This is the easiest way for readers to learn how to add three-dimensional virtual worlds to Web pages. This book describes the new VRML 2.0 specification, explores the wide array of existing VRML sites on the Web, and steps readers through the process of creating their own 3D Web environments. The CD-ROM contains a hand-picked selection of the best VRML and 3D graphics tools, plus a collection of ready-to-use virtual worlds.

$39.99 USA/$56.95 CDN   *User Level: Casual—Accomplished*
ISBN: 1-57521-143-2   *Internet—Graphics/Multimedia*   *400 pages*

Laura Lemay's Web Workshop: Microsoft FrontPage 97

Laura Lemay and Denise Tyler

The latest release of Microsoft's FrontPage not only integrates completely with the Microsoft Office suite of products, but also allows a Web author to develop and manage an entire Web site. This book shows readers how to exploit those new features on their Web or intranet site and teaches basic design principles, link creation, and HTML editing.

$39.99 USA/$56.95 CDN   *User Level: Casual—Accomplished*
ISBN: 1-57521-223-4   *Internet—Web Publishing*   *650 pages*

Laura Lemay's Web Workshop: Netscape Navigator Gold 3, Deluxe Edition

Laura Lemay and Ned Snell

Netscape Gold and JavaScript are two powerful tools used to create and design effective Web pages. The included CD-ROM contains a fully licensed edition of Netscape Navigator Gold 3!

$49.99 USA/$56.95 CDN   User Level: Casual–Accomplished
ISBN: 1-57521-292-7   Internet–General   400 pages

Laura Lemay's Web Workshop: NetObjects Fusion 2

Kabriel Robichaux and Derrick Woolworth

NetObjects Fusion has been recognized as one of the best and most advanced Web site authoring tools on the market. With this straightforward, hands-on guide, readers will learn how to effectively use it to create high-impact Web pages and applications with ease. The CD-ROM, designed to be an interactive workshop, includes a special demonstration version of NetObjects Fusion.

$39.99 USA/$56.95 CDN   User Level: Casual—Accomplished
ISBN: 1-57521-278-1   Internet–Web Publishing   550 pages

Official Marimba Guide to Castanet

Laura Lemay

Castanet is Marimba's technology for distributing and receiving Java applications across the Internet or an intranet. This clear, hands-on guide explains what this new technology is, why it's important, how to effectively use it, and how to develop content for it. The CD-ROM includes special versions of the Castanet components from Marimba, plus author's examples from the book and additional tools and utilities.

$39.99 USA/$56.95 CDN   User Level: Casual—Accomplished
ISBN: 1-57521-255-2   Internet–General/WWW Applications   500 pages

Official Marimba Guide to Bongo

Danny Goodman

Designed for programmers and non-programmers alike, Bongo is Marimba's visual tool for designing and implementing graphical user interfaces for Java applications and Castanet content. This hands-on guide teaches users how to create sophisticated, well-designed applications with this powerful tool. The CD-ROM contains special versions of Bongo, the Castanet Tuner and Transmitter (all from Marimba), examples from the author, and additional tools and utilities.

$39.99 USA/$56.95 CDN   User Level: Casual—Accomplished
ISBN: 1-57521-254-4   Internet–General/WWW Applications   500 pages

Add to Your Sams.net Library Today
with the Best Books for Internet Technologies

ISBN	Quantity	Description of Item	Unit Cost	Total Cost
1-57521-221-8		Laura Lemay's Guide to Sizzling Web Site Design (Book/CD-ROM)	$45.00	
1-57521-125-4		Laura Lemay's Web Workshop: Graphics and Web Page Design (Book/CD-ROM)	$55.00	
1-57521-143-2		Laura Lemay's Web Workshop: 3D Graphics and VRML 2 (Book/CD-ROM)	$39.99	
1-57521-223-4		Laura Lemay's Web Workshop: Microsoft FrontPage 97 (Book/CD-ROM)	$39.99	
1-57521-292-7		Laura Lemay's Web Workshop: Netscape Navigator Gold 3, Deluxe Edition (Book/CD-ROM)	$49.99	
1-57521-278-1		Laura Lemay's Web Workshop: NetObjects Fusion 2 (Book/CD-ROM	$39.99	
1-57521-255-2		Official Marimba Guide to Castanet (Book/CD-ROM)	$39.99	
1-57521-254-4		Official Marimba Guide to Bongo (Book/CD-ROM)	$39.99	
		Shipping and Handling: See information below.		
		TOTAL		

Shipping and Handling: $4.00 for the first book, and $1.75 for each additional book. If you need to have it NOW, we can ship product to you for an additional charge of approximately $18.00, and you will receive your item overnight or in two days. Overseas shipping and handling adds $2.00. Prices subject to change. Call between 9:00 a.m. and 5:00 p.m. EST for availability and pricing information on latest editions.

201 W. 103rd Street, Indianapolis, Indiana 46290

1-800-428-5331 — Orders   1-800-835-3202 — FAX   1-800-858-7674 — Customer Service

Book ISBN 1-57521-249-8

MACMILLAN COMPUTER PUBLISHING USA

A VIACOM COMPANY

Technical ---- Support:

If you need assistance with the information in this book or with a CD/Disk
accompanying the book, please access the Knowledge Base on our Web
site at **http://www.superlibrary.com/general/support**. Our most
Frequently Asked Questions are answered there. If you do not find the
answer to your questions on our Web site, you may contact Macmillan
Technical Support **(317) 581-3833** or e-mail us at **support@mcp.com**.